WORKING THE IRISH COAST

WORKING THE IRISH COAST

Mike Smylie

It has been well observed that the Irish fisheries seemed to exist for the benefit of people of all countries save and except the Irish themselves.

Fr Charles Davis in *Deep Sea Fisheries of Ireland* (Dublin, 1886)

To Ana

First published 2009

Nonsuch Ireland,
119 Baggot Street,
Dublin 2
Ireland
www.nonsuchireland.com

British Library Cataloguing in Publication Data.
A catalogue record for this book is available from the British Library.

ISBN 978 1 84588 944 9

Typesetting and origination by The History Press
Printed in Great Britain

CONTENTS

PRELIMINARY

In 1776 Arthur Young wrote:

> There is scarcely a part of Ireland but what is well situated for some fishery of consequence; her coasts and innumerable creeks and river mouths are the resort of vast shoals of herring, cod, hake, mackarel [*sic*] etc, which might, with proper attention, be converted into funds of wealth; but capital is such a universal want in Ireland, that very little is done.

Such conditions continued throughout most of the nineteenth century and into the early twentieth, up to the formation of the Free State in 1922 to be exact. If nothing else, twenty-three days in Ireland taught me at least one thing and it was this: while in some quarters, wealth was obtained from fishing the huge shoals of herring and, at periods of fruitful fishing, other species, the vast majority of this wealth never benefited those fishers that chased the shoals. No, most of the wealth was carried away to a nearby land called Britain. As were many of the other natural resources of the country. Even at a time of starvation, food that could have alleviated the plight of the inhabitants was carried off without as much as a tear. Not for the first time in world history the empire builders, in their indiscriminate and single-minded determination to build their empires, gave no thought to the destruction left in their trail. The British were no different, robbing Ireland blind during several centuries of sovereignty.

Let me say from the very outset: these writings are not intended as a thorough and complete appraisal of Ireland's maritime history. They are far from it. Given the time I allotted myself to drive the 2,500 odd miles around the Emerald Island, this would be impossible. Although I'd been planning the tour for several years, when it came to the minute planning I found I'd only a month at most to complete the circuit. I chose August because of the chance of better weather, and because of work constraints back home I could not leave until the first and had to be home before the end of the month. My intention was to combine a mixture of the documented past of the coast with my own observations and interviews with a throng of individuals whose livelihoods depend on the sea or coast. A brief historical oversight flavoured by a personal perspective maybe. Luckily I had been furnished by a host of names, especially by Joseph Teesdale and Darina Tully, and others who are members of the 40+ Fishing Boat Association, all of whom remain in my gratitude, especially Joe. However, my thanks go out to everyone I spoke to, the vast majority of whose names appear in the text. Thanks, too, to those historians, past and present, whose work has allowed me a further insight into the maritime landscape of Ireland. Finally, thanks also to the dog for keeping me company and sane during the trip.

DAY ONE

I was a year late really but that couldn't be helped. If only I'd arrived in Fishguard in August 2006 then that would have been exactly a century to the month since the opening of a ferry service across to Ireland. Yet this was 2007 and four years after my tour of the Welsh coast and the subsequent book of the coast, written long before the BBC's TV series *Coast* had attracted so much attention towards that boundary between land and sea. Still, with the dog happily ensconced in the back of the van, we were both ready for a few weeks journeying around the Irish coast, our destination fifty-four miles across the St Georges Channel.

As I drove through passport control a friendly policewoman asked for what reason I was travelling to the Emerald Isle. 'What's a fisheries historian?' she said when I told her. Good question really, I considered as I drove onto the ferry after she'd checked I wasn't smuggling people or drugs or whatever else she was looking out for when she asked to have a peep in the back. What was I in search of in my quest? It wasn't just studying fishing techniques and craft, interviewing ex-fishermen and observing what those fishing communities were up to. I wanted to discover a bit more, some anecdotal, some historical and some contemporary, about the roots of the Irish coast and its people, their habits and superstitions and their hopes.

On time, we left with a rattle and shake as the engines revved up causing vibrations to resonant throughout the ship. I was aboard the *Stena Europe*, not a modern ship by the Dover cross-channel fleet, nor indeed the Ancona to Patras Greek ferries I'm used to for my long-haul drives to Greece, but it was sufficient for the four-hour or so crossing. Somehow it reminded me of the old 'Sealink' boats working from Folkestone to Boulogne, although I couldn't put my finger on exactly why. Maybe it was the flaking paint and general lack of finesse that I observed but it was very pleasant sitting on deck in the summer sun. As Wales slipped under the horizon, I felt a surge of excitement knowing the Irish coast would soon pop up ahead. When it did, though, a haze had developed so that the landmass simply emerged out of the murky greyness rather than grow out of the calm sea.

We passed the famous Tuskar Rock to port, with its white-painted lighthouse flashing twice every seven and a half seconds. First lit in 1815, it wasn't without its troubles. A freak wave had surged over the rock during construction, washing away over thirty members of the workforce after which nineteen survivors clung to the rocks for two days before a rescue party arrived. This is according to our old friends from the Welsh coast, Mr and Mrs Samuel Carter Hall, who visited Ireland on various occasions in the first half of the nineteenth century and wrote that 'huge billows began to roll over the entire extent of the rock ... the sheds and workhouses were swept away ... every succeeding wave swept away some poor wretch ... some bound themselves by ropes to the chains ... in this condition they remained for forty-eight hours'. The whole episode sounds absolutely horrendous yet the same men finished the lighthouse – it took four years to build in all – and then went off to build others. Obviously the force of the sea was something they understood well and didn't frighten them off. Either that or there was no choice for these fellows.

Rosslare Harbour was pretty unexciting as these places often are – modern quays with housing up above overlooking the harbour which was filled with concrete and containers.

Rosslare itself lay a few miles along the coast Wexford-wise but with my intention being the circumnavigation of Ireland in a clockwise direction we'd not be there for several weeks. However the harbour itself probably hadn't always been as nondescript as it appeared. Wexford had handled most of the shipping commerce of the area for ages although the bar into the harbour restricted the size of vessel able to enter. A ferry service had run to Liverpool for many years and when the new steamer, the *Slaney*, was lost on the bar in 1885 there was a realisation that the provision of other facilities was becoming urgent. There had been the first inklings of change back in 1846 after legislation enacted in the London Parliament for the building of the railway between Dublin, Wicklow, Waterford and 'a pier in the sea or on the shore of Greenore Bay near the Town and Port of Wexford' but within months the onset of famine had concentrated minds in other directions (away from Ireland?). Further legislation followed in 1863, yet it wasn't until 1873 that the land was obtained by the Harbour Commissioners for developing the ferry link. In 1883 the first passengers were landed but only because the Liverpool to Wexford steamer *Montague* wasn't able to pass over the Wexford bar because of adverse weather. In the late 1880s, after the *Slaney* disaster, the Bristol to Wexford ferry landed livestock in Rosslare on several occasions and in 1896 a service from there to Liverpool was established, and soon after another to Bristol because the facilities at Fishguard were not completed. By 1903 the pier was ready, three years before the Fishguard service began under the Fishguard & Rosslare Railway Company, the rail connection of which was finished two years later. Thus, with a rail connection to the Dublin & South Eastern Railway that linked Dublin to Wexford and Waterford and thus Cork, to Rosslare, the new Irish link competed with the existing services between the two countries. These were, in the main, between Liverpool, Bristol and Neyland, in Pembrokeshire, on the eastern side and Cork, Wexford and Waterford on Irish coast. The intention of this faster cross-channel link was to speed passengers to Cobh (which was then called Queenstown) for a connection with the transatlantic liners over to America. As we saw in *Working the Welsh Coast*, one idea behind the building of both Milford Haven and Fishguard harbours was to attract these liners, a desire that nevertheless didn't materialise.

Whilst I was mulling over the surrounding scenery, I noticed the RNLI lifeboat station within the ferry terminal. I'd been reading on the way over about lifeboats, and therefore already knew that a lifeboat had been established here since 1896, with the boat always kept afloat. The station had closed in 1921 because of another boat being stationed at the nearby village of Fort at Rosslare Point, but this, along with all the other buildings of the Point, was washed away in a series of gales and heavy seas in 1926. The Rosslare Harbour station was once again reopened in 1927 and it remains so today. Previous to this station, another much older one was on station at Carnsore Point, the southeast tip of Ireland some ten miles away. Other than this, I'd noted that a Coastguard station had been built in 1869 and the lighthouse dwellings for the Tuskar Rock keepers in 1887.

The ship docked and vehicle drivers were called to return to the car deck and soon dog and I disembarked and as we drove off the ship I was suddenly aware that our drive of what looked like being in excess of two thousand miles was about to commence. I'd been working up to this adventure for a couple of years and the reality was now upon me. It was early evening and I'd an appointment in Kilmore Quay, a distance of some twenty miles, so hanging about wasn't an option and without any ado we headed straight in that direction.

It didn't take long to notice the housing. Once we'd left the main road and reached the rural limits, it quickly became apparent that a surge in house building had left the landscape littered with late twentieth century/early twenty-first century abscesses. Sterile mock Georgian two-storey hastily-built structures occupied otherwise green fields where cows and sheep should have been grazing. Some had pretentious porticos guarding the obviously-plastic ornate front doors whilst equally appalling plastic windows were moulded in the same style. These really were carbuncles, some fascias in brick and others rendered and painted, on an otherwise idyllic setting. Although it surprised me then, during the entire journey it was something I was to become accustomed to. And since returning, it is something that I've heard repeated literally dozens of times: the Irish countryside has been utterly ruined by this unsympathetic and possibly uncontrolled rush to build. With a peak of new builds of some 100,000 a year, over some ten or fifteen years it has been estimated that almost one million houses have been built.

I'd been warned not to drive the direct route across endless fields and new houses but to take the longer main route to Kilmore Quay but upon seeing the first road sign for it I turned left, as this quicker direct route appeared easy according to my map which I'd hastily bought upon the ship. The first few miles were simple until the road signs disappeared. On the map the road seemed to be straight but then a junction reared up ahead with no road in the general south-west direct that my destination was in. I went left but soon realised this was wrong and turned around to find another way in the right direction. This I did with no help from the map and I relaxed until the same thing happened, and again and again. The roads were a maze of confusion. Eventually, more by luck than anything else, I reached the main road at Tenacre Cross Roads and thus motored quickly, through the village of Kilmore, and down to Kilmore Quay. With its fine examples of thatched houses, busy harbour, sandy beach and air of tranquillity, this place was a lovely introduction to the Irish fishing industry.

I found John Power's house by asking a man standing outside the church. John had said on the phone a few days earlier that I should park up at the church and phone him but with this fellow directing folk inside the building I thought it unwise to park there. Continuing down to the harbour I left the van there and walked back up the hill and I guessed that the man at the church might know John's whereabouts, a guess which was correct. Entering the grounds as I'd been instructed, I was confronted with four houses around a circle of grass and dithered as to which door I should knock upon. Luckily a man appeared at the rear of one and he turned out to be my quarry. We shook hands and he ushered me inside the house.

I spent an entertaining and informative evening with John, eating sandwiches and cakes and drinking coffee supplied by his wife Trish. John had been at the fishing all his life until his retirement several years ago but has kept himself busy researching local history and taking an interest in fishy matters. He's a small guy in stature with a serious nature, possibly reticent at first but soon seemed to warm to my needs when I explained my desire to write about the coast. We spent over an hour at his computer as he photocopied various articles and photographs, the articles from the Kilmore Parish Journal that he is chairman of. He's also written a book on the local lifeboat entitled *Above and Beyond the Call of Duty* as well as a book on the Irish lobster fishing which was never published although, he says, *Fishing News* used bits of it in the past. He had his own lobster boat, working 280 pots, in his latter days of fishing until he decommissioned it in 1995. John was the first person in Ireland to introduce the 'V' notching of lobsters, a technique introduced from Maine on the east coast of America in the early 1990s by the BIM – the Irish Fishery Board (Bord Iascaigh Mhara). This is to protect a percentage of the female lobster stock by the fishermen cutting a notch in one of the flaps of their tail when caught. This is easily recognisable and lasts for two moults, ensuring that the lobster has at least one opportunity to breed and thus boost egg production and increase recruitment for future stock growth. It's now illegal to land, possess or sell such notched lobsters and it is estimated that up to 13,000 lobsters are returned to the sea each year after being notched.

John also spoke of the heydays of the herring fishery in these parts and of the Dutch and German 'loggers' that he remembers fishing in the bay. When I expressed interest in

Kilmore Quay *c.* 1870. (John Power).

the growth of the harbour he told me the first attempt to build a shelter for boats was in 1785 when a mass of loose stones and boulders were built into an L-shaped boat safe. Many of the boulders came from St Patrick's Bridge and were floated over on rafts. Long before that, though, in 1640 there were said to have been 300 open boats working from the beach though perhaps that is an exaggeration. A later breakwater was built on the exposed side of the shelter. In 1837 there were 100 boats, averaging four men aboard each, engaged in the herring, lobster and cod fishing, with some thirty houses in the village. Amongst these buildings was a coastguard station that dates from 1825. This consisted of four buildings – the four doors I'd been confronted with on arrival and now turned into houses – the centre one built on slightly higher ground for the officers, two either side for the watchers and the boathouse by the beach. John lives in the farthest watcher house and his daughter in the boathouse. In 1842 there were 154 such stations in Ireland, a year that 87 were taken over by the Board of Works. The Kilmore station was sold into private hands in 1910. It's an impressive site with fine views over the beach, to which a private set of steps leads straight down upon.

Returning to the harbour development, the first substantial structure, a pier 600 feet long, dates from 1825, built with a £4000 low-interest Government loan which the people of the barony repaid. Afterwards the harbour rose from a mere fishing station to a useful harbour, invigorated by local men investing in ships and thus the trade increased. Corn, potatoes and beans were the main export with coal and manures being brought in, the coal from South Wales.

However the harbour was exposed to storms from the east and south, often driving vessels ashore and causing a great deal of damage. Thus, in 1883, a second movement was organised which resulted in the building of an extension to the existing pier, another 120-foot long breakwater at the mouth of the harbour but not connected to the shore and the dredging of the harbour, all for £8000. However, silting up of the harbour which prevented larger vessels

Kilmore Quay and its maritime museum 2007.

from entering except on spring tides meant that, in 1910, another £500 had to be spent joining the two piers up and dredging once again. For the latter operation the Wexford Harbour Commissioners' dredger *Slaney* was brought in but its draft was too deep to enter the harbour. The local fishermen were sceptical about the work, believing that the stonework wouldn't stand up to the winter storms, one fisherman being said to have replied when asked of his opinion, 'It's like a man fitted with a new overcoat while the backside was out of his trousers!' Not for the first time did an official body take the cheapest option ending with a bodge.

Although the breakwater remained intact for the next seventeen years, the fishermen's convictions were justified when, during a particular fierce gale in 1927, the schooner *Clara* broke free of her moorings and ended up pounding against the wall, eventually breaking through and leaving a large gap which remained for many years. After large second-hand trawlers were brought into the port in the 1950s and 1960s, better protection was needed and in 1971 their needs were finally listened to with the opening of the new substantial 200ft breakwater and another 160ft extension to the existing pier. Today it houses a fleet and a marina.

I left John as darkness was falling, taking the steps to the beach. Fetching the dog, we played throwing sticks for a while, me chucking them into the sea as far as I could and him swimming out to retrieve. Then I just managed to get fish and chips in the nearby chippie minutes before they closed up and we spent a while watching the end-of-day activity munching upon superbly cooked fish and oil-free chips.

Within the harbour is the *Guillemot*, one of the old lightships of the Commissioners of Irish Lights, the board set up in the eighteenth century to administer both lighthouses and lightships within Ireland. This lightship, launched at Leith in 1923, was on station at South Arklow for some of its life until being sold off in 1968 to the Wexford Maritime Museum Committee and towed to Wexford. Subsequently it was towed to Kilmore Quay and set in concrete and is now a maritime museum, though this obviously wasn't open. Judging by the state of the ship it was hard to tell whether or not it would be open in the morning and it certainly wasn't by the time I left. An earlier *Guillemot*, again on station at South Arklow, was sunk by a German submarine in 1917.

It was time to think about sleeping so I decided to move the van away from the harbour and its bright lights, finding a quiet park along the road, with a couple of motor caravans whose inhabitants seemed to be already fast asleep. Thus, with fine views over the Saltee Islands and with the light of the Hook Head lighthouse flashing across the bay, I poured myself a glass of wine and settled down to read a couple of excerpts from the *Kilmore Parish Journal* (No 21 &22) that John had given me, these being titled *Fishing in bygone days* by Richard Roche, for which I must thank both of them.

Most of the information came from reports compiled by the Inspecting Commissioners of Fisheries and concern themselves solely with the Wexford District which is defined as being 'from the Sluices near Cahore to Fethard', a coastal length of about sixty miles when you exclude Barrow Bay and Wexford Harbour, and these reports cover a period of over a century up to 1950. They give a good idea of the state of the fishery. For example, in 1854 there were 473 fishing craft working, sixty-three of which were first-class vessels. 2,130 men and twenty-five boys in total were employed upon these craft yet only 246 of these worked aboard the first-class boats. Thus, the vast majority of the fishers are deemed to have been part-timers, working either in the river Slaney or very close to the shore. Most of these men would have fished from Wexford cots, of which we shall learn a great deal more at the end of our journey. For now it's sufficient to say these are small open craft not normally associated with deep-sea fishing.

The species caught were herring, mackerel, cod, bream, conger, pollock, sole, plaice, bass and gurnard and shellfish including lobsters and crab. Salmon, caught mostly in the rivers and Wexford Harbour and sold at one shilling and six pence a pound, was either exported or sold to the local gentry. Whereas in Britain salmon was regarded almost as the food of the poor (along with herring and oysters), in Ireland, only a few years after the Great Famine, it was not. Presumably much was exported to Britain. The overall conclusion of the report was that 'the condition of the fishing establishments was considerably worse in every respect, both as to the boats and gear, and there is no sign of any improvement whatever'. The catch was the lowest for years and the worst season ever for salmon and it noted that there were no curing stations along the coast.

By the following year the numbers of boats had drastically declined to 289 vessels employing 1,426 men and ten boys, a drop of about 35% with another slight drop in 1856. By 1871, 240 boats employed 1,089 men and 22 boys. The percentage of full-time fishers had increased with only 182 part-timers and, mentioned for the first time, there were trawlers of 15-20 tons using trawl-nets. All fish were being sold fresh for there were no ice-houses and, presumably, still no curing houses. Wexford and Kilmore are noted as being the only harbours offering protection to the boats.

In 1881 the report lists a total of 139 vessels employing 536 men and 22 boys working the coast between Barrow and Cahore. Interestingly, only 21 boats employing 80 men and 9 boys, were fishing on a full-time basis. The drop in numbers must surely be attributed to the fact that 'the want of harbours is sorely felt' although the report adds that 'the small harbour at Kilmore is better than nothing' which it almost immediately contradicts by adding that there is 'great apathy shown about Kilmore ... the pier there is no protection. It is a pity to see a sea teeming with fish and excellent trawling grounds lying waste for the want of proper appliances and the development of human energies.'

In the 1883 report of the British House of Commons Select Committee on Harbour Accommodation, compiled by Captain Alexander Boxer, Kilmore was described as having 'a small fishing pier built there but it is ... merely built down to the low-water mark ... and is perfectly useless ... any amount of fish is to be got round Ireland, but people are afraid to remain out for want of harbours or piers'. This was echoed by the Inspector of Fisheries, Major Joseph Hayes who added that

> the fishermen have to haul their large boats up in winter, at the time when large fish are to be found along the coast in great quantities, and they can only fish occasionally in their small boats ... a great mistake was made in constructing the harbour without efficient depth of water.

This lack of winter fishing was again mentioned in the 1890 report. 'Much more fish' it stated rather unkindly,

> might have been caught if the men had little more energy ... I have particularly noticed the great want of energy on the part of the fishermen, especially at Kilmore Quay where they have a practice of hauling up nearly all the boats about the beginning of November each year ... even during the summer months the boats return from the fishing ground from noon to 2pm ... so that only about half a day's fishing is done, the only reason seems nothing but sheer laziness.

In the same mouthful almost, he said that the increase in fish landed at Kilmore over the previous year was eight tons whilst the numbers of lobsters and crabs landed had gone up by 1,400 and 840 respectively. One wonders how this happened if the fishermen were so lazy and lacking energy. Moreover many fishermen set out in the early morning and returned by lunchtime, especially part-timers with land to work upon and, given the fact that the harbours were verging on being useless, is it surprising that they hauled their boats up as the winter gales approached? This in turns leads the reader to doubt his knowledge on the subject until he reads on for the Inspector later admitted 'I have only been here since June' and thus his personal knowledge on the subject was very limited. Other reasons suggested in the article for their restricted fishing were that it had to be dispatched early to the markets, there was no ice available and 'that the "satsty" or mid-day siesta was in vogue in the area'.

By 1901 the fishery was in the doldrums with only 86 vessels employing 298 men and one boy. Sixteen boats were worked full-time and 23 lobstered, the shellfish selling between eight shillings and nine and six a dozen. Ten years later there were 64 full-time boats which included 12 row boats and 43 boats working part-time. Presumably the row boats were salmon cots working on the River Slaney and Wexford Harbour for I cannot see them working out to sea. The first motor fishing vessels had arrived by 1921 – two in fact – when 34 boats worked full-time and another 65 part-time. By 1931 there were 7 motor-trawlers and 3 sailing trawlers operating out of Wexford Harbour, 6 sailing trawlers working out of Rosslare and 3 motor-trawlers and 3 sail boats in Ballygeary. From that time onwards, as in most parts of Britain, trawling increased in popularity so that in 1941 there were six trawlers in Kilmore Quay and 14 by 1950, although 10 of these were under 10 tons and the other 4 under 15 tons. It was after this that second-hand vessels were brought in, as already mentioned, and pressure applied to have the harbour improved. Today, with EU quotas and fish conservation high on the political agenda, the harbour continues to survive although I remembered John telling me 16 scalloping boats had been decommissioned in 2006. This might all be very tedious statistics, but it does a fine job at illustrating the fortunes of the fishermen, fortunes that will be reflected in many other parts of the coast, away from the few centres of fishing. Although I've included such turgid material here, I'll try and not repeat it again. Even I, after perusing the articles for an hour or so, felt pretty tired by it all. So, with my wine glass empty and the dog already snoring, I crawled into my bed on the van floor, pleased both with the evening's progress and the very fact of having arrived in Ireland, and instantly fell asleep.

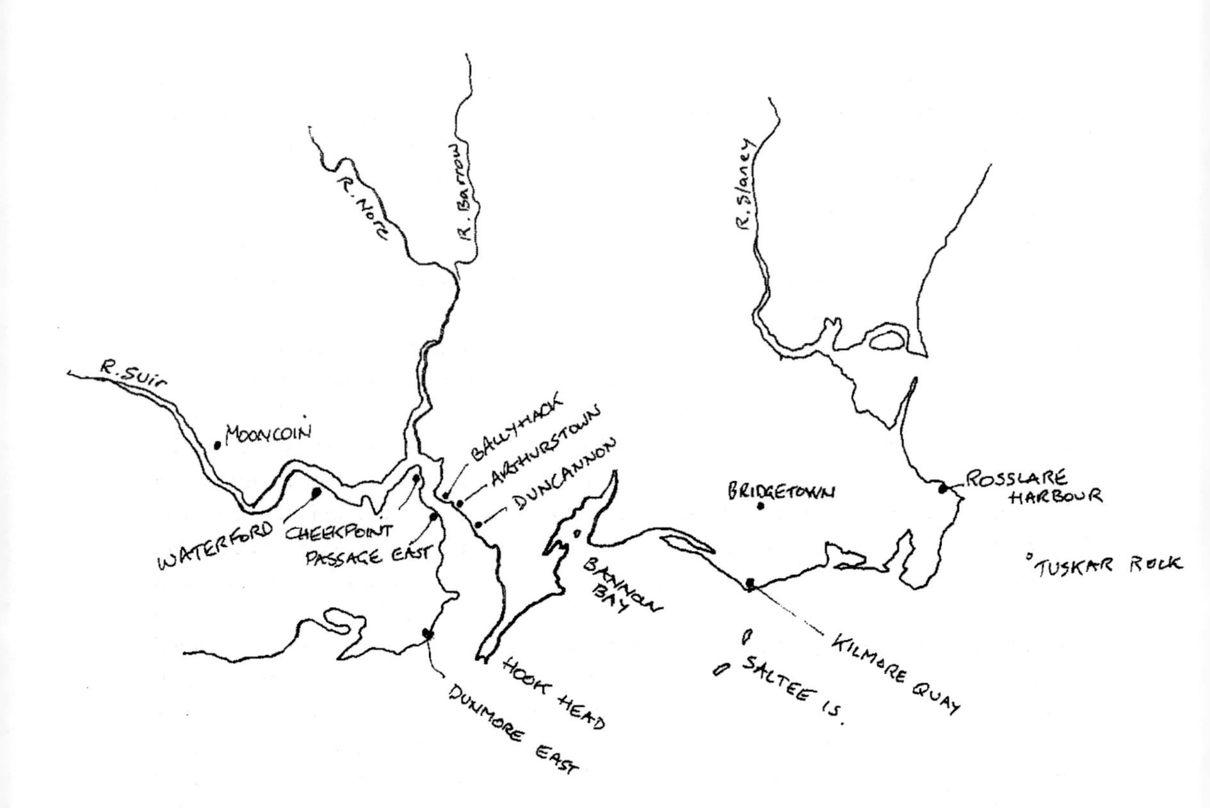

DAY TWO

There are, I'd counted, about seventy lifeboat stations around the coast of Ireland that I was very likely to pass close to over the next few weeks. This had concerned me in the planning of the trip, and as I made the slow transition from the dreamy world of sleep into consciousness on that first morning of waking in Ireland, the same worries resurfaced. It might sound a ridiculous matter to focus on at an early hour, but I'd a habit of writing a short paragraph on each station during the Welsh coastal trek. Seventy stations, though, seemed both monotonous and repetitive and certainly unnecessary. The only conclusion that could be drawn was to simply include those stations with a particular story, unique lifeboat or any notable rescues or lifeboat crew. This then I opted for. However, when walking by the harbour after brewing up my morning coffee, I couldn't help but notice the Tyne-class lifeboat moored afloat. There was an information board by the harbour that said the lifeboat was a Mersey-class boat, which it wasn't. I later discovered that the present boat had arrived in 2004 so the board was obviously a few years old. Presumably there isn't the funding to update them on a regular basis. However, the station was notable for having saved 111 lives and crew members have been awarded nine silver medals and one bronze. The same board said that a boat had been stationed here since 1847 and I wasn't surprised to later discover that, between 1847 and 1857, a boat had been on station at the request of the Coastguard and housed in their boathouse, the one that today John Power's daughter lives in. The Coastguard had been formed in 1822 by amalgamating the Customs and Preventive Water Guard and the Royal National Institution for the Preservation of Life from Shipwreck established a couple of years later with the first Irish lifeboat arriving on station in1825. But, as was often to be the case, the Institution supplied the boat and the coastguard the crew. Not only were the Coastguard responsible for organising patrols to detect smuggling, but were also involved in watching for vessels in distress and, in some cases, providing assistance. Thus it wasn't unusual for them to draw the crew from within their ranks. For those wanting fuller information on all the Irish stations, the suggested read is Nicholas Leach's *The Lifeboat Service in Ireland, Station by Station*, published by Tempus in 2005. The book not only covers the history of the lifeboat service but catalogues each station one by one.

I walked up to the Memorial Garden to the west of the village and wandered about the various sculptures, all of which were commemorative to sailors and fishermen lost at sea. There's a mock boat in stone, a whale bone and various other stone structures all creating a perfectly peaceful setting. Close by was a cleft in the rocks at sea level which, judging by its hewing, was a much older landing place, now with a stone quay of dubious age protecting the cleft from the sea. Offshore, the Little Saltee – one of the two Saltee Islands, the other being Great Saltee beyond – lies some two miles across the water. The two islands are today one of the richest wild bird regions in Ireland, a sort of staging post in their migratory flights in spring and autumn. It is thought that Neolithic farmers first colonised the islands in prehistoric times. Much later, in 1837, some twenty people lived there, including two coastguards, probably from Kilmore Quay. Today there's a landing place to where the odd fisherman might ferry any person wishing to visit even though the islands remain in private ownership.

I'd like to have hung around Kilmore Quay for much longer, perhaps even seeing if the maritime museum in the old lightship opened up for business. However, I'd another appointment at ten o'clock at Dunmore East and it seemed best to glimpse a bit of the coast along the way. I'd first contemplated driving west via New Ross to view the famine ship SS *Dunbrody*, a true to life replica of the nineteenth-century ship that carried thousands of emigrants across to America and Canada. Built in Quebec in 1845, the original boat brought timber over to New Ross before returning with thousands of those in search of a new life away from their famine-struck homeland. The Great Famine is just one sad example of the shameful and deplorable behaviour that occurred as Britain expanded her empire and, as such, has been well documented. Thus I didn't want to get into the politics of it although I knew that stories of soldiers protecting exports of spuds going to Britain when the locals were dying from starvation were sure to surface. Regional relevance to the lives of those working the coast I'd document but the idea of visiting a tourist attraction based on the era suddenly seemed mad. I decided on the coastal route.

In 1853 the Bridgetown Canal was opened, a short five-mile waterway linking the town to the sea below Duncormick. I couldn't quite grasp the reason for building a canal. Seemingly the only reason was to allow goods to be brought in and local products to be exported but building it seems a massive effort such to carry goods a few miles. Why not by horse and cart? I thought. Presumably it had something to do with the low-lying land, some of which was reclaimed by the construction of the canal. Duncormick is said to have had a 'considerable trade in slate, coal, limestone and culm from South Wales' with return cargoes such as potatoes and grain. In the 1880s another channel was cut from near Killag down to the sea at Crossfarnoge, Kilmore Quay. According to Dick Roche, thousands of people were employed in the construction earning three pence and one pound of maize a day. Men came from as far as twelve miles away to work, walking to and from work. Maybe another reason for building the canal.

Again, if there had been the time, I'd have gone in search of any remains of this canal. This lack of time was something I was going to encounter dozens of times during my journey and was entirely expected. From the outset I'd realised that it was impossible to cover every aspect of the maritime zone in four weeks, my intended journey time. All I sought was a flavour of what the coast has to offer. At Wellingtonbridge I stopped to take some photographs of the remains of a derelict abbey close to Bannow Bay, an area rich in cockles. Hook Head lies on the eastern promontory at the entrance to the beautiful Waterford Harbour. The lighthouse there is said by some to be the oldest working light in the world, a singular fact that isn't actually true. That honour goes the Tower of Hercules at La Coruna in northwest Spain. However, Hook Head is most certainly the oldest in Ireland, being built in the twelfth century. It is thought to have been financed by William Fitzgerald of Carew Castle in Pembrokeshire and, according to the Halls, one of its keepers died at the grand age of 100. 'He had been superannuated many years before his death, but was suffered to remain where so large a portion of his life had passed'. It's a tall lighthouse in a splendid, isolated setting which supposedly has a colourful story to tell which is possibly why today it contains a visitor centre which is open to the general public all year round except some holidays. Cynics might say it is the visitor centre marketing that has coloured its historical story. The earliness of the hour, and time in general, prevented me finding out. The sign at the entrance to the blue flag beach amused me: 'No learner drivers'. It seemed to me that the beach would be an ideal place to start driving rather than on the narrow roads.

Duncannon lies on the same side of Waterford Harbour as Hook Head, some eight miles upstream, and has been described as 'a poor village'. Again the area is renowned for its cockles. The extensive fort on the point which juts out into the estuary was granted by Henry II to John Talbot, the Earl of Shrewsbury and stands as one of the sentinels to Waterford and New Ross, both upstream. Today the fort houses some army personnel as well as a museum which was closed at this early hour. Below the fort is the harbour with several fishing boats alongside including one beam trawler. The storehouse alongside had been unofficially named 'Old Trafford' with another hand-painted sign declaring that Man. Utd were champions of Europe. This was something entirely unexpected in deepest County Wexford. On driving north, we passed the lighthouse snuggled into the hillside, one of two now discontinued at Duncannon, the other being in the fort. Arthurstown – formerly King's Way where James II is supposed to have passed his last night in Ireland – had its stone quay with a variety of boats alongside, including two Ballyhack yawls, the local fishing boat type of which I was keen to discover more. The terrace of old houses around the harbour created a picturesque scene which was then destroyed by the nearby modern development which can only be described as horrible. A mile on is Ballyhack, the eastern terminal of the estuary ferry service which runs over to Passage East where the ferry dropped me in County Waterford after a ten minute crossing. The Halls described the place as an 'ancient bathing place' once favoured by the people of Waterford and as 'completely deserted, although it still maintains some importance as a ferry in connection with the opposite shore of Wexford'. Although not on the east side of the estuary, it's so called because there's a Passage West on the Cork River. At this point we will jump to East Dunmore, where I had my appointment with Joe Teesdale. Joe's a member of the 40+ Fishing Boat Association, of which I am one of the two founders. Thus, I began correspondence with Joe several years ago and when I mentioned my intention of touring the coast, Joe immediately promised to supply me with contacts all around the island. Furthermore, he said he would arrange a day of interviews with local fishermen and, true to his word, this was the day.

Two hours after arriving on the ferry at Passage East I was back there again, this time with Joe, the dog staying behind for the day. The village is a cluster of colourful houses and narrow streets around the harbour with its eclectic collection of wooden craft. What I didn't know at the time and only discovered a week later was that there was a large herring smoking business belonging to Arthur Miller at East Passage. This information came to me after I received a telephone call from Arthur Miller's grandson Arthur Neiland, a fisheries economist and director of IDDRA Ltd. who contacted me because he had read my book *Herring – a History of the Silver Darlings.* He subsequently wrote *The Irish Herring Industry – One Family's Story* which is available to view on line at www.iddra.org. Most of the following comes from this paper, the use of which he gave permission and for which I thank him.

At the beginning of the twentieth century the Irish herring fishery was growing but still largely undeveloped. Arthur Miller, representing the Billingsgate firm of John L. Sayers Ltd, was one of many people involved in this development and, starting in 1900, he built fish houses at Buncrana, Killibegs, Howth, Dunmore East and Passage East. In each herring was cured – either by salting or smoking – and sent to markets in Eastern Europe and later Ireland and Britain. When John L. Sayer died in 1910, Arthur Miller went into business in his own right, based at the fish house in Passage East. Although these facts were unknown to me at the time of my visit I had unwittingly taken photographs of the building when photographing the harbour. Thus part of the fish house still exists, complete with the raised part of the smokehouse, and now functions as part of the community centre. Herring was landed directly into Passage East, or brought by road from other ports such as Dunmore East – where Arthur Miller had other fish processing sheds on the quay for salting – or Helvick, near Dungarvan, a small harbour I would subsequently visit. Some 50 cran of herring were smoked daily with a cran being the official measure of herring at 371/2 imperial gallons or 28 stone of fish (600–1000 fish depending on size). The reputation of his 'Arthur Miller Selected Kippers' matched those from the Isle of Man at Billingsgate and received a number of prizes for their quality and taste. These were packed in wooden boxes and sent directly to London by the boat train from Waterford, although later from Rosslare. However, by the 1920s, with the loss of several European markets – especially Russia and Eastern Europe – and poor catches in some years, the business was described as 'challenging'. In the 1940s a few fishing boats were bought and fished using local crews and other enterprises where taken aboard such as importing dried cod from Newfoundland, smoking wild salmon and an early attempt at laying scallops in the Waterford estuary. Arthur Miller also purchased a local licensed public house ('Millers') in Passage East. When he died in 1953 and was buried at Crooke, Passage East, the business was taken over by his two daughters and subsequently by Mr Kevin Neiland, the paper-writer's father. The period between 1950 and 1975 saw another expansion in the herring fishery but by then consumer attitudes had altered and the market for fresh, smoked and cured herring had substantially declined. Some was sold to be processed into fishmeal and much sold to foreign 'klondykers' and a boom/bust scenario developed until the herring stocks collapsed and the Celtic Sea herring fishery was closed in 1978. Today the fishery still hasn't achieved its full potential although considerable amounts of herring are landed under the EU much maligned quota system. Whereas there are some who are attempting to re-introduce smoked herring into today's consumers' diets, the vast majority seem unwilling to eat what is, in reality, one of the tastiest and most adaptable fish. Whether there will ever be another 'golden age' for the British and Irish herring fishery remains to be seen.

So it was back on to the ferry and across to Ballyhack where Joe introduced me to Tom Walsh, a salmon drift-net fisherman of the old school type. We met overlooking the harbour with its array of old wooden boats reflecting in the late morning sunshine. Tom's boat, registered W15, the 'W' being for Waterford, was moored directly beneath where we stood, a half-decker built by Skinners of Baltimore in 1936, the last they built of this design, which Tom had bought in 1960. It was painted white and dark green as it had been before he'd become its owner at the wish of the previous owner who'd asked Tom not to change the colour. Some fishermen, he told me, wouldn't have a green painted boat because of superstition, although he didn't know the reason for that particular notion. Some obviously regarded it as unlucky. Tom had been fishing since 1943 when he went out with his father. After he had died in 1950, Tom took over his salmon licence the following year and has fished every year since. Until this one, that is. In fact, he said indignantly, his grandfather and great-grandfather had been fishing salmon in the same way for years.

The trouble was this year, 2007, all salmon fishing had been stopped and this was hurting small fishermen such as Tom hard. This was a travesty. The reason for the ban was purportedly the over-fishing and the government was in the process of compensating fishermen for their inability to net. As governments are apt to, it would appear that they have gone about this in the wrong way by banning all salmon fishing. According to Tom, and many others, it is the drift-net fishers who work much bigger boats than Tom's in deeper water around the entrances to the various river estuaries that are depleting the stocks. They catch the salmon before they even have a chance of making it into the rivers to swim upstream to spawn. It was a story which I was to hear all around Ireland. Tom used to drift during the fishing season which once began on the 1 February and ended on 15 August. Over the years this season has shrunk considerably so that last year it was little more than two months long, June to August, although June, Tom said, was never any good from a fishing point of view. From an initial licence fee of £3 when he started, in 2006 it had risen to €337, a considerable rise in about

Ballyhack Harbour *c.*1900. (Tom Walsh).

sixty years. Further reducing their fishing time, they were only allowed to drift Monday to Thursday with no night fishing and no Friday nor weekend fishing.

We talked for quite a long time about the injustice of the recent ban and as to whether the fishermen would actually receive the promised compensation. Some were said to have been offered some, whereas others reckoned that if they held out against these pay-offs, a limited amount of fishing would be re-introduced in a few years time. Nobody seemed to know anyone who'd had any money though. I asked what he used to fish outside the salmon season and he told me he lined for mackerel up to the end of October and drifted for herring up to Christmas. Herring came into the estuary but locally there was no market, thus he had to take the catch to Dunmore East, either by road or sea, the latter being preferable despite there being too many big boats in the harbour. With the same big boats busily catching herring, his catches weren't as good as they had been fifty years ago. Mussels and cockles, he added, were also fished in the estuary.

Looking around the harbour there were several smaller punts, one perfect example having a black hull with the gunwales painted in green and white. 'Those were built on the slip there,' said Tom in his Irish drawl, 'Paddy Mylor, dead now, but he built hundreds with a bench saw and hatchet.' Seems he also built a 70ft barge during the war which was used to bring grain from Campile, upstream a few miles. These punts were the original salmon drift-net boats until the engined half-deckers were adopted. These transom-sterned half-deckers are better known as Ballyhack yawls, originally single-masted gaff-rigged boats which, when motorised, had the propeller on the starboard quarter to keep it away from the net which was worked over the port side, but retained a mizzen mast with a small sail to keep the boat to wind when working. Although Tom's boat was built in Baltimore, and is not a Ballyhack yawl as such, there's a distinct similarity so that any person not having an eye for river boats might easily confuse the two.

When I took interest in the Ballyhack yawls – fishing boats and their development being a major interest of mine – Tom decided he should introduce me to John Carroll. I'd already noticed Carroll's Boatyard adjacent to the harbour and when the three of us walked into the huge shed, John emerged from the workshop. I was introduced and John was keen to talk. Ballyhack yawls were without doubt a favourite of his, although they all seem to just call them half-deckers, and he led us to the rear of the shed and out to the boat storage park when he pointed out one such yawl called *Star of the Sea*. Although looking a little forlorn, this was the last half-decker John's father had built and one day he'd like to restore it. 'Better still,' he explained, 'I'd like to build a proper Ballyhack yawl, an original sailing version. Trouble is the work these days is mostly lifeboat overhauling and work like that. The fishing industry collapsed when the Common Fisheries Policy came, after our fisheries minister estimated the country's tonnage at, say, 100,000 tons when it was 250,000, so the tonnage had to stay 100,000 tons. Wrecked a healthy business. There's no wood here in the yard now, we pushed all the machinery into a shed so it would be awkward to work in wood again.' He laughed nervously, although I'm sure he would reinstate all the woodworking machinery if the work was there.

By this time Tom wanted us to join us at his house across the road for a bite of lunch. However Joe was keen to show me a 'prong', one of which was lying rotting in the mud alongside the harbour wall by the boatyard. Another one lay afloat against a trot of half-deckers out in the middle of the harbour. Prongs are small open flat-bottomed boats, usually rowed, for working nets upstream, and are notable by their pram-style flat stem. I photographed these two boats but could tell Tom was keen to get home and, as Joe told me we'd see more prongs in the afternoon, the three of us joined Tom's wife and two grandsons, who were also visiting, for ham sandwiches, coffee and scones.

After lunch and saying a fond farewell to Tom, a man I found both knowledgeable and passionate about the fishing which had obviously occupied the greater part of his working life, Joe and I walked back to his car and he pointed out the sprat weir visible upstream. It seems there were several of these on the far bank, the County Waterford side, although most were now redundant. As we'd have the chance to see one closer, I decided to leave a description of one until later.

We crossed the river on the ferry again, the third time for me that day, drove through Passage East once again and headed out of the village, up the hill in a northerly direction. All the time he was driving, Joe was telling me about the fishing and he certainly is a mine of information. His promise to introduce me to those fishing these parts was no idle promise and the day was turning out to be much more than I had dared to expect. In fact I cursed not having brought along a tape recorder for I felt I was missing so much of the nitty-gritty of the subject but hadn't because, basically, I'd forgotten it. I had thought about bringing a tape recorder several weeks before leaving but decided that most people probably wouldn't be happy with a microphone thrust in their face. It all too often has the effect of making people a bit more guarded in what they say unless they are being interviewed in a more formal setting.

We eventually, after motoring along narrow roads, past fields of grazing cows and the odd clearing with good views of the river, arrived at Cheekpoint, a small strewn-out village at the point where the rivers Suir and Barrow meet before the estuary widens out into Waterford Harbour. Its Irish name is 'Rinn na Sige' meaning 'the headland of the streaks', the streaks being the currents and eddies created in the stream. It is said to have always been a fishing village although many would have also worked the land to supplement their meagre income from the sea. Many of its inhabitants were the first deckhands to go across the Atlantic to exploit the Newfoundland cod fishery.

A prong at Cheekpoint 2007.

Here we met John Heffernan who was waiting for us and welcomed us into his house. John's a river man who has fished all his life and entering the door into the kitchen this was instantly apparent for an eel basket sat on the table as well as other signs of his business littering the room. Like Tom Walsh, he was so welcoming and talked as passionately about the river as Tom did. This was, as it turned out, something I was to encounter with almost everyone I spoke to over the ensuing weeks, but at first it was a bit of a surprise, having often found fishermen in Britain a bit stand-offish in comparison and reticent to talk until they warmed up. With John we were straight away into him describing the complexities of making an eel basket. He was, he said, licenced to work twenty baskets as well as using nets with hazel supports and could fish eels from the first of May up to the end of September. These nets were made from locally grown flax, a fact contrasting Tom Walsh's flax nets which he said came from Northern Ireland, Bridport or Musselburgh. He also used to drift for salmon and was another to suffer financially from the recent blanket ban. However, as a sort of lifesaver, a market for green crabs had recently arisen, realising the fishermen €350 a ton or fifty bags and, although he reckoned this was a lot of crabs, they were in plentiful supply.

But it was the punts and prongs, the small fishers' boats, examples of which I'd already seen, we'd come to see. Thus we climbed back into Joe's car and drove the short distance to the little quay adjacent to John's riverside shed. The ferry from Waterford to Milford Haven used to call in here, as did coal lighters from South Wales. Nowadays it's a quiet corner with a few boats dotted around. A punt on the quay had been built in about 1900, whilst another, dried out above the low water mark, belonged to John and had been built by his son Ferguson from moulds taken off an original punt. The moulds, he showed me, were hanging up on the wall in the shed.

John fished the river between here and Waterford, 8 miles upriver where he said the water was much flatter. He also has a sprat weir, a metal version of the traditional wicker ones. Because of the building of groynes in the river off Cheekpoint to alleviate the need to dredge the main channel, the foreshore had drastically altered and his original weir had ceased to work, the extensive mud banks of the foreshore at low water having appeared because of the alteration to the tidal stream. Thus the authorities had built him another sprat weir down river. These weirs operated by channelling the sprats into bag nets and had been used on the river for hundreds of years, initially under the control of the Cistercians monks of Dunbrody Abbey. Built of evergreen poles driven into the seabed in the shape of a funnel, they had a six-foot gap at the narrow end which was covered with a net to catch the fish as they swam along in the stream. The new ones replaced timber for steel. These were capable of catching huge amounts of sprats although these days this was not the case. The small number that are taken are used by John to bait his eel baskets and nets.

We drove round to the main harbour, a few hundred yards downstream, where again a variety of craft were moored. Several prongs were sitting in the mud as the tide was out. Locally,

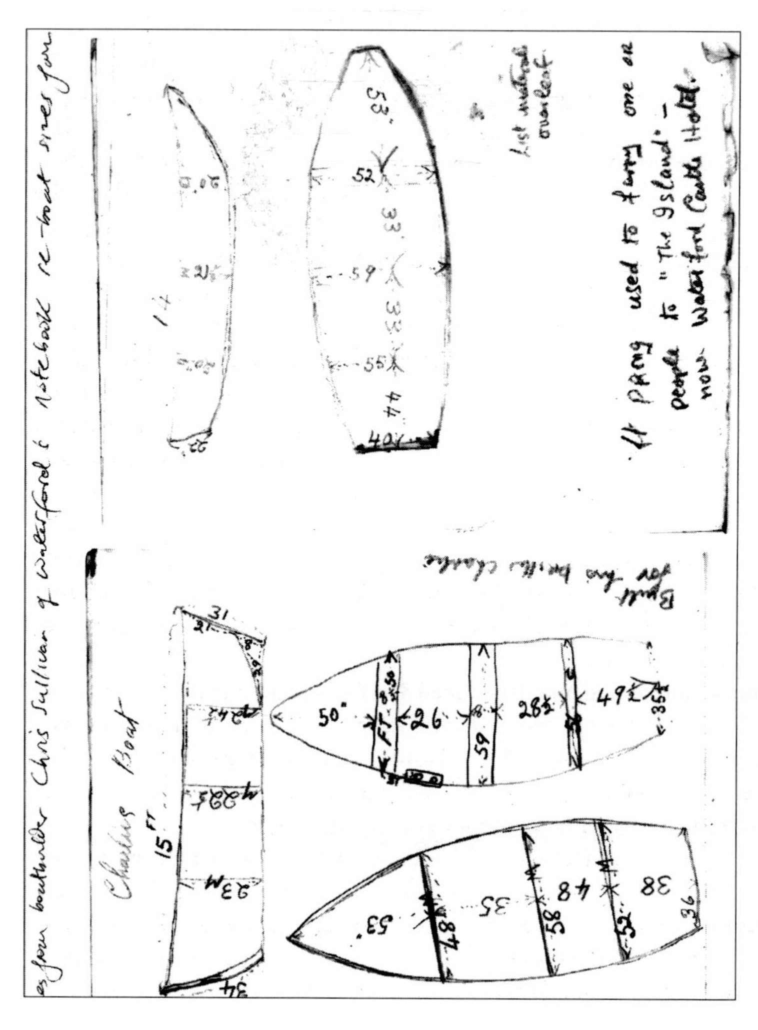

Two pages from Chris Sullivan's notebook concerning boat sizes from the 1930s.

Steam drifters at Dunmore East. (Joe Teesdale).

it is believed that the prongs developed from the currachs of the west coast and have been for generations the workhorse of the river. Most families would have owned at least one. At somewhere in the region of 17 feet in length (this varies according to builder), the prong is built in larch planking on oak frames, sometimes even of elm. Wood was sourced locally. The shape of prong, with its pram bow and rockered bottom, is supposed to have closely evolved over many years of usage on the river so that it could slide easily onto the mud without the bow lifting up and allow the occupant to step out with ease. Not that I doubt that, it's just that there are dozens of other rivers around Ireland and Britain, Europe even, that don't have such a shape.

Many fishermen built their own prongs though boatbuilders in various locations close to the fishing centres also did. In Cheekpoint there were three builders at Glass House Mill, by Belleview Point just along the river. One of these, John Lonergan, was well known because he had two club feet. He moved about by folding his deformed feet up under his buttocks and used his hands to propel himself over the ground and was as nimble and skilled as any other builder. Two brothers named Aitkins also built there and all three built punts as well as prongs. Another builder was Chris Sullivan who produced punts, cots and prongs. John showed me a 1950s' notebook in which Chris Sullivan kept his records of boats built – small pencil diagrams with a few simple measurements. There's one built for his brother Charlie and another for a local hotel. This was fascinating reading. Joe sent me over a photocopy of the whole booklet several weeks later.

He also had given me an interesting booklet entitled *The Cheekpoint Prong*, produced by the Cheekpoint Fishing Heritage Project in 2005, which catalogued the development and building of these unique craft. I could draw upon this and produce reams of facts of the prongs but that would be a bit tiresome. It seems enough to be brief and encourage further research and merely highlight the existence of both of these craft – prongs and punts.

At this point Joe and I returned to Dunmore East – passing Woodstown where the remains of a bag-net can be seen on the foreshore at low tide – where we dropped down to the harbour. The town was in the midst of some sort of international sailing regatta for small dinghies, for which activity both wind and sunshine were proving perfect, judging by the crowds watching from atop the harbour wall and the various array of flags on display. I squeezed

Dunmore East *c.*1880. (John Power).

between gazing bodies to have a quick look and take a few photos. This harbour, although extended since, was one designed by Alexander Nimmo and it was finished in 1815, complete with an elegant lighthouse at the end of the quay. Nimmo's work had a major impact upon facilities throughout Ireland and we shall learn a lot more about this man as we travel up the west coast. However, after a brief look at the fishing fleet in port and Joe waving at a few acquaintances, we didn't linger and returned to his house where I needed to exercise and feed the dog. Later on that evening Joe, his partner and her friend, and I returned to Cheekpoint for a superb evening meal at a local restaurant before driving through Waterford and on to Mooncoin where Joe had arranged to meet Peter Walsh, no relation to Tom.

Peter was another river man, a man with a constant smile upon his weathered face. Beneath his blue cap sprouts of white hair emerged. He led us down to the river Suir and where several of the river 'cots' were moored in a tiny recess or creek in the riverbank. These flat-bottomed boats were long and narrow with a very shallow draft and were quite different to the prongs. They are almost primitive in appearance and are said to be an improvement on a log boat, or dug-out, that the fishermen used until a couple of centuries ago. The argument was that the availability of whole trees to use as logs decreased and at the same time planked up timber became available. These cots have been worked on the rivers Barrow, Suir and Nore, the latter being a tributary of the Barrow. They meet just north of New Ross and all three they are often referred to as 'the Three Sisters' and are regarded as three of the finest rivers in Ireland. Mooncoin was about as far downstream that the cots were based on the Suir although a few might venture down as far as Waterford city when the river was low. A couple of cots were lying upside-down close by Peter's shed where he keeps his fishing gear. These I studied closely, noting the three planks in the construction of the bottom. The fishermen generally built their own cots and because of this it is almost impossible to specify an exact design, each man building to his, and the river's, requirements. Modern materials and techniques have been introduced in some cases. For example, although most use ribs of oak to strengthen the planking, a couple of cots have had ribs made of angle-iron incorporated into their building instead of oak.

The herring season at Dunmore East. (Joe Teesdale).

We looked into Peter's shed with its eel nets (fyke nets) and snap-nets. A snap-net was the net they used to catch salmon until the ban had taken its effect upon the fishermen here as well. It is used much in the same way as a coracle net is used in Wales. Fished using two cots, the net is stretched out between the two cotsmen who drift with the tide – both on the flood and ebb – in the hope of netting a salmon. Their use is documented as far back as 1200 and Peter's family, on his mother's side, had been fishing since 1740. Peter gave me a booklet entitled *Men, Tides and Salmon* by Noel P. Wilkins which gives a thorough explanation of the fishing method, the design and construction of the various cots and much more.

Arthur Young gives a few statistics for fishing in the late eighteenth century. Fifty boats of between 8 and 12 tons fished, the former costing £40 to build and the latter £60 and the only net fishing was for herring. Presumably these figures are for fishing downstream of Waterford. Ten mease was said to be an adequate night's fishing and forty was good. The best year on record had been 1775 when they caught 'more than they could dispose of, and the whole town and country stunk of them'. By the next century the salmon had taken precedent over herring and in 1844 Waterford exported 20,852 salmon to Bristol, this amount being independent of home consumption and that sent to Dublin. All this fish came from the Suir, Nore and Barrow rivers.

There used to be hundreds fishing in the river but this had gradually been reduced so that now there were twenty-two licences issued on the Suir, although only six or seven folk had been snap-netting until everyone had been stopped this year by the current ban. On the three rivers he said there were 132 licences in total which means twice the number of people were affected by the ban upstream. These days Peter fishes for eels and has to search for other work to keep going. It was a lovely spot down by the river. Peter displayed a mixture of what seemed to be personal charm and a particular sadness at the loss of a tradition going back generations. If only those faceless bureaucrats in Dublin would come along and see how their

Yankee Girl, a Dunmore East fishing boat. (Tommy McGrath).

Dunmore East from an old postcard posted with a King George 1/2*d* stamp. (Joe Teesdale).

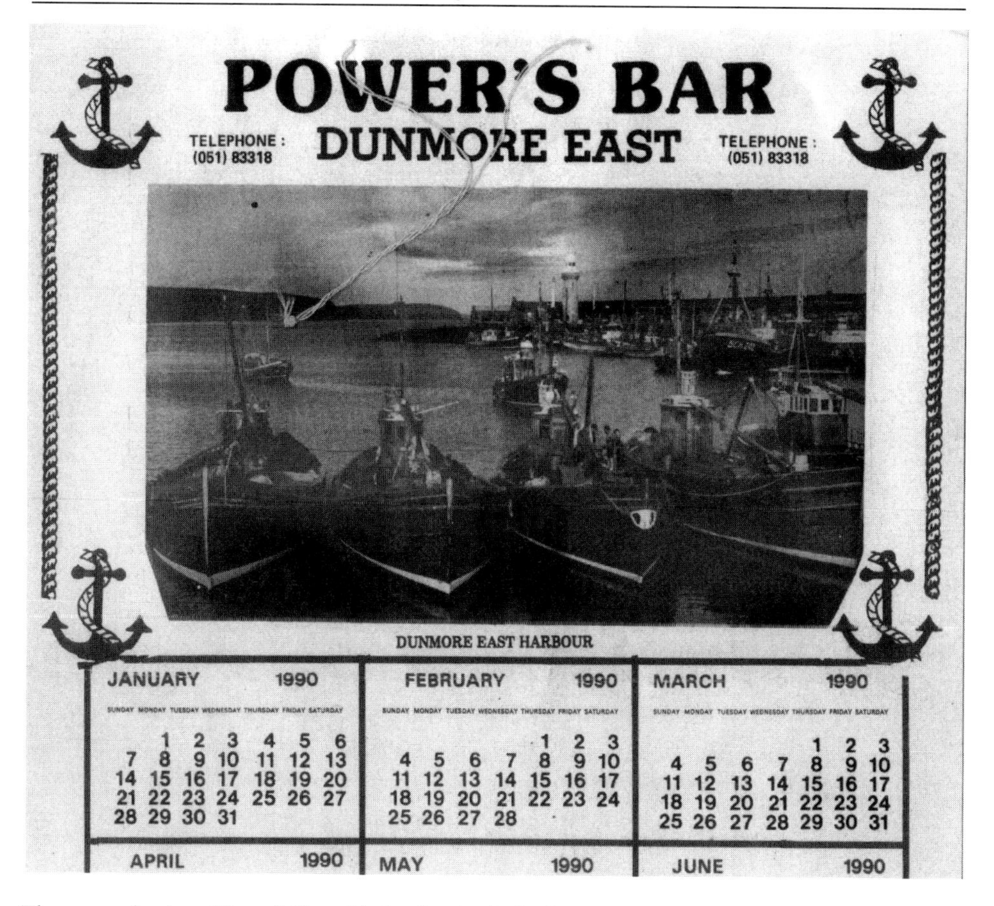

The 1990 calendar of Power's Bar with the fleet in the harbour.

ridiculous legislation affects such people as these river-folk, then they might think twice. In reality they don't care an ounce for it's the same everywhere these days, where civil servants and politicians are more interested in power and high wages than those people they are meant to be serving. I doubt there's a government in Europe that isn't corrupt. It's simply a matter of how obvious that corruption is to the people. We all know of stories of cash in paper bags and party funding crises yet regard this as piffling when compared to the corruption we are constantly told about outside Europe. Thus we accept it as part of a modern democracy.

On leaving the river we stopped at a thatched cottage alongside the road where Peter's mother had been born and where the family had lived since the eighteenth century. I'd wanted to photograph him standing at the door, which I did, although by then the light was fading as the day came to an end. After yet another farewell, on the drive back to Dunmore East we stopped briefly close by the river in the centre of Waterford City. Although it was almost dark, we'd stopped to get a glimpse of the former Dunmore East pilot boat *Betty Breen*, now converted into a yacht and moored alongside the pontoon in the river. She lay on the outside so the photograph I took was pretty useless, nevertheless it was good to see her as Joe had been showing me earlier in the day various photos of her taken during her working life.

Waterford is one of Ireland's foremost cities and, as thus, busy with night time revellers and through traffic. It is also one of the most ancient ports in all of Ireland and, in AD155, it was called Cuan-na-grian or 'the harbour of the sun'. Its modern name comes from the Norse

Vaderfjord, meaning 'safe haven', from the times the Vikings colonised it in the ninth century after destroying the earlier town. Shipbuilding must have flourished here for medieval ships' timbers dating from between the eleventh and thirteenth centuries have been excavated in recent times, these all displaying a Nordic boatbuilding tradition. After Henry II sailed up the river with 240 ships in 1171, the city became English in character and remained so until the nineteenth century. In the previous century it had been Ireland's third important port after Dublin and Cork. Trade to England increased in the nineteenth century, with woollen and linen goods being the main export. It was against a background of increasing trade and prosperity that Thomas White arrived in 1775 and his son William, married into a Quaker family, started up a shipbuilding yard in 1819. These were wooden vessels though iron vessels were built from around the mid-century at the Neptune shipyard. The Whites remained building up to about 1868.

At the same time various ferry companies established services from Waterford to England and Wales carrying both cattle and emigrants and later passengers in both directions, with steamer connections available to many piers about Waterford Harbour and along the coast in both directions. Waterford became a hub of activity for the whole county and beyond. However, nowadays, a new, very active commercial harbour has been established further downstream so that Waterford town is home to the marina with its yachts and motor cruisers we were viewing and the odd fishermen in their cots or prongs in the river. Having seen the *Betty Breen*, we climbed back aboard Joe's car, the two women not quite sure why we'd bother to stop, and returned to Dunmore East, and me to the van for a badly needed rest. From an early start observing Kilmore Quay, through three interviews with dedicated fishermen, I really felt I'd covered some ground. The only problem I foresaw, as I drifted off to a deep sleep, was that if every day was as intense as today, I'd be knackered before I got a quarter of the way around the coast.

DAY THREE

Joe described the morning as a 'soft day' which amounted to mist and light rain. Joe reckoned the expression came from American-cum-Irish film talk. Still it seemed an apt description.

We talked a little over breakfast after I'd had a shower. In the bath was a clump of seaweed which, when I asked why, was for infusing in a bath to soak up the minerals. Joe was from farming stock, inland a bit, although he'd been coming to Dunmore East since the age of five or six. At about the age of twelve he started going fishing on local boats such as the *William Edward*, *Wiseman* or *Accord*, all of which were depicted on a huge mural on the wall of Waterford Harbour and its boats which hung over the table in the kitchen. *Betty Breen* was there too, as were many larger ships. I should have photographed the mural but stupidly didn't. Anyway, Joe worked for a shipping company in the seventies in Dublin until returning to farming. When he retired two years ago he moved to Dunmore East. Having been a member of the Southern Fisheries Board for seven years, he was currently the Board's chairman which meant he was often busy at meetings or having to sign official letters.

I left Joe with a feeling of nervousness. Suddenly I felt alone in my research although I had with me to hand Joe's list of contacts along the coast. Of all the folk I met during the tour, even though everyone was really helpful in finding time to talk and supplying photographs and books, Joe really was both supportive and cooperative. Not only had he taken a day away from his normal activities to drive me around and introduce me to those already mentioned, but he'd also phoned ahead to various people so that I was expected. That morning he'd made a call to another Walsh, this time John, again no relation to either of the other Walshes, and he agreed to see me at short notice. Thus I found myself on the way to his house. On the way through Dunmore East I saw the sandy beach at Ladies Cove which is underwater at high tide as it had been on the previous evening. Today, with the tide out, children were jumping off the rocks into the calm sea which really did look inviting even if the weather was dull and misty. In fact, if I hadn't just had a shower, I might have gone in myself which would have pleased the dog.

I found John Walsh easily on the outskirts of the village and, without any hesitation, he led me into his sitting room where we sat down. Although he had retired the previous year, his had always been a life at sea. He had been a pilot for forty years, coxswain of the lifeboat for thirteen years and second coxswain for a number of years before that. His father and grandfather had been pilots before him and the latter's licence was dated 29 August 1906, this being the first licence issued. Before that, John told me, hobblers simply rowed out in search of incoming boats though, because so many were lost as they ventured further offshore, the licence system was introduced. The Waterford pilots – there were twenty-seven of them at the peak of the shipping trade – were always based in Dunmore East as they are now. Today they have just one boat with six pilots whereas many of the regular container ships visiting Waterford have their own licenced men aboard to save on the expense of bringing a pilot out. One of the pilot boats was the *Lily Doreen* which John's father had bought for £5. It was going to be used as a sail training boat but several planks sprung and the bottom was found to be rotten. Thus she was broken up on the slip at Passage East. The *Betty Breen* came on station in 1950.

The Waterford pilot cutter off Dumore.

John, like many others, also had a salmon licence so he too, was affected by the current ban. He had a huge knowledge of the tides because of his pilotage and lifeboat command and understood the movement of the fish. However, unlike those I'd met the previous day, John drifted offshore. He reckoned that, as the nets improved in quality, the men set them increasingly further out to sea. West of Tranmore, he said, the tide wasn't as strong which in turn allowed the nets to hang better in the water and thus catch more fish. The salmon fishing he said was his 'lucozade'. At other times he jigged for mackerel – 'got a box in ten minutes' – and he'd ring-netted for herring in the fifties off 'The Hook'.

We talked a bit about his time on the lifeboat and at the same time he gave me a booklet about the history of the Dunmore East lifeboats by Jeff Morris. Considering the importance of Dunmore as a port, I was surprised to find out that the first lifeboat wasn't stationed here until 1884. Tranmore Bay to the west looks exactly like Waterford Bay from out at sea in daylight and many a boat has come ashore, confusing the two, because Tranmore Bay is edged in low-lying sand. Today there are towers on both Brownstown and Newtown Heads, two on the first and three on the latter so that they are recognisable from sea and ships can differentiate between each. John remembered the coal boat *Michael*, *en route* to Sligo, which made this mistake and went up the beach at Tranmore. Luckily John and his crew had taken the crew off

Fishing boat W36 (either *St Joseph* or *Intrepid*) steaming out of Dunmore East *c.*1950 with the pilot vessel *Lilly Doreen* in the background. (Peter Powell).

before she hit the beach but he described the night as 'awful' which was probably an understatement. On other instance he remembered going out to a canoe incident, after which the wearing of reflective material became mandatory for canoers.

I probably spent two hours talking to him, even though he'd said he'd only an hour because he had to go out. We mutually decided he'd better go though both of us seemed happy to talk for another hour at least. Thus, I left him about midday after sincere farewells. I proceeded in a westerly direction along the twisting coast road to Tranmore. This was obviously a touristy town judging by the amusement arcades, the red and white striped circus tent, bars, chippers and surfers battling the wet weather. The beach of what would, in sunlight, appear as white sand, stretched away into the foggy distance. Just west of the main built-up area was a stone-built harbour with an old lifeboat shed, dating from 1858, set back a little, some fishermen's huts and the new 1997 lifeboat station. To the west of this had been a 'men only' beach where, I assumed, they were allowed to swim naked as was the norm in pre-Victorian times of the nineteenth century. From the cliff above the harbour, the towers on the headlands on each side of the bay where just visible. Passing along the coast a little later, I stopped to photograph the three towers on Newtown Head, one of which has a metal man atop.

By now the mist had thickened so much that I was having trouble seeing more than fifty yards ahead. This certainly seemed uncharacteristic of summer weather in parts of Britain and I wondered whether it was normal on the southern Irish coast. Totally unexpectedly I came across the small harbour at Dunabrattin Head. Before the late nineteenth century the fishermen from these parts hauled their boats up a small beach that was sheltered by the headland and this was generally referred to as the Boat-strand. When a harbour was built in the 1880s, the name stuck, and some still call this harbour that. It is tidal and offers little shelter in rough weather and can only accommodate small craft yet, even so, there are several small boats potting for lobsters and crabs and fishing for mackerel when in season. Salmon drifting was

Pilot vessel *Betty Breen* that was brought on duty in 1951. (Joseph Teesdale).

again practised by some fishermen. In the 1980s one such fisherman, John Murray, was sent to prison after his monofilament nets were confiscated by the fishery patrol. Monofilament, deemed best for daylight fishing, was banned although many other countries had adopted it and fishermen and their organisations were lobbying their government over it. However the leisure anglers seemed to have a stronger voice and the nets weren't legalised until 1998. Now, with salmon fishing banned altogether, the same fishermen's organisations are adamant that the government is only listening to the leisure anglers – otherwise often known as the rod and line brigade – instead of taking into account the financial needs and contribution to the economy by the salmon fishermen. I was going to hear a lot more about this over the next three weeks.

The tide was high and I wandered around the harbour with the dog sniffing new smells. A couple of these leisure fishermen were busily preparing their lines on the end of the quay. One thing I had noticed on the roads were the various road signs directing anglers to specific beaches, the signs even stating the fish normally caught there. This alone shows just how popular fishing is for those in leisure and I suppose it's not much of a shock to find out that their voices command such influence in government circles. Tales of government corruption are widespread and seem quite believable.

There's a memorial plaque against the rock next to an old anchor. This anchor belonged to the *Morning Star*, a vessel that foundered on the rocks outside the harbour on the night of the 7 October 1915 with the loss of four of the crew including the captain. The mate was the sole survivor and the saddest part of the story was that he died two months later as a result of his ordeal. The anchor was recovered in 1978 and the memorial erected in 2005.

We continued our journey, which was by now along what is now called the 'copper coast', a reference to the rich veins of copper in the hinterland. Mining occurred at various points, and at Bunmahon I came across the Tankardstown Engine Houses, a few of the buildings of which had been reinstated for visitors to learn a little about the heritage of the mining industry, helped on by a series of information boards. I wandered around the site for half an hour or so, reading the text and making notes. The place had an eerie feeling to it, largely due to the mist, which also meant it was impossible to see right across the site from one side to the other. The feeling of the isolation of the place might also have contributed to the spookiness that radiated around the site. When another car stopped I wasn't sure if I was pleased to have the reassurance of another human being or surprised that somebody else was passing through and thus suspicious of his intentions. He probably thought the same!

Copper was first mined in Mesopotamia over 8500 years ago and in Ireland about 4500 years ago which was the dawn of the Bronze Age. The region around Killarney in County Cork is documented as being the region first mined in Ireland. In Bunmahon the lodes range from a few inches to many yards in thickness and are thought to be 350 million years old. Flint mining itself is thought to be oldest industry in Ireland yet the first documented evidence for mining in this area comes from the 1740-1760 period when Thomas 'Bullocks' Wyse opened and operated a silver mine in Ballydwane, two miles to the east, although the remnant of this is a sand-filled shaft in a sea stack. In 1824 the Hibernian Mining Company and the Mining Company of Ireland both took out leases in the Bunmahon area, the latter to the east and the other to the west. The Mining Co. of Ireland discovered rich veins in Knockmahon and Ballynasissia five years later and thus they erected buildings, installing water and steam powered machinery and constructed a copper yard at Stage Cove to ship the ore off to Swansea for smelting. Coal was brought in. The deposits at Tankardstown were discovered in the 1850s when the winding house I was looking at was built to house a Cornish steam engine which drove a pair of winding drums. This mine became the hub of the industry until its closure in 1875. The ore was carried upon a tramway that ran along the cliff top and then down to sea level.

Unsuccessful attempts were made to reopen the mine in the first decade of the twentieth century but there was a period of intense exploitation in the 1970s. The site was a set of the MGM film *The Mackenzie Break*, when a lorry was pushed into the shaft and made to burst into flames. This vehicle provides the only support for soil and rubbish that have since been dumped in the shaft, and hence is dangerously unsafe now.

A brief but violent outburst of rain drew me back to the van and a few miles on. When this had stopped, I ate a pleasant lunch parked in a desolate car park overlooking the sea 300 feet below, the roar of which I could hear but the waves of which I could only glimpse through occasional gaps in the mist. The dog played with another dog that seemed to materialise from nowhere for I saw no one else nor any houses along the road. Still they were happy.

According to my journal written at the time, Dungarvan harbour was devoid of any life when we arrived, driving over the river Colligan whose bridge had been built by the sixth Earl of Devonshire. On our left was the fish quay that had once seen many a Scotch boat landing. The Devonshires built much of the town in the early nineteenth century when both the fifth and sixth earls reconstructed what was otherwise described as a poor town inhabited mainly by fishers. These two were also responsible for building many of the quays in the harbour.

Seeing Dungarvan today it's quite hard to understand that this was once one of Ireland's premier fishing towns with vessels coming from all over Ireland and Britain to fish the seemingly endless supplies of hake, cod and ling. Of course other species were available but these three were the most sought after. At the beginning of the eighteenth century Dr Richard Pococke described the place as 'a good fishing town and famous for the export of potatoes to many parts of Ireland' although the town was said to be in a state of decay with no water supply or quay. By mid-century six men in a boat could hook a thousand hake, along with other species, in a single night's fishing. The quality of the fish was considered better than that from Newfoundland and was all taken by long line. Trawling was introduced in the 1730s, but immediately condemned as damaging to the environment. The real bonanza started in about

1736 when a fisherman named Mr Doyle, sailing aboard a twelve-ton boat called *Nymph* with a crew of seven, discovered a bank some thirty miles south-east of Dungarvan, the seabed of which consisted of small pebble-stones, cockles, and other shells. The town's fortunes changed. Swimming over this bank were huge stocks of ling, hake, bream, skate and whiting which he trawled and later hauled aboard before returning back to market, overloaded with fish. The bank, named the Nymph Bank after the boat, extends some 90 miles south-west to Cape Clear. Some even thought the bank might even extend over to Newfoundland but Doyle considered this conjectural. Nevertheless, Dungarvan prospered from this discovery with 163 boats based there in 1824, employing 1,000 men. However these men were described as 'earning a poor living from the fishery' by which I presumed that the bulk of the benefit was being felt outside the town. By 1840 these numbers had increased to sixty-nine decked vessels, forty open boats and 270 row boats, all employing 1,600 men. It was about this time that the first quay was built. Fishermen, by then, lived in 'comfortable houses built for them by the Devonshires' and which were 'subject to only a nominal rent', according to the Commissioners on The Irish Fisheries report of 1836. Shipbuilding also flourished briefly during this period with vessels built above the old Railway Bridge by what is now the Civic Offices. However, with potatoes being one of the main crops of the area, the famine had disastrous effects on the whole town and surrounding countryside. By 1846, with unseasonal severe weather conditions, the fishermen were employed breaking stones. Fishing gear was pawned whilst some even burned their boats and oars to keep warm. Fish became scarce and prices went up. When the railway arrived in 1878 from Waterford in an attempt to aid the trade of the town and its economy to develop, it was too late for the fishing bonanza was almost over.

The town seemed pleasant enough as I briefly walked around, shoppers crowding the streets and the bars buzzing. I read somewhere that it was a lively modern town but that wouldn't have been my description. I must admit I was nearly drawn into one particular bar where the locals were obviously having a good time but, with intentions to push as far west that afternoon as possible in my mind and knowing the dog wanted his walk, I was persuaded against and, after visiting the bookshop and tourist information, I returned to the van and continued driving.

My next quarry was Helvick and the harbour there. I'd a contact name here, given to me by Joe, a fellow by the name of Sean Whelan, but when I phoned him he was busy and unable to come out, although he said he'd have liked to show me around. He sounded very friendly on the phone and genuinely disappointed that he was otherwise engaged. However he did mention one particular boat, the *Vega*, a BIM 50-footer, owned by Thomas Kelly, built in 1950 and which fished until 2000. Up to eighty Scots ring-net boats came here in the 1940s and 1950s to fish for herring, he told me. Sean later sent me some photographs and the book *Desperate Heaven*, published by the Durgarvan Museum Society, from which some of the following information comes.

Helvick fishermen faired equally badly during the famine, their boats being small and without sails. In 1848 a petition was signed by 2,310 people objecting to the Waterford boats using trawl nets at the expense of the ninety 'hookers' working in the bay. Presumably the term 'hooker' is used loosely here if the boats were simple rowboats. The fishermen were described as 'literally starving, not for want of fish, but for want of proper fishing boats and fishing tackle, fit for deep water'. Their boats were deemed to small, without sails and compassed. However about this time, Lord Stuart de Decies had spent some £2,000 on a new harbour at Helvick, and a curing station there so that, by 1861, a thriving small fishing village had grown up, rivalling Dungarvan. One person foremost in helping the fishermen in the post-famine years was the local vicar, the Revd James Alcock (1805-1893), who managed to get the fishermen food and loans to see them through, thus enabling them to eventually get back to fishing. Loans of between £1 and £3 were handed out and, in one case, a fisherman was said to have bought some herring nets with his money and earned £15 in two days. By 1847 there were forty-nine boats whose crews supported their families and two years later it was noted that forty-five boats caught 30,000 fish worth £500 in one month. The curing station, leased by two Scots Edwards and Lister, was capable of smoking 100 barrels of herring at any one time in its three chambers. The Third Quarterly Report from the Ring District (the Ring before the surrounding area) of 1848 gave a full description of the curing establishment which included a cooper, salting houses and office. How long it survived for is unknown.

The oldest part of Helvick Harbour was carved out of the rock inside a small stone pier and is presumably the 1840's harbour though it is thought that the 1820's structure predated this. The modern harbour, dating from 1912, has a substantial concrete pier and alongside this were a variety of boats as well as facilities including an ice plant. Nine boxes of dogfish were rotting and smelly indeed at the end of the pier. I sat nearby smoking a cigarette, observing the bay. Directly across was the lighthouse at Ballynacourty Point whilst somewhere out, under the waves, there lay the wreck of the sailing ship *Moresby* that sank on Christmas Eve 1895 with the loss of twenty lives. The ship was *en route* from Cardiff to South America loaded with coal when she lost several of her sails in severe weather. Seeing another boat, a local schooner, the captain decided to follow this into harbour, believing he was off Cork. When the schooner went aground, the *Moresby* quickly went about and split the lower deck topsails. They lowered the anchor and thought themselves safe and, although the lifeboat from Ballynacourty went out to their aid, they refused to leave the ship. During the night the wind blew up again and when the anchor cable parted, the ship was driven onto the Whitehouse Bank. Although the coxswain of the lifeboat summoned his crew once more, they didn't respond so the lifeboat was unable to put out. By daylight the crew and two passengers were in the rigging awaiting rescue. With the lifeboat crewless, the coastguard tried to get a line aboard the boat by rocket. This was unsuccessful and the man in charge attempted to get volunteers to man the coastguard boat. None were forthcoming.

By eleven o'clock that morning the ship began to heel and the onlookers could only gasp as the crew tried to swim ashore. A volunteer crew was eventually gathered but by the time they had launched and reached the stricken vessel, nobody was left aboard. The ebbing tide had taken many out to sea but they did manage to pluck seven from the sea, two of which subsequently died. Thus five survived their ordeal. The Official Report into the tragedy that followed a Court of Inquiry never really answered the questions as to what occurred that night, although three officials were made scapegoats and blamed for not communicating and anticipating the events. Why the crew of the lifeboat never mustered remains unknown although there are obvious suggestions that this was because the crew had earlier refused to leave. Incidentally, the lifeboat station was moved to a few miles west of Helvick, to Crowe Point, in 1900 and then to a new lifeboat house in Helvick Harbour in 1930.

A noteworthy event took place here in 1972 when the IRA attempted to land arms aboard the vessel *Claudia*. These had been supplied by Colonel Gaddafi of Libya to aid the 'freeing' of the six northern counties from British control, along with some £50,000 in cash. He originally had offered 40 tons of rifles and ammunition though this was reduced to five tons because of some doubt concerning the *Claudia*, which he believed to have been involved in past smuggling operations and hence was known to the authorities. Gaddafi was correct in his assessment as the vessel was shadowed by a Royal Naval submarine for some – or all – of the voyage to Helvick Head. Once the smugglers were close inshore and able to contact their comrades living ashore in a house overlooking the harbour they suddenly noticed three naval vessels closing in. The *Claudia* was arrested and taken into Helvick and later Cobh where the arms were unloaded by the Garda. The money, by a stroke of luck, managed to get ashore and was later passed on to the IRA for future missions. Three IRA men were later charged, found guilty and imprisoned for the attempt to supply the arms.

I read one report that referred to Helvick as the 'new pier' whereas the 'old pier' was at nearby Ballinagoul. However, that harbour was only built in 1848. On our return journey from Helvick Head I photographed the pier from above, noting several vessels sheltering within its confines. In the distance, on the foreshore, a gang of men were gathering shellfish that I took to be oysters which is big business around here and which are exported, as are winkles and clams, though on a smaller scale. Passing the Famine Way, we continued back to the main road.

From this road, heading south-west from Dungarvan, we turned off towards a place called 'Curragh' I'd seen on the map. I was intrigued to see if there were any currachs on the beach. The spelling of the name of this small village was equally intriguing as I've been told by currach folk that spelling it with a 'g' is an Anglicization of the correct 'currach' which comes from the Gaelic 'curach'. Thus, I wondered why this Irish village used the English spelling. I didn't find out and indeed didn't see any of the canvas boats upon the beach. In fact there wasn't much there at all except a fine sandy beach and a few kids playing. Ardmore, a few miles on, is described as 'an historic tourist town' and, judging by the acres of chalets and caravans to the east, is just that. But first impressions can be deceptive for there was a pleasant air about the place. I dropped into the local newsagent's in search of any booklets on the place but found none. Outside an old fellow was teaching a few kids how to play 'knock fist'. By the way one of the young lads was holding his hand he'd not favoured well in his lessons. The old man, rosy cheeks and greying hair and walking stick propped up against the shop window, was really enjoying himself and the boys certainly didn't seem put off by his obvious skill. I wondered whether the fellow had recently come from a bar as I'd noticed there were several for such a small place.

Ardmore is the start of St Declan's Way, a 56-mile walk between Ardmore and the Rock of Cashel following as faithfully as possible the route taken by the saint, and reaching a height of over 1600 feet. St Declan himself came back to Ireland at the very beginning of the fifth century, thirty years before St Patrick. Seems he'd been over to Rome and returned to teach his countrymen about the ways of the church. He arrived in Ardmore where he decided to set up his Christian settlement which is therefore the oldest in the country. They say that St Declan's bell and vestments were born over from Wales, where he'd come from, on a glacial boulder which today sits on a little spur of rock and that those agile enough to squeeze beneath it benefit from its amazing healing powers. One suspects, though, that those agile and fit enough to crawl underneath the boulder are probably not in need of too much healing.

Ardmore has a small harbour with a very new concrete pier and a few non-descript boats hanging about on trailers. I was quite surprised to find that a lifeboat station had been based here between 1858 and 1895 and that the lifeboat house from 1876 still stands, albeit converted into a private residence. It seems that this site was chosen because of its proximity to both Ardmore and Whiting bays. The lifeboat performed a rescue in 1860 where seven lives were saved and medals given to four of the rescuers but after that there were no call-outs. Thus the station closed, the ones of Helvick and Youghal being sufficient for their needs.

Youghal is of course famous for its potato and tobacco, for here was Sir Walter Raleigh's large estate to where he brought back his two 'discoveries'. Although potatoes were certainly cropped hereabout and exported, I don't think there's any mention of tobacco being grown here. However,

Footpath signs.

before driving into the town I turned right and followed a narrow road along the Blackwater River. I was in search of the clinker-built salmon cots of the river I'd heard about.

Let me explain a bit. Over ten years ago I'd met Darina Tully, a maritime ethnologist a bit like myself and, by chance, we met again two months before I was due in Ireland. Obviously I explained my plans to her and, saying she had an old map of Ireland in her car, we met up later that day. Pouring over the map, she pencilled in a whole host of places, names of people and types of interesting vernacular craft. Around the Blackwater she had drawn a big circle with a note of 'clinker cots'. That was all I had to go on so drove about five miles along the river until the road ended at a house. I'd not seen one boat, never mind a cot, on the river and I scoured the banks as best as I could. Returning downstream, I scoured the lower reaches of the harbour with my binoculars, again finding nothing. However the drive along the river had been lovely, trees shrouding the river, almost touching it at times, fields of different patterns and birds everywhere. Not that I could recognise any of them as I'm not good at that, but they added to what was a pleasant sight nonetheless.

The Halls were lucky enough to travel on the river by boat between Youghal and Lismore, a distance of about 15 miles, and they found no less than forty-two salmon weirs. I was jealous though I did see a line of posts sticking out of the mud that looked like the remains of one fish weir. Driving over the bridge between Counties Waterford and Cork, I was reminded of what they had written about the bridge they crossed upon. They said it was 'one of the most remarkable in the kingdom: it is 1,542 feet in length and is composed of forty-seven bays of thirty feet span. Its breadth is twenty-two feet and the height above water is ten feet' and it was Alexander Nimmo who'd designed it in the 1830s. The bridge I crossed had seven spans (I think) and was made of concrete and was built in the late 1950s. What happened to Nimmo's original bridge? I was becoming more and more intrigued about this fellow who I already knew had been responsible for all amount of harbour development along the coast.

'The Metal Man', the figure on one of the towers that stand on the western side of Tramore Bay. (Joe Teesdale).

I was surprised I liked Youghal. I walked along the waterfront in the pouring rain, amongst derelict buildings, some boarded up in rotting plywood and then I visited a Tesco store, all things I detest. The place had an air of generally falling apart but nevertheless I was happy wandering around. Even the dog, on his lead which he detests, was joyfully bounding along, pulling hard at the lease. The waterfront had an array of colourful boats – if they can look so in the rain and mist – and there were some small punts that attracted my attention which I took to be the last remaining salmon yawls that drift-netted for salmon in the estuary. Some scenes of John Heuston's film *Moby Dick* were shot here. Unfortunately, because the time was getting late, the Visitor Centre and Folk Museum were both closed and we left, passing the lighthouse which has the notoriety of being almost on the high street. The first tower here was built in 1190 but because it was called 'The Nunnery' fell into disuse after the dissolution of the monasteries in the sixteenth century. A new light was built on the same site and is still lit. There is a field close to the lighthouse where Raleigh is said to have planted the first potatoes in Europe. Perhaps if he hadn't, then potatoes might not have been so important in the Irish diet and the famine not occurred. Perhaps he's not such a hero after all and was simply a merchant keen to profit from his plundering. A bit like that other British maritime hero Sir Francis Drake who, it turned out, was one of the first traders to profit from carry human souls from Africa to the tea plantations and thus began the era of slavery. Mind you I'd be missing those baked potatoes filled with prawns if Raleigh hadn't!

In his *The Scenery and Antiquities of Ireland*, Joseph Stirling Coyne found Youghal in about 1842 as 'a place of little maritime trade; as a harbour it is chiefly resorted to by fishing-boats'. He continues by giving an early description of the typical fishing boat of the time,

> These craft, called *hookers*, are generally from ten to twenty tons burthen, and are open, with the exception of a few feet of deck in the forepart of the boat, beneath which is a small cuddy

Youghal lighthouse.

> or cabin, in which the crew repose during the brief intermission of their toil while engaged in fishing. The boats are rigged cutter-fashion, with a large fore-and-aft mainsail, a foresail, and a jib; and though without the defence of a deck, it is almost incredible in what a heavy sea they will live. The Youghal *hookers* are esteemed the best and most seaworthy boats built on this coast.

Coyne also mentions the Nymph Bank and its inexhaustible stock of fish 'both round and flat', and notes that the fishermen of the coast take little advantage of this prolific fishing ground but instead prefer to go fishing across the Atlantic at Newfoundland. Is there a degree of contradiction in this statement? I asked myself.

Ballycotton has an extensive harbour which was under repair at the time but even so it was pretty busy with fishing boats. I parked up at the head of the pier and sat at the side door watching the lighthouse on Ballycotton Rock which lies just offshore. It had just begun exhibiting its light as the evening approached and this mesmerized me for a long period as I lost myself in thoughts. I tried to phone a few people but receiving no signal on the mobile, and because of the number of vehicles driving past and attempting to find a parking spot then turning round with difficulty when they couldn't, I decided to move on and forget about sleeping the night here. Ballycotton itself seemed a very pleasant village, accentuated by the aroma of burning peat and the smell of the ocean, and would have been a lovely place to wake up.

There's a plaque on the new lifeboat shed which was erected on the fiftieth anniversary of the lifeboat's rescue of the crew of the *Daunt Rock* lightship which lies a bit to the west, off the entrance to Cork Harbour. This was in 1936 and the lifeboat was the Barnett-type *Mary Stanford*, crewed by four members of the Sliney family and three of the Walshes, all from the village. They spent sixty-three hours searching for the lightship which had broken its anchor cable and was drifting helplessly. The weather was said to have been so atrocious that the spray from the waves were breaking over the 190-foot Ballycotton lighthouse. The story has been televised and is only one example of the bravery of the

Dungarvan Quay 1951/52.

lifeboat men from this small community. The lifeboat was on station in Ballycotton before moving to another station until 1959 after which it became a pilot boat on the river Shannon at Limerick. It then passed into private hands and restored though is said to be now languishing in Dublin.

After leaving Ballycotton I managed to call David Neale, another of Joe Teesdale's contacts. David was unavailable that evening and tried to persuade me to visit him the following day. I wanted to get to Cork however, to await a call from an American friend whom I hoped was in town. We managed a few minutes of conversation. Prawns, according to David when I asked, were bad at the time as were lobsters because of fierce competition from the salmon drift-netters who, to survive, were turning to lobsters to compensate for the loss of income. The big boats were tied up, he said. 'Go slower', says David when I told him what I was up to. If only I had the time and money to do so! He continued: 'Somebody once asked an Irishman for a translation of the Spanish word "manana". Eventually, after a couple of weeks, he replied "there's no thing in Irish for such haste!"' He laughed down the phone as he told his joke and then suggested I visit Roche's Point, the eastern entrance to Cork Harbour with superb views over Cobh. I continued driving into the deepening night.

I took his advice and drove to a spot with the superb view. I was a bit shocked by all the height barriers in the car parks around there. This was another thing I was to become accustomed to. David was right, though, and the view was first-rate even if it was dark and I couldn't stay the night because of the barriers. The lights of the conurbation of Cork and Cobh, and all between, lit up the sky with its orange glow and individual lights scarpered about the dark shape of the land either side. Light pollution indeed I thought. The lights of a ship moved in the distance. Spike Island, where I'd read that the fisherman John Murray from Dunabrattin Harbour was locked up in the prison, stood out. I continued along the road, not knowing if it went anywhere until I arrived right at the point itself. This spot was fantastic, colourful houses, two terraces of them, and the lighthouse above twinkling its friendly night. The dog and I walked around for a short while before we returned to the van, I revitalised myself with a glass or two of wine whilst writing up notes and then sleep came easily.

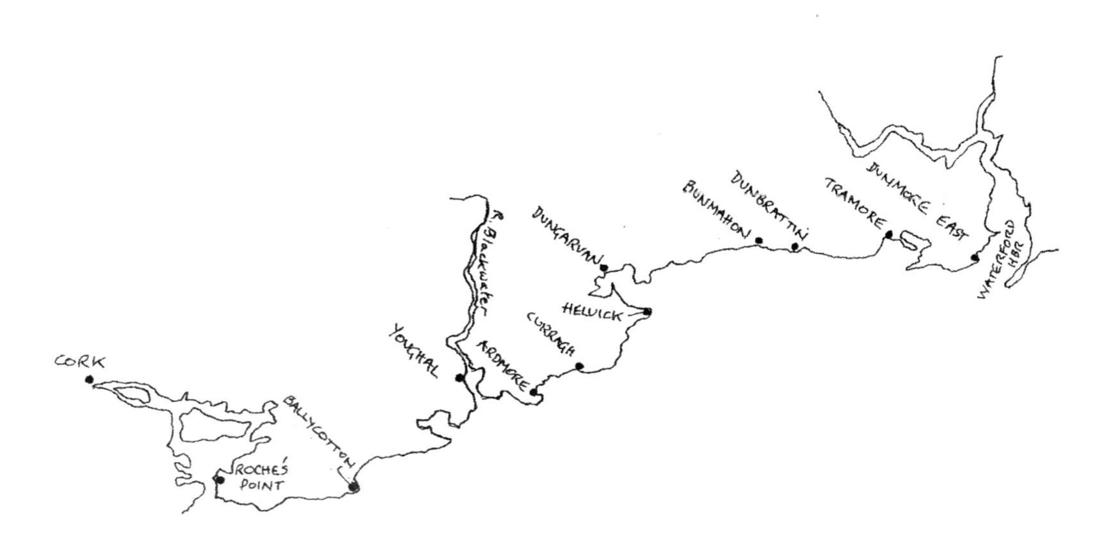

DAY FOUR

Roche's Point was even more impressive and colourful in the dull morning light, even if the greyness of the previous day still prevailed. One terrace of cottages lined the road up to the lighthouse whilst another directly faced the sea on the other side of the car park. They were even more brightly painted than they had appeared the previous evening and were all number of shades – pink, grey, yellow, red, blue, and green. The lighthouse and its corresponding buildings were all intense white, as if recently whitewashed, and above the houses nearest to the lighthouse were the ruins of God knows what. Outside, many of the cottages were surf-boards and sailing clothing which gave the impression that many of the inhabitants were holiday-makers. This was reinforced by the simple fact that I counted seven number plates with British registrations, excluding my own. Two were from Northern Ireland and the others from mainland Britain. On the beach sat a couple of sailing dinghies and one fellow dressed in a lifejacket was doing something inside one whilst two divers set out with their gear in a small inflatable from the slipway. In front of one of the dinghies was a boathouse, all shut up and closed, whilst another open-ended tunnel-like store, built in stone with the hump-back-bridge-shaped roof covered by grass, its original use unknown, housed what looked like the remains of a homemade raft. Above this, in the long grass and nettles, I found two upside-down currachs with shiny canvas skins looking recently re-bitumened. By about eight o'clock hardly anyone else had surfaced, and with the sailor having sailed off and the divers gone diving, there was no one to ask a couple of questions of. Church Bay lay directly across the mile and a half channel and over the hill the pretty harbour of Crosshaven. Dog was exercised by throwing stones into the murky water. When the coffee was drunk we proceeded on our way.

Passing the barriered car parks where I'd admired the views the evening before, the road descended to Whitegate and, seeing what looked like a shop, we drove onto the pier. The shop was closed but the pier itself had an interesting history. This was Aghada Pier, built in the years following the famine of the 1840s. During those awful years local political and religious leaders called for infrastructural works to be instigated to relieve the suffering amongst the poor and hungry. However, it was only because of Queen Victoria's visit to Queenstown (hence its subsequent name), just after the famine that produced the impetus amongst those holding the purse-strings for a pier to be built here. Perhaps they were hoping she'd come and bless this pier with her feet or was it simply just another example of the lack of investment and foresight directed towards the country people? Or was there a reason for building the pier all the time and the Queen's visit a mere excuse to obtain some funding?

For, from 1850 – just a few years later – and onwards, Lower Aghada became the hub of the eastern part of the remarkable Cork Harbour transportation system. Employing steamers, a ferry service was established between Cork City, Passage West, Cobh, Crosshaven and Aghada. Three 'Greenboats', as they were called, continued to convey passengers and goods from Cloyne, Ballycotton and beyond, via this pier, up to the 1930s when road transport started to improve.

Roches Point.

An information board informed me that this arc of Cork Harbour was one of the best in the county to see such a diversity of wildfowl for the area is a vast one of mud at low tide. Moorings for pleasure boats shared the mud and the pier was obviously an important spot for dinghy launching. It was shame the shop was closed as I was starving and eager for some breakfast. But it seemed pointless to wait so we continued driving round the Harbour anti-clockwise. Suddenly, after days on narrow roads, a fast dual carriageway appeared, carrying us along the north edge of the Harbour with no views but which took us quickly into Cork. What I didn't realise at the time was that we passed close to Rathcoursey, once a small fishing village and home to the Rathcoursey hookers (boats, not the other type) and where a couple of these are lying as hulks in a muddy creek. I'd have liked to see these remnants of the sailing age but it wasn't to be so. Instead we sped into Cork City with Rory Gallagher blaring out of the CD player.

Parking seemed a bit of a problem and, although I tend to avoid these centres of population – I believe that working people in cities are seldom employed in what is termed the vernacular zone – this time I was determined to stop. I wanted to scour a few bookshops, three of which I did though finding nothing much of interest, and afterwards, completely by chance, I found I'd parked close to the English Market on Grand Parade. The market was wonderful and totally unexpected though if I'd read the guide-book I'd have known about it. It opened in the latter half of the nineteenth century and has been well patronised ever since. It was well laid out with an excellent array of foods from all around. A banquet to the eyes and the smell throughout the place was just so mouth-watering I could have bought one of everything. One bread stall was piled high in a fantastic choice of breads and the croissants I bought beat any I'd ever eaten in France or anywhere else. In another stall the vegetables resembled a gardener's paradise with every colour visible whilst the cheese stalls were equal to any I'd seen on the continent. Grocery stalls mixed with ones selling thirty

Glandore.

varieties of olives. Cheese stalls to kill for and even butter, for which Cork was once famous worldwide. The fish stalls occupied one side and contained lots of farmed salmon and whole smoked mackerel. Although I looked closely, I didn't see any wild Alaskan salmon which we tend to prefer back home because of its sustainability. Farmed salmon might be sustainable in the short term but most of it is tasteless because it's grown too quickly and the sustainability element never seems to take into account the wastage of other fish such as herring that is processed into meal to feed these farmed specimens. Amongst the shellfish on offer were plenty of mussels and oysters but I wasn't too impressed by the number of mussels whose shells were already open.

Just as I was eating my croissants back in the van, aware that my parking ticket had just expired, the mobile phone rang. Hoping it was my American friend who was in Cork, I answered it. It was, however, a guy called Arthur Neiland who'd phoned to tell me about his grandfather and his kipperhouse in Passage East, as mentioned in chapter two. Talk of coincidence – he could have phoned me at any time over several years but he chose to call whilst I was in Ireland studying the coast. So appropriate. He also told me, as a sort of anecdote, that his grandfather happened to be in Kinsale in 1915 on the day the *Lusitania* was torpedoed by a German submarine, buying herring and mackerel from the fishermen. One of these gave him a lifebelt from the ship which hung in the company's office for many years and is now on display at the Mersey Maritime Museum in Liverpool.

Sadly my American friend didn't phone so we never made contact as I had no number for him. There didn't seem any other reason to hang about. Leaving Cork, a road sign suggested the existence of a sort of open-air maritime museum on the eastern outskirts of the city and I spent an hour looking for it. When I did eventually find the door, almost hidden in a stone wall, I realised the place had been shut for a number of years. Finding the road south, I saw a sign for Kinsale and followed it. I guess I was suspicious of these road signs especially as I had already been confused on a number of occasions previous when the old-fashioned pointing arms of signs had been pushed around, leading the unsuspecting in the wrong direction. I wanted to go to Passage West and Crosshaven but unfortunately I made a snap decision when I decided to follow the Kinsale sign. I had intended to catch the ferry from Passage West over to Great Island upon which is Cobh and to visit the Cobh Heritage Centre housed in the old railway station to learn of 'The Queenstown Story'. The story seemed fascinating for almost half of the six million people who emigrated from Ireland between 1848 and 1950 left from there. Furthermore Cork Harbour was an important refuelling point during the Napoleonic Wars when upwards of 300 ships might have been anchored. Ships with convicts bound for Australia and well as these emigrants to North America departed from here, each individual story being a sad omen for Ireland. Transatlantic liners called in as did the *Titanic* on her fateful maiden voyage in 1912. But the visit wasn't to be for, as luck would have it, the sign was correct and half an hour later I arrived at Kinsale. This was, I think, the first major mistake I made in selecting my itinerary, but not the last by any means. That's the downside of having such little time to take so much onboard. Thus, I missed Cobh and the lovely harbour of Crosshaven, home of the oldest yacht club in the world. Not only that, but I later discovered I'd missed Loughbeg where a small fleet of shrimp boats worked in the early twentieth century and maybe before. These open boats, up to 28 feet and rigged with a loose-footed gaff sail and staysail, numbered less than a dozen boats at any one time, and trawled for shrimps. They appear similar to the lobster boats of West Cork, more of which we will see later.

What I already knew of Kinsale was very little, consisting mainly of some information of the so-called Kinsale hookers, already mentioned. In his 1849 report into the loss of life after a particular gale on the East Coast of Scotland the previous year when many boats were wrecked and lives lost, Captain John Washington illustrated various types of fishing boats in use about Britain and Ireland at that time. Thus he included plans of Galway and Kinsale hookers. However we've already seen that there were Youghal and Rathcoursey hookers and, added to these, there were once Arklow hookers, all fishing craft. There are two schools of thought regarding the etymology of the term hooker. Some say it comes from the Dutch *hoeker*, being a bluff vessel with considerable tumblehome used for long-lining whilst others insist that an *urca*, later corrupted to *howker*, was a medieval fore-and-aft rigged craft of Spanish origins. These latter boats often worked off the southern Irish coast in the sixteenth century, and later, and were easily handled coastal craft. The earliest reference to Kinsale hookers comes in a letter from Kinsale in the State Papers of 1671, as quoted by John de Courcy Ireland in his *Ireland's Sea Fisheries – A History*, and he adds that these boats were developed for line fishing and was a local adaption of a Dutch design. The same letter also notes large French vessels armed with forty men with firearms causing havoc to the mackerel, herring and pilchard fisheries of the south and west coasts. Washington's Kinsale hooker version was a little under 40 feet in length and had a counter stern. When the renowned naval architect of the time, Mr James Peake, was asked of his opinion of the various craft Washington identified, he wrote of this craft:

> The bow of this boat is so full, having a long bow and a long floor, and for the purpose of deep-sea fishing and keeping at sea there is little doubt but that the vessel would give every satisfaction. Her size puts her out of comparison with the Scottish, or any merely in-shore, fishing boats; indeed she is 25 tons larger than either the Yarmouth or Hastings luggers, but a reduced form on similar lines would make an efficient boat.

In other words, he was quite impressed with these vessels. Their main use in the latter part of the nineteenth century appears to have been in the mackerel fishery, one that attracted a huge influx of craft from outside the area. For example, in 1876, there were 217 English – mainly from Cornwall and the Isle of Man – 133 Irish, 13 Scottish and 60 French boats joining in the spring fishery. John Thruillier, in his field study of the town, suggests the success of the fishery was 'due in no short measure to the Kinsale Hooker' Kinsale. It seems, had been amongst the foremost fishing stations in Ireland, with fish being exported as far as La Rochelle back in the fifteenth century. With what became known as the Kinsale mackerel fishery, the town grew in importance even more. Look at a map of the area and you'll see that fishing figured: Oysterhaven, Newfoundland Bay, Hake Head and Bream Rock are all within a few miles of the harbour's entrance. With the fishing and general trade came boatbuilding, of which there were certainly three yards at various times, one of which continued up to the 1950s. Thruillier suggests that these yards undertook repair work on boats from the Isle of Man and Cornwall and because of this, modified the old Kinsale boats on similar lines to the English luggers, losing the tumblehome and generally updating their craft into a perfected mackerel boat, known better as the West Cork mackerel boats, of which we will learn more later. Added to the general boatbuilding facilities was the Royal Naval Dockyard which built ships of war in the eighteenth century using local timber, including HMS *Kinsale* in the early part of that century.

The port, providing a sheltered and deep harbour well situated a few miles up the river Banny, dates back to at least the Viking era when it is assumed they sheltered their longboats around the turn in the river. In the seventeenth century fishing was flourishing with a decline over the next century. By 1829 there were five decked vessels, 160 half-deckers (probably the hookers), 45 sail boats and 552 row boats, the latter probably fishing for salmon in the river of which there were plenty. All in all, there were 4,612 fellows engaged in the fishing, as well as many more ashore such as 120 coopers, thirteen sail makers and 1,282 people gutting, curing and packing the fish for export. To develop this export, a branch line of the Cork to Bantry Bay railway was opened in 1863 although this was never very profitable for the train company due to the building of the station on high land above the town, which meant all goods had to be hauled up a very steep incline to get there. Nowadays it's a very different town to the days of when the fishing prospered and the fishing boats based there only amounted to a handful.

I have to say the place lived up to its expectations purely because I'd been pre-warned. A month or so before I departed, an Irish contact wrote to me by email saying, 'Kinsale, in August, will be packed with coach tours and is best left till autumn, winter and early spring'. How right he was, although it wasn't coaches that clogged the road on August Bank Holiday Saturday but hundreds of cars. Walking around, after finding a parking spot with difficulty, it was easy to understand why it was so hectic. Said to be reminiscent of Cornwall, the houses, gaily painted in pastel shades, some a bit darker, form the narrow streets similar to Looe or Fowey or Polperro. The shops and bars were welcoming although many of the prices were not. Luckily for me the bookshops were an exception in that their prices were not inflated. In places, the houses overhung the stone quays alongside the river. What was different was the hinterland of horrible housing and, oh dear, advertising boards around the main car park declaring how, wonderfully, this car park was going to be transformed into a hotel and waterfront housing.

The next sight I came across was a four-piece band playing in the street, the first real music I've heard since arriving. The four lads happily played as the punters ambled in and out of the shops. Sadly the museum was closed for the Bank Holiday which seemed a bit strange. Walking around, I found the ubiquitous decorative boat filled with flowers, the hotel blocking the quayside footpath and houses with names like 'Merlins Deep'. Blokes in white polo shirts marched around and I watched two buxom blondes climb aboard a RIB with young lads, all dressed in blue t-shirts (I couldn't read the writing on them) giving them a helping hand with anticipation and knowing smiles. Then they donned lifejackets, as is the law, and zoomed off.

Kinsale is also the gourmet capital of Ireland it is said. That alone brings prices to match, well beyond the means of many folk. Haddock and chips with tartare sauce I saw advertised in one establishment for €19.50. I'd paid €7 for the best (and largest portion) of the stuff in Kilmore Quay so wasn't about to part with that amount of money here. Amongst all this grandeur – and I did wonder whether the inflated restaurant prices brought in the moneyed folk or vice versa – I was surprised to see a funfair, although not in operation until the evening. One thing I did like was the fact that there were no rails around the harbour wall, as in so many harbours these days; such safety equipment is mandatory to stop people falling in. All in all, I decided the place was a yachtsman's paradise and a day tripper's hell although I bet there are thousands of folk who'll disagree.

To finish on Kinsale I have to include this quote from Francis Rogers, a London merchant who arrived in Kinsale from the West Indies in October 1703 amid foul weather, as quoted by Thruillier:

> the town lyeth on the river Banny, which runs far up, where is very good salmon (a fine large salmon for 8D) ... we thought ourselves in the land of plenty and just come off a long tedious starving, drink water voyage we did not a little indulge ourselves. Very good French claret, we drank in the taverns at an English shilling, a bottle ditto Brandy at 3/6 and 4/- per gall.'

Now that sounds like my sort of place!

From Kinsale I felt I couldn't miss a visit to the Old Head of Kinsale, a perfect place, or so I thought, to exercise the dog who'd been holed up in the van whilst I jostled around Kinsale. *En route* to the Head we passed the small quay at the Old Head village, stopping for a photograph before arriving at the entrance to the peninsular. A few cars were parked outside but, oh dear, what was the closed gate doing there? I parked up, seeing the six-foot stone wall with an additional bit of what looked like barbed wire atop, and a CCTV camera staring down. I peered in through the bars of the gate to see a sort of guard house with a man sitting there, obviously trained not to move when he saw the likes of me. It was a bloody golf course, privately owned and not about to admit anyone, especially someone about to write something unpleasant about the place. It was a shame because if they had, I might have written something nice on what is supposed to be a wonderful place. But to say I was disgusted is an understatement, as I really do feel it's obscene to close off such a historic and beautiful place merely so that people who can afford to do so can knock silly little balls around a field and into equally silly little holes.

For the dog-walkers and general public there was a sop to our intelligence for we were able to walk the hundred yards or so either side of the gate, along the wall and down to platforms to get a view of the sea and a little of that inside of the walls. Returning to the car I watched the gates open solely for one people carrier which I assumed to be just another bunch of golfers arriving. As I observed this, a woman arrived back at her car and as she was getting into it, we spoke briefly. She told me about the fight there had been in the courts about the closure when the locals such as her had objected. She'd been coming here for years before this, walking her dogs. The locals lost though and the gates were shut. The place was popular with Americans coming to play a round of golf, she continued, the cost being €260 a few years before. I decided I'd forego the pleasure. As she drove off, she opened the window, smiled and added as a final word, 'Money talks round here, you know!' That was fast becoming obvious.

It's a shame the place is out-of-bounds for I read that there are some historical sites to be seen. The gateway is all that remains of the de Courcy Castle whilst the remains of a prehistoric fort called Dun Cearmna is said to be close by, Cearmna being a Celtic king. Moreover two early lighthouses still exist. One of these is a cottage lighthouse, a seventeenth-century structure, in which the brazier with the fire to warn shipping was situated upon the roof. The other lighthouse is eighteenth century and the keeper's accommodation is nearby. The keeper was said to have been paid £12 a year for his services. The present lighthouse dates from 1853 and is visible from all round and today is automatic. We will hear a little more about Dun Cearmna and the lighthouse later on.

Shipwrecks of course cluster around the rocks of the Old Head, the most famous of which is the *Lusitania* which didn't sink on the rocks, rather was torpedoed some 9 miles offshore. Her wreckage, an official war grave, now lies in 750 feet of water. One ship that did run onto the rocks in fog in 1892 was the American liner *City of Chicago* with 360 passengers aboard and which broke into two before sinking. All but three of the passengers were rescued in time by the Coastguard. The cargo was subsequently washed up on the shores which proved a bonanza for the locals who, it has been said, had been pretty accustomed to smuggling in the past, using the bays and creeks of the Old Head for this purpose.

On land above, and inland, from the gateway is the old signal station where there is a memorial to the sinking of the *Lusitania* and the 1198 lives lost. However, that wasn't a good place to walk the dog so we proceeded on our journey to Garrettstown beach, a few miles west, where we spent time throwing sticks, dog lying in the shallows. Just around the corner we watched the surfers – I'd never seen so many in such a small, crowded place – who looked like little black ants swarming the beach, all with boards of all colours of the rainbow. By now the countryside had changed from the bleakness of west County Waterford into green fields of all shades, some cut, some with hay still waiting for the weather to improve. 'However', my journal went, 'it's still the unfortunate housing that interferes with the beauty of the coast'.

Passing west once more, I noted the Burren Pier opposite Courtmacsherry. We threaded through Timoleague, it being busy for some reason and came to Courtmacsherry itself, described by Coyne as 'a mere fishing-hamlet, adjoining to the marine village of the Earl of Shannon'. Here I had a stroke of luck and met Diarmuid O'Mahony.

By the time I'd parked up along the street from the harbour it was pouring down with rain. Determined to have a look to see if any interesting boats were moored up, I walked along the road in that direction and saw that the lifeboat station was open and advertising an art display of local artists. In order to escape from the downpour, and keen to have a look, I entered. Up the stairs was a room with pictures hanging all round of a whole host of different maritime scenes, in all styles and colours. In the middle was a large table and two fellows were sitting talking. I studied various paintings, some not quite my kind of picture but others I really liked in terms of both the technique and the bright colour choice. The prices seemed pretty reasonable too. After a while, when one fellow departed, I asked the other guy about the lifeboat and easily got into conversation about the harbour. He enquired as to why I was so interested and when I told him what I was doing, he said I should talk to Diarmuid. He then said he'd phone him, which he did, and the answer from the other end of the phone was that he'd be down in five minutes. I didn't find out the man's name, except that he was a volunteer in lifeboat money-raising, but he was so helpful and happy I was writing about the coast and its people, and I thank him if he ever reads this.

True to his word Diarmuid arrived within minutes, drenched from the rain. 'Come,' he said, 'we'll walk down to the harbour.' Luckily I was wearing my waterproof cagoule, and walk down to the harbour we did.

Diarmuid was born and bred in the village which consists of little more than one street lined with houses, the harbour area, and perhaps a couple of narrow roads leading off the main street. If I'm mistaken then it's due to the rain and mist with its poor visibility. Diarmuid had spent many years at sea, some as a tug skipper working out of Bantry Bay and the river Shannon. Furthermore he was coxswain of the lifeboat until 2000. However, I did sense he wasn't keen on discussing his past, being more interested in pointing out aspects of the harbour and its associated occupations. 'The railway came right up to the edge of the quay here,' he said, pointing a few yards to our right. This is a sugar beet growing area, the factory here was the last in Ireland and only closed last year. Four factories in Ireland in 1922 and they were all busy in the autumn and early winter. The same boats brought coal and fertiliser in – potash for the beet which was spread in the spring. The last schooner in here was the *Windermere* but there used to be three timber jetties jutting out there,' he continued, pointing a hundred yards in the other direction. I asked him about the Burren Pier across the water. 'Aye,' he said, 'the *Kathleen & May* was the last schooner in there, piloted by Uncle Tommy Fleming.' That was a ship I knew quite well, recounting a bit of its building in *Working the Welsh Coast* for she was built on the River Dee, and knowing she was owned for some years at Youghal and has been visiting the port every year since her restoration, until this year when the finances started running out. As we spoke, I knew that the owner, who had saved her from a certain death and spent huge amounts of money, was either looking to sell her or get financial support to keep her afloat at Bideford, where she's currently based. Another visitor was the schooner *Garlandstone*, skippered once by Captain Murdock, he recalled. 'Came with a cargo but the crew wouldn't sail when he wanted to leave. So he sailed her back single-handedly!' She's still around on the River Tamar.

I asked him when the harbour was built. 'Late 1840s, the old pier by the hotel there,' he replied, pointing again. He did a lot of that. 'They want to build a marina there now.' When I pushed him on the subject of himself, it turned out that his mother had run the Post Office and grocery shop, and Seamen's Mission. She was a great fan of sailing folk and fishermen. Diarmuid fished from an early age with a salmon draft-net, always on the ebb down by the old lifeboat house. 'The nets we used were poor, always gettin' torn, tied together and reused all the time. Caught six or seven salmon a time, though,' he said with a wry smile. Seining, which the draft-net is, finished about 1985 when drift-nets took over. He said there were twenty-one boats at one time at the fishing. The river Argideen, which drains into the harbour, translated from the Irish as 'little silver'. 'Silver as in salmon' he wrote in my notebook. Six men were involved in the draft fishing operation, two on the shore and four in the boat shooting and rowing the heavy 200-foot long net out in a circle and back to the shore. The nets were so heavy, sometimes it took two men to shoot them. Once modern nets were adopted, this reduced to two men rowing, one shooting and one on shore. At other times they went spillering, which is a general term for long-lining. In the early 1900s every one of the five men aboard the boat had his own line, baited with lugworm and redd into a wicker basket beforehand, thus easier to set.

I asked about the boats they used. 'The seine net boats. Carvel built, brought in from down the coast. There was a boatbuilder here in the village; before my time though. Also another at Galleyhead.' I took the reference to down the coast to mean Baltimore and around there. He also mentioned a 'Dingle nobby' which I took to be one of the BIM-sponsored boats built on the Manx nobby lines.

We must have spent a good hour down on the quay, him talking whilst I jotted down notes. My notebook was soaked by the time we'd finished although we'd stood some of the time sheltered by an overhanging wall. After that we returned together to the lifeboat station where we sat down and he continued his story. I was really enjoying myself, getting first-hand information, and I could see he was too, relating parts of his life, even if it was to a complete stranger.

We talked about pilotage. Different families went out in rowing boats, perhaps three boats at any time, searching for an incoming vessel, sometimes as far as Kinsale and Cork Harbour. 'There was no payment,' he said, 'but the family that got the ship also got the job of discharging the cargo. Coal shovelling for all that family, being paid 1/6d a pannier.' What other means of earning a living was there? 'The train brought in holiday-makers, the same folk each year. 'They wanted to go angling, catching massive specimens of ling, conger, white and black Pollock around wrecks. Blue sharks sometimes too,' he answered.

The lifeboat had obviously figured greatly in his life and he'd delivered many a boat. The last Watson lifeboat had been based here, as was the last Solent-class which he had taken to Poole before it was shipped to Australia where it's working today in Tasmania. Diarmuid had also taken the last Waveney-class boat from Larne to Poole during his time with the service. In 1979 he'd launched and been involved in the Fastnet Race disaster and, ten years later, had gone out during the same race to a yacht that had been dismasted. In 1999 they waited for a call during the race but thankfully got none.

As to other lifeboat projects, as he called them, the channel was dredged in 1992; they got a new Trent-class lifeboat in 1995; the pier reconstructed with a new pontoon in 1997 and a new boathouse the same year. It all pointed to a successful career. But it was time to go. As we left the building, he pointed out the house he lived in up the street. But it was still raining and I was going in the opposite direction we parted with a strong handshake and a call to drop in again if I'm ever here. What an amiable and thoroughly decent man he is still remains my enduring memory of him.

From Courtmacsherry a series of country lanes took us over to Clonakilty Bay where I wanted to go simply because of the local names which include Lion's Cove, Dunworly Bay and Dunnycove Bay. I thought it might have been a good place for walking the dog as I'd read of superb views. But it was difficult to get close to the coast and we continued on, reaching the main road at Clonakilty and passing through Ross Carbery before turning off to Glandore. There I went in search of Donal Lynch, a 40+ Fishing Boat Association member, and a person who I guessed would be able to help me. For, you see, I had various contacts in the Skibbereen area, but stupidly I'd forgotten to bring their contact details. I found Donal's house by asking the public toilet attendant who was just locking up for the night, and he directed me up the street, past a couple of busy pubs, to the blue house. Luckily Donal and his wife were in and they welcomed me inside. Donal was keen to talk but his wife let out that they were just about to go out themselves, it being Saturday evening. Thus we talked for a short while and Donal gave me all the phone numbers I needed. Then, with them late for their evening out, I left them. A shame really because I'd have liked to natter on with Donal, a mine of maritime information on Ireland as a whole. But that's the risk of turning up unannounced, knocking on doors on spec. In reality I was lucky for the second time that day. More often than not the people you are after are out.

Donal suggested visiting Union Hall, across the water, but before doing so, I walked down to Glandore's harbour, another built by Alexander Nimmo in the late 1840s. Donal had mentioned the local lug-rigged yawls that had once been used for fishing from here and were now raced, a few of which were moored off. All around are hills covered in trees which is hardly

Union Hall.

surprising since the original name for the place was Cuan Dor, the harbour of the oaks. Glandore, I read, was the first holiday resort in West Cork and held its first regatta in 1830. Unfortunately I'd missed the 2007 one.

Union Hall probably would have effused with fish if it wasn't so grey and wet. I splashed through huge puddles just to get down to the pier and the constant downpour meant that everything around, including me, was dripping wet which wasn't appropriate for taking photographs. The Kilbeg pier, as it's called, is about ten-years old and tied up alongside in a higgledy-piggledy sort of way was a fairly large fleet of fishing boats, mostly sporting red and blue paint and certainly substantial in number for such a small village. But then again, Union Hall has always been a major force in fishing in these parts, especially in the trawling sector. Much of the fishing was controlled by one family, owning several boats, and most were prawning, whitefish trawling or gill-netting whilst the small boats were presumably working lobster pots with the salmon 'on stop'. On the pier was an assortment of trailers, most empty, some attached to those petrol guzzling sports utility vehicles, I think they are called. These suggested some pleasure boat presence, though, except for a small plastic yacht on a trailer, there were no other obvious signs thus. I'd parked outside the 'Nolan smoked fish' shed, a concrete building with a corrugated iron roof, quite tall but seriously redundant. The traditional box windows were falling apart, the odd pane of glass missing. Rust coloured streaks and blackened smudges of smoke mixed with the green moss and general plant life growing out of the walls. Presumably no smoked fish had emerged from within this building for many years. If it hadn't been raining cats and dogs I'd have tried to look inside but instead sought the shelter of the van.

The evening was running away so I decided to drive over to Castletownshend, the harbour of which consisted of a short pier. A tree was growing in the middle of the road leading down to the harbour. To navigate round it, the car driver has to drive onto the pavement. Mind you, I realised afterwards, it was probably put there to slow vehicles down for a hundred yards further down the road ended with a drop straight into the sea. I didn't stay long as it was beginning to get dark. I then made a couple of phone calls, one to Nigel Towse and another to Mike Williams. Thus I made arrangements to meet these two guys, one the following day and the other on Bank Holiday Monday. Then I drove on through Skibbereen and onto Oldcourt where I'd been told, by the same fellow who emailed me about Kinsale, that I'd get a good welcome at the Oldcourt Inn. Eugene O'Neill, the owner, was a fisherman and we had a brief chat although he was busy serving customers. We arranged to meet the following morning as he said it was fine my parking in his car park for the night. After a couple of refreshing and revitalising pints of Murphy's, I moved the van as he'd suggested, cooked up what was fast becoming my staple diet of pasta with a jar of sauce, wrote up a few notes and slept, oblivious to the constant pitter-patter of rain on the van's metal roof.

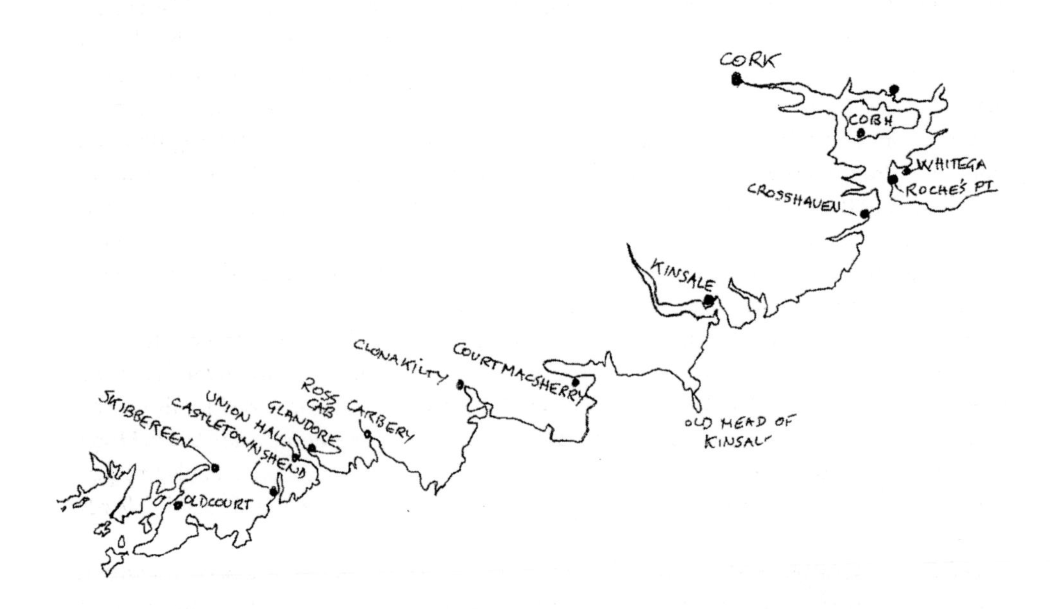

DAY FIVE

Eugene, according to his daughter, was fast asleep when I called in to the bar the next morning. It seemed he had had an impromptu family get-together the previous evening that had lasted until five in the morning. Disturbing him wasn't an option. Thus I opted to drive down to Baltimore, first dropping into Hegarty's Boatyard and having a very brief chat with John Hegarty who showed me a few of the boats in the yard and gave me his brother Liam's mobile phone number. I called him and arranged to meet him at the yard the following day.

Baltimore had the general air of another place active with holiday-makers, many of whom I guessed owned second homes there. Sleepy Baltimore must come alive in the summer, awoken from its off-season peace by those who regard the sea as their playground. It's a feeling I've felt many times before, and in this case Baltimore reminded me of Ullapool on Scotland's rugged yet beautiful west coast. There's a calm about the place yet a bustle – if that makes sense – as boaty people pursue their enjoyment. However things must have been very different back in 1631 when a horde of Algerian Corsairs entered the harbour, attacked the castle, plundered the town and carried away 200 of the inhabitants, mainly English ones, taking them to Algiers as captives. Today's harbour was pretty quiet though full of yachts at anchor, most of these boats being at the small end of the scale. I wandered around the east end of the village, the only place I could find to park. One boat I thought noteworthy of photographing I found moored alongside a pontoon. *Lucy* was a double-ender of about 28 feet, with a very narrow beam, a small foredeck and had lovely lines.

Baltimore has, I believe, grown up on the backs of fish, boosted by the fact that the harbour is another perfectly sheltered and well placed. Pilchards were landed in vast quantities in the sixteenth century when the Gaelic chiefs, especially the O'Driscolls, imposed tariffs for the rights to fish whilst the English administration insisted on fishing licences for boats. Huge amounts of revenue were taken from the fishermen as well as those ashore having to pay rents on premises – or palaces as they are generally called – to cure the pilchards. Pilchards were caught in drift-nets until the seine-net was introduced on the Cornish model by the Earl of Cork. However, in the early eighteenth century the pilchard fishery declined whilst, at the same time, the mackerel and herring fishery improved. In 1770 it was reported that 300 French vessels were fishing off the coast and in 1786 a further report sighted 200 French boats fishing between Baltimore and Crookhaven. The fact that the locals weren't fishing is put down to their lack of suitable craft, a familiar argument, though perhaps they were wise not to invest in bigger boats because the shoals disappeared in the early nineteenth century, not to reappear in any great numbers until 1860.

It was eventually this mackerel fishery that transformed Baltimore from 'a miserable town, which had drifted into decay apparently beyond hope of resurrection' in 1879 to 'a centre for a large portion of the mackerel fleet' a year later. The fishery inspector, Mr Hayes claimed that this was an astonishing feat and it must have been so, for fishermen aren't apt to change their habits in so short a period of time. Even so, the growth of the fishery was held back because of the infrastructure or, more to the point, the lack of it. Baltimore's small pier had been built in the early 1830s and was totally incapable of coping with the massive influx of mackerel so that

The harbour at Baltimore *c.*1890.

permission for a new pier was granted at the very end of 1880 and construction completed in 1883. Kinsale still dwarfed Baltimore in terms of boat numbers and mackerel landed. The 1880 landings at Kinsale were 237,436 cwts and at Baltimore 19,690 cwts, but landings of the 1881 spring mackerel at the latter increased some three-quarters whilst in Kinsale it dropped by a third. As that decade advanced, so did the fortunes of Baltimore whilst the opposite was true for Kinsale. Towards the end of the 1880s, an autumn mackerel fishery developed with much of that being exported to America where the mackerel fishery had collapsed due to too many immature fish being taken. By the end of the decade, both Baltimore and Kinsale shared an equal amount of the total Irish mackerel. The previous year there had been 148 Irish boats, 64 Manx and 14 English based in Baltimore. Twenty-two steamers were hired to take the catch to the English markets. After local lobbying, a branch line up to Skibbereen was opened in 1893 – thirty years after Kinsale had been connected to the network – but without a new deep water pier, so that mackerel had to be carried some distance to the terminus. When the new pier was eventually built, it was by then too late. The Baltimore mackerel fishery was well past its peak and, although during the First World War sixteen trains loaded with salted mackerel left every day, it was never to achieve the landings, giving it only a brief flurry of economic well-being. Seemingly, the adoption of smaller fishing boats, the West Cork mackerel boats, enabled fishermen to land at other coastal villages all around the county and that, as well as a decline in the fishery, impacted upon Baltimore's downfall as the mackerel centre of the south-west.

It was to harness and nurture the mid-1880s developing fishery that the Baltimore Fishery School was opened in 1887, at first to teach boys the rudiments of fishing but later expanding a boatbuilding and repair yard with their own slipway. The foreman in the yard was Henry Skinner who left and opened his own boatyard closer to Baltimore by the old pier. His first launch was a 56-foot motor fishing boat *Gabriel* in April 1913. With two branches of the Skinner family building in their own right, one in Baltimore and the other at nearby Rathmore, and the latter still working, albeit mostly in steel, they are continuing a tradition of

The mackerel boat *An Run*, built and owned by Nigel Towse.

boatbuilding in Baltimore that reaches back many generations.

After our walk around, I started reading and taking notes from the booklet *Mackerel and the making of Baltimore, County Cork* by Seamus Fitzgerald when I checked the time. I'm not sure where the morning had disappeared to, perhaps it was in reading all these statistics, but I suddenly realised it had. I'd my rendezvous with Nigel Towse in three quarters of an hour and I had to drive back to Skibbereen and down the other side of the River Ilen to a place where there is a tiny quay and where I was to meet him. He was sailing over from Sherkin Island to pick me up and we were going sailing. The only trouble was I got lost, ended up in Cuanamore where the ferry to Heir Island departs from and so was late by the time I reached the agreed quay. But then again, so was Nigel. Luckily!

I'd never met Nigel before, having only corresponded with him by letter too. But, when a small outboard-driven punt with a white haired fellow standing in the after end, headed my way, I knew somehow it was him. He drew alongside the stone steps of the quay and quickly handed me a poster before I climbed aboard. 'Put that in your van,' he shouted over the noise of the engine, which meant I had to retrace my steps to the top of the little driveway. The poster was one advertising the 2007 Baltimore Wooden Boat Festival which, seeing it was back in May, I'd missed. On the poster was a photo of a mackerel boat. Talking to Nigel, I guessed it was an obsession with these boats that started a chain of events that ended with some dozen traditional fishing boats of the area being able to race, along with other classics, in regattas. Once I'd stepped aboard his punt, we motored off like old friends, chatting idly. The sun had come out for the first time since I'd arrived and, with a fair wind, the afternoon promised a bit of fun and fine weather at last. We motored over to his mackerel boat and clambered aboard. I'd heard and read quite a lot about these mackerel drifters so it was exciting to get aboard one for the first time.

The lobster boats and mackerel yawls, as the drifters are locally called, were the gaff-rigged boats that dominated the lobster and mackerel fishing in the south-west part of Ireland from the

1800s to 1950s. Their more recent revival is thanks to the likes of Nigel, Liam Hegarty, Cormac Levis and Fachtna O'Sullivan. Firstly, in the early 1990s, Liam, Nigel, Fachtna and Terry Tuit lifted the lines off an old mackerel yawl, *Shamrock*, that had been built by Skinners of Baltimore in about 1910 and was amongst the most famous of these craft. At the time she lay abandoned on the beach near Schull, just down the coast from Ballydehob, where they took off the sections and measurements to allow a replica to be built. This was *An Rún*, upon which we were sitting on, which had been built both by Liam and Nigel. She was mostly built by eye and launched in October 1995. After that three more yawls were built at Hegarty's boatyard and recently one was in the South of France and another in Hegarty's. I'm not sure about the whereabouts of the other.

There was nothing modern about this mackerel boat; no engine, no visible navigation aids, no concession to twenty-first-century technology. Just the smell of timber, oil and canvas. We delved around the bilges for a while looking at the heavy oak framing and general construction but I won't bore the reader with those details. Then it was back aboard the punt and a quick motor over to Nigel's lobster boat *Hanorah*, S463. And likewise, there was no sop to modernity aboard, no refinements. A true Roaringwater lobster boat with a lovely sheer line that has a sort of short uplift at the bow, a bit like a currach.

Nigel had this boat rebuilt over several years with help from Liam Hegarty and a group of students on a boatbuilding course run by the Sherkin Island Development Committee, with funding coming from the Further Education Training Awards Council which allowed him to undertake the project on Sherkin Island where he lives. The boat was originally built on Heir Island, as many of them were, in 1893 and represents a type sometimes known as the 'towelsail yawls' because of their habit of stretching out the sail over a boathook at the bow for the three crew to sleep under for they ventured for miles along the coast, being away fishing anywhere between Cape Clear and Dursey Head, up north, for seven weeks at a time. Until relatively recently these boats were unknown outside the immediate area until, that is, Ballydehob-based teacher Cormac Levis wrote his book *Towelsail Yawls – The Lobster boats of Heir Island and Roaringwater Bay* which was published in 2002. I'd been lucky enough to have received a review copy so had avidly absorbed the book and since corresponded with the author. Since then several more new boats have been built by Hegarty's boatyard including *Saoirse Muireann* for Cormac himself.

Hanorah had been built for Con Harte who passed her down to his son Dan. After Dan ceased fishing her, she was sold on and subsequently had a foredeck fitted and a motor and pot hauler installed, one of the first to have an engine and hauler which enabled one man to control the boat and haul the pots thus reducing the crew from three to two members. The other steered the boat. By 1984 she'd a few more owners until she was abandoned in Mill Cove, Schull, after having her engine removed. And there she lay gradually rotting away until 1999 when Nigel and Liam, coaxed on by Cormac, pulled her out of her mud berth, after which she was taken to Sherkin Island to be restored. At first, Nigel seemed reluctant to let a group of students loose on his boat but the previous year he and Liam had taught a group of students while they had successfully restored a 1910-built bumboat, so he soon relented. She was launched at Easter 2005, in front of a large crowd, and was immediately a favourite. It's clear that he's happy from the gleam of his eyes when he talks about the boat. She's lovely and completely traditional with her grey and green external paint and Stockholm tar inside. She's also easy to sail as I discovered, with no complicated gear, just simply the sails to raise and sheets to handle and she's off.

The name 'Roaringwater' really does give a bit of atmosphere to these boats and you can imagine hearing the vast Atlantic Ocean funnelling up right the bay, the waves fresh and powerful from the multi-thousand mile voyage. As we cast off, leaving the punt tied to the mooring, we hoisted sail and literally shot off, roaring away towards Baltimore. It was Baltimore regatta day – not the wooden boat festival but the Bank Holiday Town Regatta

The lobster boat *Saoirse Muirneann*, owned and skippered by Cormac Levis along with his daughter.

and the big fibreglass yachts were racing further out to sea. However, come two o'clock and the traditional boats were racing. Suddenly more lobster boats appeared: *Mary Collette* in pale blue, the green-painted *Rose*, and *Mary Ann*. These were all new boats, built at Hegarty's, and finally came Cormac and his daughter in his cream-coloured *Saoirse Muireann* all the way from Ballydehob. These, although based on *Hanorah*'s lines, are slightly more beamy, have engines and a bit more freeboard to give a bit more security at sea, and a degree of comfort.

Nigel and I were a bit uncertain about the rules and regulations of the race, and the course, which didn't bode too well. The safety boat came alongside and issued us some instructions but much of what they shouted was lost to the wind, leaving us with something about 'sausages' and a 'big red buoy'. We heard a gun fire so sped through what we thought was the starting line only to discover it was the five minute warning gun. Tack around again and put a quick reef in the sail for the wind was on the increase. The sun began to get quite intense and hot, a proper August afternoon heat, which made the whole experience even more fun. I happened to tell Nigel that I wasn't one for racing really and was quite pleased when he said he wasn't either! Still, to cut a long story, we did race and found the course to be a sausage-shaped one round two big red buoys, twice round. There were five lobster boats and a smart looking yacht called *Wishbone* which was ahead of us all. Then one of the lobster boats dropped out and *Wishbone* got her furling jib in a right tangle and watched in horror as we passed her. Close to the finishing line now, and they gathered speed, hoping to catch us up. They gained, but we gathered all the wind we could and the little boat surged forth, used to the feel of the ocean and the force of the breeze. The gun sounded as we passed the line first, *Wishbone* a close second. Oh, how I bet they were upset, beaten by a small twenty-six-foot 114-year old boat, and they disappeared off, perhaps to sulk out of view!

After I arranged to meet Cormac in his brother's bar, 'The Sandboat', in Ballydehob later that evening, Cormac and his daughter departed for their sail back home and Nigel dropped me back at the quay. Unfortunately he had to get back to Sherkin Island for family commitments otherwise he'd have come and joined us. Still, it had been a pleasure to meet him and a great experience to have sailed aboard *Hanorah*, her ability to sail being impressive for such a small but heavily-built boat. To survive the Atlantic weather these boats had to be strong and capable, seaworthy yet roomy enough for three crew and some lobsters or crayfish. Their use amongst the communities of this island-splattered part of the coast continued up to the 1950s when a new breed of motorised lobster boat gained favour amongst the fishermen.

I dawdled back to Ballydehob and parked up upon the quay, alongside some old buildings lining its outer edge, which I later discovered were corn stores. Walking along the river, there was some enterprising chap renting out pedaloes in a pool formed by the weir, which dated from the 1960/70s. The twelve-arch railway viaduct over the river is impressive and was the main engineering feat on this narrow-gauge branch line and the first to use concrete for its construction. The principal reason for building this line was to carry fish from Schull to Skibbereen and was opened in 1886 with a short extension to the pier at Schull being added and completed in 1893. However, because of steep gradients and unsuited locomotives, the line was closed two years later for modifications. Only two trains each way per day ran at its peak, with extra trains on fair days over the 15-mile stretch. The pier extension was closed in 1925, presumably due to the lack of fish being landed there. However, although never profitable, the line survived until 1944, when it was temporarily closed for a year because of the fuel shortage. It finally closed two years later and nowadays much of its length is a footpath. I walked over the viaduct which, surprisingly, was littered with what appeared to be human faeces but nevertheless the views were grand.

I found 'The Sandboat', a wonderful little drinking place set amongst other buildings on the main street of the small town. As I ordered a pint of Murphy's, I noticed several pictures on the wall inside of various boats, including the sandboats of the area, as well as a framed short article, written by Cormac, on the history of the sandboats. From this I gleaned that Ballydehob quay was one of the last places where sand was brought ashore after it was dredged several miles away off Horse Island. The boats used were often no more than rowing boats though specific boats were at times built. Local shipwright John Collins served his apprenticeship with Skinners of Rathmore and returned home in 1880 and built a sandboat of some 28 feet in length and capable of carrying eight tons of sand. These boats had very flat floors which enabled them to carry a fuller load, a low freeboard for working over and little sheer. Like the lobster boats, they were heavily built with pitch pine planking on oak frames and the bigger boats usually set a loose-footed gaff mainsail and staysail. Crewed by three men, the boats would sail or be rowed to the dredging grounds before being anchored. The dredges were made by the local blacksmith in wrought iron and consisted of three iron bars out from a central link, forming the frame, the two outer bars being bent down at ninety degrees with an iron knife-edge between, forming the bottom edge of the dredge. A Hessian bag was rope stitched onto this. The dredge was lowered into the water and the boat pulled forward on its anchor rope by means of its windlass, built specifically for the purpose, thus filling the dredge. This was then hauled up on the starboard side and emptied over the gunwale. Successive dredges would allow the boat to heel over so that the freeboard was eventually reduced to a few inches so that less energy was needed to pull the dredge over the gunwale. Only then would the sand be shifted over to the port side to prevent the boat capsizing. Once full, they returned to Ballydehob quay – once called Sand Quay – or to a number of other quays, to unload. Day and night this arduous work continued for there seemed to be a constant need for this lime-rich sand to fertilise the fields of West Cork. Once back, they had to begin the equally strenuous job of shovelling the sand ashore.

Sometimes kelp was collected and sometimes gravel. At other times, especially when the weather was calm, the men went to arrive off particular beaches of Horse Island at low tide, and barrowed sand, known as 'bank' sand, was loaded directly onto the boat. With a draft of 41/42 feet and a need to keep the boat afloat, this was wading job. Two men would fill a hand barrow upon the beach and wade back to the boat and tip this over, again, the starboard side. The other man remained aboard to draw on the anchor line as necessary, help with the tipping and trimming the boat when the starboard gunwale was in danger of flooding.

John Collin's son Mike joined him in building several boats in the early 1900s though he went off to work for Skinners of Baltimore between 1915 and 1920. A few years later Mike built a boatbuilding shed at Filenamuck a couple of miles downstream of Ballydehob and built several boats there. Several of Cormac's ancestors, including his father, had owned sandboats. However the last boat landed the Sand Quay in 1959. I read about other parts of the coast and was surprised to see that Clonakilty had four sand quays in 1815 though most of the sand brought ashore was 'bank' sand. With the harbour silting up by the 1940s, some was landed at Ring but that ceased altogether in the 1950s. The same was so for Courtmacsherry, where I'd learned snippets from Durmuid, Glandore and Skibbereen, though in Cormac's subsequent text for the forthcoming and eagerly awaited 'Traditional Boats of Ireland', he mentions that Eugene O'Neill owned one sandboat on the River Ilen in 1939. Presumably this Eugene was the father of the Eugene I met as my Eugene surely wasn't old enough. Now I really cursed not waiting for him to get up. Though, by now, with Cormac having joined me and a few pints supped, I wasn't about to drive back to Oldcourt. Still, not waiting this morning was another bad decision and another I regretted.

Another casualty of my speeding around the coast was the failure to visit any of the islands of the bay. Given a whole week I'd have visited Long Island, Heir Island, Sherkin Island and, most of all, Clear Island. Not visiting this last one was a huge regret when I got home, for I really was eager to learn about the Cape Clear pilots at first hand. Pilots, I already had learned, worked out of many small communities along this coast. Nearby Crookhaven had four pilot boats whilst Cape Clear had six boats and even small harbours such as Ballydehob had one or two pilots, although these people, or mud-pilots as they were often called, were normally unlicensed and only worked close inshore. The Crookhaven and Cape Clear pilots would pilot ships into Cork Harbour or, on rare occasions, as far as Liverpool.

Furthermore, Cape Clear once had its own fleet of hookers when mackerel fishing played an important role in the local economy. These were half-decked boats of about 22 feet in the keel and up to 10 feet in beam which makes them pretty beamy. With one single mast with a gaff mainsail, jib and foresail, they fished with nets, lines and hooks. Other smacks and sprit-rigged boats worked from the island.

Whilst in the bar, Cormac introduced me to Rui Ferreira, a Portuguese boatbuilder whose grandfather had been building salt boats in Lisbon. After training as a boatbuilder at Lowestoft and meeting his now-partner Anke Eckardt, they chose to settle in this faraway corner of Ireland. He'd begun building the Castletownshend 'Ette' class of small boat, the local Irish-designed class originally built by the Mahoney brothers in Castletownshend between 1932 and 1960, though none after then until Rui and Anke launched their first in 2005. This was *Rockette*, all the boats' names ending in 'ette'. Their interest had been nurtured when they were given the wreck of *Sagette* which had been rotting in a garden. After researching their history and restoring *Sagette*, they commenced building another of these approximately 16-foot shallow drafted boats that were once popular amongst the members of the South Cork Sailing Club. Since launching the first one, number fourteen in the class, they've since built several more.

Cormac decided we'd take his car back to his house to avoid the dreaded 'drinking and driving' as he'd only downed a couple of pints. I'd already moved my van to a quiet car park alongside the river which I deemed a good overnight stopping place. *En route*, he chose to give me a quick tour of the immediate area and a little background history to this lovely hilly peninsular. We visited the site of the 1800's copper mine, with one of the richest veins in West Cork, where hundreds of people had died during the famine years. Cormac told me a story about how corn was being exported to England from here during those years under armed guard whilst the locals went hungry. Some, he said, threw themselves down the mine shaft in their desperation. They had gone to the mine looking for relief or work and when they found none they either died of hunger or committed suicide. A terribly sad and brutal example of the behaviour of British repression, and one that seemed to echo around the site. Further on was the remains of a slate mine where, he told me, a huge chimney had remained until it was hit by lightning in 2005 and collapsed. We also drove down to the little King's Quay where Mike Collins launched his new sandboats. Then it was back to Ballydehob after dropping the car off.

His wife Cearma joined us later for a meal in the local Chinese restaurant. This was heavingly busy when we first went in and we had to book a table and return half an hour later though the place had thinned out by then. Cearma's father had been a lighthouse keeper, working one month on and two weeks off. We spoke of the effect this had on family life when her mother had to bring the children up almost alone. He had spent much of his working life as keeper at the lighthouse on the Old Head of Kinsale which is where she had been born, in the keeper's cottage there. Thus her name comes from Dun Cearmna, as we've already learned about, the 'n' being dropped to make the name feminine sounding.

After the Chinese meal it was back to the 'Roses' bar across the road from 'The Sandboat'. There we sat for a couple of hours, supping away and chatting whilst all around Ballydehob awoke. Busses trundled off towards Skibbereen, loaded with folk off in search of the one night club there whilst there was a continual to-ing and fro-ing from bar to bar, each of which was packed out. A local rock band was thundering bass out from within the back room of the 'Roses'. By half past one the town was still alive and thumping, a few drunken folk stumbling up the road but no sign of any aggression that usually goes hand in hand with late night drinking in most British towns and cities. In fact, I never saw one Garda car pass by. But by then, with all the fresh sea air and excitement, I was tired and so, it seems were Cormac and Cearma. So after our farewells and my promises to come back again, thus it was me, a bit later, walking sluggishly down the road, back to van to join the dog for a well-earned deep slumber.

DAY SIX

That next morning, up early but with a bit of a thick head, Dog and I wandered down to the 'Sand Quay' again. It was far too early for the pedaloes to be out, in fact far too early for anyone to be out and about. The quayside was devoid of boats except for one small punt which bobbed around in the current caused by the river flowing off the weir. As I gazed around the quay, imagining scenes of activity of sand being shovelled ashore, I was reminded of the sandboats of North Goa that I'd watched and photographed, and indeed recorded interviews with some of those involved, some three years earlier. I remembered one guy called Satish, one of the workers, who explained the dredging system, and as he did two boats arrived loaded with sand. Basically, those boats are crewed by four men who punt the craft upstream about one kilometre where they anchor. Using a long bamboo pole with an iron hoop on the end, below which is suspended a fine-meshed bag, they dredge by one man dropping the pole onto the riverbed where the depth is in the region of 12ft, and, using a rope attached to the hoop, another man pulls the dredge along the length of the boat after which the third man hauls it up. The forth man is constantly baling out with a bucket. Once the boat is full of sand, which takes about two hours, they drift back and unload, aided by women who do most of the laborious job of carrying the sand in plastic bowls upon their heads, to form huge piles of sand which are eventually carried away by lorry. The boats themselves were double-ended, about 30ft long, and are generally built locally by imported skilled labour. The locals called these craft *vhodi*, which basically translates to 'boat'.

I recall finding one boat being rebuilt from three planks up from the keel. Out of the water they were almost Viking in appearance with long overhangs. Built shell-first, the nine-inch wide planks were bent without steam and stitched onto the lower plank using coire. At either end, these were stitched to the stem and sternpost. Frames were then added after completion by stitching to strengthen the boat. The seams and the stitching holes were caulked, no timber pegs being used here. Further downstream I'd came across two twelve-year old boys re-stitching another boat. With one lad inside and the other below, one threaded the coire through to the other who wrapped the end around a wooden peg, and tightened the stitching by levering the peg. At the same time the first boy hammered his peg into the hole to wedge the stitch tight while the other threaded the coire back to him to begin the process again. Inside this boat was coated in a substance made from the shells of cashew nuts, a liquid I had seen being used to preserve fishing boats, and well as for greasing the logs for pushing and pulling the boats upon, up and down the beach.

Sorry, I'm deflected from where I am, but why do I mention this? Well, it's just that I can imagine a sort of similar scene here a hundred years ago with boats coming in and out, others being unloaded, those working engaged in a bit of banter. Maybe a fellow repairing a boat up on the quay. Maybe it was the ghosts of yesterday making their presence felt as my thoughts wandered. I'm brought back to reality as a car screams down the road and almost does a handbrake turn before zooming off back down the road. An unwelcome morning interruption but one that brings me back to life.

Mizpah from the cover of the DVD of the film.

It's a sunny day, the first rays of heat appearing as the sun starts to climb up into a blue sky. We jumped into the van and drove back along the road to Skibbereen and down to Oldcourt once again. Mike Williams was waiting for me in O'Donovan's boatyard, upon his boat *Mizpah*, a Scottish-built fishing boat dating from 1949. She originated from the Girvan shipyard of Alexander Girvan, a well known fishing boat builder on the east side of the Clyde and was built as a motor seiner. Mike had bought her two years previously and had traced her history. She began her working life fishing out of Portpatrick before being sold in 1954 and becoming a research vessel for the Scottish Marine Biological Association at Millport for nearly twenty years. Her fishing registration was closed in 1976 when she worked out of Rothesay. In 1990 she was lying in mud on the Clyde, almost abandoned and in a state when she changed hands again and was taken to Kilkeel in Northern Ireland and afterwards to Loch Swilly where Mike found her. He and his brother Gubby built the Gubby-designed Heir Island sloops in their workshop at Turk Head, near to where I'd been the day before when Nigel picked me up. These sloops are mostly fibreglass though the first two were constructed in cedar strip on laminated pine frames, and some twenty-one boats have emerged from the workshop since the first boat was launched in 1999. Some say there is an American influence in the design of the 18ft 5in open boat with foredeck and side decks which, considering Gubby worked in the USA for some time, is hardly surprising. Others suggest a strong influence from the lobster boats although they are somewhat smaller. Though they'd built twenty-one, and had orders for another three, they'd decided to hold off building more at the present to build a motor launch on spec instead. 'A classy launch with a three-cylinder Kubota engine, you know, a '4/6d a summer in diesel' thing. We've talked about it for a couple of years now and decided it was time,' Mike explained. Gubby was off in Scotland at the time and I heard later that he'd sold his fishing boat and bought a Laurent Giles-designed 1955-built yacht called *Boomerang*.

Mike showed me around *Mizpah*, a small but lovely shaped boat that he was currently restoring. She'd starred in the Dirk Bogarde 1950s-film *The Hunted*, and Mike gave me a copy of the black and white film to watch. It's a tale of murder in London with Bogarde running away with a little boy called Robbie, an adopted and beaten child who was keen to run from home. Together they, arduously, reach Portpatrick in Scotland where the herring fleet is in (some of the shots were of elsewhere, hardly surprising as Portpatrick was never a major herring port) and where they steal the 50ft *Mizpah* and sail off. Robbie gets ill so Bogarde battles with his morals before turning the boat around and heading back, the child to the doctor and him to the police. It ends without clarification – was he justified in killing the lover of his wife or was it an accident? An entertaining if not profound film.

With Mike was Tim York, another 40+ Fishing Boat Association member who owned the fishing boat *Ribhinn Bahn*, another Noble's boat, this time a ring-netter built in 1966 and which fished from Scalpay in the Outer Hebrides of Scotland and Skye before moving south to the Isle of Man in 1986. Like *Mizpah*, she too arrived in Northern Ireland in 1990, firstly in Portavogie then Kilkeel before being brought to West Cork by Gubby and later sold to Tim. Like Mike, he was also restoring her and fitting her out as a pleasure boat. She's a bit bigger than *Mizpah* but with the graceful lines for which these ring-net boats are renowned. We chatted aboard one or other boat for an hour or so before they had to leave. Not only was it nice to meet members of the Association that I'd been sending out copies of our thrice yearly newsletter 'Fishing Boats', but good to see the new lease of life breathed back into these old but wonderfully efficient wooden fishing boats. Now that steel monsters were replacing most of the Irish and British fleets, with no let up in the amount of fish being taken from the sea, judging by the constant flow of reports suggesting that over fishing was still a major international problem, the wooden boats were fast disappearing. The only fallacy I can see in all the national governments' policy – and of course in the ill-fated and idiotic Common Fisheries Policy dreamt up by an equally idiotic and incompetent European Commission – is that removing these old fishing boats out of the industry simply means they are replaced by modern technologically efficient boats that catch much more fish per member of crew aboard. Thus employment falls and fish stocks continue to dwindle, even if so-called decommissioning removes tonnage from the European fleet.

Mike told me as we were leaving that the boat on the slip, *Suzanne II*, belonged to Eugene O'Neill. It looked like it was in for a coat of paint. Sod's Law states that I missed talking to him again. O'Donovan's yard lies across the small river from Hegarty's yard, both facing the larger river Ilen. As I arrived on time, Liam drew up in his car. Thus we spent another hour walking around his yard, him recounting to me about the boats he has stored either ashore or afloat. It's a sort of 'seven wonders' this yard, with its eclectic collection of both tired old hulls and those having new life hammered into them. Brother John turned up to rummage around in a shed before leaving minutes later preferring, I assumed, to stay out of the limelight of journalism. His brief visit reminded Liam to explain just how proficient John was as a boatbuilder. 'He prefers to work on his own, building the punts he does. Puts them together without a tape measure or anything', is all he said in a sort of non-committal way. Turns out that the punt I'd seen at Ballydehob that morning was one of John's. His current build, in a polythene-covered timber-framed shed, was a motor launch.

Liam and John's father had taken over the yard in 1948 and both had learned their trade from him. The yard itself might seem at first sight a ramshackle affair of stone sheds and strange-looking structures, but appearances are often deceptive. In the small top shed three boats were squashed in, all being restored. One was a William Fife-designed Cork Harbour One-Design called *Cygnet* and was being re-ribbed with some planking being replaced. Ten of these boats, Liam told me, had been built in the late nineteenth century and seven still remained, all having been built in and around Cork Harbour except one that had come from

Silver Spruce, the decommissioned fishing boat in Hegarty's yard, now used as a dump.

Baltimore. 'We've had three or four in', explained Liam. Although sometimes hard to understand, he never seemed to waste his few words. Ahead of *Cygnet* was a Belfast One-Design yacht also built around the late 1800s whilst alongside her was film director David Putnam's old launch that now belonged to a local woman her was doing her up herself.

'There's seven of us altogether working here', answered Liam to my questions about the yard. I looked around and wondered what they all did. But, when you see all the boats outside, I guess the answer is pretty clear. On the slip is the Tyrrell's of Arklow ex-Cape Clear ferryboat which was having a new wheelhouse added. Alongside the quay were two former fishing boats, *Silver Spruce* and *Green Pastures*. The latter had been converted into a sailing schooner by Maurice McCarthy and was soon to be heading off to greener pastures. The other, decommissioned a few years earlier, is used as a place to dump all the yard's rubbish. Off cuts of wood, big and small, metal and plastic drums, scraps of metal and aluminium, bits of this and that and even an old toilet cistern littered its decks. 'Maybe we'll get round to her,' smiles Liam.

It was here that the mackerel and lobster yawl revival started when Nigel and Liam started building the thirty-three-foot *An Rún*. Unlike Nigel's traditional mackerel yawl, the one alongside the quay, *An t-Iascaire*, was decked with a coach roof and accommodation down below. She looked a bit sad, moored there without any mast or rigging. On the quay sat the lobster boat *Fionn*, which was in need of repair after having broken away from her mooring.

We wandered around the yard as he pointed boat after boat out. This could almost be a museum, such was the number of significant vessels having implications of historical importance. There's the fishing boat *Free State*, the first fishing boat registered in Cork as C1 after the Irish Free State was established in 1922. Then there's the last sandboat that once belonged to Eugene O'Neill and worked up to the 1980s. Close by is the Tyrrell's built 1926

Lighthouse Board's old boat *Neebro* lying in the mud, a lovely clinker double-ender from the 1950s built, Liam thought, to replace the towelsail yawls when motorisation came. Seems there was a whole fleet of these working the area. Against the outer fence is the once famous *Ilen*, designed by notorious naval architect, sailor and gun-runner Conor O'Brien. She had been built by Tom Moynihan's shipwrights at the Baltimore Fishery School in 1926 after O'Brien had visited the Falkland Islands in his yacht *Saoirse*. Attracted by the boat and needing a new workboat for the island, the government there commissioned O'Brien to design the boat. He then delivered the *Ilen*, along with two crew from Cape Clear, in 1927 and she worked there for fifty years before passing into private hands, continuing to ply her trade around the South Atlantic. When she was put up for sale again, Limerick man and O'Brien follower Gerry MacMahon intervened after hearing that she might go to South America. He purchased her in 1997 and brought her back to Ireland, first to Dublin then to the Hegarty yard where he hoped to secure funding for her restoration that Liam was keen to undertake. Sadly, she still was sitting upon the quay, patiently waiting, though no one has given up on the dream.

Behind the sheds I found Graham Bailey's Cornish lugger *Peel Castle*, alongside of which was a most unusual pallet-built 'home' which presumably he stayed in whilst working upon the boat. His boat was nearing completion. Another boat was the 70-foot ex-fishing boat *Kenure* and its owner Adrian Birth, who'd bought her off Liam, showed me around. She was massive internally and will make an excellent life aboard for Adrian and his family.

I asked Liam about the future of the yard and whether he thought it secure in these days of increasing costs and bureaucracy. 'Oh, I'd love to build again,' he replied when I mentioned new builds. 'The mackerel and lobster yawls were a phase,' he explained further, 'and I'd like another phase, build something entirely new.' For sure the necessary skills abound and it's only the money that is needed. But that's the story everywhere, especially in the wooden boat world. But you never know what's around the corner. It was time to move on, though not before taking a photograph of Liam standing by the old but working bandsaw that stood outside one of the sheds. I didn't want to leave the wonderfully picturesque river Ilen, Skibbereen and Ballydehob. As I'd realised earlier, I really would have liked, more than at any time during these travels, to have stayed here much longer. But we had many more miles to cover and so, with a weary heart that was alleviated a little by the bright sunshine, we headed back along the road west, cutting left in Ballydehob, and down the road to Schull.

We drove past Schull where the harbour was deserted of vessels, although fishing gear lay cluttered all around. Before the First World War the harbour was often crammed full of French mackerel luggers but that was when the railway came down to the pier. These days, though, this is the stomping ground of teenage sailors and the international yachtie set looking to impress the opposite sex. Before the mackerel it was the pilchard. The mackerel still shoal here and chase the sprat right into the harbour. I remembered reading that the people of Schull, like Skibbereen, suffered very badly during the famine years.

We carried on past the diving centre and windsurfing school, out through the village and turned left as instructed down a rough track that followed a creek and eventually came across the remains of the *Shamrock* lying alongside a lump of rock by an ancient stone quay in Croagh Bay, just as Cormac had described to me. I guess many people, including the part-time inhabitants of Schull, wouldn't even have realised these rotting remnants were a boat, so broken up and dismal they were, never name the fragments of the once famous mackerel yawl that they'd probably never heard of. With the passing of every year more and more bits of her must disappear at high tide and one year, soon, all that will remain will be a few iron nails buried in the gravel. That might sound sad but, rather than hanging on to things for posterity, it is sometimes best that they go back into nature from whence they come. For now, in its place we have *An Rún*, a perfect replacement, or replica if you must. And she'll hopefully be around as long as *Shamrock* was.

Retracing to the main road – or at least what constituted a main road in these parts – we headed down to Crookhaven. Jerry O'Mahoney lived in the last house on the left when leaving the village, according to both Nigel and Cormac. He was, if not the last, then certainly one of the last pilots from Crookhaven. I knocked on the door but unfortunately it appeared he was out so I was unable to speak to him. Crookhaven lives up to its name. It's situated on a crook of land jutting out from the south end of the Mizen peninsula and is a perfectly sheltered harbour. Today it's an ideal holiday spot consisting of a small yet neat village in picturesque surroundings and a lovely harbour with stone quays which would once, like Schull, have been stuffed full of mackerel boats back at the beginning of the twentieth century and, even earlier as elsewhere, pilchard boats supplying the pilchard palaces. I've never seen a harbour so full of inflatables though. One pontoon was overrun with these ugly yet useful craft. The bars were equally crammed with those enjoying the tranquillity of the place.

I wandered around for while, probably looking like the stereotypical aimless tourist, bought a traditional Irish baby rattle made from reed by a local old fellow for our newborn baby, Ana – it had a pebble inside which she managed to pull out almost immediately when I gave it to her – and noticed the sign on a wall for the Rossbrin Boatyard of Schull that advertised 'restoration, repairs and build'. I wondered where it was. It was hard to imagine that this small harbour was once a vital link to shipping in that, especially during the Napoleonic Wars, sailing vessels called here for provisions such as meat, butter and grain, all produced locally. Here also Marconi came, one of many places in Ireland, and where he received his first signals from Cornwall over 200 miles away. Six months later he bridged the Atlantic, electronically speaking. His Marconi House is now a restaurant.

The wreck of the mackerel boat *Shamrock* near Schull.

At the bottom end of the bay formed by the crook is a golden sandy beach, whilst on the other side of the narrow isthmus is Barley Cove, another gloriously sandy beach. Dog and I walked down the steps cut in the rock onto the beach which was pretty crowded at one end but empty at the far end. Children were playing happily in the waves of what looked, to me anyway, freezing cold Atlantic seas. It reminded me of Wales though in so many ways – the rollers, beach backed by sand-dunes, granite rock, even the lack of housing which, for the first time, was noticeable. I also had my first really good view of the Fastnet Rock, pictures and stories of which I heard over many years but had never clapped eyes on. Even so, it was some seven or eight miles out to sea, but it was enough. I'd climbed over a fence to photograph the rock when I found myself on spongy grass which quite frightened me, not knowing whether it would support my weight. Visions of me disappearing into a peaty abyss caused me to retreat, taking the pictures whilst balanced atop the fence. I just hoped the owner wasn't watching!

Of all the lighthouses off the British and Irish coasts, the Fastnet Light must surely rank as one of the most well known, alongside such greats as the Longships, the Eddystone light, South Stack in Anglesey and Beachy Head, perhaps bolstered by the media focus after the 1979 Fastnet Race disaster and the loss of fifteen lives. The rock itself is spectacular, an isolated lump of rock measuring only some 340 by 180 feet some three miles off Cape Clear. It was the O'Driscolls (them again) who controlled the rich fishing grounds around the Fastnet and who levied a toll for those using the rocks as 'every boat which fisheth in or from the said Harbrough [Baltimore] between Fastness and the Stagges three nights, is to pay two shillings eight pence to the Lord [O'Driscoll] and fish three times every week, and if they will dry their fish for the rockes six shillings and eight pence. That all ships, except his Majesty's subjects, are to pay for their rockes to dry their fish on'.

However, in the lighthouse world, the light came relatively late for the first lighthouse wasn't completed until 1854. Before that, ships had to rely upon the Cape Clear lighthouse that was first exhibited in 1818. For the ten or so years previous to Cape Clear being illuminated, it was the signal tower on Cape Clear, built as part of a chain of signal towers after the French fleet appeared in Bantry Bay in 1796, that allowed mariners to navigate with a degree of safety along this unforgiving coast, but only during daylight hours. The Cape Clear light was 448 feet above the high water mark when it was completed and was, by 1844, considered to be too high for it was often covered by cloud. When the American passenger liner *Stephen Whitney* arrived off the coast in fog in October 1847, the crew briefly saw a light when the fog lifted, which they took as being the Old Head of Kinsale, and so they continued on their course to run aground on rocks on the north side of West Calf Island with the subsequent of the loss of 100 lives. It transpired afterwards that they had spotted the recently built light at Rock Island, Crookhaven but which the ship had no knowledge of. Pressure was brought upon the Ballast Board to either move the Cape Clear lighthouse or build another upon the Fastnet. The latter was chosen, the Cape Clear light being decommissioned at the same time, although the tower still remains.

The cast-iron Fastnet light stood atop the rock, with the light being 173 feet above the low water mark. It had cost some £17,000 to build and had a flash of 38,000 candle-power that was visible 18 miles away on a clear night. However, by 1865, it was in need of repair, the work of which was carried out. Continual rock falls close to the tower were cause for consternation and regular repair kept the structure secure. When the Commissioner for Irish Lights was formed in 1867, they began to regard the light as not being powerful enough considering its position. However it was not until 1891 that the Board decided to build another light on the rock, one 'with a biform oil light of the most powerful kind, having the same characteristics as the existing light'. This new light was to have a granite tower at its base, and Cornish quarrymen and stone-cutters were brought to the rock in 1898 to remove rock and prepare for this base, the bottom of which is six inches below the high water mark. The complete tower, first lit in 1904, is the tallest lighthouse tower in the whole of Britain and Ireland. The work had cost in the region of £70,000 which included £10,000 for the construction of a ship – the *Irene*, built specifically for the job in Glasgow in 1898. In the past Fastnet has been the first or last sight of land for thousands of transatlantic passengers, indeed it was for those ill-fated passengers aboard the *Titanic* in 1912. Those aboard the *Lusitania* had only passed it hours before the attack.

The next stop was at the Mizen Head Visitor Centre a few miles on and around Barley Cove at the very tip of the Mizen peninsula. This seemed to me to be another Cornish Land's End experience where visitors have to pay €6 to view a short exhibition before getting close to the lighthouse itself. I quote from my journal that I'd written at the time: 'a bit outrageous if you ask me after the tax payer has been funding the equipment and establishment for God knows how many years!' Needless to say I didn't pay up although I did browse around their bookshop for a few minutes though not purchasing anything. I've since discovered that when the lighthouse was automated in 1993, a local community group signed an agreement with the Commissioners of Irish Lights to open the lighthouse to visitors as the 'Mizen Vision' when some 27,000 passed through in the first year of business in 1994. Since then, it seems to have had a name change and, looking at the buildings, a new visitor centre. If I'd known it was community owned, I might have paid the €6.

Mizen Head light itself is unique in that it was not built until 1959 although a fog station had been established there in 1910. It's had its share of fatalities and near fatalities over the years. Former Taoiseach Charles Haughey nearly came to grief in 1985 when he and his crew of his yacht became lost in fog and had to take to their liferaft to await rescue by the Baltimore lifeboat. However, in December 1908, the British cargo ship *Irada, en route* from Galveston to Liverpool with a cargo of cotton, struck the rocks off Mizen Head in the dark. Four minutes after striking, her engineroom became flooded and within a few more minutes her back broken. Captain Roberts ordered the ship's boats to be launched as the ship sank close to the 400-foot cliffs. Much of the crew scrambled onto ledges at the base of the cliffs whilst the only woman aboard was crushed in a boat as the ship rolled over. The Captain and four of his crew were lost in a similar fashion. When the workmen arrived at the Fog Signal Station eight hours later they observed the wreckage floating by and lowered rope ladders down the cliff to rescue sixty-three men who had spent hours clinging on for dear life. *Irada* was the sixth large steamship to be wrecked by fog off the Mizen in twenty years. In 1995 her propeller was brought up from 40 metres of water and put on display.

I hastened a retracing of our route back to Toormore where the road north split towards Bantry. Across Dunmanus Bay was the Sheep's Head peninsula, upon which the scenery appeared fairly bland in comparison to Mizen. I therefore decided to skip it altogether, a decision for once I didn't regret. Bantry Bay appeared over the hill as we descended into Bantry itself, and stopped at the small harbour a bit east of the town where a strange concoction of uninteresting vessels lay quietly at ease. Bantry itself was, I thought, pretty non-descript, a bit depressing even.

I hadn't realised until then that Cobh, Bantry and Loch Swilly, in Donegal, had remained part of Britain after the Anglo-Irish agreement of 1921 which culminated in the establishment of the Irish Free State the following year. These three perfectly sheltered harbours were paramount to Britain's needs at a time of hostilities and remained in British hands until 1938 when, at the time of another impending war, Ireland felt an imperative to remain neutral. Having three British enclaves might have jeopardised this.

We parked up outside the Bantry Inshore Search and Rescue Association that had been founded in 1988, probably because of the lack of an RNLI boat between Baltimore and Valentia at the time though, as we will see, a lifeboat station was later established at Castletownbere Bearhaven – also known as Castletown Bearhaven. Leaving Dog behind, I walked up to Wolfe Tone Square, the main centre of the town. Theobald Wolfe Tone, a Dublin barrister, had persuaded the French Directory to attempt a landing here in December 1796 with 12,000 soldiers on thirty-five ships. His idea was for the British to be expelled from Ireland and the Republic to be formed. Ireland would then be a stepping off point for the invasion of England. However things, as usual, didn't turn out as they were expected to. Some boats didn't arrive in Bantry Bay. When a longboat was rowed ashore, this was captured. Then the wind rose up from the south-west which meant the ships were unable to sail out of the Bay and some where wrecked. Others did manage to cut and run, though a hurricane mid-way between Ireland and France caused further losses. Wolfe Tone did manage to reach France and later recorded that England hadn't been in such peril since the 1588 Spanish Armada. What might have happened if they had managed to effect a foothold in Bantry can only be imagined but, as records tell us, there were only about 15,000 British troops in the whole of Ireland at the time. The longboat captured at Bantry was on display for many years at the National Maritime Museum in Dun Laoghaire and is said to be the only surviving example of an eighteenth-century French admiral's barge. However, more recently, the boat has been used as a model upon which to build a flotilla of craft that are regularly rowed and raced by countries all over Europe.

Wolfe Tone Square was so named in 1897 to mark the centenary of the attempted invasion. In the square are several informative boards telling of the history of the place. There are some good photographs of the British naval fleet anchored in the Bay during the First World War. After 1796 the bay was heavily fortified with batteries mounted at Eagle Point, Gurteenroe, Horse Island, Seafield House and Beach Point. Nearby Berehaven and Bere Island were fortified in 1803.

The Bantry Bay Steamship Company was set up in 1883 to operate around the ports of the Bay. The old railway pier – the railway had arrived in 1892 – was extended in 1893-94 (why was it called the 'old' railway pier?) with timber to serve as a landing place. The *Countess of Bantry*, 86 tons and built in Belfast in 1884, plied the route between Castletownbere and Bantry three times a week, the fare being 3/6*d* one way and 6*s* return. For an extra shilling passengers could have a cabin. Some sailings also landed at Glengarriff and after 1906 Sunday excursions from Cork to Bantry, arriving to catch the half past twelve boat, became very popular.

But I didn't like Bantry, what there was of it. It seemed a relic from better times, perhaps a leftover from its brief flurry with oil and the wealth that comes from it. I tried to get a shower but was told the only swimming pool was at a hotel several miles back the road I'd come. Bantry might have once been a huge oil terminal, but most of the signs of it were gone. This seemed to be the problem with Bantry, it has never been as it should. My words seem to echo those of the Halls who wrote: 'a town that has been truly described as a seaport without trade, a harbour without shipping and a coast with a failing fishery'. They weren't very impressed! We progressed around the bay, occasionally stopping to admire the Caha Mountains of the Beara peninsula. Just outside Glengarriff we stopped at a campsite I saw signposted. It was huge, a mass of caravans, so we turned around and fled. The gardens of Glengarriff might have a whiff of luxuriant foliage and be loved by coaches of tourists, but, with evening fast approaching, along with the first senses of autumn, I wanted to find a place to shower and reckoned this was not it. I was lucky again though, for five or six miles out of Glengarriff I came across the Glenbrook Inn and Hungry Hill Lodge and Campsite, where, for a few euros,

I had a good shower and a level patch of grass to park upon for the night. After a pint or two in the bar, and another dose of pasta, I took my washing up to the campsite kitchen with its sinks and hot water. Whilst drying up my few items, a lovely-looking German lass of little more than twenty years of age entered. For some reason she asked me about sailing regattas at Castletown Bearhaven although why she picked on me I don't know. Did I look like the typical racing sailor? Still we got talking and I mentioned I'd been to a regatta in Baltimore. Then she asked me what I was doing so I told her. She fixed me a stare that I'm sure made me blush though she seemed in complete awe of me. Then her dreadlocked boyfriend (or so I assumed) and three other lads entered and they all listened intently as I recounted a bit about my travels over the last six days. 'Was I a professional writer?' she asked, quite seriously. 'I suppose so,' I replied which was unfortunate because the audience seemed to become even more intense, and especially hapless as I have no pretensions as to my ability. I quickly extricated myself from the group and beat a hasty retreat back to the sanctity of the van and the company of the dog. That was, for sure, enough for one day.

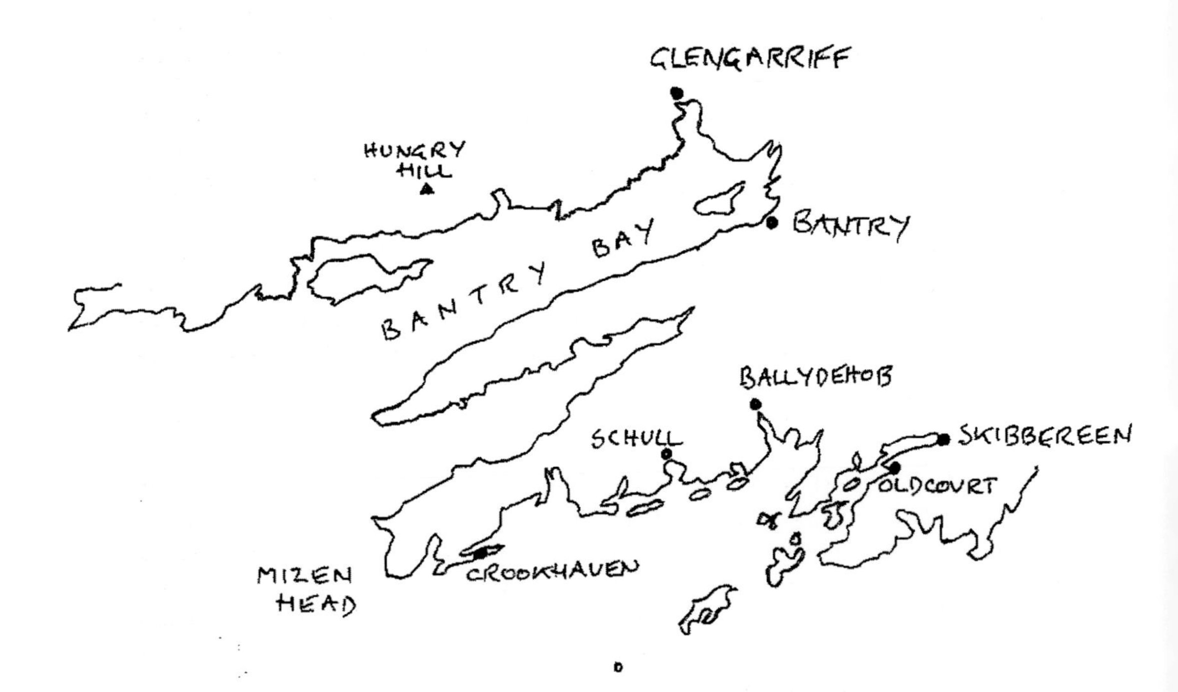

DAY SEVEN

By God did it rain during the night. I was awoken from my deep slumber by a thundering racket upon the roof and in the dark I sensed that even the dog was fazed by the din. Not surprisingly, when daylight did come, areas of the grass around the campsite were flooded even though the sun was by then shining with gusto and there wasn't a cloud in the sky. Such are the vagaries of the weather. One tent looked as if the inhabitants might have floated away though I later saw them sheltering in their car. What on the previous evening I had observed as being dribbles of water were now streams cascading down the hills all around, all in a desperate urge to get back to the sea. I had another shower. Afterwards I discovered, by talking to someone from the campsite, that the name Hungry Hill did not have anything to do with the famine, as I'd first imagined, but was simply a mis-translation from the Irish by English translators.

Like Bantry, Castletownbere became an important naval base during the First World War. However, these days it was more of a fishing harbour than anything else. The facilities for the industry were extensive: a fishmarket, ice, fuel, engineers, net and rope suppliers, general dealers and so on, with plenty of large vessels lining the main fish quay. I drove around to the other side of the harbour, across a modern bridge and onto a small island, where there's a large shipyard run by the Marine Board, complete with an equally large syncrolift system for hauling the monstrous vessels out of the water. However there wasn't a vessel of any size using the facilities at the time because, I was later informed, the dry-dock facility on Bere Island, a mile or so across the channel, is more popular amongst the fleets, and cheaper.

Even though the village is little more than a one-street affair, it was hectic with cars. Parking was a problem and I found a space wedged between two funfair vehicles. Seems there had been a fair the previous night for a few weary looking fellows were packing up their carousels and things. A sign nearby announced that the fair had been set up on the 'net repair and salting area', doubtlessly not much used these days for anything else. A shop close to the quay was run by Maisto Prekes advertising his wares as being 'Baltic Food Supplies' and seemed to announce the presence of Poles amongst the fishing crews. I spent ages searching for the public toilets – I'd drunk too much coffee that morning – and eventually found them thanks to a man having difficulty doing up his flies outside, in full view of all passers-by. He didn't seem very concerned at all. I found Pat Fitzgerald's house by asking in the garage where the overalled mechanic told me it was directly across the road. Knocking on the door gingerly for it was still quite early, I was a fairly young man. I'd expected a much older bloke. When I mentioned Joe Teesdale he beckoned me round the outside of the house and into the garden. 'Grandson's staying and is asleep. They're all asleep in fact. Wife, daughter, son-in-law. Coffee?'

Thus we sat in the hazy sun chatting about the fishing and drinking coffee for at least an hour, maybe more. Pat's grandfather, it transpired, had built seine-net boats down on the strand here. His Uncle Jim had joined him on the strand whilst Pat's father had gone fishing on Milford Haven trawlers. From west Wales the family had gone east to Essex where Pat was born though he looked as Irish as everyone I'd seen and none of the Essex-born stuff had rubbed off on him. Thirty years later, when his Uncle Jim died and he came over for the funeral, he stayed, married and subsequently did the family thing of his own.

A local woman from Valentia Island.

To begin with, on his return he worked in the building industry, but soon moved to the fishing where he's been ever since. These days he's crewing aboard the pelagic trawler *Menhaden*, a boat I happened to have photographed an hour earlier and one of several in Castletownbere's pelagic fleet. These boats fish mostly for mackerel and herring using either a purse-seine net or working a trawl net in pairs. Such is the industry today that these large boats, heavily invested in, only target these specific species and are fitted with pumps that, once the net full of fish, is brought to the side of the boat, pump the fish aboard into refrigerated saltwater tanks. Most of it is either landed locally and taken up to Killibegs by road, or they steam up themselves to where it is processed.

Some might think Pat is a reactionary due to his outspoken opinions and perhaps the fact that he was wearing a vivid red t-shirt with a hammer and sickle printed boldly upon it. I'd say he was talking sense when he spoke of the injustices forced upon Irish fishermen by the Irish government. Similar forces are brought to bear upon British fishermen so I'd heard some of his stories before. It's just that the Irish authorities, who you would be forgiven for thinking were pretty lax in their enforcement seem to be the exact opposite. They seem to be even more heavy-handed than the British Fishery Protection squad. And I thought that was saying something.

An example of this was when €110 million worth of cocaine had washed up on the shores of Dunlock Bay a month or so earlier, after the boat it was being smuggled ashore upon capsized. Rather than go and investigate this appearance, the Garda were more preoccupied raiding fishermen's houses, checking for any inconsistencies in log books and possible landings of black fish. There were, he told me, more fishery officers than drug squad members. Moreover, I'm informed, Ireland is the only country within the European Union that criminalises fishing offences, whereas in all other countries it is a civil matter.

I've got pages of jottings in my notebook that I made whilst we were chatting. One story I remember is of his grandfather who was asked to build a boat – he often went as far as Dursey Island and stayed two weeks if asked to build when there – and after two weeks someone mentioned to him that old so and so builds better boats. So his grandfather went to down his new boat and cut it in half!

Pat fished the salmon each summer for many years as well as seining for mackerel in a small 21-foot punt. Much of the catch he remembers being cured locally by the fishermen themselves whilst some was run off by road. Perhaps I shouldn't have mentioned the salmon for that brought a tirade against the authorities. Not that I was in disagreement, I just didn't want the baby woken. Pat recalled catching salmon around Dursey Island.

> They were running later and later. The Board said all farmed salmon had to be tagged. When we asked about wild salmon, that had to be tagged too. Wild fish fetched £40 a kilo and farmed ten. We got ten. They're bloody pathetic. Nets were sixty meshes deep but they made us use forty-five. The fish can see the footrope so all we could see was the salmon jumping over the net. Bloody stupid they are.

I wanted to know something about the state of the fishing in the town nowadays.

> Prawns are well down in price,' he answered, '€2.50 a kilo now, was €5.80 in April. About ten boats go drifting for tuna and some pair trawling though the dolphins are a problem. Remember when the Cornish were flying the Canadian flags when the Spanish were thrown out of Newfoundland. We put one up here and the Garda told us to take it down because the government was embarrassed. Another example of their daftness. We used to catch small fish for bait in the harbour here. Now it's illegal so we have to buy it. And their rule books. They keep changing. Six log book changes in a few years. They can look back two years for discrepancies. The weight used to be the deadweight of fish after it had been gutted. Now it's the live weight. As if we've nothing else to do but bloody weigh fish. If the politicians hadn't down played the quotas before we joined the EU we might have a better chance now.

That echoed the words of John Carroll. But what about his boat? Why weren't they out fishing now?

> We'll be away 17 September. Got our last quota in less than a week. Fuel doesn't help with it costing 54 cents a litre now and still increasing. That accounts for half of our gross takings. You should go and talk to Mick Orpen. He'll tell you a bit. Oh, and history. There's Penny Durell over at Dursey, house right at the end, red paint. She'd be another one you should talk to.

There was movement in the house and I heard a cry. It definitely seemed time to go. I thanked Pat for his hospitality and openness and my mind buzzed with excitement as I rushed back to the van to write a further few notes up. Half of what Pat told me I feel unable to add to this brief précis of a long conversation but to say it was radical might be an understatement. However it certainly left me with the opinion that there was nothing lax about the Irish government and its interpretation of European legislation. What was also becoming clear was the extent of corruption within the system.

From Castletownbere we proceeded to continue along the coast, past Cahermore and turned left towards Dursey Island. I'd heard there was a cable car across to the island and was keen to cross over. However I decided to hunt out Penny Durell first, especially as her name had also appeared on Darina Tully's map. After a few bends and turnings, Pat's directions were becoming vague. Standing by the side of the road, I saw a man so I decided to stop and ask. He didn't know, being from London and back for the holiday. 'My brother's coming in a minute to take me to the airport. He'll know,' he said. We chatted a while about the building industry in London. He'd been there since he was twenty and he must have been ten years older than I. Eventually his brother chugged up the hill in a battered looking car. The fellow asked him, adding, 'It was Penny Durell you'd be looking for?'

The brother looked at me and at the van. 'Aye,' he said, 'up here and left at the chip van. Theirs is the house at the end, one mile down.' I thanked them and waved but just as they drove off, the brother added, with a smile. 'An Irish mile, mind!'

A chip van out here made me wonder whether he was taking the piss but, a few hundred yards on and there it was. A large chip van with seating outside, parked up on a sort of lay-by. It was, sadly, closed as I'd have loved a bag of chips. I turned left and the road wound up and down, over the hill and certainly it was an 'Irish mile'. Eventually over one hill and a wonderful view of Crow Head appeared, with Dursey Island off to the right. The house was easily identified by the red paint. I parked up, noticing a 'no dogs' sign, the first I'd seen. Up a few steps and into a lovely garden where a man was weeding on his knees. I asked whether this was the house of Penny Durell, and it was. He went to call her from the depths of the house.

After introductions and explanations we sat in the front room with its shelves full of books and window overlooking one of the finest views imaginable. This, she reckoned, was the furthest inhabited house away from Dublin, excluding of course the islands. If you look at a map of Ireland you can see what she means for the Beara peninsula juts out beyond the other three main peninsulas that, along with the Beara, make up the Cork and Kerry coastline. As if reading my thoughts she said, 'It's wild in winter but wonderfully spirited. Fantastic for the bird life.' She mentioned the name of a bird that she and her husband David had seen here, the first in the area, but I'm afraid I can't remember that bird's name.

I'd come to ask her about Dursey Island and the surrounding area because Pat had mentioned she'd written a book entitled *Discover Dursey*, first published in 1996. They'd been living here not much more than ten years and had noticed a great change. 'When we came you couldn't buy much more than a loaf of bread,' she said. 'Now there's people making cheeses in their back sheds and selling and the produce. It's more cosmopolitan now.'

Dursey, she told me, had 342 inhabitants in 1842. Now, in 2007, there were four with seven part-timers. The earliest named settlers, on the other hand, were the 'Corca Luighe' who at one time owned all the land from Kenmare Bay to Cork though this was gradually reduced by others squeezing them into the south-west. The foremost family of the 'Corca Luighe' in the south-west were the O'Driscoll's who we've already heard of. But I guess no one knows exactly when the island was first settled.

The waters surrounding the island were rich in fish, still are probably. In the late twelfth century one writer wrote that 'Caoilte sings of fish of the briny sea from the coasts of Buie and Beara'. A late fourteenth- or early fifteenth-century poem spoke of 'the lands of the salmon coast, a blue water abounding in harbours, exhibiting to view large fleets of wine', a reference, presumably, to French boats trading. The Spanish came to fish as well in the fifteenth and sixteenth centuries which yielded a fine income for the chiefs of Beara. Two hundred of these Spanish boats were reported to be fishing in the vicinity, within sight of the coast. When she told me this, my mind cast back to earlier that morning. Pat had told me he'd often seen Spanish vessels unloading their catch onto massive container wagons in Castletownbere. Quite often, he said, the fishery officers would be watching whilst they unloaded their herring whilst these same officers turned a blind eye to what was happening aboard the Spanish ship alongside them. Mind you, he added, they probably didn't need to, such was the size of their fish quotas compared to the local Irish ones.

I suppose I was more interested in the events of the last 200 or so rather than the general background history, believing this to be similar to that of the rest of the coast with the Vikings coming in the ninth century, the Normans in the twelfth and the subsequent British influence. What source of income was available for those living on or close to the island?

The answer, of course, was the land and sea for the local inhabitants with the odd outsiders coming in as coastguards, lighthouse keepers and signalmen to man the signal tower. The coastguard station was established at Garinish towards the end of the 1820s and remained there until 1852, after which another was opened at Cahermore. The signal tower was short-lived. Construction began in 1804 and was only completed some seven years later, though the whole project seemed dogged by delays and collapses in the stonework. Once in operation and with Napoleon defeated in 1815, it became redundant and was abandoned like the others in the chain along the coast.

Four small islands of rock lie off the bottom end of the island – The Bull, The Cow, The Calf and The Heifer. When a site was being selected upon which to build a badly needed light, the Calf was chosen by Trinity House although the Ballast Board favoured the Bull. Why Trinity House had its own way over the Ballast Board is unclear but several respected gentlemen remarked to their lordships the error in the decision as far back as 1846. The Calf was a much more suitable place to build upon. Nevertheless the project on The Bull went ahead and, after delays and an ever-increasing budget, the cast iron light was finally lit for the first time in 1866. However, it didn't survive for long, for it was partially washed away when it broke almost in half in a particularly forceful hurricane in 1881. Miraculously, there were six survivors. They were marooned upon the island and sheltered in what remained of the structure, before being rescued twelve days later. A temporary light was established on Dursey Head whilst a new light was built on the Bull, this being first lit in 1889. Today this remains as one of the brightest lights upon this coast.

But, as already mentioned, agriculture and fishing were the main occupations of the inhabitants. It was fishing, according to Penny, which kept the hungry islanders alive during the lean famine years. With the collapse of the New England mackerel fishery in 1886, the seining for the fish in and around Dursey flourished. Added to that was the fact that some of the local fishermen were taken to the once in a lifetime Fisheries Exhibition in London to learn of new techniques. They returned home with new ideas. Thus, from then on to a peak in 1910, mackerel fishing played a huge role in the island's economy.

Penny describes the seine boats in her book as being:

> bigger then the usual type, being designed for rowing in the particular sea conditions. They had a wider belly, and the bow and stern were more raised; the transom, smaller than normal, was slightly raised out of the water. There were two oars on one side and three on the other, the stroke being on the side where there were three. In later years these boats did not adapt well to outboard motors. They were tarred each year, usually in the summer before the seining season started, and at the end of the season they were brought up on shore and 'wintered' upside down on wooden rests.

One particular boatbuilder was said to have built his own boats with such a degree of skill, with dovetail joints between each plank, that no caulking was necessary. Penny writes that this was an exception and most boats were built on commission by a fellow coming across from Kerry and staying on the island though, if Pat was right, and I'd no reason to doubt his word, his grandfather from Castletownbere also built one or two on a similar basis.

Each of the three small villages on the island – more just clusters of a few houses rather than villages – had their own seine and each one of these was divided into sixteen shares. In a similar fashion to the well known pilchard seiners from Cornwall, each seine consisted of two boats, the seine boat with ten crew and the 'follower' boat with six men aboard, and a net. The man in charge was, again like the Cornish, called the 'huer' and he sat in the stern of the boat watching out for shoals. In Cornwall he often sat upon a cliff and would make signals with his arms directing the operation. In Sicily, the man directing the operation in sword fishing used to climb to the top of a very large mast and watch from there. Once the shoal of fish had been spotted by observing various natural signs to detect its presence, the huer shouted out orders for the boat to row hard until the net was shot out around the shoal. Once the circle of the net had been thus formed its footropes were tightened to create an enclosed area from which escape was impossible. Then the fish could be moved from net to boat for carrying ashore. In some circumstances, usually when a huge catch was taken, the net was towed into shallow water for this operation. Massive amounts of fish were at times taken usual a seine net. Similar nets have been widely used, out from a beach, in many parts of the world, a method still used extensively in parts of India and Africa, and beyond. I recalled, as I read Penny's book, watching some fifty odd fishermen haul such a net in off the beach at Kovalem in south-west India, singing as they hauled upon the rope at either end. It was a mesmerizing experience and one I'll never forget.

Dursey's mackerel at that time was cured upon the beach by splitting, gutting, washing, draining, salting and packing into barrels. A few weeks later they were removed from the barrels and salted and packed again before the barrels were finally sealed and taken to Castletownbere for transportation to their distant markets in Scandinavia and the USA. Some was always retained for local consumption.

Anyway, we'd talked enough for I was sure Penny had other things to do although she'd received me into her house and given me her time without question. I bought a copy of her book which she signed, being slightly abashed when I asked her to do so. It's a good read and can only be recommended to anyone with an interest in the area. Before leaving I took her photograph amongst the lush green plants of the well-tended garden with Dursey Sound and the cable car in the background. That was my next goal.

The cable car made a major improvement in the lives of the islanders when it first became operational in 1969. A footbridge across the narrow sound had first been mooted in the 1930s but the islanders, preferring a proper bridge, decided against the plans. However, due to energetic lobbying by the Allihies parish priest Revd Matthew Keane, politicians accepted the need for some form of connection to the island to help maintain the communities living there. A cable car seemed to be the obvious compromise. Once completed, the then Taoiseach cut the ribbon to officially inaugurate what was the first cable car of its kind in Ireland. Since then thousands of islanders, tourists and well-known figures have crossed over the water in its small box-shaped car. Unfortunately, when I arrived, the operator had gone off to lunch and wouldn't be back for some time. Preference is given to the islanders when the cable car is busy, with tourists coming second in line. Some had obviously booked a trip across because a further notice informed me that the first available space for a crossing was in some two hours so I opted to abandon my idea of a walk around the island and move on. As the dog was in need of a walk, it seemed to make more sense to search for a beach.

We were certainly in luck with the splendid beach just before Allihies. However, I had previously noted the scarcity of public footpaths and the multifarious fences edging in most of the countryside. Stone walls, barbed wire and wire netting upon ancient posts seemed to enclose all the inviting areas of the surrounding scenery thus preventing access. This I could understand in areas where sheep and cattle were grazing or crops growing but in many parts there was neither sign of life or agriculture, just acres of prime walking grassland and rocky coast. Country hiking was obviously not of prime importance to the local inhabitants. Either that or they simply climbed over and ignored the 'no public access' signs.

The whiff of suntan lotion assaulted my nostrils for the first time on this, the Ballydonegan beach, after crossing the shallow stream and plodding up the soft sand that marked the start of the beach. The sun was by now hot and high in the blue sky and the dog skipped along the stream, droplets of water spraying in his wake. He found a big stick, about six feet long, and barked at me as his eyes pleaded with me to throw it. This I did, but in the direction we'd come from as the beach ahead was busy with swimmers, sunbathers and game-players. Clambering over the rocks at the far end, trying to escape his stick antics, I came across a partially hidden canoodling couple, both of whom looked up in surprise at my appearance. Retreating quickly, I did notice that the woman, who looked well into her forties, had the top part of her bikini removed whilst he, no more than twenty years of age, looked in a state of sexual excitement. Had I interrupted a copulating couple on a busy beach in south-west Cork? The mind boggled! What made this even more public was the fact that there was a huge caravan and chalet park at the northern end of the beach which, although accounting for the mass of people on the beach, meant that they actions were sure to be overlooked by someone. Still, I reasoned, I'd seen couples in the act of intercourse in more public places in the past, such as the open Downs area of Bristol! The dog ran off to the sea where dozens of hardened swimmers were enjoying the cool Atlantic whilst I returned to the van to eat some bread and cheese, my face set to the sun. The views over toward the Ineragh Peninsular were fantastic and I glimpsed the far off Skellig Islands for the first time. More on them later.

Penny had told me about the new Allihies Mine Museum, set inside the old Protestant Church that was opening later that week. Set up by the Allihies Village Cooperative, it was being officially opened by the President of Ireland. I asked one of the builders working outside if I could have a peep inside to which he replied, 'no problem'. Inside was in a state of vigorous activity as the finishing touches were being put to the restaurant and kitchen area though the actual museum part was locked and no one had a key. It was bright and airy and certainly somewhere I'd like to return to one day.

The mines in question were primarily copper mines, the buildings of one of which are situated 550 feet up the hill behind the village. I drove up towards it to take a photograph. The rust coloured streaks all around in the rock and piles of broken brown slag reminding me of the times I'd wandered around the copper mines and open veins of Snowdonia. Penny had shown me a copy of *The Berehaven Copper Mines*, a monograph written by R.A. Williams in 1991 which tells the whole story. Suffice to say, the Allihies copper mines were the most consistently productive in West Cork with a copper count of ten to fifteen percent. I later found that the Ballydonegan beach is artificial, having been formed by the sediment washed down from these slag heaps. Daphne du Maurier had famously written about the mines in her novel *Hungry Hill*.

The ore was carried down the hill to awaiting schooners at Allihies pier for transit over to the smelters at Swansea. In winter, though, the landing place was impossible to moor safely upon because of the weather, so the ore had to be taken by horse and cart to Castletownbere. Cornish miners were brought in to open the mine in the early nineteenth century and it was said that a thousand people worked there in 1838, 400 miners and 600 workers. Penny had mentioned a descendant of the Cornish miners still living there, a family by the name of Hodges. As the last Protestant in the area, he had been given the job of removing the roof from the church and dismantling the building, or so I read. I wondered whether this was the very same church that the museum was now housed in. Did he not dismantle it in its entirety? Furthermore, as I had also read the mine was never profitable. I wondered why it wasn't if the quality of the ore was so excellent.

Just outside Allihies I noticed a small slipway in a little cove, from which boys were jumping into the water, watched by their mothers. Was this the quay from where the ore was shipped out? The water looked a delicious turquoise colour and I was tempted to stop and swim too, though there was nowhere to park. We drove on. From a distance the houses of Eyeries appeared multi-coloured against the green landscape. In the village I stopped to read an information board I spotted alongside the road. This recounted the tale of Morty Og O'Sullivan. The O'Sullivans had been chiefs around the area and he was one of the best known chiefs of the clan. In the early eighteenth century he went off to France but soon returned to take up smuggling which was, as elsewhere, rife at the time. Unfortunately John Puxley had been appointed director of revenue for the whole of the south-west coast and he was very successful in capturing smugglers' vessels. He was particularly keen to capture Morty Og and on 10th March 1854, the second Sunday in Lent, they met on the way to church. Morty Og challenged him to a dual but Puxley declined. For some reason pistols were fired resulting in Puxley being killed. Morty Og fled to the hills to await a passage to back France but, just before leaving, made his way home to say his farewells to his son. An old enemy Tim Scully saw him and sent word to the soldiers in Dunboy who arrived and attacked the house. Morty Og was killed along with others and it is said that a large rusty stain on a nearby flat stone is his blood after he was flung onto the stone and the blood could never be washed away. Morty Og's head was placed on a spike outside the gaol in South Gate Bridge, Cork where it remained until his son John was granted his wish for its removal after he had caught some robbers. John was later himself killed in Eyeries. Although it seemed a quirky idea to have this story to have placed on a board alongside the road, it impressed me enough to retell it.

Around the other side of Coulagh Bay from Eyeries was Kilcatherine where some twenty seine boats were once working the waters of the bay. Ardgroom, a few miles on, seemed a sad place with a tiny harbour and extensive aquaculture smothering the bay with long lines of blue buoys which, presumably, had mussel growing-ropes attached. Then, almost unnoticeably, we passed into Kerry. It occurred to me that we had been in Cork for what seemed an age. It was now Tuesday and I'd crossed the Blackwater River at Youghal the previous Friday; thus it was only four days.

The rustic beauty of Kilmakilloge Harbour was also ruined by mussel-culture. Here the O'Sullivans had extracted huge fishing dues from Spanish boats coming into the Kenmare River to search for the pilchard shoals. The quay was substantial, overlooked by a bar which seemed close to overflowing with divers and dinghy sailors, judging by the number of dry-suit clad folk and the presence of a diving centre and a couple of sailing schools.

The road north was pleasant with fine views. We simply kept on driving, slowing to admire a particular view or headland. I decided at that point that cyclists come in two types for there were many of them. Some, clad in the full lycra gear had their head down and cycled in the middle of the road, oblivious to both other vehicles and the panoramic views. The other ones pedalled at a more leisurely pace, heads up and taking in the views. They were here to enjoy the moment though I wasn't sure why the former were. They might as well have been cycling around Dublin, or even a cycle track, for what they gained from their surroundings.

Kenmare had a quay but we didn't stop. Time was pressing on with evening approaching ad I was determined to reach Valentia that night. Records say there was once a considerable

The beach at Knightstown on Valentia Island.

herring fishery here with twelve boats of 2 tons, 14ft in the keel and costing £3 3s each. They didn't last long, being built of bog deal, and were crewed by five fishermen. The hemp nets came from 'Corke' according to Young and they were tanned locally with bark. Thirty-three years before (i.e. 1743) pilchards were plentiful hereabout.

We drove onto the famed Ring of Kerry, the state of the road seemed to be a bit of a disgrace from the start. It was pot-holed and uneven, like riding a rollercoaster. Someone likened it to having a massage on the bum without any oil! I wondered just where all the EU money had gone in Ireland when the authorities couldn't resurface such a popular and internationally famous road. Instead they had erected a sign informing us that there had been fifty-two deaths in four years. We side-tracked down to Oysterbed pier near Sneem, the surface of which was better than the main road. On and up, through Nedanone and Castle Cove we hastened, the scenery not impressively startling as I'd imagined. At the end of the peninsular the landscape improved considerably and the harbour at Derrynane was no exception. It was a shame the same couldn't be said for the road surface. Being almost landlocked, Derrynane was a perfect yachtsman's paradise and some dozen gleaming white yachts were at anchor. From the road several hundred feet above, it looked completely still and quite a picture of tranquillity.

At Waterville, where a bridge crossed the entrance to Lough Urrane and which seemed yet another holiday haven, we detoured onto a very minor road that skirted Ballinskelligs Bay until a golf course forced us back onto the main road. Ignoring Ballinskelligs because of that, we continued a few miles further before turning off towards Portmagee where we crossed the rackety bridge onto Valentia Island. Finding an almost empty car park at the south end of the island overlooking the entrance to Portmagee, where a path leads up to the old signal station, I decided to park up and stop the night. One or two more cars arrived but by nine o'clock all the walkers to the station had disappeared home and we were left to our own. The views over the Skelligs were fantastic, and I watched as a few fishing boats chugged up to Portmagee after a hard day's fishing. This was truly an idyllic spot, the best as it turned out, on the whole trip. The silence and calm, reflected in the smoothness of the sea several hundred feet below, was captivating, almost hypnotic. Cooking and eating another batch of pasta, along with a few noggins of red wine, I spent almost the entire time staring out upon the sensational seascape, watching as the daylight faded for the lighthouse on Great Skellig to begin its twinkling three flashes every ten seconds. Darkness came late, such had been the brightness of an almost perfect day and I slept with the van door open, the scent of sea and land enriching an equally perfect sleep.

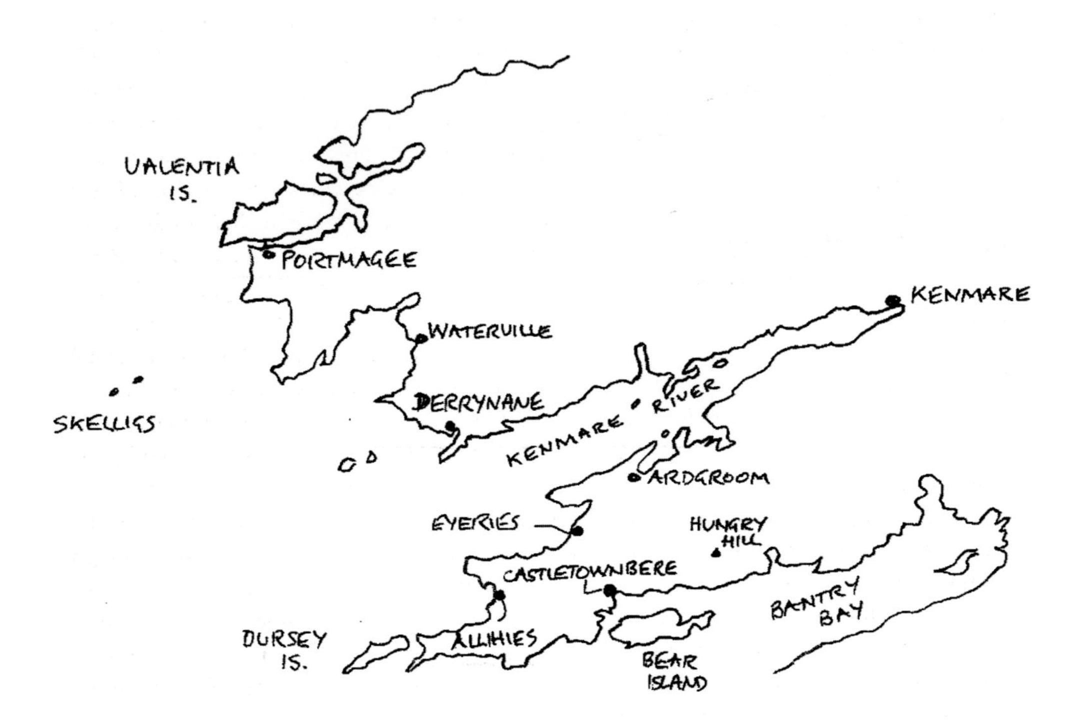

DAY EIGHT

By morning the emptiness and serene beauty of my peaceful little corner ofValentia hadn't changed. My impression of the place was as resolute as the previously evening. A haven of harmony between land and sea, with myself perhaps somewhere lost in between. Coffee was brewed whilst the dog sniffed about the grass and I became dreamily lost in thought. I'd realised just how different the tips of the scenery of these south-west peninsulas were to that inland a bit. Yesterday the east side if the Iveragh Peninsula had not impressed me whilst once we reached the end around Derrynane it was completely different. The same could be said for the Beara peninsula where I'd noticed the coast from Castletownbere, out to Garinish and back around to about Ardgroom was spectacular whilst further towards the bulk of the mainland it was less splendid. The Halls, on their journey from Skibbereen to Bantry, considered the country to be 'wild and uninteresting'. Valentia Island is, in terms of its topography, soft in comparison to other parts of the peninsula even if it does rise up to 888ft at its highest, but is nonetheless a lovely place. It is small wonder then, that many of the island's houses are second homes, filled in summer by folk enjoying its remoteness, beauty and proximity to the sea.

Afterwards Dog and I walked up to the signal station, along the path I'd watched folk walk along the previous evening. This was to Bray Head, which was about half an hour's walk; well worth it for the fine views over as far as Mizen Head. The Skelligs were clear and once we reached the signal station I had my first view of the Blasket Islands lying off the tip of the Dingle peninsula. The station itself was a square building of stone and brick, two storeys high though the first floor had long gone, possibly taken for firewood or some other recycling use. What I took for a coal bunker and water tank were built in concrete which seemed unusual. Outside, a balcony juts seaward and I stood there imagining the station signaller, on duty, watching for any signs of French or Spanish ships. He'd certainly be shocked today to see their fishing boats working within sight of the coast.

There are the scratched names of dozens of lovers on both inside and outside walls. '"Ger & Eimear" were here on the 27 December 2006' and I wondered whether they were locals or incomers from up country. They were probably, like the many thousands of people coming here, enjoying the view, exercise and each other's company. Oh, how easily useless thoughts can turn to idle judgements.

On the way back to the van we met the cows that we'd heard thundering past the van late the previous night on their way back from being milked. Perhaps they contributed to that one-time most important of exports from Kerry: butter, as this county was where the brand 'Kerrygold' had originated from. These cows eyed us suspiciously as we passed by, the sheep in the fields merely grazing unconcernedly.

The dog was happy as usual though this was more of a miracle than anything. He'd been paralysed in January 2006 from an embolism in his spine, after which the animal hospital in Bristol said he'd never walk again. The place was a disgrace, with a huge waiting room yet the tiniest sickroom where the animals are looked after. Poor old Dog was squeezed in by a washing machine continually on the go, a bright fluorescent light shining down and a phone constantly ringing shrilly. Not only that, but they filled him up with so much morphine to

An Irish black house.

distress him and then told us he was suffering from distress! Then they asked whether they should put him to sleep. Well, to cut a long story short, we got him out of that horrible place, after a bit of a fight and having to pay over £500, and took him home where he had constant attention and various alternative forms of medicine. Four weeks later we got him standing and walking after another two or so. It was a very slow process, his repairing, but he did have the inner strength to survive against all odds. As I watched him running after a rabbit I had to marvel at what we had achieved. Now, with lots of help from friends and our caring vet, I'd got my best mate back.

I digress again. It was time to leave this wonderful place and we drove back across the bridge into Portmagee. Here I made another subsequently regretful decision. It was almost ten o'clock and dozens of tourists were standing around in small groups on the quayside and I ascertained that they were waiting to board one of several small boats that were about to ferry them out to Great Skellig, or Skellig Michael as it's often called. I thought about joining them but dismissed it. No, I reasoned, there was no reason to venture out there. I would have had to leave the dog for the whole day as the boats didn't return till the afternoon and, anyway, I was intending on visiting the 'Skellig Experience' which was literally just across the water on Valentia Island. No need to waste a whole day when I had to be at Shannon Airport in three days time. So I watched them all board, about twelve to a boat and I counted ten boats, and then the boats disappeared off out to sea. Walking back across the bridge, I watched as three men in a small boat struggled to pull up a bicycle that had got entangled in one of their pots. Once they'd managed this, they motored into shallower water, to where they returned the bike. Then they set a train of twenty-five shrimp pots in a straight line, under the middle of the harbour. As I photographed them I could hear one of them say, 'oh, look, someone's photographing us.' I waved and they waved back.

'The Skellig Experience' had quite an interesting exhibition on the Rocks though I wouldn't have termed it an 'experience'. The building itself blended in fairly well with the surrounding landscape. It is a grass-covered series of concrete vaults designed by Peter

Doyle which, according to him, 'is designed to be rugged in feeling and finishes, to reflect the experience which will be undertaken by visitors'. However, closer up it seemed a bit too contemporary in my mind, and I wasn't too sure about the claim that the external stone walls tied 'the building down into the rising field'. The entrance fee was €5 which didn't seem excessive, though if you wanted to join in with one of the sea trips out to the island it cost quite a bit more. The exhibition has four themes: history and archaeology of the Early Christian monastery, sea birds, underwater Skellig, and the history of the lighthouses. I spent a while browsing around.

It is for the monastery on Skellig Michael that the island is internationally renowned, said to be the finest, most elaborate and best preserved of all Early Christian island monasteries in the world. The island is more like a pinnacle of rock rising steeply out of the sea to a height of 714 feet above sea level. It must surely be an inhospitable and hostile place to build a monastery especially with the Atlantic storms bombarding it and when, in the sixth century, the only boats available to transport the monks the seven or eight miles from the nearest part of the mainland were hide covered currachs or, more correctly *naomhóga*. There's a full-sized replica of the Kilnaruane Pillar Stone in the exhibition for the original of this had carved into it the earliest known representation of a rowing boat, complete with details of the oarsmen, their grip on the oars and the angle of the stroke-oarsmen pulling with greatest strength, all of which are considered to be accurate, indicating that the original sculptor knew what he was talking about. The monks' voyage out must surely imply both skill and determination. They then proceeded to build beehive huts and two boat-shaped oratories, along with terraces and some 2,300 steps carved in the rock. St Fionán is said to be the founder of the complex and that it remains standing over 1,400 years later is a testament to their expertise. Rain water was collected and channelled from the rock face into five storage wells and various crops were grown although the bulk of their cereals were brought in from the mainland, a sign that they didn't simply row out there and shut themselves away. Fish was plentiful and sheep and goats probably thrived to provide dairy produce and the occasional piece of meat. Sea birds and their eggs gave them a summer seasonal alternative. The Vikings raided in the early ninth century yet, unlike many other island monasteries, Skellig Michael survived though, as Gerald Cambrensis (Gerald of Wales) tells us, the monks moved to nearby Ballinskellig on the mainland. There's no certainty about the date that the island was abandoned. Gerald visited in 1185 though much of his so-called history has been found to be hearsay. Others suggest it was in 1225. It seems a bit immaterial for no matter which way you look at it these fellows survived on the rock for over 400 years. As I watched the short sixteen-minute audio visual show titled 'The Call of the Skelligs' in which I really was taken out to the monastery and had this overwhelming sense that I should have taken the opportunity to visit earlier that morning. I really did leave with a heavy heart, full of regret yet still resonating from the feeling of having the tiniest of peeps into an amazing and spiritual far-flung place. Visions of those steps winding their way around the hillside amongst the dark rocks interspersed with greenery stayed with me for much of the day.

There are also two lighthouses on the rock, built under the eye of well known lighthouse builder George Halpin and first lit in 1826. Two lights, the upper and lower, were built simultaneously to avoid confusion with Loop Head and Cape Clear. Lighthouse keepers lived at both lights, whole families who survived much in the way that the monks did, although the Valentia lifeboat (and helicopter after the building of the helipad) restocked their shelves and occasionally relieved them. One particular principal keeper, a W. Callaghan, had to bury two of his sons on the island, Patrick, aged two in 1868, and William, aged four in 1869, and subsequently he asked to be moved to another lighthouse after these deaths. How tragic is

Naomhóga.

Naomhóga on Great Blasket Island.

that? Both lights continued to function until the upper light – one of the highest in Ireland at 327 feet above sea level – was discontinued in 1870 when a lighthouse was built on nearby Inishearacht, one of the Blasket Islands. The lower light, at 175ft above sea level, continues to flash today even though the original tower was rebuilt in 1966 and automated in 1987 when the keepers' accommodation, and the island, was finally abandoned.

From 'The Skellig Experience' we drove through Chapeltown to Knightstown at the western end, before detouring up to the slate mine at Geokaun. Firstly quarried on a small scale in 1816 by Maurice Fitzgerald, the eighteenth Knight of Kerry (the title was first conferred 1261), within five years a slate yard and harbour had been established in Knightstown, designed by Alexander Nimmo specifically to work and export slate. The subsequent harbour was soon said to be a scene of 'Boats, ships, bustle and activity'. Welsh miners had been brought over to teach the locals their work and over the years the quarry had some periods of boom and others of bust. During good periods the slabs were carted down to the slate yard at Knightstown, later by tramway, and schooners with names such as *Reaper*, *Gleaner* and *Sir Charles Napier* came loaded with gravel and took away huge slabs of the slate. Some of this was used to build the old House of Commons, the British Museum and the Public Record Office in London as well as many of the Capital's railway stations including Blackfriars, Charing Cross and Waterloo. Some was even used in the construction of the San Salvador Railway. However it wasn't the best of roofing slate, being very heavy, and faced fierce competition from Welsh slate that was softer and easier to split. Valentia slate, though, had the upper hand when it came to billiard tables, fish slabs, dairy shelving, fireplaces and flagstones.

The mine eventually closed in 1878, after which many of the workers emigrated. However, it reopened again in 1900 to give islanders employment though a rock fall in 1911 caused its closure once again. However, I was surprised to see the huge grotto alive with the sound of engines and a forklift truck emerge several times with a huge slab balanced on its forks. The mine was obviously open once again, breathing new life for a few inhabitants of the island.

The heritage centre is housed in a small building and I called in to ask a few questions but I didn't linger long. What I didn't know at the time was the house next door belonged to the family of friends of mine who were living in Bristol but whose various strands of the family used the house for much of the year. Down at the harbour I found one seine boat alongside the lifeboat station though I also found a photograph in Nellie O'Cleirigh's *Valentia. A Different Irish Island* which showed half a dozen such boats on the strand, with the ornate and slightly out of place clock tower in the background. Similar seine boats worked from many fishing stations along this coast. Fishing, as elsewhere, was an important part of the island economy. William Petty's survey of the 1660s notes 160 'Saynes' fishing off the coast for pilchards and Charles Smith, in his *The Ancient and Present State of the County of Kerry* (1756) considered the harbour the best of its kind in the county. When Nimmo built his quay at the 'Foot', the original name for Knightstown, the fishing industry prospered as well as the slate mine. In 1837 there were 400 fishermen, 100 seine boats, and 150 yawls for involved, a yawl being a sailing boat of similar design to the former, though these figures must be read with caution. To crew that number of boats would take many more than any 400 men. Fishing was further expanded when the railway came to Reenard Point (later known as Valentia Harbour) on the mainland opposite Knightstown. This 39-mile branch line from Farranfore was completed by 1893 and Valentia Harbour became the most westerly railway terminus in Europe. The main impetus for building the line had come from the aspirations of some for Valentia to become a transatlantic port, it being the most westerly harbour in Ireland though a public enquiry had also identified the needs of the fishermen and farmers who needed to get their produce to markets especially in Britain. Previously most of the fish was taken by boat to Cobh. That it was an expensive line is supported by the figures: £243,627 for the twenty-six-mile stretch from Killorglin, to where the first section had already been opened since 1885. 273 skilled workers were employed along with 1149 unskilled at two shillings a day. The line passed through some of the most spectacular scenery in Ireland and consequently meant that tunnels, stone shelters to protect the line from rock falls, and substantial viaducts had to be built. The views must have been amazing, so much so that this line has been likened to Scotland's West Highland line. Ultimately however the main traffic came through fishing and tourism and, although locals continued using it, it finally closed in 1960.

Fishing was again encouraged by the Congested Districts Board set up in 1891 to develop agriculture, industry and fishing in the west of Ireland. The actual congested districts were defined statistically as places where the land available was unable to support the population living there. Thus, some quarter of the Irish population came under the board's remit. Valentia's income per family from fishing was found to be in excess of £20 per annum which was quite high at the time, though not as high as Dingle where it was £40. Along the vast majority of the entire west coast the income was less than £20. In Valentia the board paid for a pier to be erected at Tragannane, on the road to the lighthouse, another of George Halpin's and first lit in 1841. That the board regarded the Valentia fishermen expert at their work is supported by the fact that men, boats and nets were taken off to Clifden and Cleggan in County Galway to teach the fishermen there the rudiments of seining for mackerel. With an upsurge in the mackerel fishery in the first years of the twentieth century when up to half a million fish were being landed each day during the spring and autumn seasons, the Valentia fishermen thrived. Prices were good for them and those involved in the boxing the fish and carrying it to the railway station were also paid well. Most went off to English markets. Ice was brought in by barge from Norway and was stored aboard hulks anchored in the harbour. Valentia was, in fact, well established as a great fishing station, crowded with masts which, according to one report, 'were on ships or little vessels, for fishing boats had collected there from far and near that year after mackerel. Plenty of money was being made and the poor themselves didn't want for a pound'.

The first Irish-built fishing boat fitted with a Kelvin petrol/paraffin engine came to the island in 1912 and in one month in 1927 it is said that 7,000 barrels of mackerel were shipped out. After this the fishery declined. Today much of the fishery is shrimping according to one fisherman I spoke to. He and his young English mate used trains of twenty pots though he wouldn't say how many trains he set. He'd drift-netted for salmon until the current ban had come into force and reckoned that many of the other salmon fishers had turned to potting for lobsters and crabs which would, he was sure, soon deplete those stocks. The shrimps he sold to Kerry Fish across from where the ferry goes to at Reenard Point. I drove past it later, after crossing on the ferry, and saw that this establishment was Kerry's oldest wild salmon smokery.

Reenard Point was also the site of the first lifeboat stationed in this vicinity when a lifeboat house was built there in 1864. The effect was a bit wasted for five years later it was moved to Knightstown due to the fact that the only crew available lived there. In 1892 another slipway was built at Carriglea at the south of the island to enable the boat to be recovered from there in poor weather, and be carried by road back to Knightstown. That too seemed a bit pointless as the station was closed four years later. Although a temporary rescue boat was based at Valentia during the Emergency, (the Second World War, as it is often referred to in Ireland) a full-time boat wasn't stationed again there until 1946, after which a motor boat was kept afloat and a Severn-class vessel remains on station today.

Although there seemed so much to discover about this lovely fertile island, often called the granary of Kerry, time was pressing but I was keen to discover something of the cable station that I knew had been built here in the mid-nineteenth century. When the first mutterings of a cable stretching all the way across the Atlantic first surfaced in 1854, the people of Valentia were undoubtedly totally unaware of the fact. However, within two years, the effects of this great plan were already being felt upon the island for it was chosen as the European end of the project. The distance between it and Heart's Content in Newfoundland was the shortest across the great divide. Firstly HMS *Cyclops* came to survey the seabed, after which it was decided to bring the end ashore at Foilhomurrum, just below where I'd spent the previous night. In 1857 two ships were to carry the cable, one from either side, it being spliced mid-Atlantic and the first European end of it was brought ashore as the cable ship *Niagara* began paying it out. Unfortunately the cable snapped when the ship was some 330 miles out going over the continental shelf into water 2,000 fathoms deep. The second attempt was more successful and started the Canadian end so that the other end of a new cable was brought ashore in 1865 after Brunel's massive ship the *Great Eastern*, the largest vessel in the world at the time, had been adapted to carry the entire cable. Celebrations were held and the first message sent across the Atlantic by the Knight of Kerry Peter Fitzgerald, son of Maurice, announcing 'Glory to God in the highest, on earth peace, good will to men' and three cheers were called for Sir Robert Peel who was among the guests. A temporary wooden telegraph station had been built on the cliff and instantly this became busy relaying messages in both directions. Subsequently a spacious new station was built at Knightstown and completed in 1868. In the twentieth century innovative technology soon made such communication methods outdated.

Valentia has, over the last 200 years or so had a whole host of outside visitors who came to work upon the island. We've seen visiting fishermen and lighthouse keepers, staff at the cable station and miners from Wales. On top of these add coastguards, the operators of the Meteorological Station and the Wireless Station. The Meteorological Station operated from 1860 to 1867, using Admiral Fitzroy's system of weather telegraphy, after which an observatory was established by the Meteorological Committee of the Royal Society. By 1892 this had moved to Cahersiveen though it retained its original name. When the observatory was lost from the island, Marconi established a Wireless Station at Reenadrolaun Point, the northernmost tip of the island. The British Post Office took this over in 1909 until the establishment of the Irish Free State, after which it was operated under contract to the Irish Post Office on behalf of the British PO. After 1950 it was run by government departments and today broadcasts weather bulletins, gale and navigational warnings and provides a link between ships and those on land, as well as maintaining the all-important twenty-four-hour watch on the international distress frequencies and coordinating with the Marine Rescue Centre at Shannon and with the coastguards and lifeboat service.

We caught the ferry for the short ride across to Reenard Point, the only link with the mainland until the bridge at Portmagee was built in 1970. They used to say 'next parish America' for sometimes it must have seemed that contact with those across the ocean was easier than with those in Britain, especially when life was for the most part controlled by the British. Kerry itself was largely inaccessible so a couple of weeks sailing westward was perhaps nearer than, say, London. As I considered the options for those folk I was reminded of what I'd read concerning the Fitzpatrick family and their allegiance to the British Crown. They weren't all tarred with the same brush, if you'll excuse the pun, for their cousin Mary Ellen Spring-Rice, only daughter of Lord Mounteagle of Foynes, became a supporter of Sinn Féin and, as such, stood on the foredeck of Erskine Childers's gun-running yacht *Asgard* in July 1914, wearing a red skirt as the agreed signal to the waiting Republicans on shore.

I passed Kerry Fish and saw the lorry that had been loading up shrimps outside. Cahersiveen was only a few miles further on up the road and the Old Barracks Heritage Centre was easy to find. I wanted to learn a bit about the Fenian Rising of 1867 and the Barracks of the Royal Irish Constabulary seemed as good a place as anywhere for I seemed sure a museum in such a place would have some information. Three years after the Rising and two subsequent to the completion of the transatlantic link, a government, fearful that future uprisings might threaten this important link, built these imposing barracks between 1870 and 1875. However, it is believed that two sets of plans were mixed up by some British official in his haste to protect this vital communication link and that the building here was meant to have been constructed on India's north-west frontier and that a typical Irish police station is to be found in Samana, North India. Seemed a good story but I wasn't convinced although the building, four storeys high with turrets and steeply pitched roofs, did seem a bit imposing for such a small inaccessible community. It would have appeared even more out of place in north-west India.

The Fenians – a nationwide organisation of Republicans eager to see Britain kicked out of Ireland – had been formed in Kerry in 1858 by James Stephen. Over the next few years various attacks upon British interests in Kerry resulted more in imprisonment for those involved or even death, mostly through informers and bad planning. Planning for an 1867 rising continued even though the organisation was thoroughly infiltrated by informers. The rising was planned on a national scale and in Kerry those participating were to overrun the local Irish Constabulary, attack the coastguard station at Kells and break into the armoury to arm themselves and to take control of the cable station on Valentia and proclaim Ireland's independence before destroying the station. But the whole event was a disaster from start to finish, especially when HMS *Gladiator*, a British gunboat, showed up in Valentia Harbour. The men, after breaking into the coastguard's armoury, marched to Killarney where the main uprising was supposedly taking place but what they didn't know was that the uprising had been cancelled. Many of those reaching Killarney were shot by the police, some arrested and some escaped.

The heritage centre did have some other interesting exhibits on various aspects of life in the village. The harbour had been established in 1822, largely because of the 80 miles of coastline within 10 miles of Cahersiveen which gave it access to the rich fishing grounds, perhaps inspired by the success of Valentia. The main fishery was again mackerel although salmon, hake, herring, scad and pilchards were also landed. The best period in its fortunes was the early twentieth century when 30,000 barrels of fish were exported through Cahersiveen, though some had come from Valentia. At times there were a hundred boats fishing and landing, many from the Isle of Man. Looking out of the windows of the upper floor, there were fine views over the harbour and the railway bridge, one of the engineering feats on the Valentia railway. Completed in 1893, the bridge spans 947 feet across the river Fertha 'and is of an imposing design of seven side-girder main spans with two lead-in spans at either end', or so the centre blurb tells us. To be honest I'm not sure what a side-girder span is though the lead-ins at either end were obvious at a glance!

We hastened along the coast only stopping to admire some more of the engineering feats of the railway such as the Gleensk Viaduct, a high curving steel and stone structure, and one of the tunnels cut through the rock. In fact the scenery shot past so fast that we soon left the Ring of Kerry at Killorglin, circumnavigated Castlemain Harbour and arrived at Annascaul. Annascaul is the birthplace of Tom Crean who served on three Antarctic expeditions in the early 1900s and returned to build and run the pub 'The South Pole' in the village. Next was Dingle but, with it being four o'clock and my wanting to visit the Blasket Centre at Dunquin, we continued through the town, past the harbour and, after another few miles, Ventry Harbour and around the famine relief road to Slea Head where the view of the off-lying Blaskets jerks one into life, so spectacular is it. Several beehive huts sit aside the road, open invitations for passers-by to visit. On arriving at Dunquin itself, I couldn't but not stop for a look at the famous harbour nestling amongst the rocks down below. A coach-load of Czech tourists were disgorging themselves from their bus as I arrived and another of the same had already discharged. The cliff-top was therefore fairly top-heavy with people muttering in an undecipherable language but who nonetheless were evidently enjoying the perfect views of both harbour and the Blasket Islands.

And what a view it is. *Inish Mor*, or the Great Blasket, a 4-mile stretch of precipitous cliffs and jagged inhospitable rocks, lies a little over a mile out from Dunmore Head. The other, smaller, islands that make up the Blaskets lie dotted around like children of the great humped whale. Between mainland and islands is the notorious Blasket Sound where at its narrowest, its neck between Dunmore and the northeast tip of the Great Blasket, the tide is squeezed to produce some violent tide rips and an eddy in the opposite direction along the mainland shore. Today, with the sun's rays dancing along the tips of small wavelets and the sound seemingly in total silence, it's hard to imagine a more serene place. From several hundred feet above it's easy to be misled for here, on many an occasion, lives have been taken away all too often. Furthermore, hidden below the surface of the sound yet close to the midway point of this narrow neck, is situated the pinnacle rock of Stromboli which rises close to the surface, one of many such fangs awaiting unaware sailors.

One particularly tragic event occurred here on 21 September 1588. As the remnants of the Spanish Armada were trying to make their way home after the disastrous attempt to defeat the English off the French coast near Calais – and at the same time making Drake the hero of the English Navy – many foundered on the wild coastlines of Scotland and Ireland. Others sought desperate refuge in the face of a series of gales coming in from the Atlantic, to be later wrecked close to their chosen anchorages. The number of these wrecks along the Irish coast still remains a mystery though suggestions of fifty such wreck sites are probably a bit over enthusiastic. Anyway, into the Sound sailed several of the depleted Armada fleet, one of these on the morning of that fateful day being the *Santa Maria de la Rosa*, the 945-ton vice-flagship

Launching naomhóga on Great Blasket Island.

of the Spanish province of Guipuzcoa, its sails in tatters. She dropped anchor in the Sound, close to two other Armada vessels, though with the wind at gale force and the fast flood tide against this wind, the conditions were merciless. The anchor held a while but then the tide changed direction so that the pull on the anchor cable was doubled - wind and tide working together. Consequently she dragged and found herself in the worst of the boiling tide rip, fouling the anchor cable of the *San Juan Bautista* though that ship was able to set another anchor. The *Santa Maria de la Rosa*'s anchor was now bouncing along the rough seabed, almost useless and seemingly they did not have another to throw overboard. Onto the awaiting Stromboli they headed which they hit with a splintering shudder as the rock tore into the planking of the ship. Water cascaded in as the tide carried the vessel off into deeper water where, though attempts were made to sail to the nearby shore, she sank under the waves, men, barrels and odd bits of the ship being carried away off to sea by the ebbing tide. Suddenly 300 or so men and a 945-ton ship were gone although one young man, known later as Giovanni, did survive by floating ashore on a plank; he was the only survivor out of more than 300 people. Ironically, 21 September, was the day also that the first of the ships arrived back in Spain, two months to the day after they had left. Some thirty-five ships arrived back that day after sailing up to 5000 miles and several more survived out of the original 130 ships sent out to conquer England. But, for the crew of the *Santa Maria de la Rosa*, that mattered no more. They, like thousands of their like before them, simply existed no longer, except in the minds of their loved ones and, later, in the pages of history.

Between 2000 and 2002 I spent time studying maritime history at St Andrews University under the guidance of the directors of the Scottish Institute of Maritime Studies - Colin Martin and Robert Prescott. Colin had been the director of the Institute of Maritime Archaeology until this later amalgamated to become SIMS. During the first year, I spent a considerable amount of time reading about various wrecks that had been discovered and excavated. Colin, it turned out, had worked on several of these excavations over the years, including the initial search and later excavation of the *Santa Maria de la Rosa*. His book *Full Fathom Five* tells the story of this and two other Armada sites he had worked upon. As I sat there on my tuft of grass, gazing out over the shimmering sound, I thought about how quickly conditions could change, from a gentle sea one minute to raging inferno the next, and the plight of those poor sailors over 400 years ago. Not for nothing is 'the sea has no mercy' a well-known cliché.

The Great Blasket Centre – or Ionad an Bhlascaoid Mhoir - is situated a couple of miles further on, a modern low building dating from 1993 which blends in quite well with the surrounding area. Inside there's various exhibitions concerning life on the island which was inhabited over many years up to 1953. As an island community it must be unique in that several of the people living there produced some startling Gaelic literary works. That there's a sort of dreamy magnetic pull towards the islands, and especially Great Blasket where the main settlements were, is supported by the number of travellers making the effort to reach this far flung place. According to Muiris Mac Conghail, from the island you can 'contemplate Ireland or even turn your back to her and to the busy world and gaze out toward America or up at the vast expanse of an Atlantic sky for hours' whilst R.M. Lockley contemplated nearby Mount Brandon on his trip. Others did their contemplating from Dunquin as I had. Celtic scholar Robin Flower, who visited often, wrote about it and translated some of the Gaelic works into English. He said that 'seen from above you would think them sea monsters of an antique world languidly lifting their time-worn backs above the restless and transitory waves'.

I guess it is easy to turn your back on Ireland out there on Great Blasket and just as easy for people from outside to come believing them cut off from the rest of the mainland. Pierre

Trehiou must have thought that when he sailed over regularly from Paimpol in Brittany to buy lobsters and trade fishing gear and household goods with the locals. If he thought they were able to buy and sell locally I doubt he would have made the long voyage. The inhabitants also collected 'dulse', edible seaweed, which they might have traded as well. When the Congested Districts Board bought the islands from the Earl of Cork to invest the land in the slanders in 1908, and then improve the harbour two years later, facilities for landing were improved – but only slightly. It's not a lot different today.

Three inhabitants figure prominently in this literary oddity. Tomás Ó Criomhthain (O'Crohan), Peig Sayers and Maurice O'Sullivan all wrote and published their most famous books, *The Islandman*, *Peig* and *Twenty Years A-Growing* in Irish in the space of six years and each tells the story of life upon the island. The two men were born on the island though Peig Sayers didn't arrive until two days after her wedding. All are said to have portrayed life from their own perspectives. I bought a copy of Tomás O'Crohan's *The Islandman*. However, feeling a bit of a fraud for not visiting the island, I sought refuge in the brief company of Christy MacGeralt, the manager of the restaurant, another of Darina Tully's contacts and a known authority on the boats of the area.

I found him in the restaurant, and we spoke leaning over the counter of a not very busy restaurant (it was almost closing time) as he drew on a paper serviette sketches of these boats so well known far and wide. There we were, amongst the chocolate sponges and lemon cheesecakes, discussing boats as the occasional customer ordered pots of tea and buns, looking at us with a certain amount of surprise. It was Christy who explained the difference between a naomhóg and a currach. 'Call them Kerry canoes if that's easier,' he suggested as I tried to get my tongue around the Gaelic,

> but not currachs. They are the boats used in the sheltered waters further north whilst the *naomhóga* (plural) are renowned for working in more open waters. They're the longest of the skin boats. See how the bow is more pronounced and the keel is curved to take the Atlantic rollers. They were used for all manner of work, not just transporting animals and people across between islands and the mainland but fishing, egg collecting, bird hunting, you name it and they did it. A bit of salvage even. These boats were stronger than the Galway currachs, built often with a lug sail and lasted twenty-five years while the Connemara currachs seldom last more than three years. Go and see Paudi de Hora, he's a champion builder. Eddie Hutchinson is another and if there's racing tonight he'll be down at Dingle. Depends on the weather whether they do race.

He described how to get to Paudi's house, just down the road, and we parted as he wanted to shut up shop though he did add that Peter Carr (whoever he is) was currently filming a documentary about the naomhóga and a book was due out as well. Something to look forward to. I left, following Christy's instructions – that Irish mile again – and thought I'd found the house though no one was at home. A guy was cleaning the building's external faces from up a ladder so I asked him. He hadn't a clue. Said he wasn't local. If I'd been in England I'd have suspected a break-in was about to occur as it seemed abnormal that the fellow working on the house didn't know the name of the owner. Still, I wasn't convinced it was the right house anyway as there was no sign of a workshop nor any tarred vessels lying upside down. I searched along the road and couldn't find any other signs of naomhóga nor anyone to ask.

What I did discover later was that the Blasket islanders hadn't always used these hide or canvas covered vessels. At the beginning of the nineteenth century most of these were strongly-built wooden boats but these were confiscated by bailiffs in the 1880s because of the non-payment of rents. When a Dingle currach was brought in to replace the wooden boats, they were considered light and easy to lift out of the water and to carry up the beach to hide away if the bailiffs returned. The only slipway on the island offered little shelter so they had the added advantage of being to able to store the boats away from the encroaching waves whereas the wooden boats were sometimes smashed by the sea. In 1921 there were some 400 naomhóga in West Dingle and this number had been reduced to 80 by 1934. This decline is said to have come about, ironically, with the adoption of wooden boats once again and motorisation. However, according to Roderic O'Flaherty, writing in 1665, 'The ancient Irish had, besides boats and canoes, which we even use yet in crossing ferries, these small wicker boats ... They are called in Irish Corach or Noemhog'. Proof then that the term has been in use for hundreds of years.

We drove on, eager to reach Dingle at racing time. Continuing along the road around the twin peaks of Mount Eagle and Croaghmarhin, we came to Ballyferriter where, I have to say, I was quite pleased to find the regional museum closed. Four such centres in one day was surely enough for any person, never name a travel-weary soul. The twin Brandon Mountain and Peak lay ahead, lost in a mist, the brightness of the day beginning to disappear as cloud assembled in the south-west. The views were still good though over Smerwick Harbour where 600 Italian mercenaries had been landed off six Spanish ships in 1580 in another invasion attempt, though most had been killed by English soldiers.

Dingle was hectic to say the least, one of the most popular tourist destinations of the south-west. I'd read and heard so much about the place that it was almost an anticlimax to walk around the harbour and town. One shop had a big and bold sign declaring 'enough is enough and it's got to stop', a reference to the growing problem of second homes being bought up at the locals' expense. A problem I empathised with, as I had seen so much of the same thing in Britain. Somehow I thought it almost depraved, certainly immoral, to buy a holiday house in an area where the result was to push the indigenous population onto the sideline. Just one aspect of the evils of wealth, or at least too much of it. I searched out a couple of bookshops and ate fish and chips on a seat overlooking the harbour. Although the chips weren't the best and the fish a bit greasy, it was fresh and a welcome change to pasta. I considered venturing into a bar for a drink, eager to find out if it was true that there were over forty bars, some of which were in the back of the grocer's, ironmonger's and cobbler's, or so I'd read. But then I decided against it, unsure of the same writer's assurance from the barman in whatever bar he'd been drinking that the locals have three pints to warm up before arriving in Dingle. It was getting late and, although I'd searched for Eddie Hutchinson and his regatta, it was obviously not happening tonight. Mind you, the wind was freshening by the minute and the gathering clouds of an hour before had already gathered and were threatening rain.

Dingle Harbour, not as big as other harbours along the coast, is nonetheless a place of perfect shelter and only accessible from the sea through a narrow entrance. Fishing had figured important here since the heady days of the pilchard. The arrival of the railway in 1891 no doubt helped the fishing to prosper and today, though there is still a healthy fleet, the harbour is better known as the playground of Fungi the dolphin and boats of all sizes are often to be seen taking tourists out to see him. Poor old Fungi I thought, to be constantly assaulted and possibly battered by this annoying armada of prats. Why he remains is a mystery but presumably something attracts him about the place. There was something ironic about this, I thought, a dolphin enticed by the magic of the place when, as far as I could see, the only magic seducing the tourists is Fungi himself. I wasn't sure what else Dingle had going for it except the bars and surrounding mountains. Oh, and as a stepping off point for the Blaskets which I discovered when inquiring that I could sail on a return trip in the morning, staying two hours on Great Blasket, for €35. The name of the vessel: the *Peig Sayers* of course!

Dingle harbour.

I phoned Laurence Courtney, a fisherman whose name had been given to me by Adrian Birth back in Oldcourt. Surprisingly he'd heard of me when he answered. 'You're the guy who runs the 40+ Fishing Boat Association'. Hell, I thought, people do read our magazine. Unfortunately he was in Castletownbere where I had been yesterday though he had only arrived that morning to undertake some work on the boat he fishes with. Laurence had served his time in the BIM yard in Dingle. I asked him where the yard had been. 'Between the two piers,' he said, 'by the harbourmaster's office. Now knocked down but you can still see the slipway.' He'd stayed with the yard until about 1970, he told me, and reckoned they packed up building boats in the 1980s and finally closed in 1995. He'd been at the fishing ever since. 'Maybe we'll meet someday when you come again,' he said as we bid our farewells. Several people had said that to me though, as it had taken me ten years to get here, I wasn't sure when I'd be back.

Adrian had also given me the phone number of a guy named Liam. I called him to discover he was currently trawling aboard his boat the *Fleetwood Lady* some 8 miles off Loop Head. Won't be back until Saturday. 'Fishing's not bad,' he shouted into the phone over the sound of the engine, 'rays, skates and stuff but prices are low.' An oft repeated fisherman's phrase, that! Tom Kennedy, skipper of *Fiona K*, the boat I was sitting by, wasn't in. He was another of Joseph Teesdale's contacts but today was not a good contact day.

I wandered around a bit longer, photographing a couple of naomhóga and finding the site of the old boatbuilding yard. Two old fishing boats lay alongside the quay, the *Karina* and *Assumpta*, both now belonging to Alan Granville, a well known fisherman of the south coast who lived, I believe, in East Dunmore. By the time of the onset of twilight, I decided to leave Dingle which I found slightly threatening. A week later I heard on the news that there had been a massive fight in the town one evening, presumably the Saturday after my visit, in which several passing tourists as well as locals had been injured in a battle between rival gangs. Such is the peace and solitude of Dingle. That evening, hoping for a walk the following morning, I drove up the Connor Pass, a few miles outside of town where, finding a suitable car park, I decided to sleep the night at an altitude of 1,500 feet. Perhaps I hoped to bump into Eddie Hutchinson as Peter Marshall had done, according to his book *Celtic Gold*, during his circumnavigation of Ireland by boat in the summer of 1995. He'd walked up from Dingle and reached the peak of Brandon Mountain but then again he's travelled all over the world. Tonight, though, the mountains remained in cloud yet below me lights twinkled all around. In the distance the Loop Head lighthouse's flash was clear and I wondered where Liam was, somewhere out there in the dark, and whether the fishing was any better in the dark. It seemed such a hospitable place this car park high up. The odd car dropped into the car park and one particular car load of arrivals spent maybe half an hour sitting on the stone wall edging the car park, chatting and drinking bottles of beer that they subsequently threw into the field. Once they'd gone no one else disturbed me and my thoughts. We slept well, Dog and I, high in the clouds and blanketed by the warmth of the day's success.

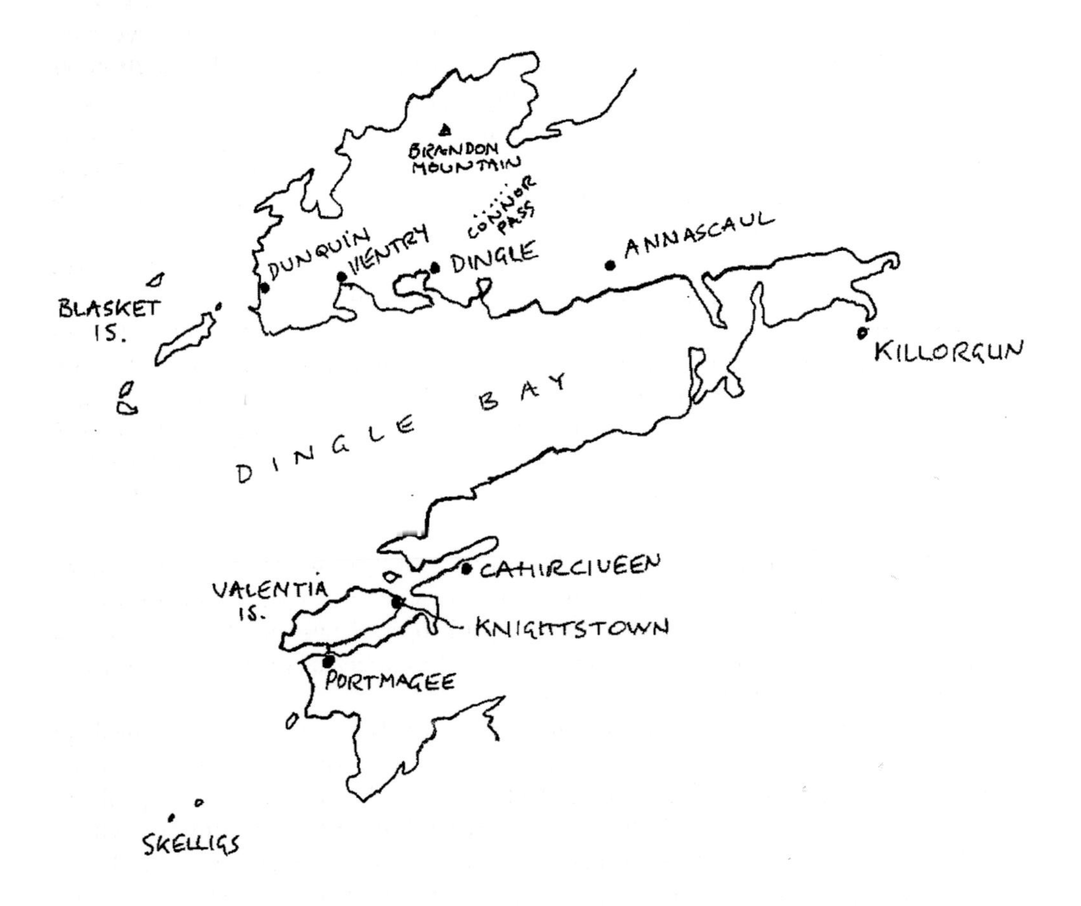

DAY NINE

Day nine started as badly as the night we'd endured. From about 2a.m. onwards the van had been assaulted by torrents of rain and an ever-increasing wind that buffeted us to such an extent I became a bit concerned. Visions of us – Dog, van and me – flying off down the valley were real in my fitful sleep. Looking out early in the morning the scenery was one of thick mist, with visibility down to a matter of yards. Merely getting outside for a pee was bad enough and Dog stayed happily in his tight corner, snuggled under the blanket I'd given him when the temperature had plummeted during the night. All thoughts of our proposed walk up to Brandon Mountain were quickly banished. What a shame though as a walk up to the summit, following in the footsteps of the pilgrims of old, would have been more than invigorating. Mount Brandon stands as one of Ireland's highest mountains. Some call it the second highest though this isn't technically correct as the highest, Carrauntoohil in the MacGillycuddy's Reeks in the east of the Iveragh peninsula, has two other peaks higher than Mount Brandon. It is one of three regarded as high places worthy of pilgrimage, the other two being Slieve League in County Donegal and Croagh Patrick in County Mayo. The remains of many of the beehives along the west end of the Dingle peninsula are thought to have been built as temporary abodes for pilgrims coming ashore, perhaps even having to wait for the mist to clear from the peak for days on end. Mornings like this were certainly not uncommon.

It was so miserable up the summit of the pass that I decided to drive down the hill even before brewing up some coffee. That's normally unheard of. The intention was to drive towards Brandon Point on the western tip of Brandon Bay. A diversion from roadworks confused me, however and we ended up Castlegregory and from there at Scraggane Point on the west side of the bay of that name. Two yellow oilskin-clad fishermen, one wearing a baseball cap and the other with a thick crop of white hair sticking out from his oilskin hood, were putting shrimp pots aboard their newish looking fibreglass boat. I watched them from the van as I supped my morning coffee and afterwards went over to talk to them. This was their second year at the shrimps they told me when I asked. They'd been making what they described as 'not bad money' which is a fisherman's way of saying the prices were really good and the profits were excellent. The last two months they'd been out jigging for pollack. For black pollack they only received about 80 cents per kilo and the fish mainly went for use in chowders such was its unpopularity though white pollack, which they considered a tasty fish, got them a much higher price.

We discussed the effect of the salmon ban in this area and White Hair recounted something he'd heard on Kerry Radio only last week, about how 180 licences were, or so the government said, getting compensation. None of the fishermen had heard of anyone being offered this money, they said. Although the fishermen's grapevine is always fast and chatty, I guess there will always be those that decline to admit when public money comes their way. They'd been drifting for salmon ever since they could remember and thought that the ban was just another nail in the coffin of their industry. Baseball Cap, the fisherman aboard the boat below us, was stacking the pots aboard the boat as White Hair picked them off the trailer behind their white van and lowered them from the quay. The pots were plastic and brand new, cylindrical and about two feet long and a bit more than a foot in diameter. Each train they said had forty pots fixed onto the line and, in total, they had 400 pots. As I watched them at work Baseball Cap suddenly stopped work at looked up at me, intense blue eyes staring.

> Tis a disgrace, I tell you. I've seen their counting methods near Lough Leane. I do a bit of fishing there. There's a counter in the river but it only goes so far out into the river Laune. Not across as you'd think. Another counter further down there said there were five fish in one spot. Funny that because we'd caught six.

I mentioned what I'd heard about wild fish being counted as farmed.

'Aye that too. We've seen that, haven't we, Joe. Their statistics are just unreal.'

White Hair just shook his head in agreement and carried on tying a pot onto a rope. One misplaced foot as the pots go over and over goes the fisherman to the bottom to drown as getting a leg out of the grip is almost impossible.

Joe White Hair seemed quite reluctant to talk whilst Baseball Cap was the opposite. When I mentioned the British weekly newspaper *Fishing News*, they both said they read it. When I said I contribute to it occasionally Joe smiled and said he'd wondered how I knew these pots were shrimp pots. I told them about my trip around and how I'd spoken to several salmon fishers.

'You'll be seeing many more on yer travels, I'm sure,' said Joe as I wished them happy fishing.

As I wandered back to the van I passed several Kerry canoes atop the slipway by the quay, most of which had been fibreglass sheathed on the outside, over the canvas. I watched as a diver dragged his small dinghy over the top of the naomhóga which can't be good for either vessel. Another group of divers were just leaving on a large semi-rigid inflatable and I counted twelve fishing boats anchored in the bay. Offshore the Magharee Islands stood guard over the bay. These were once famous for their corn but are now inhabited solely by rabbits. Across Tralee Bay, I got fleeting views of Kerry Head as it occasionally emerged from the mist, a sign that the mist was certainly thinning and might clear at any time. Likewise specks of sunlight teased us for minutes at a time.

I retraced our route through Fahamore, stopping to walk along the edge of Brandon Bay with the dog skipping about like a spring lamb. The beach was quiet except for another lone dog walker. We walked possibly a mile in soft sand with a light breeze, though not enough strength in it to blow away the clouds that hovered at only a few hundred feet. The distant mass of the mountain was still shrouded in heavy cloud, all dark grey with wisps of white. Across the other side of the bay Brandon Point was visible and, though out of view, I knew Brandon Creek lay only a few miles around that, the point of departure for Tim Severin's Brendan Voyage in 1976. Aboard a boat made up from forty-nine ox-hides, all stitched together and sealed with fat to keep the sea out, on what can only be described as a large currach, he and his crew sailed transatlantic in an attempt to prove that St Brendan the Navigator had undertaken such a voyage. Whether or not he did remains unknown though Severin did prove that such a feat had been possible in Brendan's day thus defying the critics who, up till then, refused to believe it. That Brendan sailed widely between mainland Europe and Britain and Ireland is known, so it is a distinct possibility that he did cross 'the pond' in the sixth century.

At one point, just below the odd 'third man' sculpture, a 'wooden man' constructed from driftwood firmly planted atop the sand-dunes and pointing over towards America, I found twenty-four mangled lobster pots within the space of some 100 yards along. These were all

Naomhóga in South Kerry.

Putting shrimp pots aboard at Scraggane Point.

half buried in the sand along the edge of the beach before it climbed up into sand-dunes. During the rest of the walk I saw maybe a couple more so some strange quirk of the tide must have ensured these pots all ended up in the same place. There were plenty of discarded nets also lying half buried in the sand, either destroyed during use or thrown into the sea by careless crew members. They are a nightmare for the environment.

Fahamore is a mass of holiday chalets and caravans with a few houses dotted in between. Obviously a surfers' paradise, there were novices learning the rudiments of their sport upon a beach on the west side of Tralee Bay. Across the road was a West Coast Seafood van with a display of fish. I ran my eyes over the fresh-looking fish, memorizing the species to write down later (black sole, mackerel, monk tails, plaice, turbot, cod, and brill) and though the choice wasn't great, several customers were lining up. I was tempted to join them and buy but thought better when I considered my cooking facilities: a one burner gas stove and no suitable pan!

It was five days before when I'd arrived at Oldcourt, beginning a several hundred mile drive around the south-west peninsulas, and at Blennerville we completed that journey. Here a restored windmill alerted me to some interesting history of a different kind. I'd never noticed the place on the map, never even heard of it, which makes a place like this all the more interesting and the urge for a spontaneous stop was too overwhelming to ignore which meant we ended up spending a few hours browsing the small village.

Blennerville was considered the port of Tralee until 1846, after which the ship canal leading up to nearby Tralee itself was opened. Before that, although some ships considered the facilities at Blennerville to be open to adverse weather and were reluctant to use the port, large amounts of coal, timber and iron passed through. Corn became the major export when the Corn Laws were introduced in the early 1800s. Britain was eager to convert pasture into tillage to produce grain for its growing Empire and bounties were paid to encourage this. This was a sort of reverse of the Scottish Clearances where sheep prospered at the expense of tillage and the human inhabitants. Thus Blennerville prospered as being a suitable export centre; the windmill was built about the same time. Tralee then was a small rather insignificant village whilst Blennerville consisted of 530 people in 1837, though the former must have been growing in importance for, back in the late 1820s, plans to build the canal first surfaced.

Although the history of Blennerville as a port was relatively short – nearby Barrow appears to have been a more sheltered landing – it acts as an excellent window of how agriculture developed rural parts of the country. Recent research has produced a tome under the Training and Employment Authority of the Community Response Programme and their publication *Blennerville – Gateway to Tralee's Past* has to be well recommended for anyone serious about delving into the area's past. This project received a huge stimulus in 1984 when the restored windmill was first opened and since then the ship canal has reopened and work progresses on opening more of the Tralee to Dingle railway line. Alongside the windmill, is a visitor centre with exhibits covering the famine and emigration for thousands of Irish workers left here in search of a new life in the colonies. The Windmill Museum costs €5 to enter and allows access into the mill itself for visitors to discover its workings and technicalities.

One such ship that carried people away to distant lands was the *Jeanie Johnston*, a three-masted barque built in Quebec in 1847, possibly by John Munn though one report says she was built for John Munn, as a timber ship. Within a year she had been sold to the Donovan family of Tralee and she first sailed as an emigrant ship on 24 April 1848 with 200 passengers aboard. The cost of such a voyage was £3 10*s* and she crossed over several times after that, often carrying single women excusively, some of whom worked their passage if they were unable to pay. One has to wonder what work this involved. By 1856 though the Donovans sensed a drop in passenger numbers due to the development of passenger ships specifically for the purpose and the fact that, with the advent of the railways, many were leaving directly from Cobh, and they sold her to William Johnson from North Shields. She continued working as a freight vessel until she sank in mid-Atlantic in December 1858 *en route* to North Shields from Quebec. Fortunately her crew, who had climbed to the top of the mast as she became waterlogged, were saved by the Dutch brig *Sophie-Elizabeth* which was bound for New York.

More exciting for Blennerville was the fact that for several years the town was the focus of excitement for the building of a replica of this ship. First started in 1993, the ship, a true-to-life replica, was launched in 2002 and sailed from nearby Fenit across to Canada the following year. Nowadays she's used as a corporate hospitality vessel, a sail-training ship and, when in port, as a museum vessel displaying exhibits on emigration and the famine. Ironically she had been in Bristol for the Harbour Festival a few days before I'd departed for Ireland but I'd missed her, being away that weekend. Even more annoying was the fact that, when I got home to Bristol after the tour and had downloaded my photographs, I realised that the ship I had admired so much and photographed lying alongside the Cork river was in fact the *Jeanie Johnston*. If only I hadn't been in such a rush that Saturday morning.

I wandered around the visitor centre, observing the model of a 'Kerry currach' which, although the wording might not impress Christy MacGeralt, was pretty accurate in showing the constructional details. Afterwards I took Dog for a walk along the towpath of the ship canal as the sun had decided to come out. The lock gates had been replaced with modern gear though the lock-keeper's house remained ruined. A pink gate prevented access to the gates so that we were unable to cross over onto the other bank of the canal. Young pampas grass and even a few palm trees lined the towpath which showed that somebody cared for the place, although the piles of dog shit weren't very inviting. I sat a while contemplating the scene, sun hot on my face and scent of the grass sweet to my senses, imagining the black and white painted *Jeanie Johnston* moving gracefully downstream, her oiled masts and white sails gleaming in the bright sun (though I doubt her masts were as gleaming as the replica's), her decks filled with passengers, some excited at the anticipation of their future prospects whilst others, sad at leaving, must have been watching as the last chances of changing their minds passed them by. I wondered how I would feel being hungry, being forced out of my native lands. Would I have been angry or would the thrill of setting off to sea and never returning have been too strong for me to worry about the fears of crossing the Atlantic? Stories of emigrant ships being lost with all people aboard must have been in their minds though it must be said that the *Jeanie Johnston*, I read, never lost one passenger in her short period as an emigrant ship.

The road to Tralee follows the canal as did the railway line and I noticed one particularly lovely thatched roundhouse although opposite, around the canal basin, was the ubiquitous waterfront housing development with, a little forebodingly, 24-hour security courtesy of the Federal Security Group. Almost immediately I hit a traffic jam, the first in Ireland, which slowed progress through the town to a snail's pace. Once we achieved town centre proximity, the chance of a finding a parking place was zero, a missed turning into a car parked proved this, and so we continued through, unfortunately failing to visit the Kerry County Museum there. However, having wondered on many occasion as to what the meaning of 'Go Mall' was (I'd seen it on roads and other signs and was beginning to think it was some footballer or something) I realised suddenly that it was simply meant 'slow'!

Fenit was pleasant, a harsh south-west breeze blending with the heat from the afternoon sun, giving the impression of a perfectly sheltered harbour patronised by a whole host of pleasure vessels and their owners. The harbour consists of a marina sheltered by a causeway across to a small island where a small lifeboathouse had been built alongside facilities for several fishing

The morning after!

boats. Fenit had initially been used by vessels sheltering in the lee of the islands whilst waiting to enter the ship canal at Blennerville. However, the first 'Port of Fenit' was in fact the harbour at Barrow in medieval times and should not be confused with developments at Fenit itself. A proposal was put forward in the 1840s for a pier and rail project at Fenit but this was disregarded on the basis that the ship canal to Tralee had just been opened. However, when the North Kerry railway was almost completed in 1879, the proposals surfaced once again and this time they were taken more seriously. By 1887, the new pier, the viaduct portion of which was built in timber whereas iron had originally been proposed, was completed and the Tralee to Fenit railway brought down onto the pier itself. However, because of high charges imposed by the railway company, the enterprise was never successful, vessels often choosing to use the cheaper canal option. Today, houses have been built over the route of the disused railway line which closed for good in the 1970s so that any plan to reinstate it is almost impossible.

St Brendan was born near here in 534, a man determined to carry the message of Christianity, travelling to Wales, Scotland and Brittany in the process. Up some steps at the end of the causeway, which were rebuilt in the 1970s, is a sort of memorial to the saint, called the 'St. Brendan Monument and Theme Park'. Several information boards tell his story and that of the *Navigatio Sanctii Brendani*. The park also has various replica standing stones with inscriptions as well as an example of a beehive hut. As I stood half way up the steps reading a board, an old couple clambered up.

'Oh dear,' he said to her, 'is this something new, I think?'

She didn't reply and both concentrated on climbing the steps until when, arriving at the big flat slab of granite, all shiny from its polished surface, he added: 'and is this a picnic bench?!'

In the harbour a flotilla of small all-varnished sailing boats were struggling to reach the pontoon, sails flapping as they manoeuvred in the confined space of the marina, oars being used to fend off other boats amid some cheerful banter and the occasional irate voice. I asked a woman who, too, was watching the boats in their endeavours. She informed me that these small dinghies were Dublin Bay Mermaids and that they were racing in the all-Irish national championships. The regatta lasted the whole week and thirty of these old but very pretty boats were taking part in the races.

The lighthouse on Little Samphire Island is worthy of mention. The need for a light, directing incoming ships to Tralee and Blennerville away from the out-lying rocks off Fenit, were first put forward in 1846 when the canal was opened. Two years later George Halpin submitted plans for such a light and work started in 1849. However work progressed slowly so that by the end of 1852 Halkin could only report that the tower and main walling were complete, the light apparatus under construction but the internal work incomplete. It took another two years to finish. A house for one keeper was also provided and a local naomhóg from Fenit attended their, and the station's, needs two or three times a week.

Oyster fishing in the bay had existed for 200 years with thirty-five boats taking between 10,000 and 14,000 oysters a day from the bed in 1814, the quality said to be amongst the best in Europe. Fifty years later this had fallen to no more than 3,000 a day supplied by ten or twelve boats. However this decline was said to have come about because the rowing boats were unselective in their dredging so that small spat was taken ashore and dumped as rubbish. Moreover 100,000 oysters were said to have been removed by Burton Bindon for restocking elsewhere along the Irish coast. However the fishery survived into the twentieth century with 677 tons being taken in 1977 and 190 two years later. Today fishing continues on a very restricted basis and the possibility of a revival in their fortunes doesn't look good. Mackerel and herring flourished before the harbour as built and in the early twentieth century 150 Manx boats worked from March to May for several years.

The windmill at Blennerville.

At Ardfert I stopped in a small second-hand bookshop I found at Glandore Gate. Striking up a conversation with the owner, we talked about several books he suggested I read though he hadn't them in stock. I asked him about the name of the shop and whether this place had an association with Glandore. It turned out that the answer was yes for the Crosby family who owned the estate once had land at Glandore and their summer residence on Barrow Sands was, over time, swallowed up by the sands during storms so that now it lies somewhere below the dunes and marram grass. He was friendly and offered me a cup of tea though I declined and, not finding any books to buy, left. Barrow Bay, he'd said, was where much of the footage of *Ryan's Daughter* had been filmed. At the northern end of the bay is Ballyheige.

Everywhere you go it seems there's always an advert for a 'show house' for every town or village has some sort of development with its showcase piece hoping to entice owners to buy. Ballyheige is no exception although judging by the hundreds of caravans I'm not sure whether they will get buyers. There was a lovely sand-dune fringed beach and three terraces of four traditional houses atop the low cliff at the village end. Two had been re-roofed in slate whilst two retained their corrugated iron roofs. A note in my journal states 'shame about the rest of the place'. About a mile west was a small sheltered harbour and a concrete slipway littered with evidence of lobster potting and a few small craft within the harbour.

Ballybunion is another place overrun by holiday chalets and new housing developments. In fact the whole place looked not much older than ten years though I had to remind myself that County Kerry is the top holiday resort in Ireland. Presumably much of the work that this brings in for the locals is. One advantage of all this modernity was that I came across a brand new leisure centre with a pool, shower, sauna, and steam-room to which I availed myself. Talking to a fellow in the steam-room who was on holiday here, he reckoned the winter population of the area was 1,500 which probably at least quadruples in summer. Another positive for the place was the fine beach, atop of which was an old seaweed bath. An old signal tower commands the west cliff and more chalets to the east. Moreover, one item of interest here was the railway line that ran for a little over 9 miles from the existing North Kerry line at Listowel. This line, which opened in 1888, was unique in that the trains ran on a monorail which was suspended 3ft 3in from the ground. Designed by a Frenchman, Charles Lartigue, and built by a German engineer, the system seemed to work fairly well although third class passengers sometimes had to help by pushing the train up the steep gradient into Ballybunion! I wondered what happened when only first class passengers were on their way to the seaside as I couldn't imagine them getting out and shoving. Furthermore, the rail passed through the carriage and mobile steps had to be provided for passengers to cross from side to side and heavy loads balanced each side. The line certainly attracted international attention which isn't surprising and which was good for the tourist trade for there was no other line like it. Sadly the line did not survive after damage during 'The Troubles' and was closed in 1924. A short section has been recreated in Listowel as a tourist attraction under the name 'Lartigue Monorailway'.

I was finding it difficult at this stage to find anything interesting to write about the places I visited on this part of the coast. This clearly manifested itself when, upon leaving Ballyheige, I noticed a distinct change in the landscape. After the hills and mountains, rocky inlets, colourful villages and undulating hinterland I was suddenly confronted with a view over the Shannon Estuary, over to County Clare, which appeared flat and grey. In the foreground was north Kerry, a mixture of arable fields and modern housing, which looked equally dull and about as exciting as a tea party at Buckingham Palace. Loop Head looked far away which was strange seeing how close it had seemed the previous evening from the Connor Pass. The mouth of the Shannon had an appearance of greyness mixed with anger and didn't seem very grand today. Somewhere out there in the gloom, I mused, was the lost city that sunk beneath the waves in 1283 and only appears to rise up out of the water every seven years though those fishermen unluckily enough to set eyes on the city are, within a month, dead.

I had intended to stop the night at Bunaclugga Bay; I liked the name and it looked a sandy beach on the map, but when I arrived the small car park had a height barrier guarding its entrance which was too low for the van. These barriers confused me for, given that tourism is supposedly a major contributor to the local economy and that many of these visitors come in campervans, what is their point? It's not as if there are lots of campsites as alternatives – I hadn't seen any that day – which seems to make this even more outrageous. Presumably some faceless sod in the county council offices thought that by fitting these barriers (ultimately at a cost to the tax-payers) he would stop gypsies and other travelling folk from taking over their car parks. Considering the one I was attempting to enter was totally deserted and not a house could be seen, I really could not understand the policy. I proceeded on and came across Carrigfoyle Castle, the ruins of which stand near Ballylongford but the place was overrun by midges. The castle was besieged in 1580 by Sir William Pelham and the garrison of Irish and Spanish soldiers killed. I thought about stopping here but, once bitten a few times and having second thoughts that this wasn't the place to sleep anyway for there were probably too many ghosts floating around, drove on. We passed Saleen Quay just outside Ballylongford and guessed there were a whole host of such piers along both banks of the great river and up the small tributaries, serving the small communities living by its side. Tarbert Quay is another such place though is now the southern terminus for the ferry across the river. When I arrived it was deserted and thus I decided to stop the night here. Its only downside was the power station whining away behind the trees behind us.

Then the ferry arrived, the last of the day, and my peace disappeared. A group of travellers arrived and set up their camp for the night. This consisted of six vehicles, one tent and a generator which they started up almost immediately. However, I must stress their friendliness at this point as I don't wish anyone to think I'm against gypsies or travellers. I'd be a bit of a Uriah Heep if I did, wouldn't I? No, it was the noise of the generator and the fact that one or two of them kept coming to the van door for a chat, so that any chance of reading was soon abandoned. They'd crowd around the door, eyes moving quickly over the interior. Yet they were open and talkative, happily telling me how they live in Athlone and travel for two or three months each summer. Mostly this involved roaming around Connemara – they'd come down from Clifden that day – and this was their first trek south over the Shannon and into County Kerry. I asked them how people received them, whether they had any hassle. In the north, no they hadn't though they were unsure down this way. I thought about the council officers and how their plans to prevent these temporary camps had failed. Good!

One guy tried to sell me a month-old puppy whilst another asked how much I'd sell the dog for. No chance I told him. Even though I could feel their eyes looking around the van, camera, phone, even computer in view, I felt secure that they were simply enjoying a trip whilst looking for a bargain to take home to sell. Once they'd settled down, I hoped we'd have a quiet night.

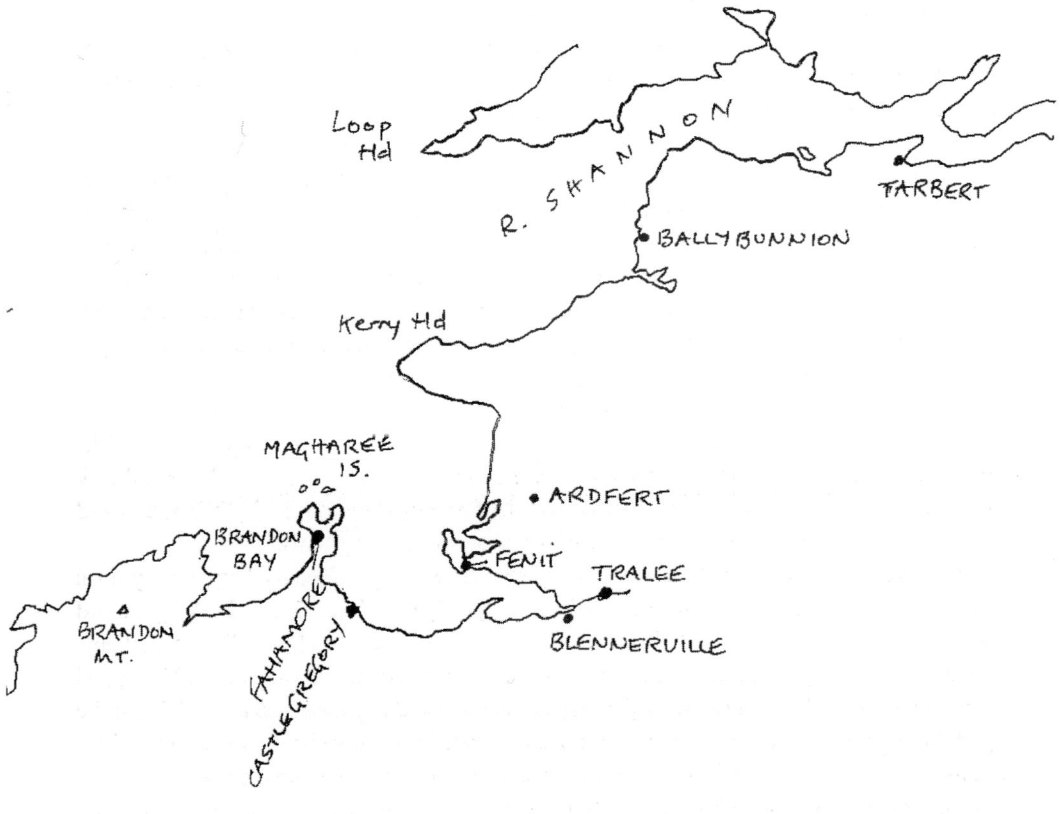

DAY TEN

It was a quiet night after all. With the generator being switched off sometime after I'd gone to sleep, as I remembered drifting off to its musical sounds. I woke early and left before there was the slightest of movement from the travellers which necessitated some dainty driving to extricate the van from the muddle of their parked vehicles. Whilst browsing around the ferry terminal at Tarbert Quay I peered through the window of the adjacent Tarbert Island Maritime Club to spy a couple of what looked like fibreglass currachs. Presumably these were raced out upon the river. An information board provided some facts on the quay, some of which I copied down in my journal and from which some of the following history is drawn.

In the early 1800s Tarbert was exporting considerable amounts of corn, butter and other agricultural produce which was being grown locally and sent onward to Limerick, not that far upstream. In 1837, 50,000 barrels of grain and 25,000 pigs raised in the surrounding district were sent away and a monthly twenty firkins of butter was being collected. All these goods were loaded directly from the shore onto a vessel.

Before the coming of the railway Tarbert was also the landing place of passengers travelling from Dublin via Limerick and onto the steamer taking them down the Shannon, and then onwards to Tralee or Killarney. The Inland Steam Navigation Company built a stone pier in 1837 and on the night of the 'Big Wind' in 1839 some thirty-seven schooners sheltered in Tarbert Bay. I wasn't sure what the 'Big Wind' represented but presumed that some storm of unusual intensity went down in history in these parts. With improvements in vessel construction that meant larger steamers were built, it was felt that this pier did not meet the needs of these larger craft and as a consequence a new deep-water pier was built between 1852 and 1858. It is now used as the terminus for the Shannon ferry. The stone for this pier came from the first battery built on the Shannon in 1794 after its demolition. Restoration work brought the pier up to present day standards in 1994.

The lighthouse on the tidal rock just around from Tarbert Quay is said to be an elegant 74ft white limestone tower built in 1831/32 when the Limerick trade with Europe was flourishing. This light enabled vessels inward and outward bound to clear the Bowline Rock and seek the safe anchorage of Tarbert when inward craft had to await the tide. Today it is automated and unmanned, and is under the authority of the Shannon Estuary Ports.

I drove eastwards as close to the shore of the great river as was possible, searching out any small quay. This was unchartered water for me as I'd normally only traced maritime links along seaward coasts. The river and its hinterland, although both working in unison and complimenting themselves in the same way as coastal settlements do, seemed somewhat dull in comparison. We stopped to brew up some coffee by a slipway adjoining the roadway and I spotted a dead crab lying at the top of the slipway, almost in the lay-by. Someone, I surmised, must have been fishing around here for this crab to be so far away from the river as I was sure it hadn't crawled such a distance.

At Foynes I called in at the Flying Boat Museum which is housed in the old terminal building and control tower across the road from the quay and railway station. Although a tad expensive at €8, it was nevertheless an interesting story. It tells of the development of the transatlantic air traffic between about 1936 and 1945. Commercial flights began in 1939 over to America and over

Shannon smacks working on the river.

the next six years Foynes became the centre of the aviation world as a transatlantic service began on an almost daily timetable and the museum gives a good insight into the business and also has a few handy anecdotes on hand. Once Shannon airport opened across the river, flying boats were superceded in favour of more traditional aircraft. The mock-up of Pan American Airline's luxury flying boat *Yankee Clipper* was fascinating as were the 1940s'-style seating in the cinema where a brief film recalled the era. However I wasn't sure why a fellow was walking around in a swimming costume in the film whilst one of the flying boats was being hauled around on shore. Was he about to swim out to the plane and pilot the plane? One peculiar little snippet I learnt at the museum was that Irish Coffee was 'invented' at Foynes in 1942 when, late one night, Chef Joe Sheridan was giving coffee to some damp and miserable passengers who had just arrived, when he thought the addition of a little tot of something warming might help them. 'Hey buddy,' said an American, 'is this Brazilian coffee?' 'No,' said Joe, 'that's Irish coffee.' How the whipped cream came to be added the story doesn't explain and I'm sure Joe wasn't the first person to add a bit of Irish whiskey into their coffee. Still it makes a good tale for innocent visitors.

Foynes itself has a large quay and small marina and much of it is now overrun with a container port. Conor O'Brien was from here, the man who set sail on his pioneering cruising yacht *Saoirse* on his round the world sail in 1925. Coming out of the museum, I was amazed to see how busy the small village had become in such a short time. When I entered the museum the place had been dead. An hour later there were cars parked everywhere, lining the streets on both sides, on any available grass verges and even filling the museum car park. Stopping for fuel just down the road, I asked the young chap in charge what was going on.

'A funeral,' he replied in monotones, before adding as a mere after-thought, 'and a wedding'. I didn't stop to give him time to explain.

I was disheartened by the lack of activity on the river and would probably have returned to Tarbert and crossed the river if it hadn't been for the fact that I had a rendezvous at Shannon airport that evening. How was I going to discover something about the traditional boats used in the river? Then looking again at Darina Tully's map of Ireland she'd given me, I realised I'd

A postcard from Foynes showing a seaplane taking off.

missed one scribble that directed me to the boatyard of Ryan and Roberts and, after a couple of worng turns, I found it down one particular lane leading off the main road near Askeaton.

Cyril Ryan runs the yard now after he and his partner Kim Roberts parted six years previously. When I arrived and spoke to one of the men working in the yard, Cyril was out. However, on asking about the 'gandelows' – the small flat-bottomed boats of the river – I was shown one particular example lying underneath a yacht alongside the fence at the far end of the yard. It seemed that this boat was being consigned to history. Today much of the time spent by the yard is fitting out Lochin hulls for the angling and tourist trade. They also engage in the wintering of yachts, their upkeep, the provision of moorings, boat sales, and the repair of theoccasional sailing dinghy. Nothing outstanding but just enough work to stay afloat and continue in others' footsteps. No one really wants small flat-bottomed open boats these days, and certainly not built of wood. Fibreglass is cheap and relatively maintenance free. Cyril though, when he arrived back, turned out to be another mine of information. With an oval face, ruddy complexion, crescent-shaped eyes and spiky white hair all on a tall and lean body, he seemed the archetypical river-man. Eye contact was difficult to achieve but it was easy to warm to his character.

The gandelow I'd seen was 21 foot in length – a typical size – and of an uncertain vintage. It belonged to someone who didn't seem very interested in it. Gandelows, he told me, were the workhorses of the river, being used to transport people and their goods, fishing, wildfowling, seaweed collecting, and even taking pilots out to incoming vessels. Built with a rocker in the planked bottom in both directions i.e. fore and aft and athwartships, the gandelows have raked sides and a tiny transom. They were thus designed to glide into the mud banks of the river and again be easily extracted from the mud similar to prongs. Some had a 'leg of mutton' sail whilst later versions had an outboard well cut into the after end of the boat.

'Those built further up the river in the city [Limerick] didn't have any across the boat,' he said, referring to the rocker which was all important in their design. There seemed to have been three families associated with the building of these craft there. Sometimes it was hard to understand all that Cyril was saying but that he had a great respect for these craft came out in the way he spoke of them. It seems that they've built a few fibreglass versions after taking a mould off an old gandelow. More importantly, he told me about a book I'd not heard of. Sir Ralph

Payne-Gallwey wrote *The Fowler in Ireland* in 1882 and in it he gives a design for a 'gondola' which is similar to the gandelow but certainly not the same vessel. It seems that the two words often got mixed up, a gondola being well known as a narrow boat similar to the elegant craft of the Venetian waterways. However, when eventually I did get to see a copy of Payne-Gallwey's book, I was rather disappointed in that it didn't really help very much. Much more useful and to the point is Jim McInerney's, *The Gandelow – A Shannon Estuary Fishing Boat*, a copy of which I obtained later that day. We'll return to the yard and expand the gandelows and their uses later.

Tristy, one of the guys working in the yard, had already pointed out the gandelow, the cranage facilities, the workshop and storage of several boats undercover. Cyril showed me an interesting boat, one of several built for the German Luftwaffe during the war and this one taken as war prize and later sold. It was a racing yacht with huge overhangs and looked the piece. There was also a Galway Hooker in the yard. We were then, after the tour of the yard, standing in the canteen, talking to the workforce present. There was John from Cheshire who had been in Ireland for thirteen years and was doing up a house 30 miles away. He'd worked in the Rio Tinto aluminium works in Anglesey, where I'd lived for twenty years. Tristy, with his constant f-words and the only Irishman other than Cyril, was an Irish equivalent of British TV chef and swearer Gordon Ramsey though he couldn't cook he pointed out when I suggested it. There were also two Poles, one Ukrainian and another Englishman on the workforce, though the latter was not at work today. The Poles and Ukrainian were still working on a boat in the far shed unaware it was lunch-time.

I mentioned Ballyhack and Cyril asked whether I'd spoken to John Carroll, to which I obviously replied the affirmative. Likewise Liam Hegarty. They obviously all know each other and occasionally keep in touch, such is the dearth of these traditional boatyards in Ireland these days. I asked Cyril about yards further north and mentioned the MacDonalds of Moville. Except for individual builders of Galway hookers and currachs, he doubted I'd find much. Flaherty and O'Connolly were names to watch out for, possible hooker builders to take stock of.

We briefly discussed the naomhóga and the differences between them and the currachs. He'd never had much to do with them this far up river though he'd like to build a gandelow again. I asked why he had Polish and Ukrainian workers.

> This guy, a shipwright, who's worked for me off and on over the years. Well, I phoned him up and he said there was a site just across the road from him. A new house. No travelling because he'd to

A Shannon gandelow at Bunratty.

> drive 20 miles morning and evening here. Same pay. 'Let's face it, Cyril, what would you do?' he told me. So I phoned an agency and they sent me one of the Poles. Now his brother is here. They are really good, work hard and good.

The boatyard lies on the banks of the River Deel, a tributary of the Shannon. When I asked about the fishing around here he said that there'd been a fish weir in the Shannon, consisting of wooden posts and hanging nets, at Glin which was downstream and a few miles east of Tarbert. Near where I'd drunk coffee that morning I surmised. They collectively, after some discussion, thought that this weir had been in use until about 1965. The conversation inevitably turned to the salmon, to which it always seemed to wherever I went. Yes, drafting and drifting occurred in the river with the gandelows. Also beach seines with lead sinkers, one man onshore and one in the gandelow, a sweep round, net on the bottom, for flat fish and flounders etc. The Deel was subject to bylaws and, as such, hadn't been fished for years. As to the drift-net, why couldn't they just have limited the size of boat and length of net instead of not issuing any licences this year. These were the sentiments of all the river people of course, and mine. That way the likes of Tom and Peter Walsh would still be fishing the way they and their forbears had for generations.

But Cyril and his fellow workers couldn't talk all day and I sensed that they were keen to get back to work after at least an hour's interruption even if they were munching their sandwiches. I left, first driving down the lane to the Shannon before returning to the main road eastwards, after which the river became obscured by trees so that half an hour later found us on the outskirts of Limerick and quickly into the city centre. Coyne suggested that the shores of the river were naked, flat and sterile which he found wearisome and I had to agree with him. Nevertheless, with time to spare and finding a parking spot close to the river, I walked to the main drag and found a good bookshop. However, after searching through their shelves for a good half an hour, I found nothing of interest concerning the river, and those living and working upon it. Feeling a bit disappointed, a walk along the river seemed a good idea and I half expected to see gandelows moored in the river. However, either I was looking in the wrong place or there were none. Then the rain started which, after a few days of sunshine, was even more disheartening. I retreated to the van and, eager to miss the rush-hour traffic, crossed the river and sped out on the N19 towards Shannon airport.

Bunratty was easy to find and, because I'd seen an artist's impression of a fish weir there, I detoured. However, I'd forgotten about the tide which was fully in so any hope of seeing a weir was instantly dashed. Stopping at the Bunratty Castle and Folk Park, I found the book on gandelows already mentioned in their well-stocked bookshop but, because the time was almost five o'clock and the park was closed, I was unable to gain access to the Folk Park. A party of banquet-goers were entering as I left, most with American accents for there's a 'great hall' in the castle where, at a good cost, these things occur. Somewhere about here a log boat had been discovered and partially excavated which was thought to be 6,800 years old. Afterwards it was re-buried. Walking across the river to exercise the dog, lo and behold there were several gandelows moored in the river and one ashore. Finally, then, after a day's searching, I found living examples of the boats that really were the work boats of the river. Fishing was obviously their main use but, other than those uses already mentioned, I discovered from the book that the Limerick Port Authority kept a fleet to be used as tenders to the various harbour workboats as well as the pilots. As the lighthouse keepers and pilots were often local men, I guess they were well used to these gandelows. At some times in the year they were used for reed collecting amongst the extensive reed beds of the Shannon just below Limerick, the reeds being used to thatch the houses.

I also learned that similar craft, called 'gangloes', had been used since before living memory at the extreme west end of the estuary, around Kilmore strand and the estuary of the river Feale, across which we'd passed the previous day. They were slightly different in shape to the Limerick boats in that they had more sheer and rocker in the keel for work in the open sea. They are assumed to have all been influenced by the same source.In the book, it is suggested the inspiration came from the Newfoundland dories used in the cod fishery there. This I find slightly dubious for, if you study most of the regional river craft of Europe, there are so many similarities between them all that it would make sense that the dories were influenced by European craft at the outset. So far I'd seen the prongs of Cheekpoint and the cots of the river Suir close up. I knew that I'd yet to check out the prams of the river Boyne and cots of the river Slaney. All these vessels have something in common in that they work in rivers and, as in the case of the gandelows, prams and Wexford cots, and indeed the Flatners of the southern coast of the Bristol Channel around Watchet and Bridgewater, occasionally out into the open sea. Having also studied other canoe-type river and estuary boats in Italy, Greece and Poland, I see similarities.

It is supposed that gandelows were popular around Limerick because of the timber being imported from Canada and Norway. Any boatbuilding of this type needs long clean lengths of spruce or pine, and Northern timber was regarded as the best due, mostly, to the fact that it is not grown quickly as much timber is these days, thus giving a knot-free and straight piece of wood to work with. With most folk living by the river owning such a boat, it was often a member of that family that gained the required skills to build their boats. A typical gandelow, if well maintained, would be expected to last twenty years whilst those dragged over stony beaches would not last half that time. The important thing was that they were cheap to build and I'm sure that on many occasion, the vital pieces of timber were whisked away without anyone seeing. Once back in Britain, it was also pointed out to me that there was another small boat peculiar around Limerick: the 'brocaun'. These were two-men craft that fished in pairs much in the same way as the snap-net fellows did. The boats themselves resembled dug-out logs. Today, none have survived in their traditional form although a more modern variation is raced.

I arrived at Shannon airport as the mist descended and heavens opened for a deluge. Luckily the airplane wasn't delayed so that soon my partner Moe and our eleven-month old daughter Ana had joined us in the van. Our intention was to spend the next day on the County Clare coast before arriving at Kinvara for the 'gathering of the fleet' of Galway hookers. Thus, eager to proceed, we drove up to Ennis, had a meal there and carried on, arriving at Kilrush at about ten o'clock, to find a suitable parking spot for the night just up from the marina. Four in the van was a bit of a squash but, with Ana fast asleep between us and dog in his place at the head of the mattress, we spent a fairly restful night though the rain continued pounding the roof throughout most of the night.

DAY ELEVEN

One drenched human and a soaked dog is sufferable in the small van but add another wet human and a eleven-month old baby (dry though not bubbling with her normal happiness) then problems surmount. The morning rain wasn't about to dampen our enthusiasm as we knew that even in the worst weather conditions it's possible to have a pleasant time. Kilrush Marina proved this when I went inside to ask about the possibility of having showers. The young woman behind the desk proved to be the most amiable person I've met in a marina. When I explained our predicament she was instantly accommodating, and allowed us to use the showers without charging us. Turned out that she was not only in charge of the marina but had to also rush out when the VHF crackled into life and some incoming or outgoing boat needed the lock gate to be opened. At other times she might be travelling the world on cruising or racing yachts, sometimes as crew and sometimes as delivery skipper. Having led that sort of life for a couple of years back in the 1980s, I can certainly see the advantages even if, to some, this is regarded as a nomadic lifestyle.

Kilrush had always been something of a yachting centre and the Royal Western Yacht Club had been based here since their first regatta back in 1832, she told me before the phone rang and she had to shoot off to open the lock gate. First I, and then Moe and Ana, had showers which bucked us up no end. On saying thanks and farewell, she gave me a pamphlet on the marina so it's only fair to add a sentence or two about the place. It is a modern complex in comparison to much of Kilrush and was, I read, the first fully integrated marina in Ireland and has 120 berths with access at all stages of the tide since the lock gates were installed in 1991. Before that it was a tidal harbour.

The rain stopped so we decided on a walk into Kilrush itself, the capital of West Clare and half a mile away. In Irish the place is 'Cill Rois' which translates to 'the church of the meadow or promontory' and a community has existed here since the sixteenth century. In 1600 it was a significant anchorage within the confines of the Shannon and just over a century later

> a very commodious haven for boats or small ships, a good conveniency of fishing which may be improved here considerably'. By 1780, according to John Lloyd, it had ' a great herring fishery. It is a handsome village with a long wide street and some good houses. The inhabitants are industrious, humane and agreeable [and] there is a plentiful market on Saturday. No less than a hundred boats of different burthens belong to this town and neighbourhood.

By this time the town itself had been planned by John Ormsby Vandeleur, the wealthiest landlord in the district and of Dutch origin. When he enlisted the help of Scots businessman James Patterson in 1802, Patterson opened a six-storey oats mill in the square. As we've already discovered, Ireland experienced a boom between 1790 and 1815 because of the Napoleonic Wars which necessitated Britain to expand her agriculture sector. Ireland was perfect for producing grain and other foodstuffs for the British army. The building and opening of factories, canals and flour mills were encouraged and, accordingly, prices rose. Kilrush was one town to benefit so that by 1808 Hely Dutton was able to report that the town was 'rising fast

A wooden currach at Liscannor.

into some consequence'. Patterson's role was acknowledged and four years later he went into shipping and by 1817 a steamship owned by him was operating a regular service between Limerick and Kilrush. Another mill, this time specialising in corn, was opened in 1811, and this mill ultimately became the town's most prominent enterprise. This company eventually established Glynn's Mills in 1874. From 12,000 barrels in 1802 to 34,000 barrels in 1812, the amount of oats exported grew rapidly. By 1837 Samuel Lewis described the place as a seaport, market and post town. The main industries by then were the manufacture of flannel, stockings, shoes, nails, bundle cloth (a cheap linen), most of these goods being for home consumption whilst corn, butter, pigs, hides and other agricultural goods were being exported to Britain. Peat was carried upriver to Limerick. There was also some salt refining, tanning and soap manufacture. Work was abundant although the labouring classes were dependent upon the potato at the time whilst it was said the poor were healthy and well fed though it was suggested that, in 1841, two-fifths of the Irish population still lived in hovels. One wonders how anyone can be reported as being 'healthy and well fed' by living on just potatoes alone. The tone of some of these reports read as being utterly arrogant, although their content is fairly thorough. The people of Kilrush, up to that point, were fairing comparatively well. When the famine came without warning in 1845 as the potato crop failed, the people of Kilrush suffered with hunger, evictions, fever and cholera reducing the population considerably. The Vandeleur family were responsible for some of the worst evictions with over 20,000 people evicted in the Kilrush Union.

During the famine years, the fishermen of Kilrush, some of whom had been operating fishing boats for catching herring until the 1830s' decline in the fishery, and who had good supplies of oysters nearby, were hoping that the future would be kinder to them, but were forced to sell their boats and fishing gear to buy food. In 1805 the only quay was the Sand Quay where sand was landed for agriculture. This was rebuilt in 1849 by the Vandeleurs and renamed Merchants Quay. With the arrival of the South Clare Railway in 1892 (as an extension of the West Clare Railway), the town's link to the rest of the country was complete. It had the added benefit of encouraging more steamers from Limerick to stop at Cappagh Quay, the non-tidal pier, where a short extension line from Kilrush ran to and this rail link enabled passengers to quickly get to the rapidly growing resort of Kilkee.

After a brief look around town we decided on a walk to the nearby Vandeleur Walled Gardens which we thought to be not far away. After half an hour of pushing the pram, we eventually found the entrance and then the gardens after another push along a long driveway. The centre was open with exhibition boards upstairs on the sort of stuff you'd expect: the development of the town, emigration, shipping and the famine. There was a café downstairs. Breakfast was welcome and afterwards, with the rain coming on again, I walked back to reclaim the van and returned to pick up the others. We left before remembering we'd not paid and when I went back in to the till to do so, the cashier looked unconcerned and hadn't realised we'd even gone.

Scattery Island – known as the Bloody Island – lies a couple of miles offshore. In Irish it is Inis Cathaigh or 'the island of Cathach'. Cathach was a legendary sea serpent who terrorised the inhabitants until he was banished by St Senan and imprisoned in the waters of Doo Lough. St Senan founded a monastic settlement in the sixth century on the island which became another of the most important sites of early Christianity in Ireland. The Vikings raided and since then thousands have come over hundreds of generations, many to perform penance though the last inhabitants left in the 1960s. The island is rife with ruins which now serve to make it an interesting and popular place to visit in summer. Boat trips run from Kilrush during the season, the same boats that run dolphin and whale watching trips. Amongst the numerous ruins are seven churches, a unique tenth century round tower – a sailor's seamark ever since – and a holy well said to have healing powers. A stone quay allows boats to land. Also on the south of the island lies the remains of a military battery dating from the Napoleonic era, part of the defences of Limerick which were constructed in various places on the banks of the great river. The lighthouse is somewhat different to those already seen for it was built as a 'movable' light. Such lights were built where dramatic changes in channels occurred so that they could be dismantled and reassembled as necessary. This one, though, was deemed 'movable' because of the army exercises and the fact that the tower was sometimes in the firing line. The War Department at first tried to block attempts to build the lighthouse but eventually failed for this was deemed a vital siting for one of the chain of lights serving the river and the channel to Limerick. The others are at Tarbert, as we've seen, Kilcredaune and Beeves Rock.

From Kilrush we drove around Poulnasherry Bay, through the outskirts of Kilkee and down to Carrigaholt, in Irish *Carraig an Cabhailtigh* which means 'Rock of the Fleet'. There are two quays here, an inner silted up, drying harbour by the village which was once a busy port and an outer quay under the castle where a couple of fishing boats were moored. Signs advertised dolphin watching trips of two hours duration and one such group of spotters, dressed in waterproofs and looking a bit miserable, was coming ashore as we arrived, the car park full, no doubt, because of more than one boat operating out of here. It seemed quite doubtful whether they saw any life out at sea at all because of the increasing mist and rain that seemed to have turned to a constant drizzle.

The fifteenth-century castle was built by the McMahon clan in 1480 and the stone quay, named Castle Pier, much later though it became the first safe and sheltered anchorage for vessels entering the Shannon. There's a fish shop with its own lobster tanks adjoining the car park. The shop itself didn't seem very exciting with its displays of farmed salmon from Donegal, farmed bass, some cod, scallops from Scotland, a bit of locally-caught pollock and some ancient-looking roll mops. Where was the mass of fresh fish the area was renowned for? With a huge amount of nutrients brought down the Shannon the estuary is supposedly famed for its supplies of fish from all levels of the food chain, from shrimps, prawns, sprats and sand-eels, through to the herring and mackerel, then bigger predators such as pollock, cod, turbot and skate, to the final larger sharks, dolphins and tuna. When I queried this with the young lad working behind the counter he simply looked blankly at me as if I was as sharp as the scales on the fish he served. And what of lobsters? Why weren't there any lobsters for sale? Again a blank look and grunt though another fellow appeared from round the back and told me that only skate, some rays, turbot and pollock were generally available. Lobsters were out of season. Out of season in August? I despaired. Presumably today's nutrients coming down the great river include the residue from agricultural poisoning of the land and thus the fish don't thrive any longer.

The village itself had a small shop that was open so, donning my trusty cagoule again, I had a quick look in but to no avail. There wasn't any information on the village unless I wanted the timings of the dolphin watches, the woman behind the counter told me with what could have been interpreted as a sneer. Luckily I'd read the board I'd seen at Tarbert the previous day which informed me that this was a small fishing village with two streets, five bars and two restaurants. I can't say I was encouraged to stay. Perhaps it was the rain making everyone miserable though I'm told they should be used to it.

Loop Head lighthouse was lost in the mist which was a pity. The present light dates from 1854 and is another designed and built by George Halpin. The current tower replaced an earlier 1802 version. Prior to that, the light consisted of a fire burning upon the roof of a stone-vaulted cottage where the keeper lived. It's said that the small room adjacent to the fireplace was called 'Smith's shop' suggesting the keeper had a dual role in life. This light is thought to have fallen into disuse around the end of the seventeenth century for the Limerick merchants complained and another light was established in 1720. Part of the old cottage remains as does the pillar upon which the fire was built. Not only was that all lost in the mists of time though, it was truly lost in today's fog!

We retraced back to Kilkee which, even in the gloom, was packed with cars and milling people and the bars on the main street were full to overflowing. The town surrounds a crescent-shaped sandy beach and there's a stone quay on the north-east side. A lot of recent building of a holiday nature and a large diving centre and water sports school all add to a pleasant atmosphere although I only walked from the car to the tourist information office, a distance of no more than a hundred yards. Smokers were crowding the tiny canopied areas outside the bars where followers of the habit gathered, their chat spilling out all along the street. Kilkee is today one of Ireland's premier tourist centres and is relatively old by comparison. By 1810 it was already growing into a resort and over the next twenty years enlargened to a hundred houses, the tourism encouraged by the steamer connection to Cappagh Quay and, in 1892, the railway from there, as already mentioned. Two years previously, the line extension from Ennis reached Kilkee directly. In the twentieth century the town transformed itself from a Victorian watering place to a friendly modern resort although some of its original charm seems to have been retained. Unfortunately the heritage centre was closed, it being the weekend when the place is at its busiest!

The railway here received some unwelcome adverse publicity from an unusual quarter. When Irish poet and entertainer Percy French was on his way to Kilkee for a show in 1898, the engine broke down and he was five hours late. Arriving at the venue where he was supposed to be entertaining the local audience, he found they'd all gone home. He sued the railway company for loss of earnings and won his case. French went on to write a verse which he sung at various other venues lauding the inefficiency of the line, some saying the negative impact caused the railway to close down though, as this happened in the 1950s, it seems a bit of a dubious claim.

The gathering of seaweed here by Coyne in the very early 1840s and his passage in the book aptly describes the endeavours:

> The strand this morning presented an unusual scene of bustle. Men and women were to be seen in all directions removing seaweed which they had cut from rocks, and brought to the shores in canoes, together with large quantities of the long-weed, which they tied together in great bundles, and which floated in with the tide, propelling with them all that was loose between them and the shore ... The women appeared quite as active as the men leaping in and out of the canoes, standing in the sea up to their waists, and in that state filling carts and creels, which they placed contiguous to the sea to receive the loadings ... This was a scene of enjoyment to the young natives, especially the little girls, who, with their frocks drawn up, and neatly fastened round their waists to keep them dry, ran in and out of the water like amphibious creatures: to young and old it appeared like the joyous scene of a harvest-home.

Whether Coyne was correct in his opinion that this was a joyous event can never be ascertained. Collecting seaweed isn't an easy job. Their favoured seaweed that fetches the highest price is what Coyne describes as consisting of many leaves, some of which are three yards long and attached to a stalk of considerable strength and which was used extensively for manuring the potato fields. Of the canoes, Coyne says they were the only type of fishing craft along the coast – he didn't seem very impressed by any of 'the boat-accommodation' in any of the bathing-places he visited – and Kilkee had a fleet of twenty vessels. They were light wicker-work covered with sail-cloth, rendered waterproof with tar and pitch and safer than timber boats upon coasts with no harbours. He also notes that it was only a few years ago that 'they were covered with horse and cow-hides', thus suggesting sometime in the early nineteenth century that they swapped hide or canvas. He had been impressed with the fishermen's general seamanship especially when judging the right time to come ashore in heavy breaking seas, a feat that currach and naomhóg seamen were generally renowned for all along the western coast. According to James Hornell who studied and wrote on Irish currachs in the 1930s, the Kilkee canoes had the distinction of being kept ashore perched upon large stones whereas in other exposed coasts posts are used suspend the boats upside-down some three feet above the ground. Not a particularly mind-boggling piece of information but one that amused me when I read it in his book *Water Transport*!

Doonbeg lies a few miles up the coast of County Clare, the maritime facilities of which consisted of a small quay on the south side of a lovely bay, alongside a ruined castle. Further north we turned off the main road to join a myriad of narrow lanes that eventually, with a bit of turning around, fed us to the shore-line. Offshore lay Mutton Island - it really is shaped like a leg of mutton when viewed from above - and close by another two Spanish Armada ships sank, one being the *San Esteban*, I think, and the other I read as being described as a nameless hulk.

Then came Quilty which used to be a centre for kelp and other seaweed collecting and where I'd heard they still gather seaweed. I sort of expected the stuff to still be drying out upon the stone walls as it used to be though when we stopped by the shore, this was just very smelly and wet with the rain still persevering. There was a small local shop open where, after asking, I was directed to the house of J. P. Downes, one of the last collectors. The bungalow's PVC front door I knocked upon introduced a modernised interior when a round faced and congenial Mr Downes invited me in. He was not what I expected – a man in his sixties formally dressed in a smart cardigan and tie – as the stereotypical seaweed gatherer which just proved once again that appearances can be misleading. Dulse was what he and his wife went out to gather at low spring tides though he said they were getting too old to keep the tradition going. Before twenty years ago there was what could be termed an industry here with the seaweed being sent for processing. The alginates thus extracted were used in toothpaste manufacture, beer, agar and certain cosmetics, he said. Nowadays hardly anyone bothered collecting the stuff. It takes a day to dry once picked but only when the weather is good. This year, with awful weather, they'd been unable to pick much. Not that there's much of a market for it anyway although the tourists bought a bit. I asked if he had any to sell. Off he went into the kitchen and I heard a shuffling of paper before he returned with a package of wrapped newspaper. He asked for €2 which seemed very reasonable for God knows how many hours work scrambling over rocks and along the water's edge before the tedious job of spreading it out to dry begins which means constantly turning and shuffling it around.

We parted and back in the van I opened up the package to find a purplish yellowish dried leaf which looked similar to dried red cabbage. White spots on it indicated salt and salty it was to the taste. As I chewed a piece the taste reminded of something but I just couldn't put my finger on it. I munched a bit more in a sort of rabid determination to like it, knowing the benefit of its minerals which included a large amount of iodine. What good iodine was to the body I wasn't sure but just certain it was beneficial to some part of it. Moe didn't fancy the stuff and, with Ana a bit impatient, we proceeded onto Spanish Point.

Between the mouth of the Shannon and Galway Bay there used to be no shelter available to vessels navigating this exposed of coasts. Even today the *Sailing Directions* for this coast declare that there's no safe anchorage between Loop Head and Black Head – the southern extreme of Galway Bay – a distance of 45 miles. Any vessel sailing is advised to stay well off shore. However, as we've seen at Kilkee, there are tidal harbours available though, in adverse weather, these are normally impossible to enter. Mutton Island has a fine weather anchorage in the lee of the island but not a place to stay should the weather turn.

Lahinch has a perfect sandy beach with surf pushed in by the prevailing south-westerlies and thus is a surfer's paradise. On a wet Saturday afternoon the place was about as exciting as a wet dish cloth. Round the bay, Liscannor wasn't much different, the lashing rain endless and debilitating. However, I did venture out to take a couple of photographs of the harbour and a particular wooden currach by the harbour. Two naomhóga sat by the large harbour that was home mostly to angling boats and other boats doing trips out to the famous Cliffs of Moher just around the corner. Today, judging by the boats in the harbour, was not a day to peer through fog in an attempt to see the cliffs from the sea. A few drenched souls wandered about looking forlorn, led on by dogs eager for a run. Mine didn't look impressed at all when I turfed him out to do his stuff.

A salmon mosaic at the smokery in Lisdoonvarna.

I just had to detour to Fisherstreet because of its name. However, on arrival, all we found was a ferry terminal for this is one of the departure points for the Aran Islands, the nearest of which, Inisheer, lies some five miles across the South Sound, though of course they too were lost in the mist. The ferries must be pretty busy judging from the number of cars parked nearby. The roads were busy hereabouts with traffic queues on narrow stretches and outside bars which seemed extremely busy.

Retracing back to Doolin, Moe spotted a sign advertising 'The Burren Smokehouse' at Lisdoonvarna so instead of taking the coastal road up to Black Head, skirting 'The Burren', we decided to visit the smokehouse. It was easy to find and had been turned in to a bit of a visitor centre as well as smokery selling all their produce (and much more). There's a short film on the smoking process which uses farmed salmon from, I think in the main, Ireland. There's a sort of silliness about smoked fish in general when the industry promotes organic salmon and other fish. Organic, though they often fail to point this out, means 'farmed' whereas I was once told by an organic smoker that there's no such thing as an organic kipper. When I pointed out that a herring fresh from the sea, raised naturally and smoked over oak, is more organic than one of his farmed fish, fed on pellets made up of grain and the residue of fish such as herrings and pilchards, he seemed to think I was some sort of idiot. Now I've been smoking herrings for over twelve years at my mobile smokehouse, and the ridiculous notion that these herrings are not so-called 'organic' just makes the whole organic labelling business ludicrous. No wonder these arguments rage within the Soil Association. When I mentioned all this to the lady behind the counter of the 'Gourmet Shop', she smiled but even so she wouldn't let me view the smokehouse itself. When I mentioned the subject of wild salmon it seemed there was none available for smoking though we did purchase a small packet of their smoked salmon. The mosaic of a jumping salmon, outside of the shop, was certainly an impressive piece of artwork.

The Burren, that plateau of limestone where the rock is so fertile that it supports over

The quay at Kinvara with Galway hookers alongside.

600 species of plants, is known as a botanist's paradise though the landscape is pretty amazing with caves, wild life and prehistoric forts that also make it a favoured haunt of holiday-makers. In the rain, though, it didn't look very inviting and we quickly drove down to Galway Bay. Ballyvaughan has a small harbour whilst Bealeclugga had just a simple quay. New Quay's was built by the Fishery Board in 1837, another of Alexander Nimmo's creations. Kinvara has a pretty little stone harbour which was alive with activity when we arrived. For the hookers had just arrived in from Galway for the annual 'Gathering of the Fleet' or, in Irish, 'Cruinniú na mBád'. Not only had we arrived just in time for the festivities , as planned, but the Lochfyne skiff *Fairy Queen*, a boat from Campbeltown on the Clyde, was propped up at the end of the quay. I'd been trying to contact the owner of this boat for several years, uncertain as to his whereabouts, and now there she was, her owner aboard. Another stroke of luck indeed. On top of that it had stopped raining and it was time to dry out.

Kinvara was a throng of activity. The narrow main street awash with cars and the bars full to bursting. In the harbour, where a couple of boats were moored alongside the quay and a host of vessels lying at anchor just off, a stage had been set up and a rock band was just finishing their set as we found a spot to park. The first thing to do was to find a bed for the night as we'd decided to forsake the van that night in search of a soft bed and a shower, a bath even for Ana. Anything to warm us up. I checked the hotels – all full and expensive at that. Then the bed and breakfasts which, too, were full. After a very brief chat with Freddie Mousy aboard the *Fairy Queen*, agreeing to meet him the following day, we drove towards the outskirts of the village in search of other bed and breakfasts and were just lucky to arrive at one which the owner, although full up, was directing a German family to a friend's bed and breakfast establishment several miles away. After a quick phone call to check that there was room for us, we and the Germans followed the husband's car to this other place. In the end we stayed the night about fifteen miles away from Kinvara, in a newly-built sterile house though with friendly and helpful hosts. For a meal they directed us to the notorious restaurant 'Paddy Burke's' in nearby Clarinbridge, a place patronised in the past by the likes of Noel Coward, Julia Roberts and Roger Moore, and many more, where we had a substantial but not outstanding meal. Afterwards we returned to the B&B and a night of comfort in a real bed.

DAY TWELVE

The house might have been sterile and characterless and the central heating a bit too hot for comfort, but the traditional breakfast served in the dining room was pleasant and thoroughly satisfying, especially since I'd hardly eaten breakfast for weeks. The coffee wasn't as good as the strong stuff I'd been brewing each morning to counter the lack of solid food. Behind the scenes our landlady was busily poaching and grilling on her stove in the immaculate kitchen, into which the smells and sounds drew me.

She didn't seem very bothered by my intrusion into her workspace and when I asked her about the surrounding area we managed to get onto the subject of fishing. She paused after carefully placing bacon, sausages, eggs, tomatoes, beans, mushrooms and fried bread onto a couple of plates and said she'd just take these into the dining room. Returning she continued by recounting how, as a family, she had collected winkles on the east side of Kinvara Bay. She was one of eight children and she recalled her father taking all eight out to fish for the tide and they'd get about £17 in total for the day's efforts. That was back in about 1965 when a man called Gibbons used to buy the winkles and send them off to Paris. Then in about 1977 clams were discovered in the bay which added to the general fishing melee. Nevertheless oysters still remain the prominent fishery in Galway Bay. These were dredged and dropped onto the shore, each person having his or her own patch marked out by buoys. The oysters were left overnight before being collected the following day. Oysters were never locked up though, never kept under lock and key, she said.

> We always kept our shed unlocked and I remember a bucket being stolen. A bucket would you believe it. It was locked after that. The front door of the house was never locked though. The latch was even broken and it was always kept shut at night by wedging a chair against it. That's how we were round these parts.

She told me this between poaching more eggs and popping toast into the toaster. 'It's all changed now though,' she added with a shrug. 'Will you be having one egg or two? Yours is almost ready now.' That seemed to be an order to take my seat.

We ate the full complement of breakfast: eggs, bacon for me, toast, cereal; you know the sort of hearty stuff designed for immediate heart-attacks. Whilst munching a piece of toast I noticed the skirting boards which weren't fixed to the wall very well. There were gaps between the boards and the plaster as if they had been fitted after the plasterers had completed, which was not the way I'd do it. This house, like the many thousands of others, had obviously been thrown up pretty quickly and cheaply, just like the even more thousands of such houses in Britain.

An elderly couple, the ones who'd received the plates I'd watched being prepared, informed me that they were on their way from Londonderry to Cork and had left their home the previous morning, driving to the bed and breakfast in about seven hours. This brought home to me the distances involved. They had managed to travel from the north coast to the half way point in seven hours, yet it was going to take me at least five days to reach the same point.

An oyster boat from Dunbulcaun Bay.

The same applied to Cork. They'd be there within six hours, they reckoned, yet I'd passed through over a week ago. Although the coastal route was obviously longer, it did seem weird that my journey was so exaggerated in time.

I wanted to return to Clarinbridge where we'd been the night before, to visit Dunbulcaun Bay, another river estuary where our landlady had told me they'd fished for winkles when she was young. This bay stretched inland as far as Clarinbridge, where an annual oyster festival held in early September is internationally known. This festival, first held in 1954, purports to celebrate all that is good about oysters at the start of the new season and has tastings, oyster opening championships and so-called heritage events, though what these were I never did find out. Much of the oyster trade is run by the Moran clan, their 300-year-old 'cottage' being run by a seventh generation family member and now seemingly on the tourist trail according to several accounts of the area I read.

We found three open black-tarred row boats, wooden punts, oyster yawls or currachs (though I'm never sure quite the difference) on the beach of about 15 feet in length close to the old stone quay that, with a layer of fresh concrete atop, was obviously still used. Though full of rainwater and obviously not used for a while, these boats, I was told by a fellow living nearby, were used for oyster dredging though the rear platform would suggest they were also used for seining for salmon at some time. When dredging, they were rowed by a crew of four men though, up to the 1920s, bigger wooden currachs were utilised and crewed by six oarsmen. Before that, smaller flat-bottomed Galway Bay 'Flats' were widely used and, although I believed at the time that no example of these craft survive, I've since discovered there's one in the collection at the Ulster Folk & Transport Museum. As a tangible reminder of the advantages of motorisation, I gazed out to sea to spot the *Medway Harvest*, G236, a modern dredger, in the process of dredging about one mile out into the bay. Metal cages at the low water mark were full of oysters presumably growing from the spat into a marketable size.

At Clarinbridge Quay we came across a very dilapidated fishing boat with a cat living aboard. Alongside, under a tarpaulin, lay a 16-foot turf boat which appeared to be in the process of being rebuilt though the project looked almost as forlorn as the fishing boat and an almost impossible rebuild. I later found out that the boat was evicted from Kinvara some time before and towed here, though the guy who lives aboard is very happy in his new, deserted home.

Kinvara was buzzing, more so than the previous evening. We were lucky to find a parking spot such was the amount of traffic arriving for the day's festivities, the main attraction being the boats racing. The tide was still low and several boats were dried out in the small harbour. I sought out Fred Moisy aboard the *Fairy Queen* to catch up on his news and his progress upon the boat which had been built on the East Coast of Scotland in 1926. Having just written a book on the history of these skiffs I was fascinated to see both boat and owner. All I knew was that he'd paid £160 for the boat in 1984 and that he'd been working upon her. He welcomed me aboard. He had been a member of the 40+ Fishing Boat Association for a few years before lapsing his membership, and apologised for this. Money, he said, had been tight. The boat has been raised up from the deck level so that she has lost much of her Lochfyne skiff looks and a huge skylight over the main cabin made her look even stranger. Inside, though, she's roomy and airy. He was hoping to get her back in the water within a matter of weeks after a long spell out upon the quay and, considering the boat is only one of three of these Scottish boats still in existence, it's hoped she'll stay afloat for many years to come.

Kinvara's first quay was built in 1773 by James French, the local landlord and merchant, over naturally occurring rocks, his intention being to promote the growth of trade in the small village. The few people who fished and gathered seaweed to survive lived in the Claddagh which was situated around the bay from the quay. The smuggling of brandy, wine, tobacco and tea seemed to be a thriving business with wool being illegally exported. Much of this illicit trade was brought in from France after several Galway merchants settled in south-west France. Geographically speaking, West Ireland is almost as close to France as it is Britain so it's unsurprising that such a trade existed. With feelings running high with Britain's domination of Ireland during the Napoleonic Wars, many also chose to support the French in their struggle. The British employed fast cutters, crewed by local pilots, to out-sail the hookers that were generally used for smuggling and to stamp out the trade. However, with a rugged and largely inaccessible south and west coast, many vessels continued to avoid the patrols, and smuggling continued on a smaller scale. Judging by the amount of drugs being discovered year on year, the trade obviously continues today and estimates suggest that for every kilo of hash, cocaine and the like uncovered by the authorities, more than three times the amount gets in to supply the markets of both Ireland and Britain.

Smuggling always attracts embellished legends of terror and violence and many more myths. Many smugglers used tunnels to bring their goods from beach to village, and Kinvara is no different. A tunnel is said to have existed between the shore and the cellar of a lodge owned by Frenchman and smuggler Captain William Delamaine. It's said that the British army seized twenty-three bales of tobacco in 1792 although there were probably many other such seizures. Delamaine's house later became a Canon's residence and a story goes that during 'The Troubles', the Black and Tans often came raiding the house claiming to have information that there was a 'cannon' there! Many spots were supposedly haunted and unsafe to be in after dark, primarily because all smuggling was undertaken under cover of dark. Likewise many bays and coves were named after the trade and in Galway Bay there's a Brandy Harbour and Brandy Point. But then again such places exist throughout Britain in similarly unpopulated and rocky coasts where smugglers once practised what many regarded as a perfectly reasonable, respectable even, trade. Who would disagree with that when governments rob us of unfair taxes such as an 85% levy on fuel!

When ownership of the fast-expanding Kinvara passed to Richard Gregory, he enlargened the pier and built a dock in 1807 and it is said that up to sixty boats arrived in one tide. As a market place, Kinvara had been having these since at least the early 1600s and Samuel Lewis, in 1837, notes two great Sheep fairs in March and October. Seaweed accounted for some £20,000 of income and huge amounts of corn passed through the harbour. Once Britain had defeated Napoleon on 1815, their armies weren't in as great a need for food and agricultural prices fell dramatically in the 1820s which had a knock-on effect on places such as Kinvara, helped along by two bad harvests. The impact was long lasting for, by the 1840s, the population was declining rapidly. The famine and ensuing clearances continued the downwards spiral so that the population of the village fell from 6,586 in 1841 to 4,268 a decade later. For most of the rest of the nineteenth century nothing improved, this being the long term effect of the famine and emigration, so that by 1901 more than a quarter of the houses were empty. In all, a third of the population either emigrated or died of fever and/or hunger.

However, by that time, the harbour was a scene of bustle once again with the quay serving the surrounding countryside and the harbour facilities were extended again in 1908. A photograph of 1902 shows maybe a dozen hookers or more alongside the shore, most probably unloading turf, as peat is called in these parts, though some were probably used to carry barley over to Galway. The hookers were the workhorses of Galway Bay and Connemara, the fishing and carrying boats that the small coastal communities, cut off by land and totally dependent on the sea for communication, depended upon for survival. As for the Aran Islands, the chain of three islands standing as sentinels to Galway Bay, the hookers brought in everything that the islanders could not grow or manufacture themselves. Before the first hooker was built - and no one knows when that was - presumably they had to rely upon currachs to cross the tricky and sometimes treacherous waters between mainland and islands.

Thus these traditional ways of life continued up to the 1960s, a time of massive change to these small communities lining Galway Bay as road transport developed and made its impact upon their world. Turf was replaced by bottle gas which overnight saw off the turf trade. Suddenly there was no work for the hookers for the lorry could serve the coast and larger motor vessels were already taking the necessary freight out to the islands although the first paddle steamer to ply between Galway and the Arans had been introduced back in 1891, mostly only carrying passengers. One by one the boats were laid up against harbour walls, to fall apart just like the old mackerel boat *Shamrock* in Schull. Some waited patiently for better times, silently retaining their pride and strength. But before we get on to these better times

A Galway hooker. (Graham Hemborough).

we'd better look at the origins of the hookers and, perhaps more importantly, the different versions of the type, of which there are four.

The largest of the hookers are referred to as 'Bád Mór', vessels of a length somewhere, on average, between 37 and 39 feet although the largest built is 44 feet and the smallest 35 feet. In general these are transom-sterned boats with a very full, apple-cheeked bow, a high degree of tumblehome amidships and a sloping sternpost. They are half-decked with a cuddy forward of the single mast, which supports a gaff mainsail and foresails set on a bowsprit. Hookers never set topsails as far as I can make out.

The half-boats or 'Leath Bháid' are so-called because they aren't half the size but carry half the load of turf than the bigger boats. Otherwise they are almost identical in shape and rig. Sizes of length range from 32 to 34 feet.

The third type, although again of a similar shape and rig, was called the 'gléoiteog', pronounced 'glowchug' and ranged from about 24 to 28 feet. Being smaller, these were more affordable to the majority of the coastal dwellers and thus were the real workhorses, being used for all manner of work. Richard Scott, in his 1983 book *The Galway Hooker*, which today remains the seminal book on the boats, calls them 'the maids of all work', a fitting description for vessels that fished, ferried people and animals, carried turf, gathered seaweed and did any other work that was considered necessary.

The last type, called a 'Púcán' and pronounced 'pookaun' was a bit different in that it set a dipping lugsail. The hull shape was basically similar though smaller at 22 to 24 feet, but they were entirely open yet they were still used in sheltered waters for fishing and carrying. Obviously they were even cheaper to build and were favoured by those not wishing to venture too far out into the bay.

The origins of these boats have been well discussed and chewed over by many a Connemara man and I don't wish to contradict the words of those whose experience of the boats is far greater than my own which, to be honest, isn't a lot. However, I do feel able to add my observations from simply studying photographs and seeing those vessels in the flesh, so to speak. Many will contest these observations, I'm sure, but nevertheless, as an outsider who has spent many years studying maritime influences all around Europe, influences that have resulted in the diverse fleet of boats from Norway to Greece, I can only make an outsider's suggestions.

The first point of note is that these vessels are unique in European waters and the only similar craft is the Baltimore hooker on the East Coast of New England, a boat that was either sailed over to the States and copied, or simply built on Irish lines by Galway and Connemara emigrants to the US, of which there were plenty during and after the famine years. What I have seen in Europe is that all boats have developed through various influences, these coming either from the outside or from within the communities they serve. Rarely has a boat come into general usage that is totally unlike anything seen elsewhere. Whether it be from a visiting boat, or a fisherman who has seen something whilst working away, or a boatbuilder new to an area, boats haven't simply arrived, they have evolved. Innovations have been imported whilst local influences such as the prevailing weather or type of harbour or beach have dictated certain restraints in their design. A fisherman might ask a boatbuilder to tweak his boat here and there, but to build something hitherto totally unknown is almost impossible due to the financial impracticalities of such a thing. This has only happened in a handful of instances. Bearing this in mind, I considered that the influences of the hookers must have come from somewhere.

The first train of thoughts leads one to the Dutch craft for two reasons: the tumblehome and the name 'hooker' which is often regarded as coming from the Dutch *hoeker*, as we saw in Kinsale. Nevertheless these aren't Dutch craft even if there are certain similarities. As I write this I have a spread of photographs scattered around the table. The huge stem resembles a Viking longboat. The tumblehome, which starts almost immediately at the bow giving them their 'apple cheeks', looks Dutch. The fine entry into the water at the bow again reminds me of Viking boats. The sloping transom, though, reminds me of the sardine boats of Brittany in Northern France. Apart from the tumblehome, the hookers are also renowned for their pretty sheer line which curves up sharply near the bow. The same sheer line is seen on the lobster boats of Roaringwater Bay, the type of boat that I'd sailed on the week before with Nigel Towse. Again that looks similar to the Viking longboats. Then I ask myself if this surmising is pure stupidity but then I say no, for the Vikings did come down to these parts aboard such craft a thousand years ago and many stayed. We also know that the Dutch came to fish as did the French in later times, trading wine and fishing for mackerel. What else do we know of the craft? They are massively built but is this unusual in a place where timber was either locally available or being imported? On a coast exposed to the full force of the Atlantic seas, boats built with huge chunks of oak cannot be regarded as out of place.

Dixon Kemp, in his *Manual of Yacht and Boat Sailing*, first published in 1878, regarded 'the profile and the lines generally to reflect the large naval and revenue cutters of the early

A Baltimore hooker from the East Coast of the US.

View of the same vessel showing the extreme rake of the transom-stern and large out-hung rudder.

nineteeenth century with a 'cods head and mackerel tail hull form'. However, I was pleased to read after I'd written the above, that he also suggests that, like the boats of the North of Ireland, the hookers and Púcán exhibited evidence of Norwegian origins. He also reckoned they were 'exceedingly lively in a seaway, but seldom ship a sea; perfectly safe in every way except when running deep, when they have sometimes been pooped, owing to their lean hollow runs'. He adds a quote from Commander Horner, R.N., who said that they were 'very bluff above and hollow beneath', and who had attempted to persuade a local boatbuilders to alter the shape and when he eventually did, after seven years, the resulting boat was a regatta winner every time. Dixon Kemp also notes that their sails 'were made of a coarse stuff called 'band linen', saturated with a mixture of tar and butter, which never thoroughly dried'. Butter was obviously in great supply as it was further south. When times were such that butter and tar wasn't available, coal tar and hog's lard were used.

I guess I could write pages about the Irish hookers just as I could about the naomhóga and currachs but that seems a bit pointless when others, far more learned on the subject, have written widely on the construction and usage of these craft. One thing is for sure though that most of what has been written about the Irish working craft in general has surfaced over the last two or three decades. When one glances back through the books published before the 1950s, rarely are the Irish boats mentioned. E. Keble Chatterton in his *Fore and Aft* (1912), only mentions Ireland in conjunction with the Royal Cork Yacht Club, the oldest in the world. No mention of hookers though he does show a Dutch 'hoeker' which bears no resemblance to the Galway boats. Likewise, in *Mast and Sail in Europe and Asia* (1929), Herbert Warrington Smyth is quite dismissive of Irish types. He regarded the hookers as the only indigenous Irish boat with a sea-keeping quality otherwise 'the native genius of the race in regard to naval architecture of sailing-craft has been confined to some not very advanced lugsail boats of canoe type, such as the Groomsport yawl or Galway pookhaun'. All other fishing boats were, he considered, mostly bought in from Cornwall, the Isle of Man or Scotland. Although much of the fleet was influenced as he says, to say that the boats are glorified canoes seems at best misguided. The Púcán doesn't resemble a canoe, nor do the Groomsport yawls nor the Drontheims from County Donegal. But more of these in later chapters. Some do mention the hookers, but only in passing. Edmund Holdsworth, in *Deep-Sea Fishing and Fishing Boats* (1874), describes them in brief and mistakenly regards the tumblehome as being 'very much in the American style, giving them a very peculiar appearance'. In *British Fishing-Boats and Coastal Craft* (1950), E.W. White describes the fishing boats of the west coast as 'heavy open boats, known as "Pookhauns", very clumsily built vessels with a raking transom stern', whilst the hookers, he wrote, were coasting vessels which had a general appearance of an eighteenth-century origin. Nothing I read is particularly encouraging about these boats which seems grossly unfair. However I'm simply observing from a distance which in a jiffy brings me back to the quay at Kinvara with the tide rising and the dried out hookers in the small harbour just coming afloat once again. It was nearly time for the race to begin. This, in turn then, brings us back to the 'better times'.

There would be many of the older folk who would dispute the term 'better times' as the old ways disappeared to be replaced with the trappings of today's world. The reliance upon sail, hard times fighting for survival, a short lifespan, the effects of famine and being governed by those that didn't care isn't what many would call better than having internal combustion engines, modern sail and net materials that don't need tanning and barking to preserve them every few months and a house which is kept warm by central heating rather than a fire in the middle with smoke rising up to the hole in the roof, but there were those that clung to the old ways. On the other hand, in 1975, Dubliner John Healion bought and restored the

1890-built hooker *Morning Star* to her former glory, not as a converted yacht but carefully to the original layout. Other hookers had been converted but these became yachts with decks and the like but when John Healion arrived in Connemara as the first hooker to return there in June 1976, he had, unwittingly, begun a revival that has resulted in plenty more of the large and half boats being restored as well as various new boats having been built. Today in Kinvara, the sun out as if to celebrate, there were five big boats about to race, three half boats and several other gléoiteog and Púcán out on the water racing. Amongst the larger boats were, *Morning Star* and *Naomh Cáilín*, *Truelight* (built *c.*1920), *American Mór* and *An Tonai*. The half-boats present were *Volunteer*, *Norah* and *Star of the West*, the latter being owned by Bairbre de Buitléar and her husband Cian.

Luckily Bairbre was not aboard the boat to race, left to look after their kids, and I was introduced to her by a mutual friend. We had corresponded through e-mailing regarding a set of three books they had published on local boats, each book describing the method of building of these craft: the hooker, the wooden currach and the canvas currach. They'd sent me a copy to review a few months previously. Thus Bairbre spent ten minutes telling me a bit about the boats and the various differences and, more importantly, pointing out which boat was which out in the bay.

The water's edge was thronged with a huge crowd as the boats sailed up and down awaiting the start of the race, the bright sun reflecting off the water in contrast to the dark hulls of many of the boats. Some skippers chose to sail almost into the harbour before tacking out again, showing off their seamanship skills whilst enthralling the crowd at the same time. Judging by the angle of heel of some of the boats, there was a fair breeze out there and I photographed many, including *Morning Star*, leaning over at crazy angles. In anticipation the bar on the corner was crowded out and glasses of dark beer twinkled in the sunlight. It was a true gathering of the fleet, both afloat and ashore.

Before the race began I had time to read about the origins of the 'Cruinniú na mBád'. The first 'Gathering' was held back in August of 1979 when eight boats had arrived from Galway with turf aboard, the first in being the *Mhaighdean Mhara* which had, aptly, been the last boat to trade across the bay in 1947. *Morning Star* had also been part of that original gathering. Thirty years later the boats were still coming to this, just one of the many festivals and regattas that the hookers attend during the year.

It was about this time, just before the race started, that I noticed a group of lads standing on what I thought were a couple of rocks appearing just off the pier as the tide receded. Somehow I'd forgotten that it was actually still rising. I wondered why these lads had been ferried out to the 'rocks' that were covered in seaweed, just to stand there with the long poles they were unloading from the punt. Then, once the punt had left them stranded, the rocks began to move. Only then did I realise that this was the *Climín* or Seaweed raft race when the two rafts are punted with the long poles along a set course. Only they didn't get very far before one of the rafts became grounded. We watched in awe as the lads pushed with their poles to no avail. The other raft sped ahead, travelling all of twenty yards in as many minutes. The second raft became free as they pushed and pulled, the sea sloshing around their feet. By this time the hookers were away in their race, sleek hulls with tan sails leaning over like modern racing yachts. Suddenly there was one boat in trouble, stopped and sails lying over into the water. Binoculars quickly reasoned the problem, the mast had snapped some ten feet above the deck, putting an end to their hopes of winning. The vessel was the half-boat *Volunteer* and she soon got an anchor down and was subsequently towed back to the safety of the harbour. Then the dreadful news spread quickly about the crowd: the *Morning Star* had capsized further out into the bay, out of sight. News soon came that all ten crew aboard had

1. Joseph Teesdale and Tom Walsh with Ballyhack Harbour in the background.

2. Salmon cots lying in a creek on the River Suir at Mooncoin.

3. Colourful cottages and the foreshore at Roche's Point.

4. Nigel Towse at the helm of *Hanorah* with Cormac Levis' *Saoirse Muireann* following behind.

5. Liam Hegarty standing in front of the old bandsaw.

6. Three boats at Oldcourt. Left to right *Mizpah*, *Signora II* and *Ribhinn Bhan*. (Photo Mike Williams).

7. Scillonian pilot cutter *Hesper* passing the Fastnet Rock in 2007. (Photo Luke Powell).

8. The Skelligs in a dusky evening with the fleet returning to Portmagee.

9. Currachs and inflatables at Dunquin, Dingle Peninsula.

10. Dublin Bay Mermaids at Fenit.

11. A Galway hooker well heeled over at Kinvara.

12. Tommy Flaherty with his model of a currach outside his house on Inishmore, Aran Islands.

13. A smaller *gléoiteog* with seaweed rafts behind at Kilkieran.

14. Young fisherman sorting his catch at Bunowen Bay.

15. Charlie Fadian alongside his currach at Dooagh, Achill Island.

16. Modern trawler at Killibegs.

17. Fabienne, Cara and Billy at Kilcar.

18. Brian MacDonald alongside one of his Drontheims at Greencastle.

19. The impressive ruins of Dunseverick Castle, Antrim.

20. The rope bridge and island at Carrick-a-rede.

21. One of Dave Donnan Jnr's paintings.

22. Captain Jim Moore in his attic with its bulging treasures.

23. Ardglass in the herring season. (From an old postcard).

24. Cockle-dredgers on the edge of Dundalk Bay.

25. Paddy Hodgens, ex-harbourmaster of Port Oriel, Clogherhead.

26. Mussel pram at Mornington, River Boyne.

27. The Tyrrell's-built *Huff of Arklow* sailing off the south of England. (Photo Cremyll Sailing).

28. Ros Bremore and *Ros Beag* at Arklow.

29. Jim Devine standing over two of his River Suir cots.

30. Dog and larger Wexford cot on the Burrow.

30. Zulu *Leenan Head* sailing in the Bay of Douarnenez, 2008.

been rescued after only a couple of minutes or so in the water but the hooker that had single-handedly begun the revival in hooker awareness had, shockingly, sunk. Only its mast was sticking out above the water. The progression and antics of the seaweed rafters were quickly forgotten as people were eager to hear more news of the tragedy. The race was abruptly cancelled and the remaining boats returned, the wet but safe crewed landed safely. It seemed that, with so much canvas set, a squall had hit the boat. She'd taken water aboard as the first wave hit her, coped but only to be hit whilst down a second time which flooded the boat. The dangers and perils of sailing these boats had surfaced for all to see. However, as an after note, I did hear a few days later that the boat had been raised from the seabed and taken ashore for the damage to be accessed which wasn't thought to be much.

After the excitement and subsequent news, the festival buzz flattened. We adjourned to the nearby O'Connolly's bar where we met Fionn McMullan, an acquaintance from the Looe lugger regatta in Cornwall who, after we'd had a couple of pints and trays of chips from a nearby chip van, invited us to park up outside his house. He even offered to allow us to sleep inside if we wished though we declined that bit. We followed him back the few miles along the narrow lanes in the general direction of Galway, where we had to be at 8am the following morning for Moe and Ana to catch their flight back to Bristol. Their couple of days on the road were almost over. I was just about half way through my travels.

Fionn, an architect, has built his family a lovely house close to the coast, inside of which we spent the remaining evening chatting over coffee on the housing problems and the looming economic downturn that many thought Ireland was facing after so many years' boom built upon European Union money. However, like religion, I promised to stay away from politics at the outset so, after walking the dog around the narrow lanes in the darkness, I climbed into the van alongside my own family and slept, happy in the knowledge that I'd managed to accomplish one initial desire: to see the hookers racing.

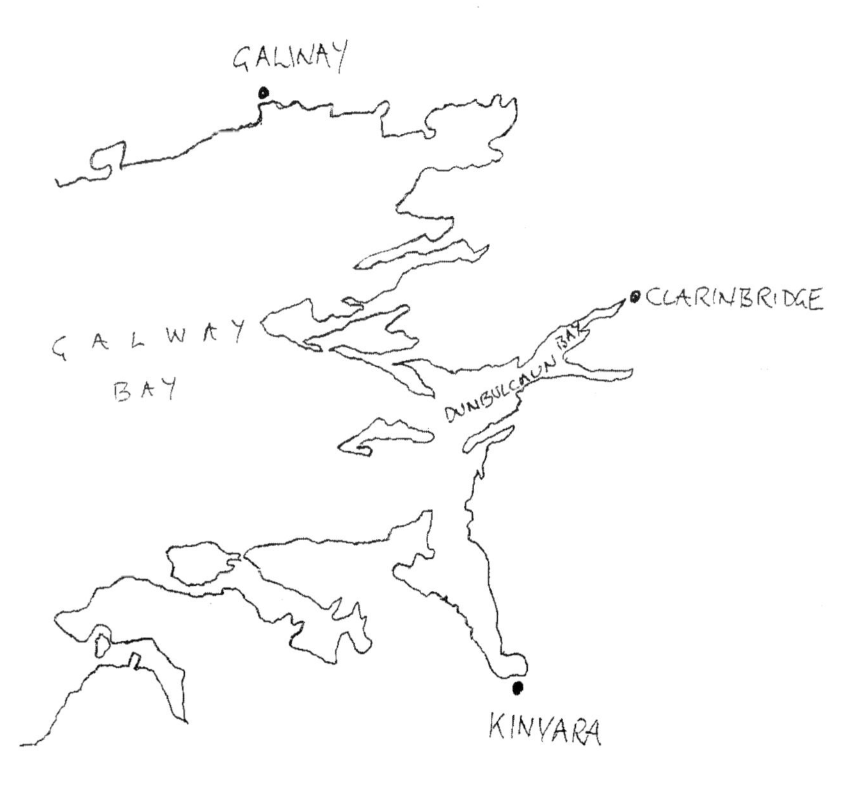

DAY THIRTEEN

If day thirteen should have been unlucky it didn't turn out that way. We made it to Galway Airport on time and Aer Arann lived up to its good reputation in the way they treated mother and child.

From the airport I joined the rush-hour traffic into the city, paused briefly at the port to take a picture and found the Claddagh of which I'd read so much. Today's Claddagh was nothing compared to its former days of history and heritage although there was an ancient gléoiteog sitting upon the quay looking a bit forlorn. In the eighteenth century this was more of a suburb of Galway rather than just part of the town, situated as it was on a beach on the west side of the town and where some 3,000 inhabitants were housed, all belonging to fishing families. That is according to Coyne though Captain Thomas Symonds, managing director of the London and West of Ireland Fishing and Fish Manure Company who wrote his *Observations on the Fisheries of the west coast of Ireland* in 1855, believed that the fishing population of Galway and its environs, many of whom presumably lived in the Claddagh, was 7,794 manning 1,811 boats and Anthony Marmion, author of *The Ancient and Modern History of the Maritime Ports of Ireland* (1858) confirmed that Claddagh was solely inhabited by fishermen. Alexander Nimmo, when writing his *Report on the Fishing Stations of the West Coast of Ireland* in the 1820s, put the number at a thousand families. Contradicting this, the Halls put the figure at between 5,000 and 6,000 although it's fair to point out that was thirty years after Nimmo. Government figures for 1836 give 105 hookers, 80 rowing boats and 820 fishermen in Galway, and for 1851 give 3,337 men and 1,083 boats fishing in the entire Western District which stretches from Mack Head, in Sligo Bay in the north, southwards to Black Head in Galway Bay. I'm not convinced that the actual number is that important and it is enough to say that was an important fishing station for, as Marmion wrote, 'This was indeed a mighty fleet for one small community'.

Historically, Galway, and in particular the Claddagh, was the centre of fishing on the west coast. Marmion notes that salmon and herring were the chief species with some ten tons of salmon being taken from the Lough Corrib and the bay itself. Herring shoals were huge and came right into the bay. Other fish such as ling and cod were also taken. However, it seems that the Claddagh fishermen claimed exclusive rights to fishing in the bay and refused entry to others. The Halls wrote that they claimed these rights over all the bays in County Galway though this isn't confirmed. These claims appear to have been what Nimmo described as their 'sundry peculiar customs' or their own law-making to suit themselves. However, even if these people, who were governed by a king they elected annually and whose insignia was having white sails on his boat when at sea, were insistent about their rights and ready to fight for them, their houses were said to be better than the average. Stories of them being big drinkers are also unconfirmed and probably exaggerated. The Halls described them as being 'peaceful and industrious' though I doubt the 'peaceful' description can be accurate. When some merchants in the town set up their own fishing company with their own boats the Claddagh fishers regarded this as an infringement of their rights and attacked these boats, cut their sails and nets and threatened the crews. Boatloads of stones were hurled at one

The fish market at the Claddagh, Galway.

point. With the stationing of a gunboat, *The Plumper*, by the Fishery Board after pressure from these merchants, their stranglehold over the fishery was eventually broken and the fishery in general soon thrived. Three hundred boats subsequently were seen to line the quays each day, all loaded with between ten and twenty thousand herrings which produced a food bonanza not only for the town but for the surrounding hinterland also, both served by hawkers on foot. When Galway was connected by railway to Dublin, it had by then certainly become the principal fishing station on the west coast.

Another particular fishery of importance, even if it was only briefly, was for basking sharks, or sunfish as they were called locally, according to Young, which was carried on by the herring boats though he doesn't specify what constitutes a 'herring boat'. Owners of the boats employed fishermen for that sole purpose and did not operate a share system as was normal for the herring. One fish could fetch £5 and, on average, they only caught three a month. Between forty and fifty boats followed this fishery he informs us.

Nimmo came to expand the harbour facilities which previously had consisted of two narrow piers jutting out from the beach and which were in a poor state. The fish market that used to be on the east side of the bridge crossing the river and was regarded as being a nuisance had been moved over the Claddagh, by the Spanish Arch, in about 1800. The main town facilities were all on the opposite side of the river and several organisations petitioned for a canal to be cut from the harbour through into Lough Corrib. Nimmo drew up plans for improvements to the two piers and the building of the Slate Pier to afford some protection to the Claddagh. Work on both of these projects was completed in the late 1820s but the canal did not progress further until well after Nimmo's death in 1832. Work started on that in 1848 and it was opened four years later.

Alexander Nimmo 's legacy to Ireland is clearly visible today and he, possibly more than anyone else, contributed to opening up coastal areas, although of course he was not acting on a private basis but under contract from various government departments. Born in Cupar, Fife, Scotland in 1783, he came to Ireland in 1811 to work as an engineer for the Bog Commission, set up to ascertain whether it was possible to turn bog into agricultural land. Within a year he was surveying Connemara, an experience he was to later draw upon. He worked for the Commission for four years before leaving in 1815 and, after a spell in Europe, returned to Ireland to set up a private business. He was soon surveying harbours in Cork, Sligo, Tramore, Dunmore East and Waterford. Between 1820 and 1824 he surveyed the whole coast of Ireland for the newly established Fishery Board and identified a whole host of small almost inaccessible communities that would greatly benefit from anything from a small basic pier to more substantial facilities. He must have worked quickly because in 1822 he sent a list to the Fishery Board with thirty-four sites where piers could be built for less than £500 which was the maximum amount of money that the Board would contribute towards any one project although, in typical government-speak, they only regarded this as being half the total cost. Soon after the Board interrupted his surveying and transferred all their surveys to the west coast so that he could continue surveying that coast and take charge of pier building projects that were to commence immediately. Thus between 1824 and 1826 he oversaw the building of piers throughout the region of the Western District which covered 107 miles of coastline. In all he was responsible for the building of forty piers. Back on the west coast semi-permanently, he was able to spend much of his time in Connemara and prepare to open up that area. Between 1822 and 1831 he also oversaw the construction of 243 miles of road. And, as we'll see later, he even developed a fishing village in Connemara though we haven't reached there yet. For the full story of Nimmo and his contribution to the opening up of these settlements, the reader is pointed to Kathleen Villiers-Tuthill's *Alexander Nimmo and The Western District*, published by Connemara Girl Publications in 2006 which gives an excellent account of his work in this region.

On the western extremities of found the National Aquarium of Ireland. This aquarium had been designed by Adrian Brooks and Mark Vollers, both friends of mine from Anglesey where Mark had been co-owner of the Anglesey Sea Zoo and Adrian had worked, the two of them being largely responsible for the development of that place from its early conception in about 1983. I'd worked in the place many a time as a building contractor in the days when building work occupied my working life rather than fisheries ethnology. Asking at reception, I was lucky enough to find that Adrian, who still works at this aquarium – Mark now has his own in Maryport, Cumbria – was at work that morning and he soon came down to meet me. I guess he was pretty surprised to see me although I'd had advance warning from Fionn, who also knew him, that he was currently in Galway. Adrian gave me a conducted tour around the site which consisted of various tanks exhibiting anything from seahorses and octopuses to conger eels and wreck fish that grow up to two metres, he said. The tanks were impressive – one simulated a lock-gate, one a kelp tank and another a wave tank whilst others simply had the fish such as rays swimming around their pool for the public to gaze upon and watch. Every conceivable species found in Galway Bay was there I guess. Most impressive was the Long Isle mackerel boat similar to *Shamrock*. Considering the folk down south didn't think there were any other mackerel boats in existence this was quite a find. The boat had belonged to Joseph Connolly and he'd offered it to them when it was obviously past restoration. They'd also a gléoiteog and, on loan, a 5,000-year old dug-out that was going to be the centrepiece of a new exhibit though it was stored away for the present. This boat had been excavated from nearby Barna. The aquarium was pretty busy by the time we'd been through all the exhibits and down to the educational centre where school kids came to learn about the deep. Then, after a cup of coffee each in the next-door restaurant, I took my leave to catch the lunchtime ferry to the Aran Islands.

Driving along the coast to Rossaveal where the ferry departs, passing through Spiddal with its Nimmo-built quay, I half expected a bit of deja-vu having been here before. Some years earlier , in about 1994 I think, I'd cycled from Galway, around the coast to Clifden and back inland during a week's holiday with my then partner. However I was surprised to find that absolutely nothing was remotely familiar. Galway had changed beyond all recognition as had the coast with its myriad of new houses littering the fringe. Previously we'd noted how new bungalows had sprouted alongside the ruined remains of the typical Connemara black houses but now it seemed that new dwellings had sprung up along almost every foot of the coast. I guess Alexander Nimmo would be turning in his grave at the damage done to the wonderful landscape. And it can't be just me whinging for everyone I spoke to regarding the housing, and many since returning to Britain, agreed. Desolate pretty coasts have been turned into a long continuous strip of ghetto-land.

Rossaveal (Ros a'Mhil) was a mass of car parking, a couple of ticket offices and an extensive harbour. I bought a ticket, €25 plus 5 to park, and wandered around with fifteen minutes to waste before departure. Again we'd cycled here and taken a ferry across but nothing was recognisable. Several fishing boats lay peacefully alongside the quay for this was the base for some thirty trawlers and well as two hookers though I didn't have time to walk round to find out the names of the vessels. Returning to the ticket office, I asked about the hookers and discovered that one was *An Tonai*, one of the ones I'd seen the previous day at Kinvara. Turns out I was speaking to Sally O'Brien, part-owner with her husband Paddy, the two of them also owning the Island Ferries Company whose boat I was about to sail on. *An Tonai* was the original provider of the service over twenty-five years ago and before that one of the last turf traders over to Aran. It would have been interesting to talk further but it was obvious the ferry was about to leave so I had to rush off. Within seconds of boarding the gangplank was slid away and we were off.

It's a forty-minute run over to Inishmore (Inis Mór in Irish) on this fast modern vessel that everyone had to either sit inside or squeeze in on the tiny after deck to have a cigarette. I phoned Joe Teesdale's contact on the island, Pat Bertie Hernon, but unfortunately he was away at Kilrush with his boat. However he gave me two names – Tommy Flaherty and Joe Joyce. Ten minutes later he phoned back to say he'd arranged with Tommy Flaherty that Tommy would meet me on the quay about half an hour after I arrived as he was coming in on his fishing boat. So, with the sun shining bright as we all embarked onto Kilronan quay, this being the capital, I sought out the refuge of a cafe with a terrace overlooking the harbour for another cup of coffee after buying my copy of the book on Alexander Nimmo that I read greedily.

Afterwards I gazed around and again Kilronan struck no chord with my memory although we'd spent the night in the hotel back then after cycling all around the island to admire its stark beauty and endless stone walls. Seeing a boat just coming alongside the quay, I quickly finished my coffee and walked back down and called out. 'Mike' came back the voice and after a brief introduction, we clambered aboard Tommy's pick-up and drove up to his house. 'It'll be easier talking there,' he added. As far as I know this Flaherty is no relation to Robert Flaherty, the American director of *Man of Aran*, one of the best maritime films ever to have been made at its release in the 1930s, and probably since. The film is shown daily in the heritage centre (I didn't have time to visit) and depicts life on the island, using local people as actors and shot all on location. It was this film along with the hardships of the islanders that brought them to the attention of the wider world. Many directors, writers and photographers followed, though none impacting as Robert Flaherty had.

Tommy and his wife have a new house about a mile outside of Kilronan and, sitting at a table, I marvelled at the fine views out over the island down to Killeany where another small quay was situated and over the sea and to the distant mainland. Both the smaller islands of

Inishmaan (Inis Meáin) and Inisheer (Inis Oirr) were visible and I estimated we must have been a good couple of hundred feet up above sea level to achieve such wonderful views. Connemara spread out away to the north and the ferry returning to Rossaveal was easy to spot. No wonder he'd picked this perfect spot to build his house. Incidentally, Killeany, according to a government report of 1833, had thirty-nine hookers working from the Nimmo-built quay and 350 people were engaged in the fishing.

Tommy had started fishing in 1967, first out of Kilronan then from other ports such as Howth, Dunmore East and Cobh. By 1972 he was back on the west coast skippering a Dublin-owned boat. These days he has his own boats, the 56-foot Killibegs-built *Ard Scia*, D55, for demersal trawling - mostly monkfish, megrim and prawns - and the larger 135-foot Dutch-built pelagic trawler *Westward Eye*, G185, both being based in Rossaveal where over half the boats are owned by Inishmore folk. We talked a while about the fishing but I hadn't really come to talk about big boat fishing, about quotas for mackerel and herring and how many Irish boats had been decommissioned and scrapped over the last year or two. I already knew that thiry-five whitefish and scallop boats had been decommissioned in 2006 and that more were in the process of going through legalities. I always find decommissioning sad because it inevitably ends up with the boat being chopped up. Whilst some boats are probably worthy of this, others aren't. An example of this was the destruction of the 1971-built BIM boat *Arbutus*, D403. Built at the BIM yard in Baltimore, this boat was typical of many built in the 1970s as wooden hulled dual purpose herring/whitefish trawlers and which were popular and successful in their work. Latterly many of these boats have been fishing for prawns but to see boats like these simply chopped up at the whim of governments in a disgrace. With current legislation, these boats could be sold on to private owners so that they could be converted in pleasure boats instead of ending up in the scrapyard. Such a waste of good materials when recycling is on the political menu.

I wanted to know about the fishing on the islands, how many were involved and what were they catching. 'Twelve lobster boats that only work in the summer,' he replied. 'Three or four fellows catch pollack for the restaurants and chip shops. They catch a couple of boxes a day for which they can get €200 a day for. Not much black pollack now, no cod or ling and even turbot is scarce. Other than that it's prawns, eighty percent of the catch.' Familiar stories I guess. 'A few use currachs to set single pots around the back of the islands,' he added after a brief silence. 'We used to hand-line off the cliffs at the back of the island for wrasse – rockfish – and get sixty or seventy at a go. We'd split 'em, salt and dry 'em and barter them.'

I asked about tourism and its impact. 'Well, they increase the demand in the chip shop and the restaurants probably wouldn't survive otherwise.' I'd seen the Supermac's fast food and doubted they'd use much fish.

> There are eight ferries a day in summer, four from Rossaveal, two from Galway and two from Doolin. That's up to 1,500 or so visitors each day and the plane carries another nine three times a day though it doesn't make a big difference. We had 30,000 visitors last year. That's a considerable trade for a small island and there are twenty-two Polish people working here because the locals don't want the jobs. Keeps the shops, bicycle hire and bars busy. Mike Mollins can hire out 1,000 bikes a day, you know.

I'd already heard that there were 200,000 Polish workers in Ireland which makes quite a difference. In Britain numbers are greater and it had been said that sixty-five percent of hotel and catering employees in Britain are Polish.

I asked about seaweed cutting. 'Yes,' he said, 'there was a seaweed factory here until a couple of years ago. It used to be collected after big seas and dried.' This reminded me of the

Curracts at the Aran Islands.

book *The Aran Islands* by John Synge, first published in 1906. He came across the inhabitants burning kelp and a ton of it was needed and the work of collecting that amount was considerable. The whole island was covered in smoke during the burning process which he described thus:

> The seaweed is collected from the rocks after the storms of autumn and winter, dried on fine days, and then made up into a rick, where it is left till the beginning of June. It is then burnt in low kilns on the shore, an affair that takes from twelve to twenty-four hours of continuous hard work, though I understand the people here do not manage well, and spoil a portion of what they produce by burning it more than required. The kiln holds about two tons of molten kelp, and when full it is loosely covered with stones and left to cool. In a few days the substance is hard as limestone, and has to be broken up with crowbars before it can be placed in curaghs [*sic*] for transport to Kilronan, where it is tested to determine the amount of iodine it contains, and paid for accordingly. In former years good kelp would bring seven pounds a ton, now four pounds are not always reached.'

We talked on a bit more, drinking tea and eating biscuits. The room with the view seemed so tranquil I wasn't in a hurry to leave but knew the ferry was departing soon. Before that I wanted to see Joe Joyce who, according to Tommy, was old but incredibly knowledgeable. 'You'd be best talking to him if you want the history stuff,' said Tommy. On standing up, I noticed a plaque on the wall. Tommy had been awarded the 'Fisherman of the Year' by the Allied Irish Bank in 1973. He laughed when he saw me looking. 'Used to be doing fourteen day trips then at the prawns. Still got some of the crew with me I had back then.'

Before we left Tommy insisted on driving me back down to the harbour. I asked to photograph him holding a model of a currach he'd built. Although he's a bit thin on top, he looks young and fit, not particularly weathered by his years at sea but intense and thoughtful. As I write this bit I'm occasionally glancing at the photo and remembering that view. What a vista with the Atlantic on one side and the Irish coast on the other, boats dotting along and the sparkles and glare of the sea. Combine that with Tommy's hospitality and kindness and naturally I experienced a really pleasant afternoon.

Joe Joyce had been ill and was still recovering so his wife thought it not a good idea for me to talk to him. That was fair enough though a shame. In the Aran Sweater Market I met by chance Marina Colozzi, a young Italian woman working in the shop. She was wondering what I was doing whilst I was taking notes from around the shop. I told her about my tour and, when she said she'd been studying the history of the island, I suggested she interview Joe Joyce when he was feeling better. She obviously tried as she emailed that he was still not well though I've heard nothing since. Hopefully she did manage to talk to him.

Aran sweaters are, of course, internationally known. The original designs are Celtic art and the tradition of knitting individual heraldic-like patterns was always done for sons of the fishing families. Newly married women would commemorate the birth of their first son by making a plain sweater with one decorative panel on the front. As subsequent sons arrived – assuming they did – new panels with different designs were added either side until the whole sweater was adorned with embellishments. These, like the Gansey in Britain, were worn by fishermen so that they could be identified if taken by the sea and subsequently washed ashore. Certain families guarded their own patterns and refused to share them, only passing them on through their daughters to her new family. When the Congested Districts Board (CBD) invested in the Arans, they brought in fishermen from Donegal and some even as far away as Scotland and the Channel Islands for the fishing season. These folk brought their wives who filleted the fish and mixed with the native women. The women were soon swapping patterns so that regional variations then appeared. Furthermore the CDB sent in knitting instructors to help the women develop their skills and these instructors also influenced their patterns. Some emigrants returning from the US added their designs to the pool so that ultimately the patterns became more widespread. With a proper Aran sweater having 400 stitches in a horizontal direction in rough home-spun wool in which twelve stitches or twenty rows make up about one inch there's plenty of work which is reflected in the price. Although all this information all came from the Aran Sweater Market for which I am indebted, I wasn't grateful enough to buy one of their sweaters!

Back to the quay then and thoughts about the new €8 million harbour development that was soon to commence. Was it badly needed as some said or just another waste of money? Then onto the ferry which was busier than that coming, although this wasn't the last of the day. I got a seat at the back and didn't really notice the man who sat down beside me. After a while I noticed him watching me write my notes and I glanced in his direction. He smiled and asked what I was writing and before long I was telling him about my mission. When he mentioned that he'd been a lighthouse keeper for twenty-six years my spirits lifted substantially as I'd already been wondering how I was going to meet such a person.

Turned out his name was Seamus O'Flaithearta and he was living in Kilronan or Cill Ronáin as he spelt it the Irish way when he wrote down his address. Being an Irish speaker. The Aran Islands are one of the last bastions of the language and has a school where kids come to learn. He was off to Galway where he sometimes worked for the local radio station. I asked whether he minded me asking him questions and he simply said 'fire away'. Stopping him talking was more difficult.

'I wasn't one of the last but decided to go when automation was talked about. Thought I could do something else, live on an island again, be a fuel merchant, do a bit of everything as you can't survive on just one thing on an island.' Tommy Flaherty might disagree but I wasn't about to contradict him.

'Yes,' he said when I asked whether the work was hard.

> Six weeks on, two weeks off, working eight hour shifts on watch. Usually four at night and four during the day. Cooked for myself with the food that was delivered every two weeks when at a place like the Fastnet. Had the pleasure of working there and the time went much faster than other places. One time I was there for nine weeks during bad weather with two other keepers. We paid for our own food which we ordered by radio. Cramped on the Fastnet. Usually had your own bedroom but not there. Then two or three hours maintenance each day cleaning the light, servicing the engines and things. Painting in the summer. Snooze time, night watch, cook, wash-up, it all took time. Sometimes it took a while to get used to the place such as Haulbowline up in the north, a rock lighthouse in the middle of a channel. When I came ashore though it took months to acclimatise. See, when I started the lights were paraffin which was a long time ago.

I asked whether the Fastnet swayed in storms. 'Was there during a force ten and I thought it didn't but couldn't swear to it.'

It turned out he'd been all over, done most of the Irish lights. He'd spent four years on the Outer Blaskets, Inishtearaght, for four years, coming off and on every four weeks. North Aran Island – there are two lights, one on Inisheer and the other at Eeragh on Rock Island or North Aran as it's sometimes called, both dating from the mid-1800s – was a pleasure, he said, because all the crew were from Aran and they were able to speak Irish all the time. Sometimes there wasn't a boat for days which could be a problem.

He'd also spent twenty years on the lifeboat crew and was now the lifeboat operations manager. 'I'm responsible for managing the affairs for the RNLI at the station. Unpaid! We brought the first Arun class boat to the island from Poole in 1987.'

He kept on saying 'carry on, next question' when I paused to catch my thoughts. What was the best lighthouse he worked at, I asked?

> Different people have different ideas. To me being on Earagh because it was close to home. I missed the family and wrote letters when a boat came out. Though we didn't always see eye to eye, we had to make do out there. It was a bit regimental, always one senior officer who was the principal keeper.

The ferry arrived back in Rossaveal as he added his last bit though it didn't stop him.

> We did a bit of joinery whilst out there. I remember making a set of step ladders once. I got stopped on the way home by the Garda. Questions and questions. What are you doing with these? they asked. What did they think I was doing, robbing. I told them and eventually they let me go.

We disembarked and I asked to take a photo of him with two wooden currachs in the background. His phone rang, I clicked the camera's shutter and he had to rush off. 'You'll send me a copy of the book,' he just had time to say with a twinkle in those uneven eyes. What a lovely man he had been.

Once back in the car and Dog given a bit of a walk, I decided to continue driving westward towards the already sinking sun. It was almost five o'clock. First stop was on the road to Lettermullen where, on the other side of Cashla Bay from Rossaveal, I photographed a collection of wooden and canvas currachs lying in the harbour alongside a mixture of more modern craft. Rejoining the main road we drove north and then west again. Here we were in deepest Connemara with turf bogs decorated with the odd stack of turfs adorning an

The Twelve Pins.

otherwise stark landscape. Way to the north the Twelve Pins towered over, clear and sharp in the intensive light. It was a very pleasant drive on roads with few other vehicles. Those that we did pass always waved at me in a sort of acknowledgement of my existence. I waved back even at those that didn't respond, unsure whether this had been a rebuttal or they simply didn't see well. At Kilkieran I found a string of seaweed rafts moored in the harbour, all tied up with colourful twine. Several more wooden currachs and a couple of what I assumed to be Púcáns which were small enough though gaff-rigged. However once again I didn't linger as I was keen to get to Roundstone several miles further on. When we'd been there on the previous visit a friend from Anglesey, Charlie Dixon, was living there and I was eager to meet him once again. It never occurred to me at that point that he might not be there any longer.

On the way we passed various small quays, many of which probably stemmed from the middle and late nineteenth century although a couple looked much more recent. The surrounding countryside was a mixture of rock, heather, lakes, sheltered bays and bogs. It was easy to understand just how inaccessible and barren the area must have been before the roads opened the area up. The best descriptions of this 'strange and beautiful corner of the world' comes from Tim Robinson's *Connemara: Listening to the Wind*, published in 2006. His words are poetic, the pictures he paints vivid in a 'magnificent testimony to a landscape and its people'. Wonderful reading.

Roundstone was a disappointment as much for its altered atmosphere as the fact that Charlie had moved out of O'Dowd's bar and disappeared to Galway, according to a couple of fishermen I spoke to. The streets were full of drinkers outside the several bars, mostly Dublin well-offs, so the same fishermen told me. Seems Roundstone has become the playground of these people when properties sell for crazy prices. A derelict two-storey house had recently fetched €1.4 million according to Tommy Flaherty. Many more houses had sprung up.

Roundstone was Alexander Nimmo's dream and before that it was nothing but rock and beach. Whilst surveying the bogs he had suggested the building of a harbour and village at the head of Roundstone Bay close to where the Ballynahinch River flows out. Later the spot was moved a few miles south where his coastal road passed through. With funding in place, he built a 150-foot quay along the south side of a bight in the shoreline and a 60-foot jetty running north from this. Work started in 1822 and when a local tenant of a nearby farm demanded compensation for damage to his land during the work, Nimmo decided to buy out the tenant at his own expense. Thus he began his own personal financial involvement in Roundstone. In 1826 this was extended to a ninety-nine-year lease and Nimmo then designed his village, renting out parcels of land for house building. Previously only a small amount of corn was produced locally, most of which went to illicit distilling though, once the harbour was completed, kelp and cured herrings passed through. He also built a stone store for the fishermen and rented out a smithy, carpentry workshop and another store, all of which he'd had built, to the government at £50 a year for six and a half years. His brother John came to live here and continued the lease after Nimmo's death in 1832. Sadly for someone described as a 'phenomenon' he was only forty-nine when he died.

The harbour was obviously successful before the rich came to holiday here. Another pier was built at the northern end of the harbour in 1830 and by 1836, during the herring season, some 600 boats were said by the former Inspector of Fisheries to visit the harbour. Today a number of boats were quietly moored alongside including several wooden currachs and the bright red painted BIM 50-footer *Dunlaoire*, D175, built by Tyrrells of Arklow in 1955. These fifty-footers, of which we shall hear more, are lovely picturesque craft and that one graces this harbour should gain respect from those city-dwelling folk for its beauty if not its tenacity in surviving over fifty years.

Roundstone harbour.

Again I wasn't lingering once I'd studied the harbour. The hordes standing, sometimes arrogantly blocking the street, didn't seem the types I wanted to converse with. Eventually, with darkness beginning its slow transition, I came across the small quay of Ballyconneely Harbour set amongst the beauty of Bunowen Bay where, immersed in the peace and solitude, I decided to park up for the night. At the end of the pier was a young lad in yellow waterproof dungarees gutting pollack. We talked a while. Some, he said, went to the restaurants but most went for bait. He worked for another man who used to have 800 lobster pots. Now he has 2,000, the increase purely because they'd lost the salmon fishing. The same old, by now familiar, story. Stop fishing the salmon and clobber the lobsters. They'd a 35-foot boat that allowed them to sail 10 miles offshore when drifting for salmon. Now they set pots in deeper water. Others had drifted in their wooden currachs so had to stay closer to the shore and now a few of these are used for potting.

I sat in the van eating the wild smoked salmon from the Burren smokehouse that we'd forgotten to eat the previous Sunday evening and listening to the squawking of the seagulls. A hundred yards away was the Connemara Smokehouse, just by the harbour which now, according to the fishing lad, bought all its fish in from Norway, Scotland and other parts of Ireland. When I asked whether any salmon was being caught these days all he would say that there's always an export market for a wild smoked salmon. I hasten to add that I'm sure he wasn't referring to this smokehouse as behaving in such an illegal way. Another wonderful spot I thought as I shut the door of the van that night. Shame, though, about the bloody awful holiday housing hereabout. It sort of ruins the beauty of the place.

DAY FOURTEEN

This day started with a lengthy walk along gorgeous Bunowen Beach. The fine white sand is backed with low sand-dunes with the yellow-flowering plant whose name escapes me though I remember capturing caterpillars off the stuff in childhood. Is it Broom? No, of course it's not. It's found all over the place in seaside locations, in dunes and seems to mix well with marram grass. The sand itself is wonderful under foot, soft and silky as I walked about in bare feet. The dog sniffed in the dunes, chasing after unseen rabbits or whatever smells excited him. The sea, calm and lapping, was bright turquoise in colour, the shade associated with hot countries. Though I was almost persuaded to swim – I could have stripped off and there was no one around to overlook, no houses in sight – the chilly south-easterly breeze was enough to put me off. The Twelve Bens, in the near distance, were shrouded in cloud above about a thousand feet and there didn't seem much chance of the sun breaking through judging by the sky.

Walking back around the rocks, paddling ankle deep just to confirm the chill of the water, a dustbin wagon appeared and a couple of men emptied a couple of bins by the pier before turning around to head back. At that point I raced back to the van, calling for the dog, as I didn't want to get stuck behind that on the narrow road up to the main road which was several miles away. We narrowly won, arriving in Clifden before any of the shops had opened.

Over that one week cycling around the Connemara coast, other than hiking up one of the Bens, all of which are unmistakable, Clifden was the only place I recognised although it was seemingly much busier and generally of an improved wealth. There's now a wholefood shop, a delicatessen, couple of butchers, good book shop, large SuperValu supermarket, a jeweller, and lots of B&Bs and hotels, bistros and bars, none of which I recall except for the hotels though even these appeared more upmarket than before.

Alcock and Brown landed close by after their Atlantic flight: the hotel I sat at writing up notes and drinking coffee went under their name. It was raining as I sat under the small umbrella outside the hotel smoking a cigarette and I did note a few strange looks from passers-by. They obviously didn't understand the absolute pleasure of enjoying a morning fag over coffee whilst planning the day ahead! Marconi himself seems to be a bit of a local hero also, there's a Marconi Restaurant, for he sent his first transatlantic message from here.

Clifden harbour was another of Nimmo's piers, begun in 1822 yet not completed until the 1830s although it was used prior to final completion. Funding from the Fishery Board was withheld for the building work differed slightly from the original plans though it was soon pointed out to the Board the advantage gained. Clifden's fortunes were founded on a thriving herring fishery, a copper mine, stone quarrying and the export of corn. Indeed the first vessel to load and depart from the pier whilst still under construction took away a load of marble. The railway from Galway helped in opening up the area to the rest of Ireland. The corn I found difficult to understand as I saw no sign of anywhere in the vicinity capable of growing the stuff. The supermarket had well-stocked shelves with everything from fresh vegetables to exotic foods though I couldn't get any of the dog's favourite dog food.

I wanted to catch the morning ferry to Inishbofin Island so had to make a dash to Cleggan instead of motoring around the famous Sky Road with its rugged coast and fine views though,

Sorting the catch of fish at Cleggan.

with the cloud already turned to rain, these views might have been exceedingly dull. Cleggan was little more than a cluster of houses and the harbour, another of Nimmo's of course. When the harbour was being constructed in the 1820s, Nimmo was sure that the site would become a thriving village even if, at that time, it only consisted of a few farms. By 1836 the village had not materialised though fishermen were living by the shore and the 1837 Report of Inquiry into the State of the Irish Fisheries found that

> All the male inhabitants of Claggan [*sic*] are more or less fishermen. They are destitute of every convenience; they live in the most wretched hovels that can be described; they are yearly tenants,

> generally holding land under freeholders, who are themselves miserably poor ... The aged are supported by their neighbours, and the widows by begging.

Things improved in the second half of that century and a pier extension was added in 1908 to further encourage growth in the fisheries. However, by that time the fishing boom was about to decline.

I parked the van up, leaving the dog with air, water and food, paid my fee to the woman who walked up from the house below to collect it, and bought a return ticket for €15 for the thirty-minute crossing. The quay was a bustle of activity as boxes of supplies in cardboard boxes were loaded aboard the ferryboat *Island Discovery*, all these boxes emerging out of cars and a lorry and carried by hand onboard. However, the ferry wasn't due to depart for some time and I wandered about aimlessly. In my boredom I started reading the information pages of my diary and discovered some useless facts: one standard barrel of dry capacity is some twenty percent larger than a barrel of cranberries and that a cord of firewood is 128 cubic feet which is 3.62 cubic metres. And a league is three miles. I never could remember that one. The stuff you learn whilst waiting for a ferry in the extremes of Western Ireland, eh!

It was a blustery ride out to the island and, as I'd supposed, the views not good. The boat bounced around a bit and I noticed a few passengers, of which there were plenty, not looking too happy. One particular group of about half a dozen young girls, probably aged about fifteen and under the watchful eye of their mentor, I judged to be part of a sports team by the way they were dressed in polyester tracksuits. One, very slim, tall and beautiful, was puking into one of those paper bags produced for the purpose. Other passengers stared in disgust and I felt really sorry for her as she retreated to the stern of the boat looking very green. Spray mingled with white horses over the sea and the hazy views over grey rocks not particularly revealing. Still we obviously maintained speed for twenty-five minutes later we were in the lee of Inishark, the small island just west, and soon entering the small bay of Bofin Harbour with Oliver Cromwell's seventeenth-century star-shaped defence Barracks on the right-hand side. A couple more minutes later we were moored up alongside the pier and disembarking. The poor girl looked instantly relieved.

I'd only a couple of hours on the island before the ferry returned, thus I made straight for the Island's Heritage Museum and Souvenir Shop, housed in a small building some hundred or more yards along the shore from the pier. It was easy to find. Inside it's jammed packed with artefacts and photographs, cutting from newspapers and acres of interesting facts which truly represented the history of the island through the eyes of those living there. I wanted to learn something about the fishing boat *Leenan Head*, a Scottish fishing boat built by W.G. Stephen of Banff in 1906 and named after the Leenan Head which is situated on the eastern entrance to Loch Swilly. She was of the Zulu design, a particular type of sailing fishing craft introduced into the East Coast of Scotland's herring fleets in the 1870s and named after the Zulu wars in which large numbers of Scottish soldiers were dying on behalf of British (English) colonialism much to the chagrin of Scottish opinion. The true Zulu boats were over 70 feet in length and had huge overhanging sternposts and upright stems and were largely regarded as a hybrid between the two established types of fishing boats on that coast at the time – the 'scaffie' from the north and 'fifie' from the south. Although not of the same size at 48 feet, *Leenan Head* was still called a Zulu, a term frowned upon by many in modern times. However she, like many of her counterparts, retained the overall Zulu shape. The reason that I was interested in this boat was that I knew she was still afloat in Paimpol, Brittany and that some of her history was associated with Inishbofin.

However it was to Inishbofin in Donegal that the *Leenan Head* came to in September 1909 to fish, a smaller island lying just off the north coast of Donegal, after a spell of fishing in Loch

Loading cattle at Inishbofin aboard the zulu *Leenan Head*.

Swilly. This boat, like many others, had been built with finance from the CDB and leased to those fishermen willing to fish at a time when the authorities were trying to pull the fisheries of the north-west coast out of the Middle Ages. Whereas the southern mackerel fishery had produced a boom for local economies, this coast received little investment and remained primitive throughout most of the nineteenth century. With a vibrant Donegal and Mayo herring fishery fished mostly by Scottish boats towards the end of that century, the CDB decided to introduce these boats to enable the local inhabitants to compete. Their older boats and currachs were unable to do this. To begin with they were built in Scotland and brought over but before long Irish boatbuilders and small yards were building their own versions. For a complete account of these boats, the reader is directed to Pat Conaghan's *The Zulu Fishermen - Forgotten Pioneer's of Donegal's First Fishing Industry*.

Further south, in Connemara, it was fishing boats built on the lines of Manx craft that were introduced into the fleets and these became known as Connemara nobbies. We shall learn more of these craft in a subsequent chapter.

Anyway, going back to the *Leenan Head*, she gradually crept down the coast between crews willing to fish her under strict CDB conditions, from Inishbofin to Downings and down to Broadhaven in County Mayo by 1915. At that time she was sold and eventually found her way to the southern Inishbofin where she became the ferryboat between Cleggan and the island. The museum had a couple of photographs of the boat and I had a very brief chat with the woman looking after the place that afternoon about it. However, the museum had plenty more to catch people's attention including the lugsail of the nobby *Dolphin* which was owned by Pat Davis in the 1920s and fished from the island.

Surprisingly, Inishbofin was once one of the most important fishing stations in Ireland back in the early nineteenth century. In those days the combined population of both Inishbofin and Inishark amounted to some 1,600 folk, a far cry from today's 200 or so, though this swells in the summer with the tourist trade. Inishark was evacuated in 1961 though is described today as 'a peaceful and enchanting place'. In the *Commissioners of Irish Fisheries Report* for 1824, they noted that Inishbofin 'is abundantly supplied with all kinds of white fish, cod, ling, glassen, mackerel and gurnet, especially in Spring, as also a few herrings' whilst the 1837 *Report* makes mention of a remarkable herring fishery. However the bulk of this fish seems to have been caught by Claddagh fishermen, echoing their belief in that they controlled all the fishing off the Galway coast. The herring fishery lasted from the beginning of January to the end of April, mackerel fishing from May through to November and glassen fishing throughout the year though predominately in winter.

More mind-boggling is the realisation that 10,000 fishermen assembled on the island during a good herring fishery, so many people, in fact, that the 1837 *Report* recommending a police force being set up to keep the peace after local fishermen with their small rowboats and those from outside with their larger sail boats with a greater fishing capability clashed. Drift-nets were often cut away and occasional brawls ensued. Probably exacerbating the situation was the lack of facilities for landing the fish; curing it, there was hardly any salt; and transporting it away, there was no pier, in the early nineteenth century. As we've seen, Cleggan pier wasn't built and neither was the pier at Derryinver in Ballynakill Bay so there wasn't a lot of hope for anyone wishing to develop markets with Inishbofin herring. Most of what was sold went to vessels coming for that purpose who sold it to merchants in Westport where it was cured.

Later in that century efforts were made to improve the fisheries, including a lobster fishery that developed in the 1820s. In 1873 there were fifty-two vessels fishing, from currachs, rowboats and Pucáns to much larger nobbies. Currachs had supposedly only been introduced onto the island in the mid-nineteenth century when the Dingle fishermen came in search of herring with their naomhóga and it is said that currachs were soon built locally to their own design. Whether this is exactly true I'm not sure because there's a general belief that Connemara fishermen were using currachs before this. Cleggan is supposed to have had its first currach around 1860 when a native of County Clare brought one in. Again this sounds a bit of an unlikely tenuous claim.

Inishbofin missed out on Nimmo's pier building and it wasn't until the CDB provided the money for a pier that one was built. In 1892 a curing station was added upon this pier where large amounts of ling were cured, under the tutelage of a Scotsman. According to a CDB report of about that time the fishermen of Inishark and Inishbofin were 'the best and most practical on the west coast'. Possibly that was why another pier was built at East End Bay, complete with a curing station, all of which was up and working by 1897. Thus with those curing stations and another at North Beach, a sheltered bay on the north coast, the fishing industry thrived upon the island, its boom years lasting until the 1920s. Inishark, though sparsely populated, also had its own small pier. It was against this background that the *Leenan Head* came to Inishbofin. Sunfish were also caught on the odd occasion and when Robert Flaherty was filming *Man of Aran*, he came to Inishbofin to shoot the harpooning of the sunfish though was unsuccessful as none were spotted. Ironically, he'd come to Inishbofin because the tradition had disappeared from Aran at least two generations previously but when he returned to the island after failing to find any of the creatures in Inishbofin, some were spotted off Aran and were duly filmed.

Inishturbot is an island lying close to the coast at the end of the peninsula upon which is the Sky Road. Like Inishark, this was once inhabited by families that wholly relied upon fishing and farming to survive. Spring was a time of preparing the ground to sow potatoes, cabbage, carrots, parsnips and turnips, all of which grew well. In summer these men used to fish herring and mackerel but in more modern times the fishing was directed towards lobsters and crayfish. For this they crossed over to mainland and camped ashore at Errismore for a week, fishing by day in their currachs and selling the catch to a local buyer each Saturday morning before returning home until the following evening. Kelp was also collected and sold on the mainland. What they did have, and didn't need to search out, was turf for the island had some of the best peat bogs. They also sold this to other islanders such as those from Inishturk, the adjacent island, and to the mainland. However this turf, or its exhausting of the supply, was one reason that the island was evacuated in 1978. Other reasons included the fallout after a nasty drowning of three young men returning to the island one night after watching a football match on television in Clifden; the lack of a shop, pub, priest and doctor; the expense of living there; and the lack of jobs which meant the young emigrated to the mainland in search of work. Today many former houses are holiday homes and some are available for hire. Luckily Inishbofin is stable enough to remain inhabited, unlike many other islands such as the Blaskets in Kerry, and with improved facilities such as the new harbour developments, increased tourism and a vibrant island community, Inishbofin will stay healthy and strong in the face of increasing hardships upon the mainland.

To these people the sea was everything, whether living upon an island or residing close to it. They breathe it, eat it, and smell it; they had a complete and utter dependency on it. But the sea gives and the sea takes. Some say this creates a balance, a repayment if you wish. I don't agree with that philosophy, believing it's simply a matter of odds. Yet there's hardly a community of coast dwellers who haven't been affected by disaster, especially in fishing communities. One of the worse to hit the Irish shore happened here in 1927 and is now known as the Cleggan Bay Disaster.

On Friday 28 October 1927 the fishing boats from Inishbofin East End and Rossadilisk left as usual in the late afternoon. Further north in County Mayo, fishermen also set out from Lacken Bay and Inishkea. An hour later, with their nets set, a ferocious storm blew from nowhere without warning and devastated these small fleets. In all twenty-five were lost in Rossadilisk and Inishbofin and another nineteen in the north and a further two off Aran. In a hamlet such as Rossadilisk that only consisted of twenty houses, everyone was personally affected though even in larger communities the effects were widespread and sincere. Fishing remains the most dangerous of occupations even with improved designs and safety equipment but in the nineteenth century the odds were almost against survival to an old age even if the average lifespan was a lot shorter than today. Returning to Cleggan later that afternoon, I stopped a few minutes at the memorial for those fishermen lost and contemplated the risks. Though what choice had these men, what other way of feeding their families and furthermore what has changed today when one part of society grows ever richer at the expense of the majority?

Leaving the museum I bought a copy of *Inishbofin Through Time and Tide*, a book written by local people and which is regarded as the most comprehensive study of the island to date. It is to be well recommended. Thereafter, on returning to the mainland in much calmer conditions, I retrieved the van from the car park and we drove back along the road to the main road and headed north once again along Nimmo's road. Letterfrack has a small pier though not one of his; he built a bridge here but it later collapsed and had to be rebuilt, and alongside I found a rusting old steam puffer as was once typical off Scotland's west coast and, alongside the other side, Kevin Walsh's 1964 Dingle-built BIM 50-footer *Ros Beithe*, D44, being rebuilt. Though the hatch was open, and the pouring rain no doubt drenching down below, there was no one aboard as I called out. Dog and I wandered the beach for ten minutes to see if anybody returned as I fancied a look inside but, given the rain and the fact that Kevin didn't, we soon gave up and continued on our way. It was at this point, with the road very narrow, that I nearly got squashed by a coach travelling too fast. The driver gave me that look to say it would have been my fault if we had collided. I returned the salute.

Spotting a signpost and almost causing an accident myself by turning sharply, I came across the Letterfrack Ocean and Country Museum which was some sort of private enterprise housed in a white building. Upstairs was the pay desk (€6.50 entrance fee) and small café and downstairs a display on the local heritage. Although much was displayed in terms of fishing, most of it was the usual paraphernalia seen in dozens of other similar establishments such as lobster pots, glass floats and netting. However, having said that, some of the information boards were interesting as were the two plans of local currachs. Thus I discovered that Edward VII visited Leenane in 1903 and Derrynacleigh pier became known as the King's Pier. In total there were eight piers in this parish, the others being at Doonen, Fahy Bay, Derryinver, Letter (the one I'd visited), Gurten, Glassillaun and Rosroe. As far as I could ascertain, only the Derryinver pier was one of Nimmo's and, though it was said that it was the only pier in Ballynakil Bay at that time, it was in a poor state of repair by 1833 even though its importance to the local trade and fisheries was recognised. Presumably the others were built later in century, probably after the famine years to create employment. As far as the fisheries were concerned, the East Atlantic Company cured fish in Dawros where the museum was, with salt brought in from Galway. Thomas Nee was the direct buyer of the fish from the boats and much of the cured herring was sent via the Limerick Steamship Company to Germany. A long hundred of herring (126 fish here) fetched two shillings and even up to the 1950s the maximum the fishermen got was *2/6d*.

Lobster fishing also thrived in the twentieth century with storage facilities being built at Glassillaun where a dozen lobsters realised 15*d* though the price dropped as low as 8*d* at times. Salted pollack, wrasse, mackerel and, as we've seen, herrings were the main fish exports. Salmon, surprisingly, were late-comers to Connemara as, according to the information, drift-netting wasn't allowed until 1968. Salmon fetched one shilling per pound weight with the price dropping down to 6-8*d* per pound in summer. I was determined to check out that bit about salmon drift-nets being illegal. Of course, as elsewhere, salmon fishing in 2007 was not happening. On a legal footing anyway!

I was keen to stop at Leenane though didn't expect very much. The quay was interesting. Two older stone quays and a newer section, though no boats took advantage of its hospitality within. Leenane lies upon the south side of Killary Harbour, Ireland's longest inlet and only fjord. In the past it was regarded as one of the best harbours for herring fishing according to Young. I considered him for a moment. He'd come over in July of 1776 and stayed until October, a period of three months. His subsequent trip the following year was much shorter and his final one in 1778 very brief indeed. Presumably he gathered most of his information in 1776 when he crossed over from Holyhead to Dublin and travelled anti-clockwise around the coast with forays inland until he reached Wexford for the return to Milford Haven. With him he had a four wheeled 'chaise', three horses and two servants. Young himself was an American agriculturist and commentator and his observations in the main reflect upon the state of the land and husbandry. Like politics and religion, though not for the same reason, I've overlooked the habits and traditions of the farmers beyond the type of products they produced and exported. Though he includes a few passages of the fishing, in the main concerning herring and salmon fishery, he presumably gets his information from the owners of any establishments he visited. I get the impression he's a bit above the normal folk. During his third tour in 1778 he stopped for the night and 'slept at Ballyroan, at an inn kept by three animals who call themselves women; met with more impertinence than at any other in Irish. It is an execrable hole.' He obviously didn't enjoy that place. I simply mention this to illustrate the sort of person he was though I'm sure not unpleasant or anything, simply a product of the upper classes who might be regarded as being more sympathetic with the poor of Ireland than many of his ilk and standing. Furthermore, Young had all his notes stolen at some point after his trip and he wrote everything up from memory. Though some facts must therefore be regarded with suspicion, his two-volume work is generally held in high esteem.

At some point from Leenane the scenery abruptly changes from rustic Connemara into green County Mayo where arable fields blend with hedgerows and grazing animals. Westport is a superbly laid out town and belonged to the Marquis of Sligo, who was once once Governor of Jamaica, who lived, when home, in nearby Westport House. Nimmo came often whilst building his road. The port was already established by then, a long quay on the river some way out of the town. This was an important fishing station for the area and statistics of 1824 give numbers of fishing boats as: decked vessels: 5; half-decked over 15 ton: 1; sail boats under 15 ton: 119; row boats: 1,117. From this we can see that the inshore fishing was the most important though details of these 119 sail boats is unclear.

Young tells us about the poor of Westport who lived on potatoes and milk nine months out of twelve and during the other two months when potatoes were scarce it was just milk and bread. All have cows and some have pigs. Why didn't they kill the pigs then? Fish was plentiful, so presumably they ate that as well, and oysters cost one shilling a cartload. Just fancy that now when one oyster costs fifty pence. Eels were available but they wouldn't eat them and herrings he described as 'an article in their food'. The men feed the family by their labours in the field and the women pay the rent by spinning.

At this point I made another error in my itinerary. I'd been made aware of the National Museum of Ireland's Country Life Museum at Turlough Park, outside Castlebar. Here I knew was a collection of artefacts relevant to Irish country life between 1850 and 1950 with displays of fishing exhibits including a few traditional working boats. However, with the time at 4pm, and knowing the place closed at 5pm, I decided to forego the experience of visiting. In retrospect, I think I should have waited. Darina Tully had impressed upon me the worthwhileness of meeting the curator Séamus McPhilib – his name was scrawled over her map in big letters – yet I was impatient to continue. I don't like delays that necessitate waiting in these cases so I drove on.

The railway north once stretched from Westport, through Newport and up to the edge of Achill Sound, to where I was heading. This opened in May 1895, the cost through the rugged landscape subsidised by the Board of Works. A train ran directly to Dublin, 187 miles away and some freight and fish was carried though it's hard to see how a line to such a remote and economically depressed area could profit from such a connection. That is was built is perhaps a testament to those who tried to open up these inaccessible and sparsely populated areas. Newport was another inlet and the only sign of fishing was the boat *Girl Jane*, G199, laid alongside looking a bit sad. Because I once owned a fishing boat called *Girl Freda*, I stopped to take a photo thinking they might be sister boats.

I read in my journal that the roads were 'like driving over a long cattle grid or an enlargened rhinoceros skin' which must mean I wasn't impressed with the bumps and pot-holes. I do remember that many of these narrow roads had been resurfaced but the pot-holes had simply been tarmaced over so that, within weeks, the pot-holes were back with a vengeance. The council had obviously taken the cheap option rather than solving the long-term problem. But then again, with talk of the Celtic Tiger economy on the way down and Europe's purses spending elsewhere, perhaps they had no choice.

The railway stopped short of Achill Island though the narrow sound had been bridged by road since 1874. Before we crossed however we stopped at the old railway station just by the

The Achill yawl *The Patriot*.

bridge because I spotted a trio of Achill yawls, one propped up ashore over beer barrels and two moored alongside the small stone quay. These yawls are another of Ireland's indigenous working craft that almost disappeared in the twentieth century although their importance in the lives of the people of what is Ireland's biggest island was unimaginable in terms of today's standards. However, like the towelsail yawls, the hookers and the currachs, these boats were the workhorses of Achill. From the mid-1800s until the mid-1900s these boats were the means of transportation and trade. They fished, collected seaweed, carried limestone for fertiliser, turf for fuel, stones for building and timber for new boats. Their fishing was seasonal again, as elsewhere, with herring fishing, line fishing and oyster dredging: in December 1867 there were 100 boats dredging oysters in Achill Sound, the shellfish which were later carried to Galway.

Original Achill yawls were about 18ft in length, carvel-planked, rigged with one dipping lugsail which was sewn by the women of the island and double-ended. The design is said to have come from the West Coast of Scotland. Nowadays they are often longer, up to 28ft, and some have square sterns to take outboard motors. Their build was said to be relatively basic due to the shortness of finance to pay for them and the hull tarred. Some had, indeed, been built with money from the CDB. In 1892 the CDB reported that there were 226 yawls and rowing boats on the island, though this doesn't specify the actual numbers of yawls, it is presumed to be substantial. However their numbers dropped to three surviving vessels in about 1980 when Dr Jerry Cowley bought an old yawl and subsequently learned how the families raced their yawls every summer. Because of this, a resurgence in the building of new craft has come about so that, this summer of 2007, some thirteen yawls raced during the Cruinníu Bádóirí Acla or Achill Sailing Festival held between July and August. Sadly, the day I arrived there was no sailing. Some of these new yawls have been built on the island by builders such as Poraigh Owen Pattern of Saulia and the O'Malleys of Corraun, though not as cheaply as they used to be when money was in very short supply. The oldest afloat is the *Cutty Sark*, said to be coming up to a 100 years old. Today's rigs, though, are a far cry from those of a century ago: modern sail cloths with radial cuts on aluminium spars. Some boats, like two I was studying, have kept their traditional black colours though many others are brightly painted and some come from Clare Island to the south.

Crossing over the swing-bridge, I decided to chance the Atlantic Drive that follows the coast around the south-western portion of the coast. At first the road follows the sound where I saw lots of currachs though many had been fibreglassed on their outsides. At the very tip was a sign declaring the Clare Island Sea Farm which seemed to be a very secretive place judging by the fencing. The drive along the coast facing the ocean was simply fantastic. I stopped at one point to immerse myself in the dramatic view of the rugged coast and even the dog seemed to be unusually prone to stopping in his chasing rabbits to gaze out to sea. Clare Island was bright and clear several miles offshore, another place I'd have liked to visit but time constraints disallowed. Even so, knowing there was still something of a fishing industry there, and plenty of fish-farming (or aquaculture as some prefer to call it so that it sounds less intensive), and one remaining currach builder so I'd heard, it was another regret not doing so. The Atlantic Drive itself is about five miles long, a few hundred feet above the sea, Clew Bay to the left and America somewhere ahead beyond the cliffs. The coast is a mass of jagged rocks, vertical cliffs and green terraces with sheep wandering about like little white dots in the far off distance. The sea was pretty crazy as it had been this morning and the wind strong as I stood staring out at the vista. Though exposed to the full brunt of any Atlantic storm, there is a certain stark attraction of places like this even though it would be hard to call it beautiful in the way that, say, Connemara is. Remote, bleak, cold and abrupt some might call this coast. With hardly a house in sight it could be termed paradise though I did stop and photograph a lovely restored 'black house' with new thatch and red painted windows and door. At the far end is Dooega where I counted seventeen currachs lying upside down alongside a house. Cutting back across the island to the east side at Cashel, joining the main road, I eventually ended up at my goal of Dooagh.

I found Charlie Fadian by asking at the shop where I was directed to his sister's house. Charlie lives next door and he came straight out when his sister told him somebody was here to see him. His shoe laces were undone as if he'd made a quick exit to discover who it was. I mentioned Darina Tully – Charlie was on her map – and he immediately welcomed me into his house. When I apologised for interrupting he said he was just reading the paper. The house , in which he'd been born, was small but homely and I sat by a fire that wasn't doing too well, just a tiny bit of smoke coming from a couple of turfs. Charlie disappeared, to return with a can of paraffin which he poured on with a startling effect.

Not knowing anything about Charlie's history as Darina had simply written his name as a man to meet, I began by asking about the Achill yawls. 'Only on the other side of the island,' he replied, 'though they only race now. They were used to fish and all sorts of other things, carry turf, sheep. They were rigged with a sort of latten sail. Oh, it's currachs and boats round here. Not many use currachs now.' He lit one of his Benson & Hedges, so I rolled a cigarette.

Charlie has an Orkney day boat with an inboard now. Thus he's not used his currach this year and now there's a lad that he allows to use it. Fishing consisted of draft-netting for salmon before the ban, and mackerel, herring and whitefish for, as he put it, a feed as there was hardly any market locally. Those that ate fish normally caught it themselves as most fishermen were part-timers, combining fishing with work on the land even if this was amongst the most unfertile in Ireland. He also has forty lobster pots down in the summer. But, although he fished throughout the seasons for whatever was in, it was the shark fishing that excited him beyond all doubt.

Charlie didn't refer to these basking sharks as sunfish though the main season seemed to be in the summer when the sun was highest.

> April to September we got 'em in Keem Bay, 28-foot sharks in an 18-foot currach. We'd net 'em, get them tired and all a'tangled and then get their head up onto the transom. We'd row 'em up to the rocks and stake 'em to the rocks and cut out the liver which could be a ton in weight. That would go to the shark factory at Purteen for turning into oil.

Shark fishing was an ancient tradition, as we've seen, on the Galway and Mayo coasts, as Young had commented upon. Hely Dutton, in his *Statistical Survey of County Galway*, estimated that one shark was worth £45 and part-time fishermen generated over £5,000 of income from their livers. Another writer, Hardiman, in 1820 suggested that 'Next to the herring fishery, that of the sunfish or basking-shark, beginning in March and ending in June, is the most important, and, if cultivated with sufficient industry and skill, would prove highly valuable.' Wallop Brabazon, in his *The Deep Sea and Coast Fisheries of Ireland*, published in 1848, assigns a whole chapter in his book to sun fishing and, though he says that it 'is very little worked at present' suggests that the Sun Fish bank which lies about 100 miles west of Clew Bay, about a day's sail from land, has 'Fish of a very large kind of shark – they are of a light colour, like a dog-fish, with the same rough skin, and have measured nine yards in length and nearly four yards in breadth as they lie on the shore – they are found in great numbers ...' However, evidence shows that the Bank is much nearer, being some twelve miles west of Achill and stretching from Slyne Head to Erris Head and which was rich in herring, for long-lining and for basking sharks.

Shark fishing had recommenced, after years of stagnation, in 1946 when Joe Sweeney took over running a salmon fishery in Keem Bay because these sharks were destroying his salmon nets. At first he shot them, up to twenty a day, until he and others began netting them with manila nets that stretched as they battled within so that escape was impossible and the shark tired. The net was anchored close to where the sharks came inshore and thus swam into its clutches. Once those waiting onshore saw this, the currach would be launched and rowed alongside the desperate victim so that a lance could be thrown to cut his spinal cord just behind the dorsal fin. Miss first time and the shark can roll, upsetting currach and those within. Sometimes it took ten or more throws and on one or two occasions the currach was capsized, the crew having to swim ashore.

Currach design changed slightly from the typical North Mayo coast currach used from Blacksod Bay, the Inishea Islands and along the north coast as far as Sligo Bay. Here three-, four- and five-man currachs were in use for fishing but when Connemara lobster fishers arrived in their three-man heavier currachs, the Achill men adopted these which gave them increased stability even though slower and less reliable in roughs seas.

Charlie and I jumped into my van as he was keen to show me a few sites before the light faded. We headed west on his instructions, up the hill and into nothing, with me wondering where he was taking me. Had I missed the turning I thought. Until, that is, a perfect beach came suddenly into view below us. This was Keem Bay, as far west as you could drive on the island, and it was here that many of the Dooagh folk fished for sharks. We drove down the steep road, the beach cleared of any sun seekers at this time of day though it was easy to see what a perfect spot this would be for swimming and snorkelling. If it hadn't been so cold I might have thought of returning later to sleep here and swim in the morning. The sea was a brilliant turquoise colour, so clear and the beach of pure white sand, as perfect as any Pacific paradise. Charlie pointed out the little house they'd sleep in at night whilst waiting for the

Shark fishing at Keem Bay, Achill Island.

sharks to entangle themselves. The holiday trade, he added when I asked, would be dead in a couple of weeks and the islanders would be left in their peace. The only trouble with this was that there was little to earn from which is why many left during the winter in search of other work. Charlie himself had gone to London to work on more than one occasion.

We drove back along the coast road, the sun dropping below the hill tops, leaving us in shade. Then to Purteen where Sweeney's oil factory was up to the last Achill shark being caught in 1984. Upwards of a dozen currachs lay upside down alongside the harbour with a few boats moored alongside. Lastly he showed me his currach in 'The Pens', as they call it, in Dooagh, where some half dozen boats were tied upside down with blue rope fixed to heavy stones either side, with little pieces of scrap wood between rope and skin of the currach to protect the fabric of the skin. Charlie's had 'KEEM BAY WT242P painted in shaky white capitals on each bow. He asked me whether I wanted to buy it, an innocent look as he suggested it was worth €1,000. 'I'm getting too old for it now,' he smiled, 'needs a patch at the back where she leaks a little. Take her back to England.'

I might have done if I could have got it in the van and I had €1000 to spare though I was sure he'd have taken a lot less for it if I'd pressed him. It had been built by somebody who had lived just up the road before he had died a few years earlier. Both those Achill boatbuilders mentioned earlier are, I believe, still building currachs. I wasn't keen on the fibreglass but presumed that it could be removed. I imagined the look on my friend Simon Cooper's face if I had returned with it upon the roof. Simon has built a couple of currachs himself, though nothing like this one.

It was dark by the time we returned to Charlie's house. He invited me in again though I thought I'd better go in search of somewhere to sleep. I'd seen a campsite and was desperate for something to eat and a shower. He must rank amongst one of the most endearing folk

I met during this trip, though, as I've said before, everyone I met was of a similar ilk. I guess it was the way I'd interrupted his evening in front of a lovely warm fire yet he insisted we go for a tour. That and his throaty endearing laugh.

I did go to the campsite at Keel, a couple of miles back along the road, where I was charged €17 for the night and on top of that had to pay another €1 for a shower token. I was too tired to argue but believed it way too expensive. After all it wasn't much more than a field by the sea with some facilities. I'd only stopped there for the shower though I assume that they have to give out tokens otherwise folk would stop outside and walk in for a shower. I know I would. Still, having cooked some more pasta, I decided the shower could wait till the morning and fell asleep with the wind on a slow increase and rain threatening once again.

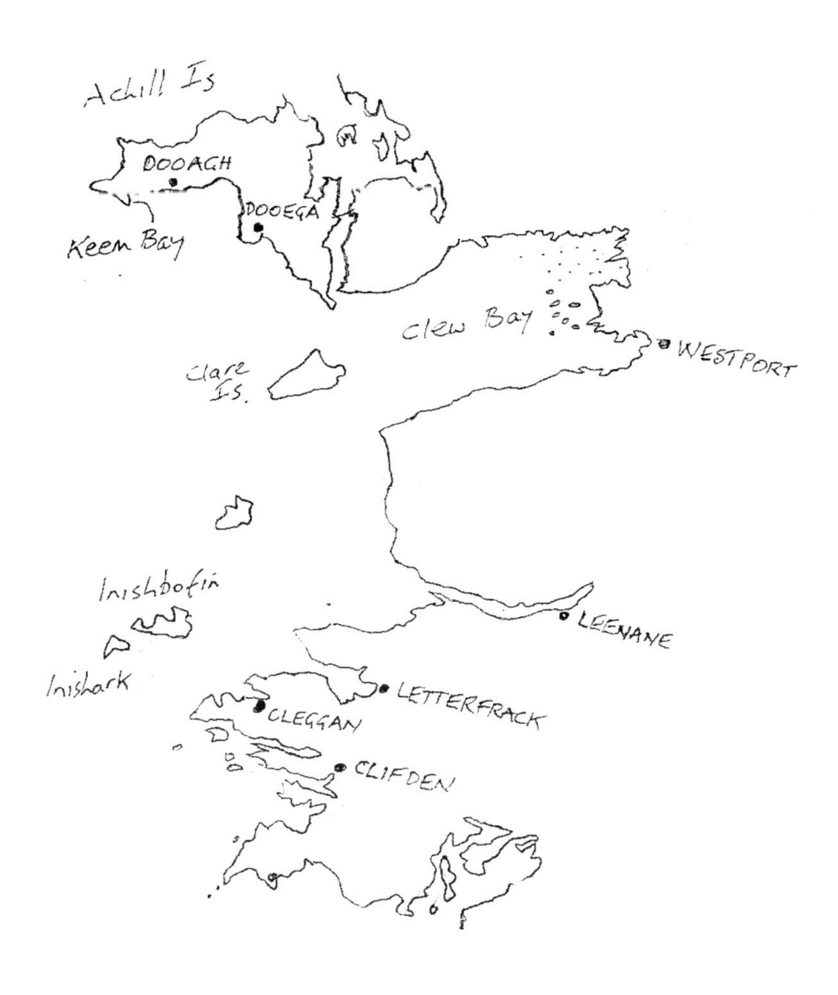

DAY FIFTEEN

The shower was cold. After a wakeful night with the Atlantic wind tearing in over the low dunes of the beach and buffeting the van around, the shock of having to have a cold shower was a bit much. I complained to the management who were apologetic and gave me a refund of €3, though I should have demanded more seeing the only reason I called in was to have a shower. A hot one I presumed. Heading off Achill, I spotted an Internet Café above a bookshop. I called in to see if there were any interesting messages as I'd not checked since leaving home. Calling in the nearby supermarket I was slightly surprised to hear two of the assistants there speaking Polish.

We stopped briefly at Ballycroy and almost detoured to the island of Inishbiggle where I'd seen a festival advertised. I was intrigued to know what sort of festival was being held there and I'd also heard that there was a cable car connecting the island to the mainland, much like the one at Dursey. However, I later discovered that, although there had been a plan to build such a structure back in the late 1990s, this was finally abandoned in December 2005 for several reasons: lack of finance, lack of a partner to build and operate it, the recent provision of new piers and, finally, the fact that the island's population had declined from eighty odd when the plan was first put forward over thirty years ago down to twenty-five in 2005. Thus islanders must still cross over by boat to Ballycroy.

Ballycroy and the area around it is considered to be one of the most unspoilt and scenic landscapes in County Mayo. To me it seemed to be merely a mixture of peat bogs and sheep. In the days when there were no roads, the sea was the only trade route to other parts of Ireland and the rest of Europe. Blacksod Bay was a place of refuge though pirates roamed and plundered merchant ships.

One local chieftain was Grace O'Malley (Gráinne Mhaoil) who was born into a sixteenth-century seafaring family whose motto was 'O'Malley Invincible on land and sea'. She displayed maritime skills and a daring for adventure and was well able to extract a living from the sea. She commanded a fleet of versatile sea-going galleys and large currachs, and traded with Europe on several occasions. For those entering her so-called territorial waters, she charged a toll and often pirated and robbed unsuspecting ships. She was said to be extremely bold and a brave, war-like chief, like no Viking ever had been. Caesar Otway, in 1840, referred to her as the 'heroine of the west'. Much of her strength came from two marriages, first to the O'Flaherty clan, locally feared, and after his death to Sir Richard Burke. She certainly had a dynamic life, had several places of abode including castles on Clare Island and on the shores of Clew Bay, was imprisoned in Limerick, then Dublin, before being allowed to sail to London to petition Queen Elizabeth to allow her to attack ships of Her Majesty's enemies. Once successful in her petition, she continued raiding in her name willy-nilly, including the Aran Islands, survived the times of the Spanish Armada, and eventually died at about the ripe old age of seventy in around 1600. Her story illustrates just how strong maritime links were along this coast. Visiting ships were common and along with that came piracy and, of course, dirty dealings between individuals and governments.

Several years ago I came across the replica galley *Aileach* in western Scotland and this boat was built by the McDonalds of Moville (whom we shall meet at a later date). In 1991 this boat successfully sailed from Westport over to Stornoway in the Outer Hebrides to prove that such a 40-foot vessel could undertake such a voyage.

Another of the Spanish Armada ships, *La Rata Sancta Maria Encoronada*, a 35-gun, 820 ton ship with 419 men aboard, was wrecked on nearby Fahy Strand. This vessel was the unofficial flagship of Don Alonso Martinez de Leiva, the commander of the Armada's vanguard. He had decided to enter Blacksod Bay to undertake some repairs and find fresh water and he eventually anchored off Fahy. He had underestimated the force of the tide and the ship soon dragged onto the Strand and became fast. She was abandoned and the crew brought ashore and the ship set alight by her crew before Grace O'Malley and her followers could reach it. The crew then marched 25 miles to join another Armada vessel, the *Duquesa Santa Ana*, which was anchored at Elly Bay (how did they know?). Both complements sailed off aboard her only to be wrecked off Donegal two days later. Their tale continues with both crews coming ashore safely and making their way to Killibegs where they found the damaged galleas *Girona* under repair. A month later 1,300 men sailed aboard this small vessel towards neutral Scotland, a safer bet than Spain in such an overloaded and unseaworthy vessel, Don Alonso reckoned. Yet again, for the third time, the *Girona* was wrecked close to Giant's Causeway in Antrim where all but a handful of the men perished, including Don Alonso himself. A sad story indeed.

Northwards, the road was unexciting and eventually we reached Belmullet. However it was festival day and the main road was closed due to the presence of a huge market. I later learnt that this was it was patron saint St Dervla's Day which accounted for the market and possibly every car from several hundred square miles around being parked up. The Garda were blocking the road and I followed their diversion, following the car in front, but once he had parked up I had to find my own way out the other side. It was busy here for sure. Though once part of the mainland, the Mullet Peninsula is now an island, thanks to our friend Nimmo who built a short ship canal across the isthmus, thus directly connecting Broad Haven with Blacksod Bay, the former being noted as a 'fine harbour' by Marmion. Nimmo had also built the road I'd travelled along from Achill though presumably the route is slightly altered since.

Once across the canal – a road bridge prevents any boat taller than about ten feet from sailing through – we were upon the Mullet Peninsula, a very flat land with fantastic beaches of glorious white sand, fringed one side with clear water and the other with sand-dunes. On the western seaboard, the landscape is one of low, flat, windswept Machair: plains of sand, often flooded in winter, and again backed by sand-dunes. Offshore, the two Inishkea islands, North and South, lie to the south-west. It was from here, remember, that nine fishermen were drowned in the unexpected 1927 gale when their currachs were overturned by the ferocity of the sea. Today the two islands remain uninhabited though they are renowned for two facts – firstly for their collecting of seabirds that led to a huge quantity of feathers being sold and, secondly, that their whiskey was said to be one of the best around though this was accounted by the fact there was never a Revenue officer about according to William Maxwell in his *Wild Sports of the West*, published in 1832.

We drove through Binghamstown, a town built in 1796 by Major Denis Bingham, the local landlord who had his estate nearby. He had built a castle at Elly Bay the year before completing his town. When the road from Erris arrived in 1824, another family of wealthy landlords, the Carters, built Belmullet as a rival settlement and which later grew from having a larger and more popular cattle market. Sensing he was losing out, Bingham tried to prevent his townsfolk from attending that fair by building a 'great gate' blocking the road north so that anyone taking his cattle out had to pay a toll. His policy failed and by the end of the nineteenth century his 'town', which was little more than a village by then, gradually fell into disuse though nearby Saleen harbour continued to be used by emigrant ships carrying some of the local population away to North America. Today's Binghamstown, now called *An Geata Mór*, was just a cluster of new houses along the roadside and around the cross-roads. Not a lot else though I gather there are plenty of building sites for sale. Elly Bay lies a few miles south, where we stopped for the dog to run on the beach. The remains of Bingham's castle lie somewhere along the north of the beach though these remains are little more than grass-covered foundations for a portion of it was deliberately pulled down in 1929, perhaps because what remained then was a reminder, after 1922, of English colonisation. I thought about that Spanish ship anchored in the bay in 1588 and wondered what the locals would have made of it.

At Aghleam, near the south of the peninsula, we stopped at the recently created Heritage Centre where the curator was more than helpful in directing me to various records of coastal activity in the these parts. Before entering I'd been pleased to see an old wooden open boat outside the museum which, though it looked worse for wear, had undoubtedly to be a salmon boat, judging from its after end platform. Once inside, and reading through the files the curator busied herself kindly extracting for me, a group of local workmen came into the room which doubled up as a café and proceeded to order their breakfast, their conversation being all in their native Irish.

The Arranmore Whaling Company set up the Inishkea Whaling Station at Rusheen, a tiny tidal island east of Inishkea South in 1907. This company, Norwegian-owned, built a stage, slipway, and jetty of large baulks of timber, fitted steam winches, sheds with boilers and a grinding shed to grind up meat and bone into manure and cattle food, oil storage facilities, a cooperage and an administration building to oversee the operation. The whaling steamer, the *Erling*, skippered by Captain Bruum, caught whales and sold them exclusively to the Company. However, the enterprise was never successful as whales could only be slipped two hours out of every twenty-four. Added to that were labour problems due to the inaccessibility of the island. Only seventy whales were caught and processed in the first year. When the Whale Fisheries Act came into force in 1909, catches were licensed. Under this legislation whales could only be caught between April and October, the whalers were prevented from operating less than three miles from the low water mark and each vessel had to display a distinct mark: a black harpoon on a white rectangular background. They also had too keep one mile away from any fishing boat or anchored craft. It is said that between twenty-six and forty locals took up work though these people demanded higher wages during the lobster season when they could earn £52 between two men in a currach. The following year the Blacksod Whaling Company got a licence after it was set up by Bruum when he left Inishkea, the latter closing in 1914. Blacksod faired much better due, largely, to its position though it wasn't without its share of early problems when influential locals feared foul smells and damage to the local mussel and oyster beds. The site was taken over in 1914 by the Admiralty who used it as a petrol base until the war ended. Afterwards the Norwegians continued whaling and, at its peak, 125 whales were landed in 1920.

Whales were towed in after killing and moored to a buoy before being dragged up the slipway by means of a steel wire attached to its tail. The flenser then stripped away the blubber blanket which was cut up into blocks and boiled. Three successive boilings in eight hours, with the oil run off each time, extracted all the oil possible. Meanwhile the carcass was gutted and the meat removed. This was also boiled and the residue, along with the bones, ground up to a powder. Sperm whales were boiled separately as their oil was more valuable.

Three years later though Blacksod also closed, after a disastrous fire swept through most of its buildings, a fire thought to have been started by three locals who had been refused work there though this was never proved. The Arranmore Whaling Co., based of course on the island of Aranmore off the west coast of Donegal, finally wound up in 1914. In total 295 whales were processed in Blacksod between 1910 and 1914.

Our final call was at Blacksod lighthouse though it was closed. It is situated right in the south of the peninsula, and was first illuminated in 1866. It was here that the second longest serving lighthouse keeper, Mr Edward Sweeney, came in 1933 along with wife Maureen who ran the local post office and his mother Ma Sweeney, as she was called. Edward, or rather Ted as he was known as, had a sort of round the clock meteorological station in his back garden which consisted of 'an ingenious method of strategically placed pots, jam jars, weathervanes and an intuition gleaned from years of experience', according to Richard Taylor in *The Lighthouses of Ireland.* On 4 June 1944 he, aided by his two local female assistants, placed his usual hourly weather reports to the Met. Office at Dunstable by phone, informing them that a front was coming in and that he had recorded winds of force six. Meanwhile back at Allied Headquarters, as the final plans were laid for the invasion of Normandy, chief forecaster Group Captain J. Stagg was having doubts about the weather. Once he heard Ted Sweeney's report and had asked that Sweeney double-checked, Operation Overlord was delayed by twenty-four hours until 6 June. Ted Sweeney was right, of course, and if the invasion had gone ahead on the 5 June, the seaborne fleets would have had to cope with force seven winds and heavy rain which would, in all probability, have caused the operation to fail. It's strange now to think that a couple of upside down jam jars had perhaps altered the whole course of history in Europe. Incidentally, some 12 miles west of Blacksod is Blackrock lighthouse which was built before Blacksod even though George Halpin advised the building of the latter. Eagle Island, off the north-west of the peninsula, was the first light off this coast, first illuminated in 1835.

Particularly high-quality red granite was quarried here and brought down by tram to a pier at Blacksod and shipped away. The narrow-gauge tramway, first built in 1889, operated partly by gravity and partly by a winch on the shoulder of a hill between quarry and pier. Operations ceased in 1910 when the line was relocated to Pickle Point, Belmullet. The harbour today though was home to a few currachs and a couple of other boats. At Fallmore, with its fine views over towards Achill Island, I found a most interesting currach with a flimsy wooden cabin built at its fore end.

With a long drive ahead north, we didn't linger. I had intended to drive up to Glenlara to view a lovely natural boat landing in the rock but I missed the turning. So it was back to Belmullet where the last vestiges of the market were still at it. Richard Taylor, in the days when he worked as a keeper at Blacksod, reckoned that the market here was the best in all of Ireland and that you could get a drink here at any time of the day or night. I bet there would be some hefty celebrating tonight, I thought, as I was once again diverted down the Shore Road and around a housing estate to reach the main road east.

At Ballina I should have gone to Killala to view the harbour with its small fleet of fishing boats in what is described as a wonderful place. The French invasion of 1798 landed hereabouts at nearby Kilcummin Pier. They were under General Humbert and, combining with Irish forces, took control of parts of the countryside until they were pushed back and eventually defeated a month later, again at Killala where some 500 people were massacred by the English troops. Today 1798 is known as the 'Year of the French'. Horse racing on nearby Lacken Strand is said to make it worth the effort of visiting. But it wasn't to be and we crossed the bridge over the river Moy, which is said to be the second best salmon river in all Ireland, only bettered by the Bann.

Killala was once the main port of this part of the north Mayo coast until it was outdone by Ballina which itself became a considerable port. Exports, mainly to Britain, were bacon,

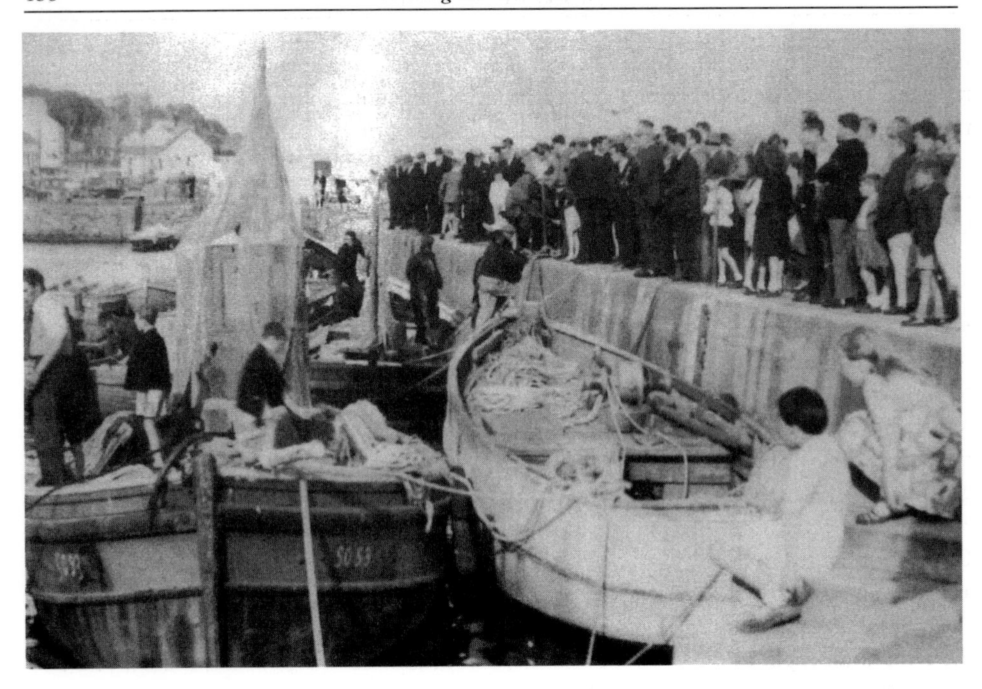

Boats at Killibegs.

Curing mackerel on Kelly's Quay, Killibegs *c.*1890.

pork, butter, salmon, flour, meal, wheat, barley and oats which suggests a healthy farming industry. Likewise imports, mostly from Britain again, were tea, coffee, sugar, tobacco, coal, iron, salt and general manufactured goods, these again according to Marmion. Why coal and iron? Poor quality coal had been mined for 400 years up to 1990 at the Arigna colliery across in County Sligo and an ironworks established there in 1788 by three brothers of the name O'Reilly, according to Samuel Lewis.

We followed the narrow coastal road for some time around Dromere West simply to get a few photographs of the superb line of surf fringing the shore before quickly arriving at Sligo. Having been on narrow roads for days now, the dual carriageway suddenly became frightening and, as abruptly as we'd arrived, we'd left the town, once famous for its salmon fishery. In 1851 this area employed 475 fishing boats with a crew complement of 2724 though this had reduced to 216 vessels and 1269 crew two years later which proved the area had a substantial, if not fickle, fishing industry. Again the road north is fast and well surfaced and took us quickly around Bundoran and through Ballyshannon, the birthplace of that fantastic blues/rock guitarist Rory Gallagher whose music I had listened to since my school days. Although Cork is considered to be his home town by many, he had been born here in the local hospital and moved to Cork with his parents at the tender age of eight.

Donegal was pleasant and reminded me of a Lake District town. I parked up alongside the river and sought the only bookshop in town though found nothing of much interest. Scared of getting a parking ticket as I'd not paid, I dashed back after the disappointment of the bookshop – I'd expected to find something relevant to the coast – and travelled on, heading west for perhaps the final time, to Killibegs. The harbour, the home of Ireland's largest pelagic fleet of fishing boats, was full of these vessels as most seemed not to be fishing until the mackerel fishery began in September. A number of twin-rig trawlers lined the harbour as well though this number had declined over the last year. Although Killibegs remains the premier fishing port in terms of tonnage and value of fish landed (87,000t, €33 million in 2007), whitefish activity was reducing so that the port was increasingly reliant upon the pelagic sector. Sitting in the van, avoiding the rain that had come on, I phoned Joachim Doogan, one of Joe Teesdale's contacts, but he was on his way out. When I recounted my travels, he suggested going to see James McLeod in St Catherine's Street, one of the pioneering fishermen of Killibegs and one of the earliest to use an echosounder and radio according to Joachim. I found St Catherine Street easily and knocked on the doors of every house along it which amounted to eight doors. No one answered at all. Could they all be out I wondered?

Disheartened, we drove west towards Teelin where I already knew that the first Zulu-type fishing boat had been introduced into the Irish fleet. Coming up the hill from Kilcar I was met by a woman, struggling with several bags of shopping, and her two children who seemed pretty exhausted, all hitch-hiking from the middle of the road in true Irish fashion. I offered them a lift and, as it was, they only needed to travel another mile or so to where they were staying. Fabienne, as I discovered her name, from south-east France, was staying in an idyllic thatched cottage, outside of which was a sign telling passers-by that this was 'Cara's Hostel'. She offered me a glass of wine which I readily accepted and before long I was happily ensconced in their kitchen, in front of a roaring stove, eating tea and supping the wine, to which I contributed I hasten to add for seldom do I travel without a bottle or two of wine, talking to Fabienne and a Frenchman named Matthew. Then a man came in, elderly and short, and wearing a woolly hat, and sat down in front of the fire. He didn't say much to start with though he seemed to have a perpetual grin on his weather-beaten face. Fabienne was teasing him and his eyes had a warmth matching the fire. This was Cara, I discovered, who owned the place and who had lived in the house with his mother until she had died and

Steamboat Pier at Killibegs, 1907.

Scrubbing the hull of fishing boats at Killibegs, 1958.

now lived in another bungalow on land just above the cottage. During the season he rents out beds, not rooms mind, at €7 a night and I was surprised to discover when he showed me around that, in the front room of the cottage, there were five beds whilst in another room, which can only be described as a large shed, he had another four double beds and two singles all squashed in. How visitors took to the cosy and unisex sleeping arrangements I wasn't sure. Matthew was sleeping in the front room, Fabienne and her family in the tiniest of rooms out the back which was just able to hold one double bed in which the three of them slept. I didn't ask how much they paid. When another German girl arrived, she chose the shed down the way over sharing with the Frenchman whose passion, I discovered, was for river fishing. It all seemed chaotically Irish in the nicest of ways and a bloody good money spinner though equally a great deal for the travellers.

Outside, the view was worth a million pounds, a superb perspective over Kilcar Harbour and across the expanse of Donegal Bay to the distant Sligo coast. Inishmurray was just visible, a small island off North Sligo that, according to Marmion, had one hundred inhabitants, all of whom 'exist by fishing'. As darkness fell through a haze of too much wine the view gradually faded into obscurity. We chatted well into the night, Cara, Fabienne and I, though with the night silent and sleeping, I refrained the offer of a €7 bed and retired to join the dog in the van parked alongside the cottage.

DAY SIXTEEN

The views the following morning were equally exquisite and I drank coffee with Fabienne and her entourage whilst enjoying every bit of the panorama. Weatherwise the day was another of those that begins with good intentions, sun avoiding skidding clouds, though the threat of later drizzle was always real. We sat on cracked and crazed plastic chairs outside the cottage, with Dog sniffing around in the long grass, waiting for the occasional car passing along the road for him to bark at. The Frenchman, Matthew, appeared with his rod, off in search of a trout in the small stream above Kilcar. I jokingly asked if he had a licence to fish and he looked at me blankly, as if he seriously had never heard of such a thing. He and Fabienne muttered something in French. Then her kids awoke, moody girl just reaching puberty and blonde haired boy, all sporty and keen to go surfing. I asked whether Cara was up. 'No,' replied Fabienne, 'he never surfaces before eleven. You should interview him.'

The same thoughts had occurred to me for, although he'd spoken about his life the previous evening, I was either too slow to take notes or affected by the alcohol to remember much he had said later on. However I needed to continue so, instead of forgoing an opportunity to question someone born and bred by the sea, I decided to drive down to Teelin, where I'd been heading the previous evening, and return here later to talk to Cara when he'd risen from his slumbers. Fabienne, after much discussion, was off to Killibegs to hire a car to take her children off for the day so I said my farewells and left.

Teelin lies on the far side of the harbour, under the mass of Slieve League where impressive cliffs plunge down into the sea from a great height, the highest in Europe at almost 2,000 feet. I didn't make the extra effort to have a look, however, even if Fabienne had suggested it and she seemed to know the area pretty well after just a week staying with Cara. The village, if you can call it that, was strung out along the road that bordered the harbour, winding around the houses. The odd boat was moored alongside various rickety wooden jetties. At the far end, where the road ends, there's a substantial pier with the Gallagher Brothers' fish warehouse, the same company name I'd seen in Killibegs. One of the firm's employees was on the harbour and seemed reluctant to talk, and when he did it was in monosyllables.

'We just marinate herring here.'

'When does the herring come in?' I asked.

'Beginning October I guess.'

'Do you do anything else with it?'

'Bit of canning in Killibegs.'

'Do they can all year?'

'No, not much over the last couple of years. A bit maybe.'

'What happens when there's no herring?'

'Not much, bit of cleaning up and that.'

Then another fellow comes along and rolls a Golden Virginia fag.

'Good weather!' he imparts.

'That your boat?' I ask him, pointing at the blue and white boat alongside the pier.

'For sure.'

Cara on the donkey with his mother and father on left of photo. (Cara Cuinnghim).

Herring man left us at that point with a nod.

'You do trips out in that?'

'For sure,' blowing smoke in rings.

'Where do you go, take them?'

'To the cliffs, fishing.'

I wasn't getting far here though I was intrigued to know how busy he was because there wasn't another soul in sight. Herring man was no doubt cleaning up. I thought I'd try once more.

'How many times a day do you go out?'

'Depends.'

'On what?'

'How many folk come.'

'How many today?'

'Ah, that'll be telling.'

I gave up. Walking back towards the van I saw some leaflets on the side of a small hut-like building by the slipway. I looked like one of those little cubicles at motorway toll booths. I took a leaflet. The boat was the *Nuala Star* and ran sightseeing trips to the Bunglas Cliffs below Slieve League, diving, whale and dolphin watching, and angling trips. At the bottom, on how to find them, it read '5 km to Teelin Pier and talk to Paddy'. Well, presumably I had and it hadn't got me very far.

Then suddenly three cars sped down the road and emptied its load of ten passengers. Paddy walked towards the boat, past me.

'Ah, that's the ten o'clock crowd,' he says. I look at the clock on my mobile. It was 10.45.

'They sleep in late,' Paddy says and climbed aboard before ushering the passengers on, starts the engine and off they went.

By the harbour were the remains of an old boat, a clinker-built motor boat with the stern-tube still in place, although not much else was left of the boat itself. A few sad frames and forlorn planks. Above on the hill were the ruins of a large stone building. I wondered whether it was some curing station though it seemed in an odd place. Later I discovered it was the remains of a coastguard station built prior to 1813. When it was fully operational there were five men employed whose families lived in the compound. In 1920, the IRA attacked the station and killed George Kennington. The Free State Army arrested a number of local people and in retaliation the IRA burned it down.

Teelin was at one time, around 1889, Ireland's foremost cod fishing port. That's hard to believe now. The pier was built between 1881–1883 and cost £3,000. The money came from the House of Lords at the behest of Lord Bradford who was a regular visitor to the area and who often stayed at the Glencolmcille Hotel in Carrick, just up the road. I stopped at Carrick on the way back to collect a bit of breakfast and discovered really good croissants which I bought.

Returning to the little cottage, Fabienne was still dithering about whether to hire a car or buy one. Cara was still asleep. Seems he had put the word out for her and somebody had phoned to say he'd a car for sale for a few hundred pounds. It didn't sound like it was anything she'd be able to drive back to France in. She made us more coffee, again sitting outside for the sun was still avoiding the scudding clouds and warmly shining. Soon Cara arrived and the three of us munched on the croissants, though Cara with a degree of hesitation, his perpetual grin not being lost for the occasion. Thus I got him talking about his life once again, perhaps in more detail than the previous night.

His full name, he assured me, was Cara Cuinnghim. He'd moved up to the cottage in the 1930s with his mother and father. I never did discover his age but he must have been over seventy though he didn't look it and was as fit as a fiddle. He'd lived a life between sea and land throughout and, and though he didn't speak much of his father, I presumed that's where he learned the ropes from. I asked first about the types of fishing.

'My brother left school at fourteen but I left earlier. He was two years older than me. We went out with Daddy. Four men in a draft boat for salmon in Teelin Bay. We beat the water with a stick, called it 'magapota', the stick. A bit of 'dullin' for mackerel and long-lines in the early Spring.'

Teelin.

I asked what 'dullin' was.

'Making the ring around the mackerel.' He ate another mouthful of the croissant that looked it might last him all day. 'Started drifting for salmon in about 1950. We 'ad a yawl by then, belonged to Paddy Boyle, an uncle of Daddy's. Also a 17-foot punt.'

'What was the yawl like?'

'One of them northern types, pointed, four oars and we'd sail out to the lines.'

I presumed a Greencastle or Moville yawl, the type I was keen to learn more of the further north we travelled.

'Used the yawl for the 'erring too. Brother caught pollack. Ever had a Rusty Mackerel?'

'No, what's that.' Fabienne had mentioned a pub around here of that name.

'Salted herring, head and tail on, in a barrel and left for seven days before being packed in wooden boxes.' It sounded salty but I'd eaten far saltier herring.

'Where did you fish the herring?' I'm always interested in herring fishing.

'Out in the Bay, set a net 200 yards long, anchored each end in the entrance. You could see the headlights of cars on the cliffs at night. Courting couples up there. During the day we'd dig the spuds, cut corn, whatever, whilst watching for the herring. Then we'd sell it to Nolan's in Killibegs. Got some lobsters too.'

I turned the conversation over to home life.

'I milked the cattle and Mum made butter. She put a design on it so we had to cut it straight. We sold some. Had sheep in the fields. Bought flour to bake bread. I remember the flours: "Pride of the West", "Millacrats".' He paused whilst he recalled the third.

'Yes, "White Heather". Sometimes bought "Brewster Loaf", a white soda bread. We never ate brown bread like now. Just white. Brown's only been around seventeen or eighteen years. Then the doctor told us to eat brown bread.'

'Did you feel better for it?'

'I feel all right.'

What about growing things?'

'Potatoes, onions, cabbage, turnip. Hay we cut by hand. We'd no machinery see. Eggs from the hens. Had a donkey in the 1940s to carry things. We'd barter for bacon. Dear bacon and scrap bacon. There was a choice.'

A car arrived and another friendly face joined us. This was Billy Boyle who sometimes fished and sometimes worked in the processing factory during the winter season.

'Got fifty sheep too,' he smiled. 'Cara here's the local hustler. Did he tell you that? Sings well too. During the festival he'll be out in the pub every night singing to six or seven in the morning.'

'He was singing the other night in the pub till four in the morning,' added Fabienne in her French sing-song sort of voice.

Cara looked at her, his grin fast spreading into a wide smile as he laughed. I wasn't sure whether something was going on between these two but they obviously liked each other and anyway I didn't really care. He looked over at Billy.

'Billy here was the last man I fished with. That was five years ago. Since then he's salmon fished, haven't you Billy? Fished the salmon since a kid. Now he's fifty odd and can't.'

I was hoping we'd get round to the ban on the salmon.

'I remember being in the boat one week without any salmon,' Cara offered. 'Several "dulls" then shifted to another place after that week and caught ninety-three in one dull. Got one and six per fish.'

'Once got 139 in one,' countered Billy, 'though one got away!'

'They are offering €10,000 in compensation. That's nothing to what we could get years ago.' Billy seemed angry, quite rightly, with the government not issuing licences.

'Not only that but a few people in isolated spots are still fishing. Where the TD wants votes there have been exceptions.'

This was the first I'd heard about this, that some were allowed licences, though wasn't sure whether it was true.

'Them politicians are bent,' he continued, 'Irish politics is full of corruption, all those in power.' Whereas I couldn't agree more I was still doubtful. All politicians, to some extent, are corrupt as British politics had proved over the years. Sleaze, cash for questions, not declaring donations, employing family as researchers, various sexual activities, you name it and they are up to it.

'So what about your family, Cara?' I asked.

'Mum died at ninety-four. Never sick in her life. I loved her and never married. But she didn't keep me back, I didn't want to marry. No fruit on the tree. If I was married now I wouldn't be running a hostel.' He laughed again and his deeply etched face beneath his woolly hat, a wonderful work of art in itself, sparkled with life. Fabienne was teasing him about him having had more than his fair share of conquests over women.

'Mum died in 1986 when we'd nearly finished the house. Everyone said "move in" to the new home but I wanted to stay where Mum had lived. Stayed a week and then moved in my own time. My brother came a couple of days after she died, he was married and lived in Belfast. He has two daughters, my two nieces, who come to stay with me in the house most years. Brother had a heart attack and lived for five years afterwards.'

'How long you been renting out?'

'Started 1990, I think. Gives me something to do, some income now that I'm not fishing or on the land.'

You get the impression with Cara that he has lived a near idyllic life, a lifestyle we'd all strive for given the right conditions. These conditions exist on this remote and largely ignored coast, where beauty surrounds you at every turn, where the constraints of society are far flung. His life, as he portrays it, was not one of just survival, it was more than that though, I'm sure there were plenty of hardships. How many times have I spoken to working people of a similar age, especially fishermen, who wax lyrical about how it was 'back then' even if they survived through danger, poverty and little comfort. It suits us today to largely ignore those views by declaring that the old times are best gone, they didn't have what we do today. But exactly what do we have today other than greed, crime and a lack of understanding of our surroundings? Ipods and wide-screen TVs. Debt and constant fear from so-called terror. Manipulation and control from governments, as much idle money-based pleasure as you need and a blindness to all the wrongs in society.

I was interrupted in my thoughts by another arrival in a van with 'AlgAran' written on the side. Cara's neighbour Michael McClusky got out and we were introduced. Seems he's now a partner in organic and wild seaweed products which was what AlgAran was. Funnily enough I'd seen their products in the Aran Islands, and told him so.

'Yea, we produce some out there. We export to Germany, Italy, Spain and hopefully France soon. My partner is Italian and we've one worker. I was foreman on Killibegs Pier before this. Now I collect seaweed, process it – we've a place on the upper road – and sell it.'

I asked about the seaweed itself.

'There's 800 different types of seaweed, you know, but we only use 30 types and all of it comes from the west coast here.'

800 different types! I hadn't realised there were so many. Michael gave me one of his brochures which detailed those products available as well as some information on the seaweeds themselves, some nutritional stuff and some recipes. Dulse, or dillisk, was there as was Atlantic Spirulina but I'd never heard of Calcium Seaweed which is the best source of calcium in nature. I had another croissant and persuaded Fabienne to make some more coffee. Cara was

busily trying to sell her his mate's car.

'Lovely car,' he was telling her, 'got doors and wheels,' with that now familiar grin right across his face. I wondered whether he slept in his woolly hat.

I could have sat there for days and was really reluctant to leave but I knew I must. I wanted to go to the Maritime and Heritage Centre in Killibegs which I'd found the previous evening but was closed. Fabienne decided to rent a car so asked for a lift in. She had to get the bus to Donegal as that seemed the nearest place to hire a car. She wasn't persuaded by Cara's description of the car with doors and wheels. And so we did leave, saying fond farewells though I heard afterwards that Cara was sad I'd not paid €7. Fabienne had laid into him because I'd only slept outside. However, reading through the lines, I guess he thought I'd not talked to him enough. I was sure I had though I'm positive I only scratched the surface for there must be much more to his life than he can recount in a few hours. Cara, if you read this, I hope you are satisfied!

So back to Killibegs it was where I said goodbye to Fabienne, her children having earlier departed to the beach. Rain seemed to be in the air so I doubted the beach would be much fun for long. The Killibegs Maritime and Heritage Centre was an odd place to say the least. Housed in an old carpet factory, it seemed to combine fishing with carpet-making. However, having said that, what photographs there were, were excellent as were the documentary films. It just seemed an impersonal sort of place lacking character and also appeared to have a dearth of artefacts in the fishing field.

Killibegs was a sleepy railhead in the second half of the nineteenth century. In Arthur Young's time, in the 1770s, fishing for herring occupied fifty or sixty odd boats. These were lightly built of local fir with a length of 19-21 in the keel, 7ft 4in in beam and 3ft 4in in depth. They cost £18-20 and were crewed by six men. There were two seasons: the first between the end of July and beginning of September and a winter fishery from October to early January. Young informs us that the hemp nets, brought from the Baltic, cost £3 to £3 3s each.

However competition from the Swedish and Scotch fisheries meant that the fishery didn't develop as much as it could have. Young suggested they needed to elect an Admiral to organise things as the Scots did. He gives us some useful information of the habit of importing

> Gottenburg [*sic*] herrings in quantity', paying the duty and selling abroad. 20 Swedish barrels, when re-packed, fill 25 Irish barrels, so with the duty paid on the 20, they can re-export them to the West Indies at a profit, a process he described as mischievous. There was a bounty payable of 2s 4d to export herring but taking account the duty paid, the merchant only received 11 1/2d and 'so clogged and perplexed with forms and delays, that not many attempts to claim it.

He also noted a whale fishery hereabouts, first established by Thomas Nesbit of Kilmacredan in 1759 with a 140-ton vessel.

By 1891 the Congested Districts Board was beginning to fund fishing from Killibegs though without much success. Up to 1920 it is said that there was no fishing industry as such. The Killibegs Industrial School was set up about the same time to teach general woodwork, beginners' geometry and to learn how small boats were built. Before long they were building boats and by the late 1920s a small yawl with two oars cost almost £9 and was expected to last sixty years. Thus the port developed for there was nothing like it on the west coast for protection. Scottish herring gutters arrived too to strengthen the industry.

In 1936 James McLeod started fishing with a half-decker, a boat that had been a watch boat. This was his first introduction to fishing and he soon had his first boat, *Martha Helen*, paid for with money loaned from his father. He believed there was a future for fishing and, even if things were primitive at the time, they would develop. How correct he was. Just before the 1939 war flying-dragging was introduced though he went off to war, captaining a ship for the duration.

Boatbuilding continued during the war using local timber. Scots fir was preferred inside and larch outside. Afterwards, even though wages were low, the school was busy and at some point the boatbuilding yard was taken over by the BIM. James Stafford, the designer of the BIM 50-footers worked here for several years. By the late 1960s a 'network analysis system' of 'rationalised boatbuilding techniques improving the manner in which they were built' was developed. Better techniques linked to faster times so that a boat of about 50 feet could be built within thirteen weeks. When Ireland joined the then EEC in the 1970s the government didn't understand fishing and bartered away Irish rights for agricultural gains. Priorities weren't directed at fishing, as was so in the UK. To counter this, and because there was no national organisation for fishermen, the Killibegs Fishermen's Association was formed in 1972. Change came abruptly from then on, with quick freezing and packing facilities. This meant fish could be washed and sorted in boxes, filleted by hand, then frozen overnight, graded and packed. Today it remains the main west coast fishing port with its large fleet of huge pelagic trawlers.

I wandered around looking at the fine collection of photographs, one which showed herring gutting at Kelly's Quay in the 1890s. In a back room there's all manner of carpet-making looms and tools which I ignored but I did spend some minutes in the reconstructed wheelhouse of a 1950s trawler where a short film showed scenes of pair trawling. On each trawl they came up with a really full bag.

Again I was keen to move on as usual. I'd been excited about arriving in Donegal, a place that seemed surrounded in a certain amount of mystery, though when I considered why I thought this, I had no answer for myself. Perhaps it was the remoteness and inaccessibility of the place, the fact that it is hidden away from much of the Republic of Ireland, with only a tiny strip of land connecting it. Somehow it seemed covertly sequestered away, squeezed into a corner if you must, by Northern Ireland.

Driving north then, away from Killibegs, the scenery was pleasant until Ardara. Here I saw the Heritage Centre with a strap line of 'from fleece to fashion'. Luckily it was closed. Looking at the map I realised I'd missed out visiting Glencolmcille on the western tip of the county, a place with a small quay and a very rural tradition. There's an internationally known Folk Village Museum founded by Father McDyer that advertises itself as 'reliving 18th, 19th and 20th century Ireland'. That no doubt would have been interesting, but too late now. Another regret. The coast road via Kilclooney to Clooney was closed so I had to take the inland route. Once arriving back on the coast, it was as I'd been well warned: a mass of new housing strewn about the place like some scene from a far-off planet.

At Dunglow I entered The Rosses, where Marmion had noted as having a vibrant herring fishery in the 1780s with some 400 sail boats and 1,000 small boats chasing the shoals. 23 million herring were caught off here in 1782 whilst two years later vast quantities were boiled down for oil and sold at ten pence a gallon as there were no curing facilities. Marmion continued by saying that, even though this part of the coast was teeming with herring, little or no fishing occurred in the late nineteenth century. It appeared there was no use for them.

Burtonport, my journal described as 'not a very exciting place'. Fishing mainly consisted of salmon, lobster and crab, according to an information board by the harbour which was eminently out of date with the restrictions on salmon fishing. Looking around Burtonport today it's hard to realise that this was, twenty years ago, a busy and thriving fish harbour which was one of the largest exporters of whitefish in Ireland. A few boats dotted about offshore and a couple of fishing boats lay alongside the harbour wall along with several more small day boats. A man aboard an inflatable was trying to start an outboard whilst his woman friend was

Fish curing at Ardlara.

The harbour at Bunbeg.

leaning over holding the boat to the quay, showing off a large percentage of her shapely bum. A loaded car ferry was in the process of leaving for, presumably, Leabgarrow on Aranmore Island, where incidentally the longest serving lifeboat station on the west coast is situated. Though not the first – a boat was stationed in Westport between 1857 and 1862 – between Bloody Foreland up north and Slea Head in the south, this station has run continually since 1883. Fenit's boat might have been stationed earlier, in 1879, but the service was abandoned between 1969 and 1994. There's a memorial and plaque to the eleven young men lost at sea in the shipwrecks of the vessels *Evelyn Marie* in 1975 and *Carraig Una* the following year. Two shipwrecks in consecutive years must be almost unheard of these days and must have a sour effect upon every family in such a close-knit community.

Bunbeg – Bun Beag in the Irish – I expected to be a miserable place and was pleased to discover the exact opposite was true. It was a lovely little harbour, well protected and thoroughly used if one counts the number of boats there. What I took to have originally been a four-story grain store stood alongside the quay. On the slipway was a grand assortment of wooden craft of all shapes and sizes though the majority were what would generally be termed yawls but are in fact modern descendants of the 'Drontheims', the traditional working boats of this coast. Indeed, this type of vessel was indigenous right along from Donegal to almost Belfast. Most were double-enders though some sported transom sterns. I wandered amongst them, photographing bows and sterns, profiles, constructional details and various other idiosyncrasies, in fact so much filming that a group of lads sitting nearby gave me some strange looks. There were boats with names like *Philomena*, *The Olive* and *Erin's Hope*, all of which weren't very Irish.

What I didn't know at the time of my visit was that there was still a currach builder, Jim Boyd, living and working nearby. The Bunbeg currach is a small currach, evolving to cross the waterway or inlet that Bunbeg lies upon. These currachs are small enough so that they can easily be carried on the back of one man, much as the coracle fishermen of Wales carry their coracles. The best, and most recent, source of information comes from *The Donegal Currachs* by Dónal MacPolín, an ex-teacher who lives in Moville and who has spent a lifetime studying the traditional boats of Donegal. Indeed, his first book, *The Drontheim – Forgotten Sailing Boat of the North Irish Coast* I shall refer to later.

In *The Donegal Currachs*, MacPolín notes the existence of five separate and quite distinct currachs in use in Donegal over time. The first of these is the Donegal 'paddling' currach, curach céasla in Irish, which is unique in that it is Ireland's smallest. It is 8ft in length and is characterised by the fact that it is often paddled by one man crouching in the front of the boat because it lacks thwarts (seats). Furthermore it was said to be crudely built.

The second is the Tory Island currach which was used primarily for fishing from the off-shore island though similar examples were common on the mainland opposite and the nearby Inishbofin Island. These were extraordinary boats in that they were rowed great distances for Tory Island itself lies some eight miles offshore. They were characterised by the addition of a shallow keel and rubbing strakes on the outside of the hull.

Third is the Bunbeg currach as already mentioned. Fourth in the list is the Dunfanaghy or Sheephaven currach from the waters east of Horn Head. Being one of the largest of the five types, it was renowned for its seaworthiness, though weren't they all? Finally there's the Fanad or Ros Guill currach, Ros Guill being the headland to the east of Sheephaven whilst Fanad Head lies a bit further east. This currach is basically a different version of the previous type; its differences lying in its construction. Now, not wishing to go into any fine details in these craft – any reader should consult MacPolín's fine book – I only mention them to illustrate that these small communities living on the edge of the Atlantic were accomplished sailors. In Tory Island, for example, the Congested Districts Board subsidized the building of wooden craft at the expense of the currachs, though some have survived. Thankfully, with three traditional builders of the craft still working and a resurgence in interest in these extraordinary craft, examples of each are easily to be seen nowadays.

We headed north again to Bloody Foreland, the north-west tip of Ireland. As I rounded it Tory Island was clearly visible in the fading twilight. Inland, the area was a mass of new housing, mostly bungalows, just like little boxes in a bland sort of way. It was quite depressing, and it took the flashing lighthouse on Tory Island to lift my spirits. Amongst the non-descript homes were occasion architect-designed 'superior' houses, two storeys and with hanging baskets gushing forth colour and crisp green lawns laid out in perfect contrast to the surrounding heather and rocky ground, all trying to disguise their intrusion into the landscape. I wondered whether people lived here all year round or did they spend the majority of their time in Dublin working for the pharmaceutical companies or whoever had arrived from America. Presumably so and their presence would undoubtedly be overwhelming for local traditions, if any were left. Then I noticed the abundance of yellow-backed Northern Irish number-plates on the cars which presupposed they all came from across the border. Do these people own or rent properties? Perhaps they come for the fantastic views which really are wonderful. Many of the small offshore islands are equally dotted with houses too. The tumour has spread widely!

We turned east at last, sure that we were well over half way in our journey, probably almost two-thirds. The road was beginning to get hazy under the headlights of the van. Mist. Yet the light of Tory Island was still visible through the gloom which seemed a bit weird as it seemed to descend from nowhere. The lighthouse is one of Ireland's oldest, coming on station in 1832 and was the creation of our old friend George Halpin. I drove out to Horn Head where Halpin's other light Fanad Head was visible to the east with Tory Island still bright and flashing westward. One flashed four times and the other five. Just back from Horn Head, above a white cottage, I parked up in a small lay-by. Below, as I ate my late tea, I watched as the lights below seemed to twinkle their evening message, that first sign of mist having disappeared. Headlights pierced the night in the distance and lights were switched off in the far-off houses as sleep encroached over the land. Though I tried to write up some notes, the same sleep trespassed into the van and both Dog and I soon succumbed to its persuasive powers.

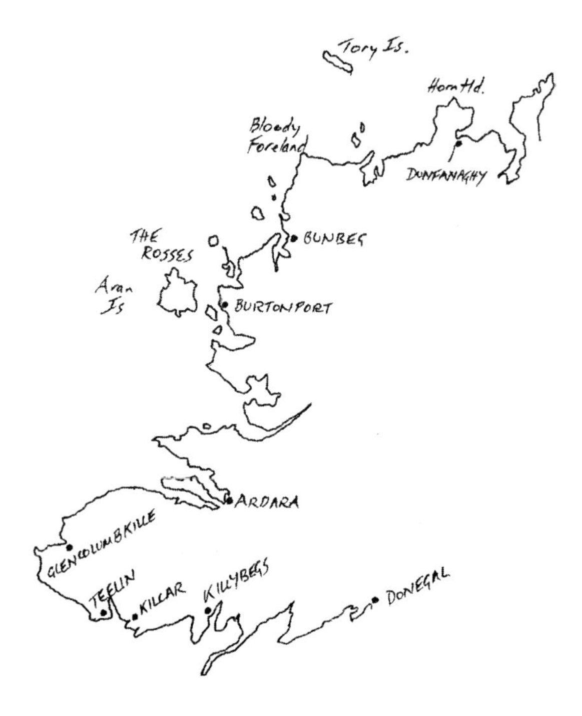

DAY SEVENTEEN

We awoke early as usual, the sun already peeking out over the distant hills of Inishowen. After a brew of coffee I decided we'd drive down to Killahoey Beach, down upon which I'd been gazing the previous evening and again observing its extent and loveliness that morning, and which was situated about a mile east of Dunfanaghy. Perhaps I'd spot an odd Dunfanaghy currach though I doubted it.

The beach, wide and quite sheltered except from northerly winds and backed by sand-dunes, was another of the Blue Flag beaches. I'd seen plenty of these during the trip, a testament to the quality of water coming in from the Atlantic. I walked along the beach which was deserted at this early hour and the dog freely chased birds and, later, sticks. At the eastern end of the beach there's a stream running into the sea, winding its way through a gap in the dunes and along the beach fringe. At certain stages of the tide a deep pool is formed several yards before the stream meets the surf though there wasn't much of a sea running today. Thus, with no one in sight anyway, and in desperate need of some revitalisation and a wash, I stripped off to my nothingness and, suitably prepared with soap, cleansed myself in the cool, peaty-brown water. Having last suffered the freezing shower in Achill, this cold entrance into the day was not quite as severe. I lay in the pool watching the soapy froth disappear seaward, getting lost in the breaking wavelets whilst enjoying the silky soft feel of the water against animate skin. Then, feeling bold and confident of no one around, I ran out into the small waves, letting the saltwater refresh and energise a tired soul. I lay there for several minutes, tingling from the cold and forcing myself to stay in. Usually I'm not good at this but this time I was, concentrating my thoughts by gazing up at the white cottage on Horn Head, just above which I'd slept the night. The headland was basked in browns, greens and purples as the sun lifted its head over the golf course to my right. Only a few houses dotted the headland, unlike the myriad of dwellings further west. But a few minutes of the icy cold was enough and, after a brief rinse in the fresh water once again, and a rub down with my towel, which I had thankfully remembered, I partially dressed before sitting down on a rock to write this. The beginnings of the sun's heat warmed my naked back. It was going to be a nice day.

Back at the van I prepared for another day. We headed in the general direction of east once again though to be begin with the road went south-east around the south of Loch Swilly. For some strange reason that I still do not know the answer to, we didn't head out to the Ros Guill peninsula nor towards Fanad Head. I'd wanted to visit the small fishing village of Downings, often known as Downies. Though there isn't much commercial fishing these days, just a few potters and more angling boats for the tourist trade, there was once a considerable herring fishery here. But we didn't go there.

Driving between Creeslough and Kilmacrenan, I came across the old railway extension that reached as far as Burtonport. With the pillars of the viaducts solely remaining as silent reminders of this pioneering era, the track follows the road (vice-versa I guess really) for several miles, through gaps hewn out of the rock by hand. The Co. Donegal narrow-gauge railway system was the largest in the British Isles and ran between Ballyshannon and Killibegs via Donegal in the south, Burtonport to the west, the Inishowen peninsula in the north and all connecting to Londonderry in the east. All 125-miles of line up, down, around and through the hills. This Burtonport stretch had opened in 1905 but by the late 1950s had passed its sell-by date and seen its last trains.

The road is high in parts and the gradient steep. I imagined the engines awkwardly puffing uphill like something out of Thomas the Tank Engine. As I think back, Ireland's history is a bit like that, harsh extremes of conditions over generations of British control, war, turmoil and famine. Then along comes the Free State, the Republic and the Common Market. The Celtic Tiger economy winds up, some things are started, some finished, factories arrive for Ireland largely. Houses appear everywhere, politicians get fat. But, with the bubble about to burst – some say it burst four years ago and that the country has survived on credit – before the railway engine gets to the top of the incline, the brow of the hill, one wonders whether there's enough energy in the old puffer to get her those last few steps to the top or whether she'll lose all momentum and slide back down again, down the way she came. Whatever does happen, and whichever way she goes, its downhill all the way. The only difference is, if she fails, she'll have another chance. Maybe.

Beyond Letterkenny there were a string of 'pavement strengthening' road signs though no pavement. Was the hard shoulder, which they called it further south, a pavement here I wondered. Again the roads were pretty rough and ready, the signposts a bit erratic which is perhaps why I missed a turning to Ros Guill. However I did manage to see a left turn a few miles short of Derry, and follow the coast of Loch Swilly up to Fahan.

Here the Lough Swilly Marina Ltd run the '406 berth marina costing 8 million euros - the largest flagship marine leisure and tourism project undertaken by private developers in Co. Donegal ...', or so the huge sign painted onto the side of a red trailer read. It went on ...

> has to date:-
> NOT been assisted by Donegal County Council or by any local Fianna Fail councillor
> NOT been promoted by the Chairperson of the Dail Committee on Tourism Deputy Cecilia Keaveney
> NOT been assisted by the Department of Communications, Marine and Natural Resources
> NOT been funded by any of the Funding Agencies established to promote inward investment and employment in this economically deprived border area.

Were they trying to get a message across I belligerently thought? I've never been a very keen supporter of marinas as I always believe they attract the wrong sort of boat to the sea. Worse still are those fancy marinas surrounded by so-called 'waterfront housing', but then again I'm biased. Here the marina was away from everything, the nearest thing being the old disused railway line on its way once to the northern reaches of Inishowen. Still the sign was a reminder of the oddities of politics for it was obvious that the powers that be were very much against coming to their aid. Presumably though, they had been given planning permission. Perhaps not. It wasn't surprising really to find the marina office tucked away in a small lock-up container. I was going to ask, but the lock-up was firmly locked up.

In the marina, though most of the boats were non-descript and plastic, I did spot a nice converted lifeboat, the *Julia Barry* and a lovely, sprucely painted, 50-footer fishing boat *Shenandoah*, SO606, the latter still having her otter boards alongside though looked too well painted to still be fishing. Alongside the old, half demolished wooden pier was the mussel dredger *Annie*, looking a bit forlorn.

Inch Island lies across from Fanad and Arthur Young wrote of the herring fishery there.

The fishing fleet at Downings.

He says the fishery ran from the middle of October up to Christmas and that 500 boats were employed there in 1775, the year before he arrived. Of these he wrote:

> The farmers and the coast inhabitants build and send them out, and either fish on their own account, or let them; but the latter most common. Five men take a boat, each man half a share, each net half and the boat a whole one. A boat costs 10l. on an average, each has six stand of nets at 2l. In a middling year each boat will take 6000 herrings a night, during the season, six times a week, the price on an average 4s 2d a 1000 from the water. Home consumption takes the most, and the shipping which lies here for the purpose the rest ... Ships on the station for buying are from 20 to 100 tons, and have the bounty of 20s a ton ... By the act they are to be built since the year 1766, each has one or two boats for fishing; also for the first 20 tons they must have eight men, and two to every eight ton about 20. The merchants who have the ships both buy of the country boats and fish themselves, they both cure for barrel and in bulk that is salted in the hold of the ship, a ton of salt will cure 10,000 herrings. 500 herrings in a barrel of those of Loch-Swilly, but 800 at Killibegs. They made their own barrels of American staves, but now of fir'; 1000 staves, Philadelphia, will make 8 ton or 64 barrels and the price 6l. the 1000, making 11d each barrel, 20 hoops to the barrel, at 6d ... Mr Alexander began the fishery in 1773, when he employed two sloops, each of 40 tons. In 1774 2 sloops and 1 brig, the latter he sent to Antigua with 650 barrels.

He goes on to describe a salt house erected at Downing which he states is on Inch Island (I cannot confirm that though there's no mention of it on my map. Is he confusing his geography here?) and was built by this Mr Alexander. It consisted of two stone rooms for storing salt in, a gutting shed, a cooper's shop, various barrelling and salting sheds, a store for the boats when not in use and accommodation for, presumably him and/or his fishermen and staff.

This fishing station, when completed, would have the facility to cure 100,000 herrings in a day, use 10 tons of salt and employ seventeen or eighteen boats with ninety crew, according to Young. On top of that, he estimated that there would be six men employed to carry the fish from the boats to the gutting house, forty boys, women and girls gutting the fish, four more to carry between gut-house and salt-house, ten men to do the first salting and pack the fish, eight to 'draw from the vessels and carry to the barrelling-house', presumably carrying barrels, ten more packing the barrels, kept busy by five coopers, six men drawing off the pickle and another eight to carry the barrels to the ship's boats. That's 186 folk employed in total which makes it a grand affair. Young reckons Alexander would get about 20-30 shillings a barrel for his herring in the West Indies market and hoped to export 1750 barrels there each year. In 1775 one of his sloops went ashore at Blacksod Bay and though it wasn't wrecked, 'the country came down, obliged the crew to go ashore, threatening to murder them if they did not, and then not only robbed the vessel of her cargo, but every portable material'. Supposedly the cargo consisted or 40 tons, or 160,000 herrings. The mind really does boggle as to what the robbers did with so many barrels of herring and how in fact did they make off with them.

Of the quantity and quality of the herring he states:

> In 1775 there were about 180,000 barrels exported besides Mr Alexander's. There were that year fish enough in the Loch [sic] for all the boats of Europe. They swarmed so, that a boat which went out at seven in the evening returned at a eleven full, and went out on a second trip. The fellows said it was difficult to row through them; and every winter the plenty has been great, only the weather not equally good for taking, which cannot go on in a stormy night.

This substantiates any claim that the herring fishery was massive around the Donegal coast in the late eighteenth century though it seems to not have survived into the nineteenth on such a scale. According to the eminent John Molloy in *The Herring Fisheries of Ireland 1900-2005*, this decline coincided with the Act of Union between Britain and Ireland in 1800 and that an Act of Parliament had to be passed in 1819 in an attempt to stimulate the fishery by introducing the bounties. Like in Scotland, this only encouraged the so-called buss fishery though from twenty-seven vessels and 188 men fishing in 1819, these numbers jumped dramatically to 27,142 boats and 49,448 men by 1823. Molloy quotes these figures from a paper entitled *The Herring Fisheries of Ireland*, dated 1866 and written by William Andrews, Chairman of the Natural History and Museum Department of the Royal Dublin Society. These statistics suggest boats had less than two men in their crew which seems a bit doubtful. One wonders where over 27,000 boats came from in the space of four years. That some fishing occurred in the late nineteenth century is confirmed by Conaghan who notes that nine fishermen, all from one boat, were drowned whilst going out to the herring in 1890. Molloy also notes that the most successful herring fishery in the first decade of the twentieth century was off the Donegal coast with some 17,300 tons being, on average, landed yearly over several years.

Young also notes that he considered the fishery as being a great nursery for seafarers and that Mr Alexander's enterprise was a magnetic pull for all the boats in the county that came to sell their fish. It is a shame that he doesn't give any details of the small local boats involved.

Buncrana, just a few miles up the coast, is the 'Gateway to Inishowen – the angler's Paradise' or so the sign read. It had a quay with several boats alongside including two lovely clinker double-enders, the all-weather lifeboat and the Loch Swilly ferry. Here, the reader might remember Arthur Miller from chapter two, who had built a fish house in Passage East and had also opened up another here. However we drove on to Drumfree where I spotted a bar called 'The North Pole' which reminded me of Tom Crean and his 'The South Pole' pub. Later on,

The herring fleet at Buncrana 1930s.

I tried to find some link between this bar and the North Pole and could only find references on the internet to cyclist meetings and a government report concerning several bombings and murders with statements from various people that two of the perpetrators of one particular bombing, with resultant murder, had been seen in the North Pole bar, Drumfree. The bombings' report did make interesting reading because it hinted that the British Army were behind some or all of those bombings mentioned. However that's nothing to do with this trip and remains well publicised.

Malin is one of those places that every British seaman has heard of through the shipping forecast. In actuality it's named after Malin Head which lies about eight miles to the north If I had gone the extra way to the headland, I'd have had a good view over the small island of Inistrahull, another of those evacuated, this time as late as 1987. There's an occasional ferry from the pier at Malin Head and another from Bunagee Harbour for the island is now a major tourist attraction. The lighthouse, another of George Halpin's, was built in 1813 and its presence was largely due to the amount of shipping passing into and out of Loch Foyle. There is an interesting fact about the island: when it was inhabited the principal fishery was for turbot. For this the fishermen sailed some 30 miles out to the sandy Hempton Bank and set lines which they left down for about an hour before hauling in. Once home by the evening, all the fish was loaded onto one boat which they sailed out 15 miles to meet the Derry to Liverpool steamer onto which the live fish was placed. Once home again, they'd reset their lines along the rocky island coast to catch ling and conger for their bait for the following day. The turbot they caught was said to be the very best in all of Ireland and would arrive at Liverpool market some twenty hours after they were caught. This they did every day except in stormy weather. If the turbot could not be delivered to the ferryboat for any reason, then they were kept alive by being tethered to a line attached to a hook placed in

Yawls at Greencastle.

their snout, and the other end tied to the derrick on the landing. Turbot could be kept swimming around like this for several days. Any that died in the process were either eaten or given to the lighthouse keepers.

The village of Malin was pleasant enough though fairly small. There's a lovely ten-arched stone bridge over the river and picturesque white-washed buildings, a far cry from the trash upon the coast on the west. This seemed to be a really rural part of the coast. Between here at the coast of Loch Foyle, we passed the fine sandy beach of Culdaff Bay and drove along roads fringed in hedges of fuchsia, all in red and orange decor amongst the green grass. I stopped to photograph an ancient water pump by the side of the road, spotting a small clinker yawl stuffed away in the shed of a cottage opposite. Over the hill to the north was Kinnagoe Bay where another of the 1588 Spanish Armada ships, *La Trinidad Valencera*, ran aground and which, after discovery in 1971, was excavated over several years between 1973 and 1983 under the archaeological direction of Colin Martin who, you will remember, directed the excavations of the *Santa Maria de la Rosa* in the Blasket Sound. Was I tempted to go and view over the rocks she sank upon? No! I was keener to get to Loch Foyle, the coast of which we joined at Moville and soon were parked up in the busy main street. Walking down to the harbour which consisted of a single pier, alongside of which I counted seven mussel dredgers, I asked where the yard of the McDonald brothers was, only to be told they'd moved to Greencastle several years before. Thus, after a quick look around the local bookshop, I returned to the van and motored the mile or so along the shoreline to Greencastle.

This is a busy harbour with various workboats mixing with a plethora of pleasure boats. Several fishing boats lay alongside and a couple of mussel dredgers including the *Bonny and Kelly*, one I'd sailed upon several years before when she was working out of Port Penrhyn, Bangor, North Wales whilst owned by Myti Mussels. The harbour is also the base for the two Foyle pilot boats. It was easy to find the McDonald's boatbuilding shed whose business I'd heard a lot about.

Walking in, I asked whether either of the two brothers were about. The man I inquired upon, who was about to plane down a bulk of timber, pointed out Brian McDonald, a man in a bright blue t-shirt. As it turned out he was affable to visitors who walked in to talk. He's a big man with an equally big aura surrounding him. He'd the stubble of a grey beard and short wispy greying hair. We got chatting easily and he showed me around. On the floor of the yard was a fibreglass hull, a 34-foot Cygnus, which they were in the process of fitting out.

'We've done hundreds of these,' Brian told me. 'Most go down to Cork. A few in Galway I think. Mostly used for lobster and crab fishing though some would have salmon drifted. The other boat is a 22-foot RNLI tender for the Aranmore lifeboat which we are servicing.'

They had moved from Moville to these new premises in 2000 after the yard had been established there by James McDonald way back in 1750. It must be one of the oldest established boatbuilders in the whole of the British Isles.

'We're the sixth generation to practice boatbuilding. Me and brother Philip over there,' he said, pointing to another fellow working with some timber.

However it was because of the Drontheims I'd come.

'The yawls, yes, we've built hundreds of them too. This one here, the *James McDonald*, belongs to the museum. Built it about 1998 but they let it go so we've had to restore it since. This one, the *James Kelly*,' he said leaning over another, 'was built about the same time. Most finished fishing in the 1950s though we've built several others since.'

Although often called Drontheims, Brian referred to them as Greencastle yawls. Today a yawl is about 26 feet in length, a clinker-built hull of larch on oak frames with an inboard engine. Before the days of sail things were different, however. How the yawls came about is an interesting tale.

On the north coast of Ireland, Norway yawls (boats probably similar to the square-sailed Lista boats that were commonplace all along the Norwegian coast) were being brought by ship because, it has been suggested, the country's timber supplies began to be exhausted in the middle of the eighteenth century, mostly due to over-exploitation by the British Navy in expanding their fleet of ships. These boats arrived as supplementary cargo and were sold off by the timber-ships as they progressed around the coast. This seems to have been the case throughout the north and west of Scotland as well as the north coast of Ireland. Thus the Norway yawls were then in use throughout this coastline and generally reflected the craft of Gokstad, Norway, Shetland, the Faroes and Iceland. There is a painting by J.W. Campbell in the Ulster Folk & Transport Museum, dated 1822, of Portstewart, Co. Derry showing one such yawl, thus supporting the above supposition. The vessel has very curved ends and, at a guess, is about 15–20 feet long. There is no sign of any mast or rig. However we can at least gain a picture of these eighteenth-century vessels in general use around the whole of the north-western Atlantic seaboard. The Drontheim developed through innovation in the same way as the Shetland sixareen did, a vessel used for the offshore long-lining fishery.

Edgar March, in his seminal *Inshore Craft of Britain*, tells us that, in the words of John Smith, boatbuilder, 'many of them came across from Norway [to Shetland] and were improved upon to suit the requirements of the haaf fishermen, being made deeper by the addition of a top strake … the boats from Norway were built with three boards to a side and were very cheap'. In Ireland the builders reduced the sheer, believing the high bow to catch the wind, and used narrower planks to enable local timber stock to be used. Regardless of its origins, the Drontheim was typical of the craft right along the northern coast of Ireland. The Groomsport Yawl, described as 'a whale boat … imported from Norway', carried two dipping lugsails, while the Killough yawl just had one. Skerries yawls were Drontheims in the same way as

Greencastle yawls were. These latter boats were used in the Islay fishery where they were referred to as Irish skiffs. These were introduced into the area for the sole reason that Islay was closer to Rathlin Island and the Irish coast than it was to any harbour of significance on the mainland. A voyage to Campbeltown necessitated navigating around the Mull of Kintyre, infamous for its fog, strong currents and variable, sometimes violent, winds. The result was that boats were bought in from Moville or Portrush and later built on the island to the same design: there is no evidence that the Norway yawls were imported direct to Islay. These skiffs invariably set one spritsail, occasionally two, and when racing, resorted to a standing lug so preferred by the ring-netters in their Lochfyne skiffs. The boats were 26 feet in length, although smaller 22 feet versions were used when fishing off the Mull of Kintyre. The Campbeltown fishers called these Irish skiffs 'Greenies' after the Greencastle skiff. Records tell of skiffs being brought over by steamer from Ireland and dropped overboard off Sanda Isle to be collected. However, Kintyre, Islay and Colonsay were the geographical limits of the distribution of these craft in Scotland.

Brian led me up a ladder at the back of the shed, up to a second floor platform where a small punt was under construction.

'This is a small 15-foot new build. I've four more to do when I've the time.' he smiled as he spoke.

'Who builds them, you?' I asked.

'Yes, that's it, just me. Moulds are always on the thwarts except at the extremes. Six on a 26-footer and three on these 15-footers. They used to be better for inshore fishing, easier to launch and retrieve, and often complemented a larger yawl in the fleets.'

He was right obviously as this small punt had three moulds from which he used his eye to shape the boat. Some say that these boats resemble Viking longboats whilst they are under construction and you could really see it here. I could also see that Brian was the brother with the boatbuilding skills.

I didn't want to take up too much of Brian's time as I could see they were all busy. He pointed

Yawls at Portrush.

me to the museum which lay across the road almost. This is the Inishowen Maritime Museum and Planetarium (I missed that bit) and is housed in the former coastguard station overlooking what the blurb says is 'one of busiest fishing fleets in Ireland'. I paid my fee and entered what, when I'd completed the circuit, I considered to be one of the best maritime museums I'd ever been in. Pride of place in the fishing section was the Drontheim *The Violet*, a yawl from Inch Island and thought to be one of the oldest fishing boats in Ireland. It was registered to James Brown of Inch although believed to have been built at Moville between 1870 and 1880. Amongst the other craft on display were a Fanad currach and a recently built Dunfanaghy currach. This one had been built the previous year by Dónal MacPolín and was built with double hazel rod ribs (called couples) in the traditional style. These currachs had been used for lobster, long-line and salmon fishing up to the 1960s though some also traded with passing steamers and trawlers. Most had been built by the Colls, Robinsons and McElhinneys.

The McDonalds weren't the only boatbuilders in Moville I was surprised to learn. The Beattie brothers also worked from there. Another building centre was established at Portrush with builders Hopkins, Kelly and McCaun. The McDonald family had come from Scotland prior to 1750. But then again, that didn't surprise me!

Interestingly, model boats used to be raced on the Foyle for many years in regattas in Stroove (some seem to call it Shrove) and Colmore. The tradition was that these models of yachts were made from the staves of the herring barrels and thus the length of the models was restricted by the length of the stave itself.

Displayed upon the walls, there were an impressive number of lines and construction plans of local traditional boat types drawn up by a Mr Harry Madill of Portadown. These included: South Downs herring boat; Lough Foyle punt; Donegal punt; Groomsport yawl; Killough, Co. Down, yawl; North Down yawl; Newcastle line skiff; Ardglass line skiff; and a Kilkeel skiff.

Having seen the two pilot boats, I already knew that Greencastle was a pilot station. In 1831 there were already twenty-nine pilots licensed by the Ballast Office Committee. Today it's the Londonderry Port and Harbour Commissioners who operate two stations though, according to the information in the museum, these are at Tremone Bay, near Culdaff and Stroove, Inishowen Head. Presumably Greencastle now operates all the vessels. During the Second World War, when Derry was an important base for the Atlantic convoy escort vessels, although the pilots were based in neutral Ireland, they were awarded the 'Atlantic Star' for their contribution to the Battle of the Atlantic.

Other exhibits centred on emigration, the Irish Lights, the Coastguard and their rockets, shipwrecks and the Irish navy. There was also a superb collection of photographs dotted around the walls. All in all it's a wonderful place to spend a couple of hours wandering around. Outside is another yawl, the *St Margaret* looking worse for wear and a salmon punt, though no one in the museum knew from where it came.

I caught the ferry, which cost €10, across to the other side at Magilligan which is in Northern Island. The ferry here goes back at least 150 years and was the main transport route between Inishowen and Coleraine. Flax was grown, spun and woven in the Greencastle and Stroove areas and men and women walked the 13 miles from Magilligan to Coleraine and back for the market. The ferry was a simple rowboat though when the weather made crossing impossible, sheds at the Point provided overnight shelter. Philip McKinney was the main ferryman for decades, living at Greencastle. During the Second World War it was Hugh McClenaghan's turn as he was the only boatman allowed to land at Magilligan with a special licence. Today's ferry, though, is very different, a drive-through type of boat which runs a continual shuttle service from early morning to about 10pm. The ten minute voyage saves some 30 miles of driving. The only regret was that we weren't to visit Londonderry and the Foyle River.

Marmion has some worthwhile facts about the Foyle salmon fishery, to which the Irish Society claimed exclusive rights as far up as Lifford. These rights came about after they had been conveyed to the Corporation of London by James I and eventually passed to the society. Annually, 130 tons were shipped to London, Liverpool and Glasgow in Marmion's time. There were120 men employed in the taking of fish. Marmion also notes that, in 1835, Derry merchants went to the Orkney Islands where they cured 5,800 barrels of herring that year.

There wasn't a lot at Magilligan Point other than a slipway, a few houses and a bar. Thankfully there were no police to greet us any longer although judging by the tall steel fencing at the terminal, there used to be. The spit of land is wholly occupied by a Military Firing Range. Further along a high concrete wall with occasion steel gates built in edges along the road, making it look like the Berlin Wall. There are cameras everywhere and fencing and a sort of rolling steel top to the concrete wall. Not a sign of any military presence though, the last left Northern Ireland a few weeks before and the signs are encouraging for they declare 'demolition in progress'. It wasn't clear exactly what was being demolished. Part of the camp still contains a prison though this now houses Northern Ireland's criminals rather than its political prisoners.

At Coleraine we stopped to have a look at the River Bann, said to be the greatest salmon river in the whole of Ireland. This is regarded as being because the fish spawn in all the rivers that run into the Bann, and because it is the main drain-off to Lough Neagh. The fish swim to sea until January, says Young, 'when the return to fresh water and continue so till August. This is when they are netted'. The fishing in 1776 fishing proved to be the best yet and 1452 salmon were taken in one haul, he wrote. He himself saw a catch of 370 fish in one haul. Like the Foyle, all rights were to the Irish Society all the way from Lough Neagh to the sea and the fishery was worth £6000 a year. At Coleraine itself it earned £1000 and a similar amount

The harbour at Portstewart.

came from the eel fishing. No nets or weirs were allowed after 12 August. Marmion adds that 21,660 fish were taken in 1843 and 15,011 the following year. Of the latter, 13,464 salmon were exported to England and 1545 sold locally. 300 bailiffs were employed to guard the river and its tributaries from poachers.

We rushed a bit through Portrush though I did stop to photograph the pleasant if artificial harbour. The lifeboat *Katie Hannan* was afloat in the harbour. Although Portrush has had a lifeboat since 1860, the boat has only been kept afloat since 1981. This lifeboat, however, hit the news headlines at the time of writing this book in January 2008, months after my visit, when she got into difficulties off Rathlin Island whilst she was attempting to rescue three men from a boat. The weather was awful at the time, and the freak wave grounded her on the coast of the island. The crew were eventually air-lifted off but the lifeboat was left to the mercy of the sea as the gale force winds continued throughout the following week, preventing any hope of salvage. Luckily the three men in the boat were rescued by coastguards. As the RNLI spokesperson echoed, there are occasional instances that these volunteer crews, whilst risking their own lives to save others, get into trouble too.

I also sought out the Portrush 'Herring Ponds' without success unless the pond in the rocks just outside the harbour was I was supposedly looking for. I followed a signpost but the trail went cold after finding no others. The place seemed a mass of bars and God knows what and I wasn't keen to find out more. Portstewart was even more hectic with traffic jammed solid and I lost patience with queues of crawling cars. I guess it was such a culture shock after two weeks or more away from traffic. Both towns, though, once had thriving maritime trades. Now they simply rely upon tourism for every penny they can extract.

Portballantrae seemed a bit different, calm and secluded after the mania of the previous places. We stopped by the harbour, Dog eager for a sniff whilst I admired a couple of yawls, one being a McDonald's boat, the *Clare & Louise*. This one must surely be old, I decided, for the sternpost was sharp and had been cut away to form an aperture for a propeller, suggesting it was of pre-motorisation vintage. It wouldn't survive many more years judging by the way it was rotting. Two more sat outside the Portballantrae Boat Club's premises. Close by to Portballantrae are the remains of Dunluce Castle which date back to the fourteenth century though the site itself is much older. We didn't visit though I did read that the south wall of the castle, facing the mainland, has two openings cut into it which were built to house two cannons that were salvaged from the wreck of the Spanish Armada ship *Girona*, mentioned in chapter 11, and which foundered nearby with a massive loss of life.

Bushmills was next and I swear I could smell the whiskey from the well-known distillery which towers above the rest of the small town. The Old Bushmills Distillery is the oldest licensed one in the world, having started its grainy business back in 1608 when James I granted them permission though it is assumed they'd been at it for hundreds of years beforehand. Guided tours are available, after which the visitor gets to drink a wee shot of the stuff. I've been round several distilleries in Scotland and enjoyed each visit though I'm sure they only hand out the youngest of the malts. Some now charge (I didn't know whether Bushmills did or not at the time though I later discovered that there was an admission charge) which seems a bit cheeky and extreme considering they hope the visitor buys a bottle at the end. I guess it's a matter of if they can they will. However, as it was well past 5pm, I was confident that any tours would be well finished for the day. And anyway, with further distance to drive, I didn't feel that partaking with a dram, however small it might be, was perhaps the best of ideas.

Coming out of Bushmills, I spotted smoke coming out of some trees. Dark smoke it was, the stuff Victorian times are remembered by. I thought the trees were alight until a steam engine puffed into view. This was the Giant's Causeway & Bushmills Railway that only

Collecting seaweed on the Antrim coast.

opened in 2002 but was, in fact, much older. The idea of a railway along the north coast from Ballycastle to Portrush had surfaced in the 1870s, to provide a means of shifting the industrial mining products to the harbour at Portrush. These included limestone, coal, bauxite, basalt and even iron. The lack of finances ensured the project was shelved though a narrow-gauge line was built from Ballycastle to Ballymoney on the main rail line between Belfast and Derry, and opened in 1883. The same year the Giant's Causeway Tramway opened, a short stretch of a hydro-electric powered tram system, the first in the world, though steam locomotives were also used. The principle reason was to attract visitors to Giant's Causeway and it remained in operation until 1949.

At Giant's Causeway itself, I was horrified by the number of coaches, the multitude of cars and hordes of visitors. I ran away, well, quickly drove off though not before I'd sweetly asked the guy on the car park if I could quickly run into the information centre to view the books on sale. Again there was nothing of interest so I beat my hasty retreat. I wasn't particularly bothered about viewing the 40,000 basalt columns, and equally not concerned with missing out on the UNESCO site that is Northern Ireland's premier tourist attraction I was reminded of Thackeray's words at discovering he was looking at the site in 1832: 'Mon Dieu! And I have travelled 150 miles to see that!' However, I would have liked to walk down to Portnaboe purely because I have a photograph of yawls pulled up upon the stony beach there. However, with the time ticking on, I had a much more exciting and interesting coastal wonder to visit.

On the road east we passed the impressive ruins of Dunseverick Castle still clinging to the headland some couple of hundred feet above the sea. Someday, presumably, part of it would collapse and fall, just like the kitchens of its more famous and well visited neighbour of Dunluce Castle. Portbradden is a tiny harbour with a few houses and a couple of stores on the west side of White Park Bay. The Irish 'bradán' translates to 'salmon' thus telling us that this was originally a salmon port. Today it was nothing but quiet. Ballintoy was quiet too although the man in the red van selling his paintings probably didn't want it that way. Neither, presumably, did the café owners, there to quench the thirst of those walking the coastal footpath. Two bikers turned up with a roar instantly destroying the repose. The extensive and well-protected harbour was built in the mid-eighteenth century, though rebuilt years later. Lignite (wood coal), burnt limestone from the massive limestone kilns overlooking the harbour and basalt for making roads were all exported. Fishing boats were also based here, fishing salmon, herring and cod. In 1803 a report listed the parish of Ballintoy as having eighty-two fishers, twenty-one salmon fishers and ten fish carriers. Today any fishing is probably for lobsters though sea-angling is much more lucrative.

Then to our goal, Carrick-a-Rede, a place I'd heard and read about and was determined to see for myself. This part of the sea was a particular rich spot for salmon as they swam around the volcanic headland on their migration. This accounts for the high number of fishermen in the Ballintoy parish, which includes both Carrick-a-Rede and nearby Larrybane. Carrick-a-Rede literally means 'the rock in the road' which refers to this obstructing the salmon's migration as they seek out the Bann and Bush rivers. The rock itself is an island, separated from the mainland by a vertical gap of maybe 60 feet. Local folk have been fishing this spot by boat for generations, at least from 1620 and probably before. In 1755 the first rope bridge was erected across to the island, about 80 feet above the sea, so that one end of the seine net could be attached to the rock. When the bag-net was introduced to Ireland from Scotland in the mid-1800s, the fishermen adopted this method here, building themselves a net store on the island. Today, though fishing stopped in 2002, the rope bridge remains and crossing it is popular with visitors, 185,000 of which came last year though not all crossed over. Many come just for the bridge and have no knowledge, or a desire for any knowledge, on the salmon fishery. So far this year the numbers were 225,000,

Quarrymen at Brockie Quarry near Carrick-a-rede.

according to the people collecting the admissions fees, and the site is the UK's second most popular attraction. Were they taking the piss, I thought? More popular than those London attractions such as Madame Tussaud's or the London Eye, or the Giant's Causeway indeed. I doubted it. Perhaps they meant fishing attraction.

It's a mile or so walk along the headland from the car park after paying your £3 to enter, a very pleasant walk even if the rain had started. The colder the wind blew, the faster I walked. I wasn't the only person out, and when I did arrive at the bridge, I had to wait five minutes as the first group crossed and another group returned, the crossing operation controlled by the 'bridge-master'. Once across, I wandered about the island, gazing down at the hut and imagining how things would have been during the summer season when they fished. In winter the bridge was dismantled and stored away until the spring. There were plenty of birds flying around, the names of which I do not know, but I was aware that the island is frequently visited by orthnologists for its colourful bird life.

A stream of visitors have been here over the ages. Naturalist and clergyman Revd Dr William Hamilton came in 1784 and wrote, 'I went a short way off the beaten track to see a whimsical little fishing rock, connected to the main land by a very extraordinary flying bridge'. Our old acquaintances Mr and Mrs Hall came here in 1840 and described what they called the 'hanging bridge'. They weren't too impressed for

> The day on which we examined it was very stormy and we declined to cross it. One of our attendant guides ran over it with as much indifference as if he had been walking along a guarded balcony, scarcely condescending to place his hands upon the slender rope that answered the purpose of protector – the 'bridge' all the while swinging to and fro as the wind rushed about and under it.

In those days there was only a single rope handrail unlike today.

At its peak, they were catching 300 salmon a day though this slowly declined over the years as stocks depleted, largely, it is believed, because of the huge number being caught in drift-nets out at sea. This is the only part of the recent lack of licences that makes sense, as already mentioned. Stop that unselective fishing and the benefit for the river fishermen of, not only Ireland, but England and Wales too would be a hundredfold. There's an ice house above Carrick-a-Rede where ice was stored after cutting in winter, enabling the fish to be sent off to Belfast and England. Back at the car park, a bit drenched, another quick walk took Dog and I down to Larrybane in the opposite direction. Hard dolerite was quarried here and rectangular setts carried across by a wire pulley to the small island of Stackboy just offshore, before being sent down a chute into the hold of steam puffers that carried them across to Glasgow where they paved the streets. More recently, in the 1930s, limestone was also quarried before being burnt in the huge kiln above the car park though most of the resulting quicklime was carried away by road. Today the whole area belongs to the National Trust.

Young has a few notes about salmon fishing hereabouts which he says was considerable.

> The fish are cured in puncheons with common salt, and then in tierces of 42 gallons each, 6 of which make a ton; and it sells at present 17*l* a ton, but never before more than 16*l* average for 10 years 14*l*. The rise of price is attributed to the American supply of the Mediterranean with fish being cut off.

From Ballycastle I had a good view of Rathlin Island and the Mull of Kintyre. Ever since sailing up the west coast of Scotland, passing the Mull, have I wanted to visit Rathlin. It's only

6 miles away from Ballycastle and a ferry departs daily. Known as the 'Stocking of Ireland', it has three lighthouses, the remains of a kelp store, a tradition of model boat racing that is at least a 100 years old, the site of Marconi's first commercial radio transmission across water in 1898, a good harbour, and a modern visitor centre.

That evening, completely unannounced, I knocked on the door of Pat Nolan, one of the Fishing Boat Association members, and he and his wife instantly welcomed me in. Pat is a wizard when it comes to the BIM 50-footers and I was keen to learn from him. He hails from Union Hall in the South and has a wide knowledge of the fishery, including publishing a small booklet of his own about the fishing down there in West Cork entitled *Sea Caress* (since then Pat has written *Sea Change* (Nonsuch Ireland, 2008) which documents the history of BIM 50-footers). What I didn't realise until we talked was just how much of a wizard he was and so he and his knowledge surpassed my greatest expectations. After a cup of coffee Pat and I 'retired' to his upstairs room, or 'engine shed, as he called it, where all his data was kept. These 50-footers, as they've become known, were designed by James Stafford, a naval architect employed by the 'Comhlachas Iascaigh Mhara Na hEireann' (the Irish Sea Fisheries Association) in 1946. It wasn't until 1952 that this became the less of a mouthful corporate body 'An Bord Iascaigh Mhara', now widely known as the BIM. Stafford had served time with Tyrrells of Arklow from 1931. Subsequently, the BIM had interests in yards at Baltimore, Dingle and Killibegs as we've seen though the first boat of this type was launched in Killibegs in 1949 where Stafford was based. These boats, designed to be 49ft 8in in overall length – though, says Pat, you had to give or take the odd foot – cost about £4000 at the time and the fishermen were expected to put a down payment of ten percent, the rest being paid to the BIM over a period with minimal interest. This had been usual in the fisheries since the days of the CDB, a sort of hire purchase, common today. Far too common, some say. However it's worth remembering that it was possible to make a packet of money from fishing in that period and some skippers managed to pay off their debt in a couple of years. In all, Pat reckoned eighty-eight of the boats were built in total, twenty-one each at the BIM yards, eight at Meevagh, nine by Tyrrells of Arklow, six by W.G. Stephens of Banff, East Coast of Scotland, one by Henry Skinner of Baltimore and the final one at Sisk's boatyard in Dun Laoghaire. Furthermore Tyrrells also built the *Vega* which was wholly owned privately. By 1952 they were costing £5,500 and over £7,000 two years later. By the time the last one was running down the ways in 1970, its full cost was £22,000. Pat estimates that seven boats are still working at the fishing and seventeen have been converted such as the Dingle-built *Ros Beithe* that I'd seen in Letterfrack alongside the old pier.

Still today many regard them as the prettiest of fishing boats belonging to that era and were a pillar to the development of the fisheries. Certainly in Ireland that must be true though it's hard to compare them on such a scale as some of the boats that appeared from the Scottish yards, especially some of the ring-netters from folk such as Millers of St. Monans and Alex Noble of Girvan. I doubt there will be people who disagree with the statement that they are a thousand times more aesthetic as the boats being built by today's designers and builders in steel.

I left Pat's quite late after we'd chatted for hours. It was very dark and raining again as I headed east once more. It was too late to follow Ballycastle's heritage trail. The harbour had been a significant landing place since the 1400s, called Port Brittas. The McDonnells, chieftains of all of Antrim, watched their galleys sail in and out of the little harbour from their castle on a neighbouring hill. Many different harbour schemes have been implemented since landlord Colonel Hugh Boyd began his first operations in the 1740s, building a wooden pier and inner harbour. Boyd himself claimed that one time there were sixty ships in the harbour loading his locally mined coal for Dublin. Whilst building his harbour, to move the heavy chunks of stone, he built a special wooden tramway, 310 yards long with a three-foot gauge, the rails being of oak and fir. This is considered to have been the first 'railway' in Ireland.

Salmon were also taken hereabouts and an ice house dating from 1823 still survives, though not in its original form. Other fishing consisted of cod, coley, herring and mackerel whilst the salmon drift-netting occurred off the mouth of river Margy, at the west end of the beach, in the late spring and summer. The present harbour dates from the 1990s and the ferry to Rathlin is the only thing that departs from it on a daily fashion though there are of course the various angling boats operating in the season.

A few miles out of Ballycastle, headlights full on, I chanced upon a campsite at the edge of Ballypatrick Forest. I might have missed the small sign if my headlights were dipped because of the pouring rain. Watertop Farm advertised pony trekking, boating, farm tours, an assault course, scenic walks, a tea room, fishing, archery, caravans and camping. I turned down the long winding down to a yard with various buildings and found a door to knock upon which was eventually opened by an elderly woman who first looked at me with suspicion. When I explained I was a latecomer, it was well after 10pm, she relieved me of £8 and told me to park in the yard because it was too wet. Deciding to have a shower after cooking some pasta, I searched high and low for the facilities, both for washing up and showering. They were not in the same building but nevertheless I completed my mission, though the rain would probably have sufficed for both operations. It threw it down cats, dogs and all. The roof of the van was bombarded; the din inside once again making sleep difficult though, eventually, not impossible. Even if I had snored away through the night, I doubt even a partner in the bed next to me would have heard it, such was the clatter. The dog slept peacefully throughout.

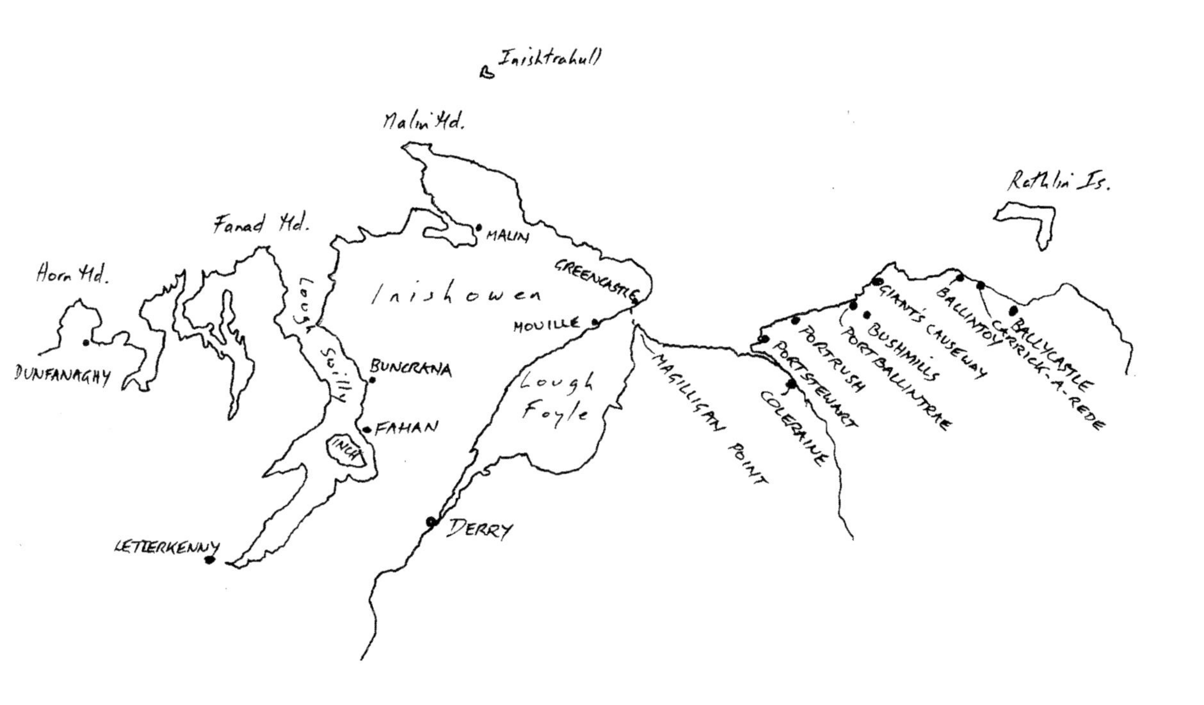

DAY EIGHTEEN

The summer of 2007 must surely rank as one of the worst on record. Floods, global warming and ruined crops made the headlines. Headlines that declared that prices would have to go up world-wide to compensate. More pain, more rain. Pitter-patter went the rain on the roof to press the point, even if it had slowed down to a steady but fine drizzle. The night's ricocheting had meant a fitful night, not helped by the dog's dreaming at which times his paw shakes, rattling the side of the van. I addressed the day through blinkered eyes, or so I thought on first impressions. I was wrong; it was thick mist.

I wasn't sure how high up the forest is but at a guess this was over 700 feet. Departing – I never saw a soul and I'm sure I could have escaped paying a cent but that's the trustworthy sort of guy I am – the road was encapsulated in the mist, so much so that it was impossible to see more than a twenty yards ahead. We crept along and so, luckily, did the other users on the road. I had considered retracing to Ballycastle during one of my periods of wakefulness during the night, but the weather certainly put the lid on that idea. This was midwinter weather, chilly too, and we were supposedly in the height of summer. It's not carbon dioxide that's causing this global warming, I cynically thought, but the hot air and piffle from all the bullshit that is spoken about it, especially in politic-speak and their multitude of advisers the world over! Build on flood planes and expect flooding. And, let's face it, companies, and especially the supermarkets, don't need excuses to raise their prices. They just do it whatever the weather.

We were well into the Glens of Antrim now and by the time the road dumped us back at the coast the mist had cleared. The Mull of Kintyre was clear, the sun even shining on the purple heather. Sanda Island was equally clear and I recalled the few days that my father, a friend of mine, and I had sheltered in the lee of the island after being engulfed by a sudden gale whilst attempting to round the Mull in my father's boat. That was probably in about 1970, a long time ago, but the memory came easily. More recently I'd walked on parts of the Mull, especially on the west side where friend Angus Martin from Campbeltown had taken me to one of his favourite haunts, the Inans, a particular valley of pure virginity surrounded by high hills. That was back in 1992 and since then I've had several hikes out over those hills. I'd even walked to the lighthouse on the Mull one blustery day with American Brad Johnson in, I think, 2000. From that Scottish side, I'd often contemplated the Antrim coast and now here I was.

It was just a shame that cloud still hid everything behind me higher than about 200 feet. There would be no walking up Glenariff or Glenballyemon or Glenaan or Glendun. Cushendall, cushioned between seaboard and hill, had been a popular stopping off point for those travelling up to the Giant's Causeway, the attractiveness of the place being appreciated since the early 1800s. Around then, the village had its first hotel, the 'Glens of Antrim', in Shore Street which, as you'd expect, is close to the shore. Others soon followed and then came boarding houses. The Cyclists' Touring Club were frequent visitors as members pedalled frantically around the coast. Between 1888 and 1930 a passenger rail service ran between Ballymena and Parkmore at the head of Glenariff, passengers alighting there to take a horse

The limestone bridge at Carnlough.

and carriage, and later a motor car, down to Cushendall. In the twentieth century the shoreline receded by 150 feet as coastal erosion took its toll, especially on the beach that shrunk accordingly.

Glenariff, or Waterfoot as it's otherwise known, lies a mile further south around Red Bay. The quay here had a coalyard, suggesting the import of coal from Scotland. Strange limestone columns sat by the road, the remains of a bridge though it didn't seem to go anywhere except into the sea. Presumably it was a tramway from a mine, the coastal erosion destroying its hope of survival. The ruins of another quay further around the bay consisted of a couple of lumps of rock and concrete, one with a substantial bollard in its midst, surely a sign of more industrial workings. This quay had been destroyed by a storm in 1901.

Then came Carnlough, around Garron Point – the road hugged the coast all the way and, with the first signs of the sun coming out here, the whole coast warmed to my heart – with its limestone trade and harbour. Here I happened to drop into McKillop's shop on the main street, completely by chance and fell into conversation with its owner. He happened to have a cousin Felix McKillop who'd written a book about the area entitled *Gencloy – A Local History including Carnlough*. The shop itself was sparsely stocked and its owner didn't seem bothered about the lack of customers and happily spent time recounting to me much of the history of the place. He spoke of 'the Otter', the engine used on the tramway bringing limestone down from the hills, from the time of its purchase in 1898 up to 1930 when diesel locomotives were used instead. Although quarried limestone had passed through here from the early nineteenth century, and perhaps earlier, the quarry above the village didn't open until 1851 when the first shipment left from the harbour for Scotland. There was a quay, Gibbons Pier, in 1831 though this was in a state of dilapidation. Vessels that used it were small 15-20 ton craft, bringing in the Scottish coal as well as local goods from Belfast. Amongst the exports listed are potatoes, grain and limestone. In 1835 the inhabitants were, according to James Boyle of the Ordnance Survey,

> either engaged in fishing or agriculture, or in some sort of dealing. They are mostly of a lower class... Their principal support seems to be derived from letting of lodgings to the crowds of the lower order who swarm here in the summer from the inland country for the benefit of sea bathing.

Lewis (1837) echoes this, describing it as 'a maritime village ... containing 213 inhabitants. This place, originally a small fishing village, is pleasantly situated.' However, with the new mine working, the harbour was vastly improved and with it, the fortunes of those living there. Once the coast road was completed by the early 1840s, more visitors of a better class came. The effects of the famine between 1845 and 1847 were mild here in comparison to most parts of Ireland. The reason for this is said to be because of the generosity of the Marchioness of Londonderry who owned most of what existed. However, that's not to say Carnlough didn't suffer from starvation and emigration.

By 1854 a tramway had been built bringing limestone down from the quarry into the harbour, over the famous limestone bridge which still stands in the middle of Carnlough, spanning the road, the harbour by then having being expanded. By the time these works were completed, the limestone industry was experiencing a boom with 2,600 tons being exported in the first five months of 1856. The industry expanded to its 1890s peak and survived into the twentieth century though now all remains is the harbour, bridge and track of the tramway, all of which still attract tourists. The harbour seemed fairly widely used, judging by the various day boats within it, and two fishing boats whilst another, *Flora of Belfast*, was out of the water and appeared to be an East Coast of England coble, a type of open beach boat traditionally peculiar to Yorkshire and Northumberland.

Glenarm, the last of the nine glens, also had a harbour from where limestone was once exported though today this is a marina. The Halls described this place as 'beautifully situated. The small bay affords a safe and convenient shelter for shipping, and the mountains look down upon it.' How true! But now, sadly, we were about to leave this dramatic coast; in fact from here on back down to Rosslare, we were to see none of the beauty that we'd experienced over the last two and a half weeks. Though not unpleasant, the east coast does not have the same splendour and emotional vividness of the south, west and north coasts, even though each of these separately have their own individual impressive qualities and really are quite breathtaking in parts. Or so the dog told me!

Ballygalley is another sheltered little spot tucked around the head of the same name. In times gone by there was a thriving kelp industry which was a welcome additional income for some for the large brown seaweed is plentiful along this coast. During the winter and spring it is washed up on the shore by the gales. Up to the twentieth century it was collected and dried before being carefully burnt on iron bars placed over a shallow pit paved with flat stones, this being called a kelp kiln. The resulting hard mass after hours of burning was also, confusingly, called kelp and was broken up into lumps and mostly shipped over to Glasgow for further processing. It was valued as a source of soda for bleaching and in soap and glass manufacture. Its iodine content made it useful for medicines, dyes and photographic materials. Dulse, the seaweed I'd eaten in County Clare, also grew upon the kelp and was regarded as a local delicacy. There's a sad story here. Manna Jane, really Jean Parke, was the wife of a local farmer who spent time at sea. One night, whilst he was away, she dreamed that he drowned. Thus she spent more and more time on the beach watching out for his boat to return. When he didn't, she became obsessed with waiting for his return and consequently their farm became neglected and she was eventually evicted. She built a shelter on the beach from stones, driftwood and seaweed, living off seafood. Many of the locals started calling her a witch. However, she drowned one stormy night as the sea carried away her shelter and her with it.

Of Larne, the Halls said it 'has little to recommend it'. I would certainly agree and it seems to survive solely as a ferry port to and from Stranraer. It once thrived through the export of limestone, the quarries of which were said to be extensive inland here. We sped through. At the bottom of Lough Larne we detoured back up the other side of the Lough to Portmuck, a lovely little harbour overlooked by the small village which seemed to be in the process of being patronised by holiday-makers. Children were splashing around in the water of the harbour whilst a couple of jet-skis were buzzing about outside the harbour just like the annoying wasps these things imitate. Portmuck gets its name from the island offshore, Muck Isle which in turn comes from the Irish 'muc' for pig as the island is said to resemble a sleeping porker. The harbour itself dates back to similar times as Carnlough and was built to facilitate the export of limestone from Islandmagee, the name of the north pointing peninsula. In time Portmuck has had a monastery, an old fortress, a coastguard station and a revenue station. It was also a renowned smugglers' haunt, though where isn't along this coast. By the 1920s the pier was ruinous and, at a time when grants were available for the renovation of such piers if a certain number of fishermen used it, it is said that there were a number of deceased fishermen who were supporting locals in their application for such funding. Whether they got it, I do not know, but the canted pier is certainly not in a ruinous state now though the harbour has silted up over the last five decades. This is, in fact, a really pretty little place and I sat for a while, enjoying listening to the kids screaming though loathing the jet skis which luckily eventually zoomed off to haunt some other poor souls. The sun was warm and soak-upable which was extraordinary given the awful morning's rain. A ferry sailed out from Larne. I watched it sail off to the Scottish coast which was vaguely visible in the distance. Offshore I thought about herrings as I remembered the Halls writing that the 'Larne coast is remarkable for its herrings'. They saw fishermen using artificial flies to catch them, the flies themselves being of 'a very rude imitation of nature – nothing more, indeed, than one of the feathers of a sea-gull tied to a large and coarse hook'. That is quite surprising because herrings aren't renowned for taking bait in this way, though they do, occasionally, land on feathered hooks when fishing for mackerel.

Carrickfergus has an impressive castle which is one of the first things you see. You can't miss it. Beneath the castle is a large new marina in an even bigger harbour, the marina being fringed with the waterside housing that I need say no more about. I ventured into the reception to find out some information and was amazed to be handed a sort of nylon document holder. Inside was a number of documents and brochures: one about the council services, another about the history of the town and another with the rules of the marina, plus the scale of charges and more bits and bobs, oh, and a DVD. The cost must be significant so that if I was a local tax payer I'd be horrified to see these folders given out willy-nilly. I can't say I learned very much from what was there though the DVD was obviously aimed at American visitors highlighting, as it does, that Andrew Jackson, the seventh President of the US was born here, as were the US Rangers who spearheaded the Allied Invasion in 1944. The John Paul Jones connection is also mentioned. I did visit the new museum which entertained me for half an hour or so.

With regard to the fisheries though, in 1812 John Dubordieu, in his *Survey of County Antrim*, described how 'the fishery in the bay employs many boats and men who mostly inhabit the Scotch quarter; the fish taken are several flat kinds, as well as cod, ling, haddock, red and grey gurnard, and remarkable fine oysters'. No mention of herrings then. It seems the fishery was helped by the construction of a pier in the Scotch quarter in 1831, and more substantial pier extensions were added in 1885. James Boyle, mentioned above and who worked for the Ordnance Survey, found that the main manufacturing in the town was 'a distillery, two flax spinning mills, a flour and corn mill, one corn mill, two tanyards and two brickyards'. In the second half of the nineteenth century salt mining began at Duncrue, French Park and Maidenmount though the Halls mentioned a 'Salt-hole' at Ballycarry as existing in 1840. These three mines were controlled by the Maidenmount Salt Mines and the salt was mined and brined after which it was piped down to the saltworks in the harbour where it was evaporated in salt pans and finally manufactured into white salt for export. Some continues to be mined today.

Carrickfergus' other maritime commodity was shipbuilding. Paul Rodgers had his own shipyard after he took over the running of his father-in-law Robert Johnson's yard in 1878 at which he was previously the manager. He and his workforce gained a fine reputation as designer and builder of ships, especially schooners. In 1885 the yard smoothly made a transition from wooden ships to steel vessels, as was the trend of the day. In all, Rogers produced twenty-nine ships in his yard. However production ceased in 1892 though the yard, under a different ownership, undertook ship repairs between about 1895 and 1901. After that, shipbuilding, and its ancillary industries, ceased in Carrickfergus.

From there we sped easily into Belfast, Van Morrison's 'Stepping Out Queen' playing loudly on the player – he was born here if you didn't already know. Somewhere I passed the Harland & Wolfe yard though I didn't see it. I was in a deadly hurry by this time, having lingered too long in Portmuck, to get to the Ulster Folk & Transport Museum at Cultra on the other side of Belfast Lough. It was Saturday afternoon and I knew it would shut by five and I needed at least two hours there, so the delights of Belfast were, I'm sorry to have to admit, ignored. Anyway, as I've already said, I hate large cities and do my best to avoid them. They don't offer much when it comes to coastal dwelling and time constraints gave me the perfect excuse to drive through.

I was not as impressed with the Folk & Transport Museum as much as I thought I would be. I'd heard so much about the place that perhaps my expectations far outweighed the reality. However, having said that, there are some wonderful exhibits about the place. It's split into two really, separated by the main dual-carriageway road between Belfast and Bangor, the Transport Museum on one side and Ballycultra Town the other, where each building has come from various parts of the Ulster landscape, pulled apart and reconstructed to show how life used to be. This half is a sort of folk town, full of these wonderful buildings, though the setting seemed strange. More of that in a minute.

The transport section is housed in two separate collections of buildings adjoining each other. For £7 I was allowed past the barrier by a pleasant and affable fellow who was keen to help. In the first set of buildings were the Irish railways, bicycle and motorbike collections and road transport galleries. The collection of vehicles is simply stupendous. In the railway hall there are various steam engines and diesel locomotives that visitors can climb aboard. I've never been aboard a steam engine though like everyone else, I wanted to be a driver as an infant. There's something so solid and reliable, so archaic even about steam engines. It is easy to imagine the fields rushing past, the heat from the boiler with soot covering everything, as the night express sped towards its destination. The first proper railway in Ireland – though not Hugh Boyd's tramway – ran the eight miles between Dublin and Kingstown (Dún Laoghaire) in 1834 but by 1853 the network had expanded to 840 miles. The first line in Ulster ran from Belfast to Armagh in 1839. The whole system peaked in 1920 to 3442 miles and if you look at a railway map of Ireland, you see the whole map covered. It's hard to imagine just how important to the development of, especially, agriculture and fisheries, this system was. The only trouble was the overall intention by Britain to bleed the country dry of all its commodities to feed the mother country.

The Irish navvy has become a by-word for workers building railways though its real origins come from the canal building era when these men were regarded as 'navigators'. The railway building era was a dangerous time for these workers (was not the canal era too?) for they worked in shifts around the clock, seven days a week, in all weathers. They lived nearby the workings in shacks they built themselves. The pay was poor and irregular and often they lived through the 'Truck system' in which they had to buy all their food and drink from shops owned by the contractors. In remote places they paid well over the odds for these basic necessities. In the years after the famine, when as we've seen above, the system expanded throughout the British Isles, about a third of all navvies in England were Irish and half in Scotland. Of course they built the Irish lines too.

I could have spent the two hours mooching about that one hall. Bicycles and motor vehicles don't throw me into ecstatic throes of delight though I have to say the condition and number of trams, bikes, fire engines, coaches, lorries and vans, milk floats, and cars was incredible. The first all-Irish car was built by Chambers Motors Ltd of Belfast in 1904 and that company survived until 1928 building more cars and commercial vehicles. In the second set of buildings fanning out from a lobby with a small book and souvenir shop, there are exhibitions on early transport including sledges, early forms of the wheel and animal transport (donkeys carrying seaweed!), the horse-drawn gallery, the hackneyed *Titanic* exhibition and something to do with space which I ignored. Outside was the schooner *Result*, a vessel built by the aforementioned Paul Rodgers in 1893 as the last sailing vessel built by him. This boat had seen action in the First World War and was the last boat working British and Irish waters under sail when she finished working in 1967 under the command of Capt. Peter Welch of Braunton, North Devon. By then she had a shortened rig and a diesel engine installed. The museum bought her in 1970 and she has sat outside for a number of years. How long she'll last is anyone's question though rain and storm do not do wooden vessels any good. They need saltwater to keep the planks wet and rot out. I do know that the museum has stored away somewhere the last remaining fishing 'nickey', the *Mary Joseph* (more of these in time), though what state she is in I hate to hazard a guess. That is the only trouble with many museums: they gather old boats but do not have the finances and technical ability to be able to restore them. Except in some cases, these boats are often best left in the hands of private enthusiasts who put endless hours and pitfuls of money to keep the craft afloat.

Ballycultra Town's Summer Fair was already coming to a sodden end when I arrived towards closing time. Whether the day did end up being a magical one I do not know but the vagaries of the weather almost always affect these events. The fair was a mixture of Victorian dress and a market, a programme of all day events, traditional music and fun around the buildings in the centre of the 'town'. I wandered around a number of the buildings which, given the right circumstances such as sun, would be interesting. With rain dripping down the back my neck, wet feet and a general feeling of cold, it wasn't. I did persevere, walking away from the central cluster of edifices for a short while to view some of the agricultural buildings, but it was no use. There are fifty buildings in all ranging from a bicycle repair shop, railway porter's house and shoemaker's house, all from Dromore, to various agricultural buildings such as a flax mill, a cottier's house, a forge and a byre-dwelling. A brilliant collection though, as I said, obviously out of place. What disappointed me most was the lack of information about how these inhabitants of the buildings led their lives. And, with regard to the sea and those living at the edge of Ulster, there was simply nothing.

Bangor was much as I had expected, a large marina. The rain again. I photographed a couple of large newish pelagic trawlers for posterity and some mussel dredgers and spoke to a skipper of the dredger *Maria Lena* from Kilkeel. Mussel spat from wherever – Waterford, the Irish Sea etc etc – was laid in Belfast Lough and then transported to Holland. In fact he was just back from a trip there to collect another load. He said that business was fair in a true fisherman's understatement. *Bonny & Kelly* had obviously followed me down because she had also just arrived from Greencastle.

I walked all the way around the marina in the wet, past the nicely laid-out gardens and the Victorian housing suggesting a bit of wealth. The St Ives-built *Silvery Light*, a herring boat I knew pretty well, was moored on the outside of the marina with no one aboard. She looked a bit uncared for, the sails were off the booms and brightwork fading. Behind her was the herring drifter *Dundarg*, built in 1939 by Nobles of Fraserburgh. I shouted over to a guy aboard. Turns out his boss had just bought her. She used to be a dive boat but they were off to the slipway in Portavogie for three weeks to strip off the paintwork of the hull and re-caulk her before repainting. The intention was then to fit her out as a luxury charter boat though, with more and more boats getting into this field, it would be a competitive market for them. Good luck I say as it is wonderful to see such a special and lovely boat of that age being put to such good use.

Back at the van, I noticed the old harbour, the Long Hole, over the harbour wall to the east. Judging by the way that the boathouse, now a restaurant, is away from the harbour, the car park I was standing upon was once the beach. A Colin Archer design in the boatyard called *Our Sagittarian* looked as if she had had a bit of a collision with either another boat or the harbour wall. There was a nasty hole in her. I phoned David Adair, another 40+ member, who unfortunately was undergoing a full house restoration so that all his records were stashed away for the duration. He suggested I go and see David Donnan in Portavogie the next morning and even kindly made an arrangement for me to go there at 11am, saying he'd phone David himself. People here are so kind and amenable, I thought once again.

I wanted to go up to Groomsport a mile or so east. I'd a couple of photographs of Groomsport yawls though when I got there I could find no one or nothing about them. The lovely harbour is built around Cockle Island which suggests cockle fishing. It is perfectly sheltered from all but the stormiest of winds. Cockle Row Cottages is a museum which was obviously closed. However, inside it is laid out to portray what life was like a century ago for a fisherman. In fact, so I discovered later, if one searches the internet at www.northdowntourism.com and navigates to 'cockle row cottages, one is able to enjoy a 360 degree panoramic view of the inside and outside by webcam. Oh, the beauty of technology No wonder there was no entrance fee! From the harbour wall, the rain briefly stopped and Dog exercising, it was possible to see nearly a dozen flashing lights from lighthouses and lightships from this spectacular harbour, such was the clarity of the air. The lighthouse on Mew Island (built in 1884) was just visible to the right, a place I remember during my youth when navigating these waters for, in the days before Decca Navigation and GPS, we used radio direction finding, and one of the strongest transmitters was on the island. I recall many a time tuning in and plotting a bearing from Mew Island to find our position. As elsewhere, the harbour was void of any working boats and the place solely relies upon tourism for survival. The fish and chips were pretty good though.

Portavo lies between Groomsport and Donaghadee in the shadow of Copeland Island. The names come from the French 'Que portez-vous', a reference to smuggling, according to the Francophile Delachorois, as this is what the traffickers would ask each other as they bundled their cargoes ashore on moonless nights. The Copeland Islands were regarded as a staging post, even a warehouse, for this part of the coast. Tobacco, spirits and silk, as well as more mundane items as sugar, soap, and window glass were brought ashore. In 1823 the authorities seized eighty-eight sacks of tobacco on Lighthouse Island with a duty value of £1,307.

The harbour at Groomsport.

A Groomsport yawl.

Orlock was also a favoured landfall. Gin and other liquors, and tobacco, were landed at North Kea. The goods were stashed in caves since collapsed and a light in the window of a house would guide the boat in. Groomsport had half bales of tobacco on open sale - a bit like buying tobacco in the pub these days where it's been brought in from Belgium where it's a third of the price it is in the UK. Serves the government right for being greedy, I say!

Early attempts were made to stamp out smuggling in the 1820s. Coastguard stations were built here on the Ard peninsula, as elsewhere, six by 1825 at Groomsport, Donaghadee, Millisle, Ballyhalbert, Cloghey and Tara, all manned by fifty-five customs officers and boatmen. The local Revenue cutter was the *Kite* based at Donaghadee and crewed by thirty-four men, costing as much as running the six stations. The government took this loss of tax seriously. A small vessel was kept moored off Copeland Island because the owner – Dick Ker, said to be a smuggler although he always denied it – refused permission for it to land. Portavo also had good oysters, scallops, mussels and other fish. In the eighteenth century new oyster beds were discovered off Balloo. Kelp was generally imported from Scotland though loads of it washed up ashore here. This was 'shamefully neglected' according to the Belfast News Letters section in 1789. In the 1837 Ordnance Survey report, Boyle recorded that 'a great many fishers' lived along this coast. Boats sheltered on the south side of Portavo Point where there were cabins for the fishermen to reside in although Ker, who owned here also (probably gained his land from smuggling!), preferred if they didn't. Today nearly all of this 'fabled fishing hamlet' has disappeared save for one fisherman's cottage.

By the time I arrived in Donaghadee, I was tired. Colourful houses circle the bay with a paddling pool and large harbour. We passed Grace Neill's famous bar, said to be the oldest in Ireland and an inn since 1611, on the right. The harbour wall actually ends on a bank in the middle of the bay so that it is exposed to the north, facing Copeland Island, and runs along the back of the harbour, where it dries out, thus being open to the west as well. Within this is

A nickey steaming into Belfast *c.*1920.

the site of the older harbour that dates back to the origins of the packet service between here and Portpatrick across the North Channel, which this was demolished in the nineteenth century. In 1617, this harbour, a simple short quay, was described as the 'most usuall and frequentit for passage between Scotland and Ulster'. Within ten years another, better, harbour had been built and an improved mail service established in 1662. Then, in the 1780s, John Smeaton was commissioned to build a new harbour at a cost of £10,000. However, with the introduction of steam-driven paddle steamers another harbour was deemed necessary to cope with the increased trade. Not only was Donaghadee a packet harbour but also a busy trading harbour especially for the export of live oxen to Scotland and thence England. The famous engineer Rennie was asked to build a new harbour, the one that exists today. In 1825, just after the harbour's completion, a paddle steamer was placed on the route across the 22-mile stretch of water. The service continued up to 1849 at which time the mail service was transferred to the Belfast-Glasgow route. Rennie's lighthouse on the end of the southern quay was only completed in 1836. The railway arrived in Donaghadee in 1861 and, in 1900, a bold plan was put about to build a tunnel under the sea to link Scotland and Ireland. Although various tunnels under the sea had already been proposed, no-one had yet taken seriously the proposal to dig such a long tunnel. The designer deemed all the problems associated with such a project surmountable. The only uphill struggle he had was the finance which he estimated at between six and sixteen million pounds. To date, no such funds, much more in today's figures, have been found. Donaghadee therefore remains a town relying upon tourism.

We drove south once again and came to a perfect place to park overlooking the sea and the harbour of Ballywalter. The beach was sandy with rocky outfalls and, with the van door open, I lay in bed watching the lights out to sea twinkle away. The wind was fresh but the sky clear, a whole garden of stars to muse on. A trawler plodded southwards, possibly to Portavogie, its green and white lights occasionally disappearing in the northerly swell. Most of the immediate world around me was sleeping whilst I was still buzzing from the day's gathering of knowledge. Even a few glasses of red wine wouldn't calm my mind, so I simply continued staring out until sleepness came in the form of fitful dreams. Luckily I managed to close the door before the rain came on once again.

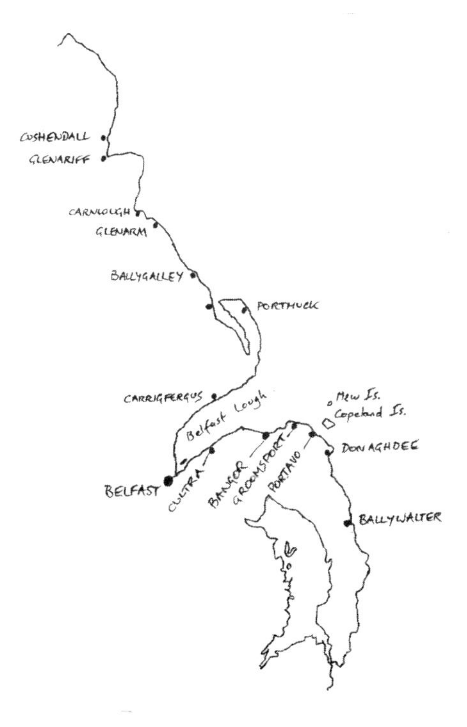

DAY NINETEEN

Oh joy upon joy, the sun was out when I slid the van door across the next morning. The tide was well out and a huge expanse of sand spread out below me like an amphitheatre full of gold. Several folk were out walking with their dogs and mine jumped straight out and shot down over the rocks to introduce himself to the locals. I brewed up coffee whilst watching him run in circles, chasing birds and skipping as if he was a spring lamb. Once the caffeine had refreshed my mind and he'd returned, we walked together along the sands to Ballywalter harbour. This consisted of a long arm jutting out into the Irish Sea with the old lifeboat house atop the slipway. The drying harbour was full of small craft though none of interest to me. The harbour was built in 1851 or thereabouts, as it seems the whole of this coast was actively engaged in fishing. The limestone kiln was built the same time, supposedly to burn limestone for the mortar for the construction of nearby Ballywalter Park. The lifeboat house was built a bit later, in 1866, when the first lifeboat was placed on station. Up to the 1890s this service was a busy one. Its most notable rescue took place in 1883 when the brig *Euphemia Fullerton* was driven ashore onto nearby rocks at night. The pulling lifeboat *Admiral Henry Meynell* was launched but she, too, was driven back ashore at launching and three oars were broken. Another successful attempt at launching was made the following morning, at which time the lifeboat brought ashore the six crew from the brig who had been hanging onto the rigging for most of the night. Between 1897 and 1906, when another lifeboat, the *William Wallace* had been stationed there, only one call-out was answered and the decision was made then to close the station. Today the lifeboat house is occupied by HM Coastguard.

Ballyhalbert, formerly called Talbotstown after the Talbot family who occupied this area after John De Courcy's Anglo-Norman invasion of the late twelfth century, is a spread of housing around a stony bay all looking out to sea. Many seemed to be 'for sale' with boards outside. Its harbour lies just around the south edge of the bay, tucked in under Burr Point, where the substantial structure is protected by a 200-yard long quay. A few small boats lay alongside. In 1836 the inhabitants of Ballyhalbert were mostly fishermen and this had been built in the 1850s, principally for these fishers, though potatoes were exported and coal brought in. I don't quite know why, but I spent some time making a rough plan of the harbour in my notebook, perhaps because I had time to waste before my appointment with the Donnans.

I also had time enough for a brief look over Portavogie harbour, the mostly easterly harbour in Ireland. I'd sailed into here with my family whilst a kid though couldn't remember much about the place though I have vivid memories of sailing passed the South Rock lightship that is anchored off and is, I think, Ireland's one remaining lightship though even this is about to be replaced by a buoy. In the nineteenth century Portavogie was regarded as a major herring port and today its importance is no way diminished. It being Sunday the harbour was full of pretty fishing boats with names that conjure up thoughts about the sea such as *Sea Harvester*, *Bountiful*, *Elegant*, *Faithful Friend IV*, *Golden Ray*, *Argent*, *Day Dawn* and *Bonnie Lass*. There are two good slipways for large vessels and a mural depicting the Scots herring girl that

The BIM 50-footer *Ros Guill*, built in Scotland for Schull fisherman Dan Griffin and later sold to Belfast.

The yawl *Mary Elizabeth*, built for herring fishing and owned by William Close, lying in Portavogie harbour 1925.

I use on my 'herring exhibition'. The poem upon the mural was written by Portavogie man Captain Jim Moore, which reminded me to phone him and ask for an interview.

I found the Donnan house with difficulty, having to ask a neighbour of theirs for directions. There are two Dave Donnans, father and son, and they were both at home. Comfortably sat in their front room, a big mug of coffee in my hand, we talked for a couple of hours about their involvement in the local fishing. Both had fished, senior Dave having retired whilst younger Dave works in the fish processing factory mostly all year round though, he said, the work can be seasonal. Most of the landings these days in the harbour are prawns, the mainstay of many a fleet around Britain these days, though three or four boats were trawling whitefish.

'Fished from a 20-foot yawl,' said Dave dad, 'built at Murnin's of Strangford.'

'Murnin?' I asked.

'Aye, there were a few boatbuilders around here. In the early days folk built their own yawls. Then Palmer worked from Ballyhalbert before he moved to Portavogie. Albert Palmer was working in the 1940s and built the *Glorious*. He built many 50-60 footers but stopped many years ago. Colin Mahood and his brother Brian fitted out wheelhouses and the electrics and stuff. Still do it in the yard. Stewart's another. They were to the north, Palmer in the middle and Mahood in the south where the existing slipway is. You'll see.'

He showed me a photograph of the *Glorious*, as well as many more.

'So how old is the harbour?' I asked.

'Captain Jim Moore'll tell you more. 1904 I think. Though before the harbour the boats anchored off the rocks, in the roadstead. Last year they found the remains of a nobby, the anchor chain heading north-east. Jim's written a bit about Portavogie.'

I told them I'd already phoned him and was going to see him afterwards.

'There two parishes here really – Ballyfrench, town of the French, and Portavogie, port of the bog,' he said when I mentioned my difficulty in finding their house. 'Portavogie is more of a townland than a village.'

Aboard the *Glorious*, built by Palmer of Portavogie in 1940s for herring drifting and ringing.

Those words were echoed by Hugh Robert Coffey later that afternoon, another fisherman I visited in Portavogie. I asked about how things were today.

> Lots of potters. Probably 2,000 creels laid hereabout. The mosquito fleet we call 'em. Forward wheelhouses and all the same boats, all one-maners. Bit of mackerel jigging and some lines on a small scale. No fishing in Strangford Loch, no dredging and trawling, though some creels allowed. Five or six boats work the clam fishery in winter. Used to be plenty of whiting and haddock, used to give it away, though now rarely see it. The cockles were hammered about four years ago. Certainly no herring and if there was it would go to Ardglass though the herring fishery used to be massive here. Things used to be taken for granted though that's changed. On reflection we did wrong, taking berried and undersized lobsters for example. Now no one does as it's stupid.

They sat next to each other on the settee most of the time. Father and son, and how alike they were. So friendly, so genuine, I felt an impostor. Dave dad, as I called him, had such a picturesque face in which his kindness was clearly evident. Dave son was an accomplished painter and his dad told him to go and get a few examples. The ones he showed me were all of the sea, fishing boats, a lighthouse, but mostly fishing boats. I later photographed a couple including one of the boat *Silvery Light* I'd seen the previous night in Bangor. They were true to life and true to detail, both important attributes. They told me about two or three places I should visit after Capt. Jim Moore.

> Tara, there's a coastguard station there. Was going to be a harbour. Stop before the rocket house as he doesn't like people driving past, and walk down. Ratalla, it's a bit south of Portavogie harbour. They used to say there's Ratalla boats in the bay. And there's Kearney. It's a fishing village. Worth a visit about five miles south.

I never did discover exactly where Tara was. At first I took it to mean Cloughey though then realised that there had been coastguard stations at both places so they must be separated. I should have asked for clarification. Anyway, though I could have sat there all day, I had to leave. I can still picture the expressions on Dave dad's etched face. There seemed to be some sadness there though he didn't say. Only two people wouldn't let me take a photograph of them after I'd spoken to them; he was one. The other I hadn't yet met and in total I reckon I interviewed between fifty and sixty people. Dave son wasn't so inhibited and so I took one of him in the doorway of their house. Before I did leave, and as I've said, I was sorry to go, they handed me some really interesting papers with various facts about the Ard peninsula and Portavogie fleets, some of which I shall attempt to convey across.

One of the papers concerned boatbuilding in Ballyhalbert. One open air boatyard was near the graveyard and the most prolific builder was William Mahood who built some of the vessels from Springbank on the edge of McCammon Sands, Ballyhalbert. It is said he built them in six weeks. There's a whole list of vessels built between 1886 and 1926, some twenty-six vessels in all. These were variously described as luggers, ketches and nobbies. Amazingly, many of his craft ended up all over Ireland, in Belmullet, Baltimore, Westport, Cape Clear, Arklow, Dingle and Union Hall. However this paper also noted builders at Cloughey, Ballyeasborough, Stable Hole and Warnocks Road, the latter three being within what is now Portavogie. Stable Hole was in fact the oldest settlement here, back in 1555, a time when the area was settled by fishermen from across the Irish Sea. Cloughey lies a bit south of Portavogie.

Another concerned the history of the harbour which before 1904, as Dave had said, didn't exist. The main jetty in use at that time had been built at John's Port, a mile north of today's Portavogie and this seemed to have been a well patronised quay. In 1822 there were three cutters, thirteen smacks, twenty-three wherries and two yawls based there whilst at Ballyhalbert there were five sloops, fourteen smacks, unspecified number of wherries and twelve yawls. In a moment I will explain the difference between these types of craft.

Fifty years before this Arthur Young noted the summer fishing off the Ard peninsula which, he wrote, was largely for home consumption. There were, he estimated, 400 boats from the coast, each 4–5 tons each and costing £15 each to build with the cost of a set of nets being £10. On average each boat caught a mease of herring a night which sold for £8 8*s*. But, as usual, the fishing was precarious. In 1774 it had been very good but very bad the following

Adam, Tommy and Samuel Parker aboard the *Essie Cully*.

year. 1776, the year of his visit, had begun well though we don't know how it ended. The barony of Ard were fishermen, sailors and farmers, by turns, he wrote. He also noted that boats went to the Loch Swilly herring from here. Imports were coal from Whitehaven and timber and iron from Gothenburg and Norway.

By 1886 the fleets had expanded. Cloughey had nineteen sailing luggers and thirty row boats, Portavogie forty luggers, Kircubbin fifteen luggers, Ballywalter eight or nine row boats and Portaferry eight luggers and twenty row boats. However, this is still a far cry from Young's 400 boats, many of which presumably came from other parts of the coast. Whereas the luggers might be 4-5 tons, the row boats weren't. What is interesting about the 1880s was the growing demand for a proper harbour along this coast, the only ones being at Donaghadee in the north and Ardglass in the south, which meant fishing boats often missed their rail connections if the winds were light (Even though the railway had reached Donaghadee, Ardglass wasn't connected to the rail network until 1891.) Cloughey was the favoured spot and a railway was suggested running down the Ard Peninsula.

By the end of the nineteenth century, Ard fishermen were travelling to the Kinsale mackerel fishery as well as the herring fishing in Maryport and as far away as Shetland. Alexander Nimmo had been through in the early part of the century and suggested Stable Hole as a suitable site for a harbour though nothing came of it. After years of disagreement, it wasn't until 1898 that funding was made available. Work started in 1900 and was completed by 1904 though the structure was damaged 15 months later. Repairs weren't commenced until 1908 and completed by 1910, at which it was named St Andrews Harbour though why I never did discover.

Time, then, to clarify fishing boat nomenclature in a few very brief words. Cutters and smacks are single-masted craft, the main difference being the number and way of setting the foresail(s). This only refers to the rig and not the hull. Luggers are lug-rigged vessels and generally refer to the Cornish and Manx luggers. Here's a further confusion. Luggers had been built in Cornwall for generations and when they were adopted by Manx fishermen they were called nickeys. Basically they are the same with minor localised differences. One Cornish builder, though, William Paynter, originally from St Ives, set up a business in Kilkeel in 1875 and built several nickeys for the Isle of Man, Campbeltown and Irish fleets. However many of the Manx nickeys were being built on the island so business wasn't as brisk as he'd hoped. When a disastrous fire swept through his premises a couple of years after his arrival in Kilkeel, Paynter rebuilt his premises and persevered though he never received the number of orders he had hoped for. Thus, in 1883, he returned to Cornwall. Nevertheless, the term 'nickey' stuck in the Isle of Man and Northern Ireland. Wherries were a particular type of boat in use throughout the Irish Sea and, in general, can be regarded as coming in two sizes. Big wherries fished off the coast, even sailing as far as Shetland. Many were used for smuggling between the powerhouse of the smugglers in the Isle of Man to all four countries surrounding it. Smaller wherries fished inshore, especially in sheltered parts of the coasts such as in Loch Fyne, Scotland. All wherries, though, were rigged with two masts with a schooner rig. I will explain these craft in much more detail in a later chapter. Nobbies, of which we've heard a fair amount about on the west coast, were imported from the Isle of Man after the 1880s when they replaced the earlier nickeys on the island. These were lug-rigged vessels with a hull shape that was, in turn, copied from the ring-net herring boats of Loch Fyne, known as Lochfyne skiffs. Row boats, often called punts, don't need further explanation.

Captain Jim Moore welcomed me into his house and we sat down to talk. What soon became apparent was that he was a good talker and he also knew his stuff. At seventy-four-years old, he'd been around, he said with a smile. He was short with a round face and bald except for two tufts over each ears and bushy grey eyebrows. His red knitted sweater seemed slightly too big. But he had a mysterious air about him.

I began by asking him about his book on Portavogie and he showed me a copy: ***Portavogie: A History***.

'Sold about 600 copies. £8 to you and all the profit goes to cancer.'

I bought one. Then he briefly ran over the history of the harbour, much of which the Donnans had pieced together. I asked him about his history.

> Left school at fourteen. My father had a boat, a Stewart-built 52-footer, *Girl Isabel*. Before that he'd owned the *Lady Brooke*, also built by Stewart in 1942. Stewart packed up building about 1950. So I started fishing in 1947, sixty years ago. We were netting hake all around including over to Peel. Diesel was cheap then, no pressure on owners. Nothing in the wheelhouse but the skipper. None of this electronic wizardry they all rely upon these days. Five of us in all aboard. We worked ten to six, all the lines redd up by six. Summers seemed best. I enjoyed those long summer evenings, the smell of kippers and the Scotch herring fleet going out at night. Northern Ireland had a massive fleet then, all the boats in pristine condition, gleaming and beautifully varnished boats. If the fishing was poor some went off to the Merchant Navy though came back for the herring season. Oh, they talked of foreign places so I wanted to go off there. So when I was eighteen I joined Lairdferry in 1952 in Belfast, the Burns Laird Line. The next twenty years I sailed all over the place though mainly Canada and the Mediterranean runs. Got seven certificates. Left in 1968 because I'd been married seven years.

He seemed confident in the way he spoke, almost as if what he said was rehearsed. He continued after drinking some of his coffee.

> Trawling had started here as the seine-net was too expensive. I bought the *Kincora*, built in Arklow in 1949 for Jimmy Thompson of Buckie. Kincora was the palace of the last king of Ireland who was murdered by the Vikings. Jimmy Thompson had two boats from Tyrrells financed by the Dublin lot when he taught the Southern Irish to use the seine-net. He'd also taught in Canada. Well, I bought the boat. 11am on the 23 of March 1968 and I had her until August 1981.

His memory was fantastic for he recounted everything without consulting anything. The way he recalled dates, and even the exact times, was incredible. Well rehearsed maybe.

> Trawled and fished for queenies. Isle of Man, Douglas and Ramsey most, Isle of Whithorn. Sold her to Ardglass in September 1981. I'd already bought the *Sandpaulin* from Killibegs on the 4 July 1981 and kept her until 1983. *Mayflower* next, a Herd & Mackenzie boat built in 1957. Bought her on the 6 June 1984, the anniversary of D-Day. Gave he up her on the 11 November 1994, Armistice Day, and retired. Son took her over until September 2006. She was in our family for twenty-three years and she's still in Kilkeel.

We talked a little bit more about the fishery and then the conversation got round to earnings and here he was equally lucid.

> In 1940 we made £30. But say with the *Kincora*. She grossed about £580 a week on good weeks after auctioneers fees. She'd cost £10,300 as a seine-netter so I had to spend another £700 for trawling gear. £11,000. Paid £1000 deposit. So, £580 less expenses left £500. Divide that by ten

> equals £100. Each man got £50, half a share. £250 left over and £150 went to the government mortgage and £100 to the boat for upkeep and the nets. By the time I'd finished fishing the expenses were £700 a week. The government took tax off the skipper but the skipper never took tax off the crew. If you did he'd not be there on a Monday. I paid the *Kincora* off in two years and was laughing after that.

'What about life aboard the boat?' I asked.

> The man with the least sea time was cook. Breakfast was always good, bacon and eggs, plenty of fried bread. Everything cooked in one pan. Sometimes it rolled onto the floor but he put it back into the pan. Lots of tea made with condensed milk. Two holes in the tin! Lunch was a sandwich and mug of tea. The evening meal was always a good proper meal, meat, veg. All wholesome food and plenty of it. Good food. Chocolate biscuits and tea during the day. A grocer knew his boats. In Campbeltown he'd come down to the boat and ask what you needed for the next evening. Coffee too, and lemonade. Fishing boats were very uncomfortable. We ringed for herring too, landing catches in Peel. Away from home from Monday to Saturday. Breakfast was fried herring then, boiled herring with potatoes for lunch and kippers for tea. No bacon and stuff. If we were away for a long time we'd get the women ashore to do our washing. Pay them with some mackerel or herring. When dredging queenies we'd be at it twenty-four hours a day. Two dredges out but needed the engine power for that. Could get up to twenty bags an hour at times.

I could relate more. However after a while he said come and have a look. I climbed up a ladder into his roof and I was staggered. Inside the attic, everywhere was literally stuffed with memorabilia. I would not have thought it possible to get so much stuff into one attic. Benches stuffed with models of every conceivable type of boat from liners, steamers, Thames sailing barges, Clyde puffers and, of course, lots of fishing boats. Posters everywhere. His second love is football and there was plenty of that too. Photographs everywhere too, cigarette cards of boats, model lighthouses, fishing gear. I had trouble taking a photograph trying to capture some of the atmosphere with Jim in the picture it was all so crammed in. But I had to leave him, as with the Donnans and so many others, I'd have liked to stay a while. But I wanted to drive down to Kearney and walk the dog. We said our farewells, him telling me to call again if passing. I will for sure.

Kearney dates back to the eighth century when it was part of the 'petty kingdom' of Ulechach Arda when the abundant fishing and light soil attracted settlers. In 1177, after John De Courcy had conquered the whole of Ulster, Kearney passed to the Savage family who built Quintin Castle a few years later. By the late nineteenth century the Orr, Hastings, McMullan, McNabb and Cavan families held most of the Kearney townland, all interrelated by marriage and class, though they established a strong social network. Kearney was booming with three windmills, two flax mills, eleven grinding corn, and a school that only closed in the 1920s. In 1836 the population was 150 but, a century later, this was twenty. One of the most influential and prominent figures in the village was Mary Ann Donnan who lived from 1841 until 1939. She was the mid-wife, flowerer of linen, layer-outer of corpses and the captain of the *She-Cruiser*, a fishing boat crewed entirely by women that worked lobster creels. Her belief was that the wind always blew in the east when someone died and just before she died she asked what direction it was blowing. The answer was from the east.

The village has been owned by the National Trust since 1965 and is open to visitors. It has a lovely calm atmosphere with whitewashed houses in a traditional manner. No TV aerials or satellite dishes are allowed on the exterior of the houses. We walked along the coast for a mile or so, enjoying every moment of the sea air and fine scenery. Returning to the village I found the tiny sort of museum that seems to be open through the day though no one was in attendance whilst I visited. Inside were some information boards and photos of the wildlife. There was one interesting one about the South Rock Light. This part of the coast was a busy sea route with coal, hardware, textiles and tea the main cargo. Many ships were lost on the rocks that jut well out from the coast though the locals benefited by scavenging these wrecks. Some say they even lured vessels onto the rocks but that's a tale well told throughout coastal areas. It might be true and might not, no one has ever proved it either way though meaningless experiments with lanterns have been done.

The first lighthouse had been built by Thomas Rogers and first illuminated in 1797 and continued to flashed for eighty years until, because of continuing shipwrecks, it was replaced by a lightship further out for the lighthouse did not mark the end of the shoals. Today it remains the oldest remaining rock lighthouse and even though the light no longer flashes it is a well known and used landmark. To replace it, a lightship was stationed further out.

The first keeper of the South Rock lighthouse was called McCullogh and he lived there with his twelve-year old son. One day, on the boy's first trip to civilisation, the boy kept asking questions, as they do. His father promised him a present, probably to shut him up. He asked what he wanted. Earlier the boy had seen two girls who his father had teasingly called goats. So the boy answered by saying 'there's just yin thing da, I'd like you'd to buy me yin o' them goats!' Or so the story goes.

I hastened back to Portavogie to meet Hugh Robert Coffey. Like Jim Moore, he started fishing in 1947, herring out of Portavogie.

'Should have gone away,' he said in his broad Ulster accent which was at times difficult to understand.

> The Scots knew about ringing and were hard to compete against. In the winter and spring we seine-netted up the Clyde, up to Rothesay and as far south as Dublin Bay, the Lambie Deep there. Still making good money from it, more in a week than I ever made in a season.

Again I asked about the harbour and he echoed some of the words I had heard earlier.

> St Andrews harbour, Jim Moore knows about it. Locals called it Piet harbour. Before boats laid inside the McCammon Rocks and one lot in the bay here. Yes, Ratalla is a bit south of the existing harbour. So they built the harbour where it was as a compromise. Halfway between the two. Boats sank though in the harbour because of the spray and so they went back out and anchored off until the harbour was improved by 1910, I think.

We talked about the boatbuilders and again he echoed what the Donnans and Jim Moore had said about the Stewarts, Palmers and Mahoods. Colin and Brian who were still working at repairs were the original Mahood's grandsons. At one time, though, he added, there were two Mahoods working separately, William on the north side and James to the south. They built what he called 48-foot 'sternsheeters', by which he meant nobbies. They could build one in six weeks he added, echoing earlier words. Then came superstitions, many of which were the same I'd heard in Scotland.

> Never mention or bring a salmon onto the boat. He's the 'red fellow'. A rat is a 'queer fellow' and a pig a 'curly tail'. Red haired women were avoided like the plague. Once, when such a

> woman was on the quay one Monday morning, some of the fellows went home when they saw her. If ya' broke a net you'd lose a net. Mentioning a man's name was deemed unlucky. Don't put the brush on top of the net when swabbing the deck. Many more superstitions. Let me think.

Hugh reminded me of Dave Donnan Snr in many ways. They had similar looks though Hugh was older and shorter and his hair much whiter. Dave's was almost still ginger. Hugh's movements were slow which were accounted by the fact that he'd had a heart attack in the 1980s and had to retire from the fishing. He seemed to forget about the superstitions and carried on in another vein, a sure sign that he was quite keen to talk and reminisce.

> Yes, I really enjoyed good times though it was a hard time. Loved fishing out of Peel, a handy place for the herring drifting. Good people over there. It's 30 miles over there though it's nearer to the Free State. Monday mornings could be bad. Needed to settle the stomach so we used to get a few prawns, large ones, and twist the tail off and eat them raw. That would settle the stomach for sure. Sometimes we'd roast them on top of the stove for a couple of minutes and have them in a sandwich. That's all they seem to fish these days: prawns. Remember going to Whitehaven. Used to get flounders there, de-head them and hang them up on a piece of string along the length of the boat to dry for two or three days and then them eat raw. Great taste and a change from herring three times a day. Maybe a kipper in the evening. We'd swap herrings for kippers in Peel. I remember being on the *Golden Dawn*. A young fellow wouldn't share his lemonade. I had some limeade so I put some Fairy Liquid in lemonade and watched the guy creep down and take a few swigs. You should have seen his face. It was a picture. We were always playing tricks. I sold a box of mackerel three times once, the first two buyers forgetting to take it away.

Suddenly, he got up and went into the next room. I could hear some rummaging about and he returned with a bell-pull he'd made out of rope which he gave me. I've got it hanging on the wall here as I write.

> Make 'em these days to pass the time. Rope work's a pastime and hobby because I get so breathless when walking out. When I started some of the fellows had their own nets but that phased out. The share system came in so I didn't have any nets of my own. Started as a boy on a half share on the wee boat *Mirantha*. *Aigh Vie*, know her? She's a nobby and I was on her a while. Used to be a few nickies around too. The *Mary Joseph*, she had roses growing out of her. Campbeltown you say. They used to ask to get the street lights turned off because there was so much herring near the harbour. Just outside it. Oh, I fished there and in Kilkerran Bay.

I'd asked whether he'd ever fished from Campbeltown.

Sadly I had to leave him as he said the last ferry across from Portaferry to Strangford left about 10pm or maybe 10.30pm. As it was half an hour away I had to get a move on. Hugh is another lovely fellow. I know this sounds repetitive but it's always true. There must be something about Irish fishermen or maybe it's just the Irish in them all.

Hugh was almost right. The last ferry left Portaferry at a 10.45pm so I caught it. The five minute crossing cost £5.30 but saved about 50 miles of driving. About a mile outside of Strangford Lough, on the Ardglass road, there's what looked like a fish weir across the mouth of a small bay. Set in a straight line across about 100 yards, the first section was built in stone, a low wall about three feet high, and the rest a series of posts, presumably once having brush and woven hazel rods, or perhaps netting, as infill.

I stopped in a car park, cooked and ate overlooking the Lough. In the dark a car drew up alongside. There was a knock on the van. Police? No, a man was there with a podgy face, rat-like eyes and swaying. He was drunk as a fart and as he asked me a question or two as he peed against the van tyre. He was muttering about the dog and whether I was alone. Three other guys were in the car but only he got out. Eventually he got back in and it turned out that he was the driver! Off he drove across the grass leaving deep ruts in the pristine grass of the picnic area. Pillock, I thought. I think this was the only time I felt a bit vulnerable and decided to move off to Ardglass. Parking up on the quay, I read until at least 1am. It was almost worse there. There was a lot of squealing tyres, speeding cars on the road with loud exhausts. Suddenly there was much shouting of both men and women and a great chorus of honking car horns and general hubbub. I just couldn't believe the noise just down the road. Eventually the place quietened down though one car came up the quay and disappeared around the corner which I knew was a dead-end. At that I fell asleep.

DAY TWENTY

Hugh Coffey was wrong about the weather. He had explained that, as a lad, he had been told that when the South Rock Light Vessel was down on the horizon, half hidden, the weather would be good. If it was high the opposite was the case. As we had gazed out at the lightship the previous evening, just before I had left him at his garden gate, it had certainly looked low, almost as if it was indeed hiding under the horizon (perhaps from those due to remove it from service). On waking up to the familiar drumming on the van's roof, I knew we were in for yet another wet day. God I was fed up with them. Furthermore, last night was the first night I'd been cold, even wearing a jumper to sleep. And this morning I could see my breath as I wrote up a few notes. Autumn is upon us already and it's not the end of August. This must surely be the summer that never was, I'd written.

Ardglass was calmer in the morning and everyone seemed friendly despite the rain. I searched out the café by the harbour where the fishermen gather but by the time I found the right one – a coffee bar within the local shop – they'd dispersed. The shop assistant was almost apologetic though why I did not know as it was certainly not her fault. At the marina I had a refreshingly hot shower and the manager refused to charge me. There's also a fine picture on the wall there of various nickeys and a couple of Scots boats dating back

Ardglass in the 1920s from an old newspaper.

from about 1870. I photographed it with his permission, but the result turned out to be completely out of focus. Even the fellow I spoke to outside the Northern Ireland Fish Producers' Organisation's office commiserated with me when I asked whether Dick James was about. Dave Donnan had suggested I search him out here though unfortunately he was off north somewhere.

Ardglass, from the Irish for 'green hill', is one of the ancient settlements in the Barony of Lecale. As in the case further north, these lands were given over to the Norman knights after the invasion, in which they built a series of castles. It's a perfect harbour tucked away in a small bay just north of St John's Point, the southern tip of the Lecale peninsula and was one of the few natural harbours of refuge along this coast before quays and piers were built here and at other places. Marmion lists it as once ranking 'second to Carrickfergus of all the Ulster ports' with exports of cattle, corn, linen, flax and butter. As to fishing, he says it was 'the most extensive fishing station on the coast', employing 4,000 tons of shipping and 2,500 men and boys. However, prior to the middle of the nineteenth century, little fish was landed here unlike today when it is the premier port along this coast.

The first attempt to build a pier was in 1812 after John Rennie had surveyed the bay and he again oversaw the extension to this in the 1830s though not without mishap when the new lighthouse collapsed in 1838 after a storm. By the second half of that century it had become the centre of the East Coast fishery with 500 Scottish, English, and Irish boats coming to land during the herring season. This fish was gutted and barrelled by a hundred-strong army of herring girls, many from Scotland, and the barrels exported far and wide. However, it wasn't until 1885 that the harbour works were finalised with the completion of the outer pier.

Today's fishing fleet is a shadow to those times. Signs of upheaval in the fishing industry were visible close to where I'd parked the van the previous evening where the remains of a couple of fishing boats lay that had been scrapped. The wheelhouse of one, BA374, sat on the old quay alongside the wooden stems of two boats, complete with the rabbet line looking as fresh as the day it was cut to receive the plank-ends. A couple of long, straight keels, with bolts sticking out in all directions, added to the general sadness and the whole scene could quite easily have been submitted for judging for the Turner Prize. Lots of other fishing debris lay outside redundant warehouses, one of these being advertised for sale. I wondered how long it would be until the site was cleared and housing sprouted up. With the marina just yards away, this seemed a very likely outcome. The fish quay itself was pretty extensive though not busy at that time of day for presumably all the boats were out with only two moored alongside. Nets and trawl boards lay propped up against walls and the market hall looked ready to receive its next load of fish. Outside of the harbour I could see the Isle of Man clearly (the rain did stop so maybe Hugh was right after all!) and the Calf of Man looked as if it was almost touchable if I reached out. I counted nineteen fishing boats offshore, probably all catching prawns. I later found out that there are about twenty-five boats in the Ardglass fleet and, as I had perceived, they were all busy catching prawns.

I looked for Michael Howland who owned a shop called Milligan's up the road after this was suggested by the fellow outside the NIFPO. Michael is researching the history of the town for a book he intends to publish. He has an extensive photograph collection and after I'd asked in the shop and they had phoned him – I think he had been asleep – he came down and led me back to his house a few doors up. There, we went through his library of pictures and papers over some coffee. He then phoned one of his associates in the book project, George Rice, and we went over to see him.

George and I discussed the history of the harbour which interested me most though perhaps I should say I listened whilst he spoke. George is a retired psychiatrist who lives permanently in Ardglass now which gives him time to work on his side of the project, part of which is the development of the harbour facilities. Now I'm sure he wasn't giving away too much but I listened intently.

There's no evidence that a prehistoric harbour of any form existed here, he said. The place to land vessels seemed to be a couple of miles further north at Ballyhornan where there's some shelter afforded by a small island. As late as the famine time the inhabitants there were asking for their pier to be restored. Killough, just around the corner, was a tidal bay and wasn't deemed suitable for development until the 1820s.

'But why Ardglass?' I asked him

'The answer must lie in William Ogilvy who owned the castle.'

I'd already read about him at Michael Howland's house. He had acquired the Ardglass Estate through his marriage to Emilia Mary Lennox, the dowager Duchess of Leinster. The castle George was referring to was now the Golf Course Club House. There are in total seven castles or fortified houses in Ardglass dating from the fourteenth and sixteenth centuries so it's important to get the right one! I visited the Club House afterwards, on George's advice, venturing inside to look at some photos on the wall, almost tip-toeing about in fear of being slung out by the ear. I viewed them in the bar in fact and afterwards I counted the offshore boats from the golf course, avoiding the flying golf balls of course. A few people seemed to resent my presence which pleased me no end for I was reassured in my being there because I'd been given permission by an official though I had left the dog in the van.

> Firstly that structure dates back to the thirteenth century. Archaeologists regard it to have been a fortified storehouse. But Ardglass was then difficult to get into from sea, especially in a south-easterly. Once in it wasn't very safe. Thus it fell into disuse. Secondly there's the human reason. Ogilvy had two daughters. Perhaps he was looking for a marriage settlement for his daughters. He had 3,000 acres about here. He employed Rennie in 1809 to survey the harbour. Remember it was the only place between Drogheda and Belfast that's not tidal, safe or not. He brought the main stones in from the Isle of Man with local infill. The entrance was a continual problem though. He was keen to rival Donaghadee for the packet station trade and he got to Rennie before they commissioned him to survey the coasts in 1814. He was a man of influence and had a Duchess as a wife.

I wasn't sure where all this was going. Looking at a map, Ardglass seemed the obvious place to build a harbour but not very well situated to operate the Mail Packet as the distance to Portpatrick is further, and Ardglass is also further away from Belfast. But some interest stirred deep down.

> You see if the archaeologists think the golf course was a merchant's store then it's likely they were curers and salters. In the middle ages there was a gathering of fish here; this coast has been renowned for its herring shoals. A herring station. Ogilvy wanted salt pans in Ardglass because most of the salt they needed was coming in from Chester and a bit from Carrickfergus. That's why we'd like to borrow your copy of the *Welsh Port Books*. Herring was being sent back to Chester and Bristol. Ardglass was being defended, with five or six men in the Tower House. No, there's a powerful argument for the Golf Club being a sort of medieval 'Woolworths', a market house, specifically for fish though not entirely. Cattle and potatoes were also being exported and slate and coal brought in. Ogilvy died in 1832 you know, before the harbour was finished. His last words before dying were 'I married a beautiful Duchess but am unable to tame the waters of Ardglass'.

I think I eventually worked out what he meant. I think the general consensus between him and Michael – they may correct me if I'm wrong – is that the castle originated as some medieval trading post where goods were exported all around the Irish Sea for which vessels were needed. These vessels came to Ardglass, even if the harbour was dangerous to enter in some winds, and not a particularly safe place once inside. However, it is the only natural one and, as such, was probably one of the safest along this open and exposed coast. Ogilvy expanded on this, building his harbour because the options were limited. Ballyhornan was exposed and Killough tidal. Ardglass wasn't tidal. It all seemed a bit long-winded though a useful and interesting exercise in investigating options. When I got home I did send Michael the pages of the Port Books as they requested and I hope they helped them to confirm George's theories.

Ardglass is the second of the County Down fishing villages, the others being Portavogie, Annalong and Kilkeel, the latter two laying ahead at this point. There's a wee booklet entitled *A Guide to the County Down Fishing Villages*, produced by something called 'The Co Down Fishing Villages Network' which I thought unusual and probably unsurpassed in the whole of Britain that anybody would bother to publish a book on fishing villages. This must surely attest the importance of fishing hereabouts when, according to the booklet, 94% of Northern Ireland's fishing fleet is based in these four ports though, with decommissioning hitting the fleets, I'm sure today's fleet is smaller than the 179 boats it mentions. It probably decreases almost on a daily basis. I did enjoy reading writer, poet and historian Tom Porter's short poem *Ghost of the Long-Line Men*, one of a collection of his in the booklet.

Killough, as George had said, is tidal but now totally silted up and disused though in 1744 there were fifteen ships belonging to this port so it must have been well used back then. The harbour is formed by two piers, one 600-foot long and another shorter one from Coney Island across the way, which date from 1821-4 and were built by Alexander Nimmo at a cost of £17,000. Lord Bangor owned and financed its building ten years after Ogilvy built his harbour and I doubt he would if he had regarded Ardglass as a threat to his investment. Barley was a major export and the harbour was said to have been 'the chief point of export for the grain-growing country of Lecale in the nineteenth century', according to *The Industrial Archaeology of County Down*. Marmion adds that the pier was good and that there was shipbuilding in the harbour though soon after, in the 1860s, the piers had been breached by storms and were falling into rack and ruin. The 600-foot one wasn't any better at the time of my visit and funnily enough I can't even remember the other one from Coney Island. Maybe it had been demolished. The battery of my camera had gone flat and I was busily charging it from the cigarette lighter, the consequence being I hadn't taken any photographs since being inside the marina trying hard to capture that photo, flattening the battery in the process.

The road cuts inland from St John's Point, for me the area being immortalised by Van Morrison in his song 'Coney Island', 'Stopping off at St John's Point ... over the hills to Ardglass ... stopping for a couple of jars of mussels and some potted herring ... heading towards Coney Island' and along the edge of Dundrum Bay. There is of course a lighthouse at St John's Point which dates back to 1844. It is a stout phallic-like structure, the archetypical lighthouse, painted white with three black bands. Further on around the inlet is the tiny harbour at Dundrum itself, consisting of a quay with modern waterside housing, the original quay dates from 1807-08 though was lengthened shortly after 1830. The housing is more 2006, and seemed mysteriously out of place in such a backwater as this. The principal exports in the nineteenth century were potatoes with coal and slates being brought in. A sign that the bay has oyster beds was the presence of the Dundrum Oyster Fishery though there seemed to be no one about when I called to discover more.

Newcastle, on the other side of the bay and sitting beneath the bulk of Slieve Donard

A Newcastle skiff.

(at 2788 feet the highest mountain in the Mourne range) was originally the crossing point of the river Shimna. It was developed into a tourist town in the 1830s when Marmion described it as 'a modern watering place with some export trade'. However, before that, it was evidently a magnet for the wealthy who wished to enjoy the sights of the mountains which appeared to touch the town. Today it was busy with visitors and roadworks alike. I walked along the promenade, which is quite new with stainless steel railings to stop folk dropping onto the stony beach, a new pedestrian bridge across the river, stainless steel waste bins, lampposts and lights and fancy oak benches. It all looked very impressive and as if a huge amount of money had been thrown at it. Sadly, there had been a power cut so the bookshop was closed though the open-air swimming pool at Blackrock wasn't and sounded very busy from the screams of delight, or maybe cold.

The harbour was small and full of pleasure boats. No signs of the Newcastle skiffs that once fished from here. These small double-ended boats, clinker-built by local boatbuilders, were similar to the yawls from the north though the Newcastle men preferred to call them skiffs for some reason. Perhaps because they were smaller for coping with the tidal harbour. They were used to set long-lines in the bay, catching whiting, codling and haddock in winter, plaice, turbot and sole in spring, and mackerel and herring in the late summer. However, unlike the boats from the north, they generally only set one dipping lugsail. The harbour itself dates from the 1820s, being built to replace an earlier quay used by the fishermen who lived in squalid huts on the seashore. The chief reason for building the new pier was to expand the export of Mourne granite. This was first quarried above, on Millstone Mountain, after the quarry was opened in 1824 by John Lynn. He built a tramway, known as the Bogie Line, to bring the granite down to the harbour to be exported. Some was used in the construction of Belfast and Liverpool docks, and some went to London. In 1859 a richer quarry was opened on Thomas's Mountain, to which the tramway was extended. As in Dundrum, coal and slates were brought back. It is said that Newcastle was one of the first places where the thatched roofs were replaced with 'Bangor Blues', the slates from North Wales, which arrived aboard ships coming to load the granite. Tens of thousands of tons were produced every year, the peak being in the late nineteenth century. The industry had disappeared by 1939. With the arrival of the railway in 1869, Newcastle was reached from Belfast within an hour, bringing with it hordes of day-trippers and holiday-makers. Today it survives in much the same way, though having to compete with package holidays abroad.

Annalong sounds such a lovely name for a place to live in. It translates to 'the ford of the ships' which may refer to the Viking raids upon the coast. The village itself seems to date from the seventeenth century and the harbour built by 1740, said to be the best of the harbours on the Mourne coast. During the first half of the nineteenth century it was expanded specifically for the export of local dressed granite though this was enlargened more again in the 1880s to accommodate bigger vessels. It was also paramount in importance in the building of the nearby dam in Silent Valley in the 1920s, thus creating a reservoir that supplies Belfast with its drinking water producing, these days, 30 million gallons of water daily. A railway was built from Annalong to transport all the necessary material needed for the construction.

However, it had a much murkier, some would say exciting and profitable, past in the eighteenth century when it was close to the centre of smuggling activity along this coast. Though not operating on the same scale as Rush and Skerries further south, of which we will learn more, the Mourne coast was deemed perfect for the illicit trade in commodities

The harbour at Annalong with nobbies alongside.

Yawls at Kilkeel.

that were otherwise heavily taxed by the government and there is no doubt that the trade was extensive about the Irish Sea. This was in no way different to most of the coast of Europe were taxes were equally high. In the days before computers and radar, the movement of vessels was very hard to observe and control even if the coastguard service did stem from the combining of the Preventive Water Guard and the Revenue Service set up to counter smuggling. Today's drug smugglers are a far cry from the bringing in of tobacco, wine and brandy in a business that was regarded as totally reasonable by the majority of people. All smugglers needed was a place to run ashore quietly at night, to move and hide their goods, and have a ready and preferably large market to sell their goods. Although profits were high – though they had to obviously make sure they sold their goods on at a lower price than the taxed counterparts – they did suffer losses through the Revenue men. With the central storehouse of the Isle of Man just across the water, the Mourne coast was prefect for their purpose, with Belfast and other developing parts of Northern Ireland, their intended markets, not far away. The general state of the coast road connections was poor and much of the goods were carried through the mountain passes, again away from prying eyes. With increased effort to stamp out smuggling in the nineteenth century many ex-smugglers turned to fishing for a livelihood and, with the abundant supplies of herring just offshore, Annalong became a fishing harbour in about the middle of that century, the principal one at that, as it was the only harbour of any significance between Carlingford and Newcastle at the time. It remained so until Kilkeel was built.

Dog and I walked around the harbour which is, as all the literature says, very picturesque. The nineteenth-century Corn Mill was of interest as it was one of the last working water-mills in Ulster at its closure in the 1960s. In 1983 the local council bought it and a restoration began that took two years before it was opened to the public. We looked in but didn't have the tour round. A couple of fishing boats came into the harbour as we gazed around, though they only had a couple of boxes of mixed fish for their troubles. One person of interest born here was Francis Rawdon Chesney (1789-1872). At twenty-five he saved several fishermen's lives when they had been caught out in a storm. He was a British soldier and explorer in Asia and demonstrated that the building of the Suez Canal was feasible, bringing about its eventual construction. He also proved that the rivers Euphrates and Tigris were navigable.

Kilkeel was another place I'd heard so much about, mostly with regard to the fishing However, Kilkeel was, in comparison to many of the fishing towns and villages we'd visited, new. When Alexander Nimmo surveyed this coast he thought the mouth of the river Kilkeel not suitable for a harbour, preferring Greencastle and Derryogue, the latter an established fishing community. Kilkeel, he considered, suffered from having a gravel bar which he regarded as obstructing access into any cut of the river mouth. Derryogue, just south of Kilkeel, did have a quay built and became a major yawl harbour though not accessible to large craft. It certainly existed in 1834 and probably fell into disuse, as Annalong did, once Kilkeel was up and running. Today the 'little harbour of Derryogue, some distance west of Kilkeel, which afforded indifferent shelter to the small fishing crafts in northerly and westerly winds', as it was described, has all but disappeared except for a line of stones that used to be Andrew's Quay. On report notes that Derryogue yawls were built locally. One builder was William Norris who built them between 26 and 30 feet in length, another being Duncan Scott, though no dates are given.

In 1740, Kilkeel was described by Harris the great antiquarian as, 'a small village and a church situated between the foot of the Mountains of Mourne and the sea, in a narrow vale, which extends for some miles along the coast, the sea good and the country well inhabited'. In 1835 it was inhabited mostly by fishermen who fished close to the shore in 'canoes', which we can assume were currachs, as there was no shelter for craft. By 1846, though, it had grown to five streets and 230 houses 'for the greater part well-built and comfortable, and nearly all are occupied by a hardy, temperate and courteous population estimated at 1270'. But it still had little industry for the locals. However, there was a hotel which was popular and the need for a harbour was becoming more vital. In January 1843, a squall hit the fishing fleets out and resulted in eighty fishermen being drowned from Newcastle, Kilkeel and Annalong. It was subsequently believed that the haddock deserted Dundrum Bay as a result of this storm.

By the 1860s a very basic pier had been built at the mouth of the river below Kilkeel village but this was inadequate and had to be improved in the early 1870s. With more demand, and over 1,000 fishing boats working this coast in 1879, this again had to be enlargened so that by1887 the harbour was able to accommodate 100 luggers at any one time, with 300 said to be landing during the herring season. Today it remains the premier fishing harbour in Northern Ireland.

It was bright and breezy by the time I arrived in the late afternoon and the harbour was pretty full though many of the boats were presumably out.

'No, not as many as you'd think,' said Leslie Warnock, 'the haddock quota was exhausted last week so now the choice they have is to lay up or go to the prawns with a twin-rig trawl. Many have chosen the former as you can see.'

Leslie is the owner of the Kilkeel Fishing Supplies and as he's a member of the 40+. I decided to call in and introduce myself. He took me into his office and we chatted for ages. He also showed me his photograph collection. He's keen on old fishing boats.

'How may boats then working from here?' I asked.

'Fifty odd though there used to be a lot more. When the herring was running. Decommissioned plenty, some scrapped here.'

'Yes, I heard. Bloody disgraceful isn't it, chopping them up. Good old craft with life left in them. Lovely old ringers smashed up on beaches, others set fire to. Legalised vandalism I call it.'

'It's the ring-netters I love most,' he agreed, 'with their varnished hulls. They were just so

The nickey *Mary Joseph* motoring into Kilkeel.

Kilkeel harbour *c.*1900.

pretty, sleek vessels.'

What person able to appreciate the gentle curves and skill going into a fishing boat's construction wouldn't agree with him? We talked of Paynter's Yard and he pointed out where it had been situated at the other side of harbour.

'He built the *Mary Joseph* you know here in 1877.'

I said I did and wondered whether he'd heard more about her than I had.

'Heard they, the museum, were going to do her up. That was ages ago. I've a good picture here of her somewhere.'

He found it and I copied it, as I did several others.

> MacIntosh had a yard here too, you know. He built boats including the *Peace*, M20. She was fitted with two second-hand engines before being sold to Eyemouth where she became the *Bethel*. The two engines were swapped for a single unit. I'd love to know what happened to that boat. It's possible that she went to Southern Ireland.

He was the first person I'd heard up in the North that didn't refer to the Republic as the Free State. We nattered on for a while before he said I should go and have a quick chat with Lenny McLaughlin who worked next door and who has the largest collection of photographs of Kilkeel. Leslie went back to helping his blokes with the setting up of a net that I'd interrupted them doing, or thought I had anyway. I went to meet Lenny briefly. He was about to shut up shop and seemed in a rush. He seemed to know who I was and said he'd been meaning to join the 40+. He said he'd thousands of photos and he said he'd help me though I never heard from him again even though we exchanged addresses.

From Kilkeel I drove up into the mountains intending to take the dog for a hike. It was really windy and very wet underfoot. Whilst lifting the dog over a particular awkward stile, the button holding my trousers up flew off. I found two halves of it amongst the grass for it had snapped in two! The walk was aborted much to the chagrin of the dog who was happily splashing through the wet, and we returned to the van, the wind trying its best to remove the trousers.

Thus we drove on, back to the coast and along, past the nineteenth-century watering place of Rostrevor, arriving at Warrenpoint on the edge of Carlingford Lough, where there's a harbour dating from 1767 which was the principal place of trade for Newry. A wet dock was built at the same time. The harbour was improved in 1830 but the Newry Ship Canal was opened in 1850 which affected a decline in the Warrenpoint harbour. Today it's touristy with a pleasant breakwater to walk along, an open-air swimming pool (cor, two in a day) and a modern port a bit upstream which dates from the 1970s. I watched a ship steam slowly down river and out to sea on its passage over to Heysham whilst the dog sniffed around. The breakwater was completed in 1974 to protect the new harbour. The town itself is very Victorian in design with its grid system and it is thought to be one of the best planned towns in Ireland. It didn't do much for me, I'm sorry to say. Offshore here is the Haulbowline lighthouse that Seamus O'Flaithearta had mentioned back on the ferry from the Aran Islands. This is a rock lighthouse, built by George Halpin in 1817 and is one of the oldest on the coast. The accommodation is in the tower, brightened no doubt by the tiny windows in the solid structure, a stone one a 100 feet high, acting as sentinel to the entrance to Carlingford Loch. Today it's a natural stone colour though it was, for its first 130-odd years, painted white.

We drove along the canal to Newry and crossed over the river and canal, returning along the other side. The canal could have been built in 1703 when Captain Francis Nevill suggested the idea of linking Lough Neagh with the sea. Construction did start nearly thirty years later and the first canal to Lough Neagh opened in 1742, the first major one of its type in Ireland,

William Paynter's boatyard at Kilkeel.

in the British Isles in fact, the first two vessels along it carrying coal to Dublin. However it was plagued with problems and faults and several attempts were made at rectifying these without much success. In the 1820s Alexander Nimmo was asked to survey the canal and he suggested abandoning it and canalising the river up as far as Newry. Eventually, John Rennie was employed to deepen the channel to a new lock and the old canal was enlargened and deepened, the work finally completed in 1850, at which time Rennie boasted that this, what became the Newry Ship Canal, was 'the largest in Great Britain, or in any other country, with the exception of the great canal from Amsterdam to the Helder'.

We stopped briefly at a small quay where I'd spotted a few boats. Amongst several steel craft was the mussel dredger *Ketten*, WD213. Then at some point we passed back into the Republic though I wasn't sure exactly where. Suddenly I noticed the post-boxes were painted green and the road signs different. It certainly didn't feel any different. We passed Carlingford with its marina and Victorian town dominated by the Norman castle overlooking the Lough and its harbour enclosed by two great piers. Oysters were once exported from here – the beds lie along the beach from Narrow Water to Greenore Point – and these were considered the finest in flavour, superior even to the Purfleet oysters of Dorset which were the best in England. Greenore is the main port on the Irish side but we sped past with the light fading, past Gyles Quay, an old boomed harbour formed by enlargening a natural hole in the rock where today a small fleet of potters is based, and through Dundalk though I did photograph the fish quay with its bunch of uninteresting boats lined up three or four abreast, many being suction dredgers.

We drove on to Blackrock where I hoped to find Charlie McCarthy at 'The Point' although I wasn't sure why I was to talk to him. He was another name on Darina's map. I asked in the shop and they hadn't heard of him. So I sat in the van contemplating the scenery in front of me which was the expanse of Dundalk Bay. According to an information board the sea goes out miles and the beach is said to be popular with children because of its gentle slope. On the other hand, seeing how quickly the tide will flood in, I find this a bit dangerous. Having said that there are signs all along the promenade warning beach-goers not to venture out and over (or through) the river channel which runs parallel to the shore. Obviously if anyone becomes trapped offshore of that on a rising tide then they are in grave trouble. It's a sort of mini-Morecambe Bay, renowned for its treacherous sands. The other pastime here seems to be bird-watching. There's a 'Cockle Hill', a low wetland with no hill and, I wondered, maybe no cockles any longer. Somewhere out in the bay lie memories of the lug-rigged yawls that once fished there, mainly for herring though sometimes for lobsters. Despite having the same construction in the hull as the northern yawls, these southern yawls favoured the dipping lugsail. Another type of local boat was the salmon flat which I assume to be similar to the flat-bottomed river Boyne craft which are yet to come in this journey.

We moved along the coast to find a resting place for the night and parked up on some grass overlooking the Irish Sea along the southern edge of Dundalk Bay. There was a quay in the distance which seemed to be a protecting arm to a small river. It was too dark to work out and I thought I'd leave that to the morning. Posts in the water marked a channel suggesting some recent usage. Offshore a yacht was anchored in deeper water with two little boats dried out on the beach. In the twilight they looked like a couple of stranded beasts. It did seem to be a very exposed position although sheltered from the north-west through to southerly winds. A good easterly gale, I thought, would do a fair bit of damage here and, according to the Portavogie men, not that infrequent. Staring out over a muddy foreshore, the lights of the north shore twinkling across the bay, I considered the past few days.

Northern Ireland has some sense of Britishness although there are pockets where it was missing entirely. Before you shout out, remember I've only whisked along the coast. It's hard to define what this Britishness actually is though it seems to be just a feeling of organisation, of control even, of the orderly fashion that Britain has to suffer. Ireland, on the other hand, would like to be orderly in its new European face but somehow can't quite manage it. Oh, yes, the Garda are more forceful these days, government more intrusive into people's lives and laws have been introduced, but these only depend on who you know and how much you care. There's nothing of the quaintness about the place any longer, and it seems that the East Coast is going to be even more straightforward in so many respects than its western counterpart. Dublin only lies 45 miles to the south of where I was but thankfully, that night anyway, it still seemed a lifetime away. Thoughts to go to sleep with.

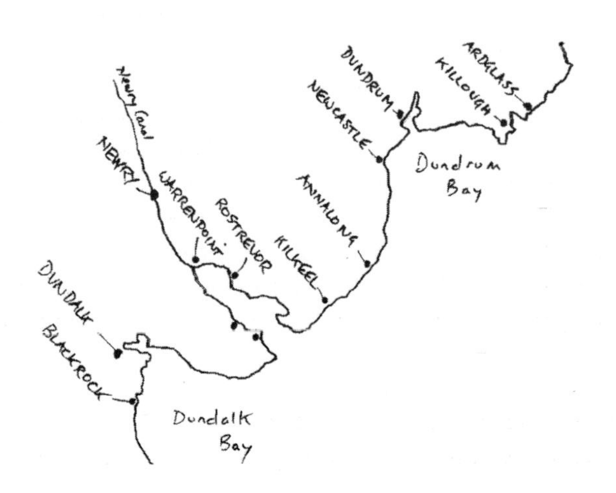

DAY TWENTY-ONE

Mornings have become a routine: wake up, stroke the dog who's lying across the floor of the van next to the head of the mattress, get up, roll up the bed, put the seat back, fill the kettle and put it on the stove to boil. Make the coffee, let the dog sniff around, drink said coffee, write notes, think about what the day will bring, pour over my map, pour another coffee ...

This morning was no different. There was the metallic sound of rigging slapping against an aluminium mast floating across the water from the anchored yacht. The tide was lower than the previous evening and the two boats no longer look like stranded beasts, simply uninteresting run-of-the-mill dayboats. The eastern horizon was a pastel wishy-washy yellow colour under grey clouds with the occasional shaft of brightness highlighting their ragged shape and slow drift across the skyscape. A fine drizzle splashed patterns on the front windscreen. The dog gave a soft growl as the owners of the house across the road made their way to work. I wonder whether they minded me parking on the patch of grass directly across from their view out over the Irish Sea, whether they consider it their patch. Not that there's a fence or anything though someone keeps the grass mown. It suddenly occured to me that I didn't notice any public footpath signs in Northern Ireland either so I wonder what the rights of passage over private land are there. After three mugs of coffee I am ready for the day's travelling to begin so I pack away everything that might move and drive on. Time, in the words of Rudyard Kipling, to take hold of the wings of the morning.

The quay I'd seen the previous evening in the twilight turned out to be a harbour, hidden behind a house. Twenty odd fishing boats were lying alongside the quay, on top of which was a large hard standing where more boats had been lifted out. These boats, in the main, were cockle dredgers, mostly steel workboats designed with one purpose in mind. I studied one to describe how these boats operate when at sea. There's a suction dredge hanging over the stern which is lowered to the seabed with a flexible pipe of about nine inches in diameter, leading to a dredge pump. The dredge itself has skids on the bottom to allow it to run over the sandy seabed smoothly as it's being towed. Seawater is added to the dredge through another pipe, dislodging the cockles and sucking them into the contraption. Eventually the cockles (well, I presumed cockles) are pumped up from the seabed and into a cylindrical revolving sieve so that the remaining sand and water drain away and the cockles are then bagged. The double winch controls the dredge and the large pipe leading off it. There's not much action around this morning though. The quay itself looks to be newly refurbished, with street lamps and a concrete surface. The odd container loafed about probably being used as fishermen's stores. A nearby limestone kiln was an impressive affair with unusually ornate brickwork around its corners and arch but otherwise appeared to be completely derelict. In fact, the whole area seemed pretty abandoned with rubbish strewn along the edge of the scrubland and a few boats that wouldn't be going to sea again. Even the boats in the pool against the quay looked pretty run down and uncared for though the owners might disagree with me. Certainly they didn't have the same sparkle as many other similar boats I'd seen.

I wasn't exactly sure where I was. Somewhere close to the Loakers Wetlands, a protected area famous as the most important site in Ireland for wading birds. I never did discover the name of the harbour. Further down the coast, just past Annagassan, I observed a group of people, perhaps twenty in number, raking the sandy foreshore presumably for cockles. Port, part of the parish of Togher, is a fine sandy beach with Blue Flag status, a convenient public toilet and a medieval church somewhere about. We walked along the beach for some time, my waterproofs fighting against the rain, and then returned back to the van through the sand-dunes. Coastal erosion is an obvious problem judging how the dunes were being eaten away.

I'd arranged to meet Paddy Hodgens in Clogherhead, a fishing port tucked south of Clogher Head. The harbour is actually called Port Oriel Harbour and I was quite surprised when driving down the hill to find a completely refurbished quay, complete with acres of shiny-new concrete. Paddy was sitting in his car as he'd described on the phone when I'd called him the previous evening. He was yet another of Joe Teesdale's contacts.

Paddy used to be the harbourmaster here so he knew the place probably better than anyone alive. Born in 1929, he'd started fishing at the age of sixteen as cook on the 53-foot herring drifter *Gola* out of Howth. During that first year they had fished out of Howth to begin with, then moved up to Ardglass to fish off the Isle of Man, getting home at weekends. Afterwards they'd gone seine-netting off Newcastle, and down to Dundalk Bay which was good, he said, because they got home every night. Paddy spent five years at the fishing before coming ashore. He didn't look old enough to be 78 though I didn't disbelieve him. Obviously the weather here keeps one young. Under his baseball hat, with his rounded shoulders, he looked a good ten years younger, more maybe, with a fresh glowing complexion, ears sticking out from light grey hair and head always seemingly tilting a wee bit to one side.

'Spent three summers on the *Brae Mou*,' he said as if I should have known the boat.

'She was Tom Sharkey's boat, he brought her from Lossiemouth in 1938, a dual purpose seiner-drifter with a motor. Sharkey family had owned the *Family Trust* which was the first motorised boat here.'

I asked about the new pier.

> Just opened, 17 May back, after two years work. They spent €12 million on it. There's twenty to twenty-two boats working out of here, most from France, twin-riggers working over the stern, all controlled from the wheelhouse. The French ones seem to suit us best here. Sixty to seventy per-cent prawns, we have a good quota, probably about a third of the total Irish prawn quota. Bit of a cod by-catch, up to five percent, the same for monkfish. They work the West of Ireland between March and July, landing in to Dunmore East and then around the Smalls in winter

I'd read in the booklet *Clogherhead Port Oriel – A Brief History*, by Kathleen O'Brien Briggs (Paddy kindly gave me a copy) that prawn fishing started here back in the 1950s when everything else was in decline. Prior to this, prawns were regarded as having no commercial value until scampi became popular. This whole coast, indeed much of Scotland, hasn't looked back since. The book also charts the growth of the structure of the harbour. Though a harbour was mentioned in the 1476 Statute Rolls of the Parliament of Ireland, this was slightly west of the existing one. Every fishing boat entering paid a mease of herring, though no more than once a year. The present inner harbour that Paddy showed me dates from the 1820s though this was, like many other small harbours of the time, tidal. At the time the fishermen fished in their yawls, similar to those we've seen all along the coast. That these yawls were in use here surprised me because, as I have earlier stated, I had previously believed that these craft worked the coasts from Co. Donegal to Co. Down but I was beginning to discover that their use on the East Coast was much more widespread and that there were similarities to the so-called 'baulk yawls' of the Isle of Man. All these boats were influenced by the original Norway yawls, previously described in an earlier chapter. This is proof that the Norwegian influence was considerable and far reaching.

These yawls were hauled up at both this 'new' harbour or Dock as it was referred to, and the older Port-a-Wadda during the winter for safe-keeping. When two larger boats were introduced into the fleet here, these probably being of the nickey type, they were too big to be taken ashore and were submerged in the Dock over the winter and dried out the following year. The Dock was excavated in 1837 but it wasn't until 1885 that funds were provided for a decent pier to protect the harbour. Once this was completed there was a certain amount of disillusionment as the locals had been expecting a new fishery harbour when all they got was an inferior Harbour of Refuge. I couldn't quite understand the difference mind you. Since then more work has been carried out in the Dock with booms provided to close it off during storms and, in 1964, a mechanised crane to lower and raise these. Paddy described how this was done when the wind was anywhere between north-west and south-east in direction. He reckoned they could fit seventeen to eighteen 50-footers in there.

He became harbourmaster in 1950 though he remained involved in small boat fishing. As harbourmaster his duties were to collect harbour dues, light up the lights, lower the booms as he thought necessary and generally keep the place tidy. He retired in 1996 and since then the job has been done by a young lad whom Paddy introduced me to. He was picking up the rubbish.

'If I don't do it, no one else will,' he said as he stooped to pick up an empty crisp packet.

Above the harbour were three new industrial units.

'One processes crabs, another is a mechanic cum engineer and the other is a fishmonger who sells at the farmers' markets,' Paddy answered when I inquired. 'The crab processor has a small boat of his own though he buys a lot of crabs from Gyles Quay, Skerries or wherever and makes crab meat. You can see Gyles Quay under that white cloud see,' he continued, pointing away north over the sea. 'Kilkeel is under that blue hill over there.'

Fishing boats at Clogherhead *c.*1920.

Fishermen and representatives at Clogherhead with motorised vessels behind.

I squinted to see but couldn't work out which blue hill he meant as they all looked blue! Nor which white cloud as there were many scudding across the sky. Paddy carried on talking.

> There used to be a bigger processor here. Derek Younger. Redsail Fish Processing and Frozen Foods. He opened up in the late 1970s, bought everything that was landed and sold it to markets in France and Spain. He died about five years ago so it closed though the Fishermen's Co-op bought it. It's for sale again as we've a new auction building. Boats now land wherever: Howth, Dunmore East, Clogherhead, especially Rossaveal in Co. Galway. And it's sold here every Monday and Thursday. No processing though. Just four workmen, one manager and a girl in the office running the market. When Derek Younger had it, he employed 130 people.

He pointed to one of only a handful of boats alongside the quay, the biggest one at the end.

> That's new here, belongs to Seamus and Niall Connolly, the *New Grange II*. They have three boats now. Bought this one from France. We've had a succession of new and second-hand boats coming into the fleet here over the last few years. A sign of investment which must mean success partly because of the fishery and partly from the harbour development. Look Seamus is there, I'll introduce you.

Seamus told me the boat had been the *Notre Dame de Rocamadeur*. He'd bought her three weeks ago and had been working on her as she was being surveyed the following morning for her licence. She'd cost about £850,000 in total and he'd had to sell another boat to finance this one. The crew, I noted, were busy removing old signs in French and replacing them with English versions. He said to have a look around but then his mobile rang and, after a brief chat, said he'd have to go but would be back soon. We waited a while though he didn't return.

Paddy pointed out a white cottage across the bay which he said had been a coastguard station back in 1922 when it closed. This was 'Watch House' though there was another signal station atop the hill behind the harbour. The harbourmaster's office used to be a wooden hut near the present ice plant but that's gone since the new works. Suddenly, Paddy decided we'd drop in at his house up the road as he wanted to show me a picture of the harbour as it was. Then he said he'd introduce me to one of the lifeboat crew who he reckoned would be down at the station in Clogherhead itself which as, in fact, about a mile or more away from the harbour.

Padraig Rath was in the station. He was, I guess, in his forties, bespectacled with short greying hair on a fairly square head. After he'd make his introductions Paddy decided he'd go so I said farewell to him. As he left he said he wanted a copy of the book in exchange for the booklet he'd given me. Padraig took me into the lifeboat shed where the Mersey-class lifeboat *Doris Bleasdale* sat on her trailer attached to the tractor ready to roll out at a moment's notice. Upstairs, in the office, he made me a cup of coffee whilst talking about the station. The first lifeboat was stationed here in 1899 in a corrugated galvanised iron house and the present building dates from 1992 when it was built specifically for the existing lifeboat which was brought onto station in 1993. Padraig was the second coxswain and mechanic and thus was the only full-time crew in this station though many stations have two full-time crew.

'That would be the coxswain and the mechanic though depends on the geographical position rather than the size of boat', he said.

He'd been with the lifeboat for twenty-five years and was responsible for much of the day-to-day running of the station.

> We average ten calls a year though have only had two so far this year. Most calls are to fishing boats ten or twenty miles off. We exercise every two weeks regardless. Yes, we do work with the coastguards, we have to. There are four coastguard helicopters: Dublin Airport, Waterford Airport, Shannon Airport and one at Sligo. Each boat has its own special field almost, Howth deal eighty percent with pleasure boats, more often inshore. Dublin has a lot of suicide jumpers because the bodies float down the Liffey and are often found under Howth Head. Have you heard about the Boyne Fishermen's River Rescue?

I said I had but didn't know much about it.

> The salmon fishermen started finding bodies in the Boyne where they can take ten weeks to surface. Fishing the river in their salmon boats they know each nook and cranny in the river from the habits of the fish. They decided amongst themselves to start the river rescue. When alerted, they'd go out onto the river, use their nets to find the body, staying out until it was found. Sometimes it took weeks. Now they have a dozen boats or so, RIBs, and fifty volunteers who get no pay and they go all over when needed.

I asked about the boat itself, the launch.

> We can launch in seven minutes, ten if it's less critical. We let go the chains on the whistle and the tractor pushes the boat out into the water. Only need a little over a couple of feet to float off. Coming back, it takes about fifteen minutes to retrieve the boat.

He described the way they brought the boat ashore as well as saying that the RNLI were developing a new class to replace the Mersey, a boat with water jet engines. Then he mentioned that the Viking replica long ship *Sea Stallion* had arrived here a fortnight ago from the Isle of Man as part of their sailing from Roskilde in Denmark to Dublin. He'd seen the boat and he'd been mightily impressed. There were sixty-five crew aboard, all of different nationalities. We nattered on a bit more about life in general. As a mechanic, though, he seemed to have plenty to do and was soon off again on another call. A few weeks later he e-mailed me a few photographs of the lifeboat at the Blessing of the Fleet in the improved Oriel Harbour held on the 5 August, a couple of weeks before my visit. The harbour was full of boats.

After he'd driven off I sat on the beach a while enjoying the sun that was out. Somehow it reminded me of Anglesey in my childhood. There were a few folk around and a couple of kids splashing in the sea. The beach is sandy for four miles, right down to the entrance of the Boyne River. I wanted to get to Mornington on the south side of the mouth of the river, on the other side, which necessitated a drive through Drogheda. I only stopped to get some money out of the hole in the wall though it didn't seem very busy which contradicts Young's description of the town as being one of the busiest market towns he'd come across. Things change in time.

At Mornington I was after examples of the river fishing boats I'd heard about, sometimes called 'prams' though some fishermen seemed to refer to them as simply canoes or boats. Despite being unusual craft, they were not that different to the prongs of Waterford, but definitely having their own individual characteristics. Just below Mornington the river widens out before taking a double bend out to the sea. Here, afloat, on the mud and amongst the grass, some in fairly good condition, some derelict, I counted twenty-five prams.

The prams, as I'll call them, were the salmon and mussel boats of the river. Though they were similar there were subtle differences between those that fished the salmon and those that raked up the mussels. Built mostly by the local fishermen themselves, and most would have one of each, both have the same basic shape with a fairly flat but rockered bottom. They are keel-less and clinker-built from local deal in the main. The transom is strangely circular in shape whilst the bow is almost truncated in that it looks as if it's been cut off in the same way as a pram dinghy does, which is where the name comes from. On the bottom of the hull there are runners along the entire length to ease their pulling in the mud. Can one be used as the other then? In the absence of anyone about to ask, I had to discover for myself.

The salmon boats are easy to recognise as they have a stern platform for holding the net. From that, I worked out that the average size of these was about between fourteen and sixteen feet. The mussel boats on the other hand are generally bigger at between 19 and 21 feet to carry the extra load. They only have one thwart though some have a large platform near the bow upon which the fisherman stands whilst dredging. Salmon boats have two thwarts. Thus these have more beam and two extra planks either side. With mussel harvesting halted in 1998, because the river was being dredged, and the beds being re-seeded afterwards, it was hoped to recommence collecting in 2003 yet still, four years later. I'm told it hasn't due to the lack of reproduction. Such stories of poor harvests occur all over mussel producing areas so it is possible that they will come back again. I found what I deemed to be the mussel boats turned upside down with old carpets and other fabrics covering them until such time as the fishery starts up once more. As to the salmon boats, I counted about a dozen definites though a couple of the rotting boats were hard to decipher. There were a couple of salmon boats afloat as well, though, with this year's lack of licences, they can't be getting much use.

Salmon fishing is by a draft net, taken out from the shore where one man holds the end of the net, and the boat letting it feed out as the oarsman rows around in a loop before returning

The Boyne fishermen's banner.

A Boyne coracle.

to the riverbank. There used to be fifty salmon licences locally. In mussel fishing, practised in winter, the fishermen use a long rake about 18 feet in length to lift the mussels. It's a method rarely used these days though the mussel fishermen of Conwy, in North Wales, still practice the age-old tradition. As to my own query about whether one boat could be used in place of the other type, I ultimately decided that they couldn't except in desperation.

There's also a Boyne currach which was used for draft-netting for salmon in the lower reaches of the river and was one of the last currachs to be covered in hide. These vessels are almost circular in shape and show some resemblance to the coracles of Wales though two men would be aboard, one rowing from a kneeling position and the other paying out the net, whereas the Welsh coracle only ever carried one man.

Dog and I wandered about as I studied these craft. It was funny watching him bound around in the long grass. He probably thought it equally funny to watch me measuring these rotten old boats. Eventually we reached the river entrance where a groyne on the south side sticks out into the Irish Sea. Several stumpy towers depict the northern channel edge whilst another two towers are situated onshore, presumably once as leading marks. The square Maiden Tower is situated by the old lifeboat house which, until recently, was derelict and has now been restored. Looking like some folly from the past, an old wooden lighthouse structure sits on wooden stilts upon the flat roof of a nearby house. Whether this was the remains of the patent screw pile structure, invented by blind Belfast engineer Alexander Mitchell, I wasn't sure though I read somewhere that the piles, once screwed into the sand, supported a timber structure so it is possible.

The coast between here at Balbriggan was one of an endless sandy beach, a bit like the one to the north. The road was fringed with tourist shops, amusement arcades and other unsightly elements necessary for a coast-wise holiday in these northern climates. Caravans and chalets jostled with bars and gaudy hotels and hostels.

Balbriggan is about to be invaded by thousands of houses being built on its northern edge. Just the thought of this instilled horror in me. More housing! Where do all the people come from to inhabit them? I learnt that there was a huge amount of local opposition to the project. Houses aside, what of the harbour? This stems back to the Hamilton's family purchasing the area. They wished to develop the small settlement. Between 1761 and 1765 he funded the building of a 600-foot quay of limestone which formed the first harbour at the mouth of the river. At the same time a lighthouse was erected by John Hamilton in 1769. The first keeper is said to have been a clergyman: Reverend George Hamilton, possibly a relative. When Young passed through he stayed with the Hamiltons and wrote of a pleasant harbour that 'subsists by its fishing boats which [Hamilton] builds; has 23 of them, each carrying seven men, who are not paid wages, but divide up the catch'. The commercial harbour was also a local focal point for trade with corn and timber being exported whilst Welsh slates, coal and culm were imported from across the water and Cheshire rock salt. Whether this salt was for the herring curing isn't clear but it's quite likely. Hamilton's lighthouse was later demoted to a harbour light in 1860 with the building and illuminating of the Rockabill which is situated on the southerly and larger of the two rocks called Rockabill that lie about 3 miles off the Skerries. The lifeboat house is of interest for it was built in 1890 beneath the railway viaduct carrying the Dublin to Drogheda. Sadly the station closed eight years later though the building still remains.

It's ironic that the harbour at Skerries – known at Holmpatrick at the time – got permission in the fifteenth century to build a fortified harbour because of pirates being provided a base on Lambay Island that lies just offshore because in later years Skerries became a centre of smuggling operations all around the Irish Sea. However, before that, there was mention of a harbour at Holmpatrick in 1315. John Hamilton, owner of Balbriggan, also gained possession of Skerries in 1721 and he renovated the pier in 1775 creating a thriving fishing industry. I'm curious to know if Hamilton had a hand at the smuggling seeing how much money he invested in these harbours. The Skerries wherries were a particular type of craft regarded as being native to the area and I'm fairly sure that the vessels that Young referred to were such craft.

These vessels have been documented to some degree by Holdsworth who describes them as peculiar and much used in the district to the north of Dublin. He examined one in 1864, in Balbriggan, used for trawling, another suggestion that they were working from there as well as Skerries, although he added that few were used by then in the fishing, the majority being employed carrying cargo in the coastal trade. His description was as follows,

> a lumbering craft, half-decked or entirely so, and some of them we believe were over 30 tons. These wherries are the only fishing vessels we have seen on any part of our coasts which had the schooner rig; but some were in the course of time converted into smacks, and that is now the usual rig of the larger fishing boats, except those used in the drift-fishery.

Of the smaller fishing boats in use, he notes their similarity to the Norway yawls and reckoned the Norway trading vessels many years ago introduced them.

The 53-ton wherry *Mary Gold of Skerries* fished, as did many others between 1812 and 1818, out of Tobermory, taking aboard 320 bushels of salt on the 7 February 1814 and returning a week later with the same salt and no fish. Brabazon states that he preferred the wherry rig to the cutter rig as these craft avoid the huge weight of one single mast, two smaller ones being much lighter, and also makes them easier to work in heavy rolling weather, and they set a boomless main which aids working aboard. The advantage of loose-footed sails was well known by the fishermen around the country, the Thames bawley being one most notable example. Numbers of wherries working the Irish coast in 1802 were: Ringsend 7, Howth 7, Malahide, 3, Rush, 16, Skerries, 36, Balbriggan, 9 and Baldoyle 9. They were noted as being chiefly employed in long-lining, where they could shoot the lines under foresail alone. Some were decked and others only half-decked. In 1820 there were fifty-two vessels ranging between 20 and 57 tons. Some were smack rigged whilst others were two-masted wherries, both of which were considered the best type of vessel for the western fisheries.

Referring to the fisheries of the West Coast of Scotland, Walker notes these wherries in use in Barra, whose native boats, which he called 'yauls', were too small and insufficient. These were from Rush and he describes them as being the most expert in the cod fishery. They were half-decked and from 6–10 tons and were 'the proper Vessels to be used upon this Barra Fishery'. Anderson makes the following observation regarding the wherry rig,

> All the fishermen agree, that wherry-rigged vessels are the only proper ones for the line-fishery ... wherry-rigged vessels would also answer perfectly well for the herring-fishery after the Dutch method'. This was in 1785, so do we infer that he did not come across any wherry-rigged vessels engaged in the herring fishery during his travels? Of Shetland he suggested that 'the only vessels that have hitherto been discovered, that can possibly be employed for these purposes [the long-line] are such as the wherry-rigged; for, with such vessels only, can the sails be worked with the facility that is necessary on these occasions; and with such a rigging alone, can a vessel of any considerable burthen be so worked as to be capable of shooting and hauling a long-line under the easy management of a foresail.

The harbour at Skerries.

He notes that the fishermen of London, Yarmouth and other parts of the East Coast of Britain, as well as those of Rush and the northwest of Ireland use such a vessel. As an example he quotes Captain Kyd who ascertained that wherry-rigged vessels were more efficient at catching fish than other boats, suggesting that each 'wherry man caught nearly as much fish as four men in boats'. However, in direct contradiction, he states in his addendum that, although fishermen seemed to be unanimously of the opinion that the wherry rig was the optimum rig for vessels bigger than a boat, he had come to the conclusion that this wasn't strictly true. He continued, 'A vessel that is to be employed in fishing for herrings at sea after the Dutch method, requires probably a peculiar built and possibly a particular rig also, for lying in the water'. It was important that at least one mast be lowered, he said. However, he admitted, wherries were the simplest and easiest to work of all the vessels he considered.

These wherries also fished Shetland and around the coast at Killibegs. It's a shame that little is known about them these days. By the late 1870s the wherries had largely been superceded by the nickeys and later nobbies. Loughshinny is, I guess, a similar place when it comes to smuggling, a small harbour in easy reach of Dublin. The beach was lovely and the quay pretty deserted. However, it is Rush that is said to been the real active centre of the smuggling trade in all of the Irish Sea.

As I've said before, smuggling was, and still is in some quarters, regarded as a legitimate trade in goods, simply avoiding unfair duties imposed by the state. In the Irish Sea, in the eighteenth century, it was the Isle of Man that became the storehouse for goods that were to be smuggled into Britain that would otherwise attract dues if imported in the state-recognised way. The island was perfectly situated in the centre of the Irish Sea and, under the jurisdiction of its proprietor the Duke of Atholl and not the British Government, it could charge whatever import duty it wished. Thus items such as tea, coffee, tobacco, wine and spirits were brought from Europe by various Manx merchants to be forwarded by boat into Wales, Western England or Scotland. Salt was sometimes brought in from Ireland. The slave-traders brought goods such as coffee and rum back from the West Indies.

The favoured craft used to transport the goods from the Isle of Man across to the mainland was termed the wherry. Evidence is strong of the existence of such a class of vessel, but there appears to be much confusion as to what exactly constitutes a 'wherry'. A wherry has been described as a light boat with two masts, with a fore and aft rig and in use in the Isle of Man until the 1830s when the dandy rig was introduced.

However, the problem with the term 'wherry' is that in the past it has been used with a customary lack of precision. Often such vernacular terms require a fine critique to clarify their definition. What exactly does the above definition refer to? Is it the hull-form, or a rig, or 'just' a boat? That wherries exist is clear from the documented evidence but more investigation is required to properly define such a vessel.

When the Revd Dr John Walker set sail from Greenock to Campbeltown during his tour around the Scottish West Coast in 1764 (he later wrote *A Report on the Hebrides of 1764 & 1771*), it was aboard the 'custom house wherry'. Presumably, this wherry, belonging to the Customs and Excise Service, was larger than a simple open boat. In 1766 a 'large wherry from France discharged 650 ankers of brandy at the Troon' which again suggests a large decked vessel.

Philip Higgins was employed to list every vessel entering Douglas Harbour in the 1750s/1760s and in his thorough compilation he names hundreds of boats. Amongst these are a fair proportion coming from Rush in Ireland, the home of the Skerries wherries – we shall discuss this type of vessel later and in general two sizes appear in use. The smaller wherries are classed as being 6 tons and the larger ones 18 tons. Out of a sample of 150 wherries, only nine carried cargoes, rather than arriving in ballast. The cargoes of these nine were individually: a horse (2), a bullock, a cow, two cows (3), ballast and beef, beef tallow. One vessel, the *Happy Return*, coming from Drogheda, had a tonnage of 35 tons. The wherry *Mary and Ann* arrived in Saltcoats from Balbriggan in November 1766 with only ballast aboard and took on eight cartloads of coal and proceeded to Ballycastle. The Higgins list includes a *Mary Ann* as being 18 tons and over a six-month period she called in at Douglas on at least four occasions. From other sources we have the Whitehaven wherry *Mary* that was registered as 24 tons in 1812 whereas the smaller *Peggy* was 6.58 tons. In comparison, the sloop *Peggy of Ladyburn* was 29 feet long and 10 feet 6 inches in beam and was regarded as a small sloop.

A.W. Moore, in his *A History of the Isle of Man*, quotes from a letter written to the Board of London by the Collector of Customs at Liverpool in 1740 that gives the particulars of one large wherry as being 16 or 17 tons burden carrying ten or twelve men. This vessel, it seems, was from 'near Ribble and Wyrewater' and was 'constantly employed in carrying prohibited goods from the Isle of Man to those parts'.

That wherries were used for smuggling is undisputed: in 1765 there was seen 'a wherry at anchor and a great many horses and casks upon the shore...the casks carried back to the wherry in yoals ... the wherry weighed anchor and went to sea'. Their use in smuggling was due to their speed. In another letter to the Board, the Collector of Customs at Liverpool wrote of a captured one: 'She is a fair boat about 16 or 17 tons loaden and sails comparatively well and carries 10 or 12 men always armed'. This echoes the dimensions above.

L.M. Cullen, who wrote various papers on smuggling in the Irish Sea and beyond, noted that Rush was considered the centre for the smuggling trade in the northern Irish Sea and that fifty such vessels were from there. Indeed, the Irish Revenue Commissioners informed their British counterparts that Rush-built wherries were responsible for the entire contraband trade.

Evidence for the smaller wherries is more forthcoming and the dimensions of one are given. Of boats condemned in 1778, after being arrested for smuggling, there were

> small boats that none were decked ... boat number 11 measuring 19 feet 12 in and 8 feet 2 inches in breadth is computed in the said certificate at seven and one fourth tonnes though by his computation it should only be seven tonnes.

In contrast the wherry *Heads of Ayr* is 52 tons. In 1777, fifteen wherries were said to measure 82 tons, calculating to 5½ tons.

The Isle of Man wherries were fish carriers but there appears to be no evidence on the island to support the theory that they fished. In the eighteenth century these two masted 'wherries' were used by fresh buyers who would meet the fishermen at sea and buy herring for a quick passage to ports in England and Ireland, especially Dublin or Liverpool, or back to the island.

The island of Arran had its own unique type of wherry if the description below is correct. This was the yachtsman Robert Buchanan, in 1883, while sailing off the east side of Lewis:

> The Arran wherry, now nearly extinct, is a wretched-looking thing without a bowsprit, but with two strong masts. Across the foremast is a bulkhead, and there is a small locker room for blankets and bread. In the open space between bulkhead and locker birch-tops are thickly strewn for a bed, and for covering there is a huge woollen waterproof blanket ready to be stretched out. Close to the mast lies a huge stone and thereon a stove...rude and ill-found as these boats are, they face weather before which any ordinary yachtsman would quail.

Wherries were also used to fish off the English coast. A portrait on a porcelain bowl, painted in underglaze blue, depicts the fishing vessel *Isabella* fishing with a net hanging over the stern, and is dated 1779. Three more schooner-rigged vessels are shown in J.T. Serres' views of the Mersey and in 1796 the ferries from Liverpool to the Wirral were two-masted open boats. At North Meols, a similar type of vessel was used for fishing. The *Betty* was a two-masted schooner, built at Hoole Marsh in 1817 and measured 32.3 feet x 10.9 feet x 14.70 tons. She was sold to Whitehaven in 1840. Stammers, in *Mersey Sailing Ferries*, gives iconographical evidence for these vessels.

However, we must guard against the confusing or erratic use of terminology. Mackenzie, in his *The Book of the Lews* (1919), refers to 'the straight-stemmed wick wherry' in contrast to the Buckie boat, as being one of the East Coast boat types, when presumably he was referring to the scaffie. In Hampshire and around the Isle of Wight wherries were two-masted craft, often with transom sterns that set either sprit or lug sails. They were often used for smuggling in the nineteenth century and a painting by George Chambers, now in the National Maritime Museum, shows one such sprit-rigged vessel that has a hull-shape with a strong resemblance to these Irish Sea wherries. Whether there is a common link, or this is mere coincidence, is unclear.

In conclusion, there does seem to be some evidence that the term wherry referred to the hull as well as the rig, although the general consensus is that a wherry is a two-masted vessel of any description. This is supported by evidence from Bangor where the sloop *Petrel,* built there in 1866, was subsequently lengthened and re-registered as a wherry of 24 tons and sold to Scotland in 1883.

Evidence of the smack-rigged trader (wherry?) working in Manx waters can be seen through the model of the *Athol of Douglas*, dating from 1790–1800. The hull is clinker and has a roomy forecastle which allowed plenty of foredeck for working the headsails. The model is considered to be a true replica and is suggested to be of a Norwegian or Scottish aspect, although it shows a certain resemblance to medieval boats on the seals of Dover and Poole. Gretton, who wrote an article on this boat which was published in *The Journal of the Manx Museum* in 1957, believed this to point to Norman influences and thus 'the relationship to the Viking ships can be assumed'.

I liked Rush immensely and not just for its smuggling history even if readers think I've overdone the history bit here. No, it was a place without a sense of time, a sleepy little village with a lovely harbour. I sketched it. Then I decided to clean out the van and suddenly the dog was gone. I searched the car park, the surrounding area, even the beach. Then I saw him, lying in the sea, just his head above water, cooling off though it wasn't that hot.

I guess Malahide once upon a time was a nice peaceful place. Now, although there's a bit of a Mediterranean feel about the centre of the town, it's a mass of expensive restaurants, tennis courts, waterfront housing (and so so much more on the periphery) and a large marina. It has swallowed up whatever heritage it had. It's both touristy and in commuting distance of Dublin. It has tram stations that lead as far as Balbriggan where even there I saw car parkfuls of cars awaiting their commuter owners to return and Malahide is no different on that score either. Still, it's quite pleasant in the sun and I think it's the foreign accents that give it its present Southern European flavour.

We really are into the Dublin zone now. I quickly visited the fishing harbour at Howth with its huge harbour. There's a huge platform for bringing large boats out of the water and massive trolleys to carry these equally massive fishing boats (70–80 feet at least) into the nearby shipyard. Boats galore in the harbour of all sizes and some fish shops where I managed to buy some marinated herring. The harbour itself dates from the early nineteenth century when Howth was the main packet station for the Holyhead ferry. By 1813 there were signs of silting up. In 1818 the sail boats were replaced with the first steam packets that reduced the travelling down across from Holyhead to seven hours. Dun Laoghaire took all the ferry trade after 1833 after which the harbour fell into disrepair until the twentieth century and the coming of the fishing fleet. Another infamous visitor to Howth was, in 1914, Erskine Childers' yacht *Asgard* with its cargo of rifles to arm the nationalists.

I didn't imagine I could drive through a capital city so quickly but Dublin I did. Even quicker than Belfast. Before I knew it I was on the road around the south of the river, heading out to Dun Laoghaire which was probably a good thing as darkness was beginning to fall and I wanted a brief look over the town. From a history point of view it had its first pier in 1767 for the landing of the ferry from Holyhead though it wasn't until the 1820s that the harbour was really developed with more quays added in the 1850s. More recently in 2001, further breakwaters were built and a new ferry terminal. Young arrived here in 1776 from Holyhead after a twenty-two-hour crossing. Today it takes about two on the fast boat! The National Maritime Museum used to be housed in the Mariner's Church here though it is presently shut and I'm not sure when, or if even, it will reopen.

Of much more interest to me was the lovely little harbour of Sandycove for, even in the late hour with the sun well gone, the kids were still jumping off the pier into the sea and swimming around. The crescent-shaped cove is sandy indeed and the man-made structures simply close off the seaward end except for a narrow entrance. In the early nineteenth century, Dun Laoghaire's first lifeboat was placed here by the Dublin Ballast Board but it was soon considered an unsatisfactory place and it was moved into the main harbour. Nearby, below the

Martello Tower, is the open-air seawater bathing pool called the Forty Foot Pool, named after the regiment Fortieth Foot that was stationed in the tower. A morning swim became a ritual. It used to be for gentlemen only who could swim naked though pressure eventually opened it to women even though the 'forty foot gentlemen' strongly objected. The compromise was that 'togs must be worn' after nine o'clock in the morning. Before that nudity prevailed as I believe it still does in the allotted time. There are three such harbours in Dalkey, where I was, the others being Bulloch and Coliemore, but those were for tomorrow, for now I was off to see Darina Tully who lives nearby with her husband John.

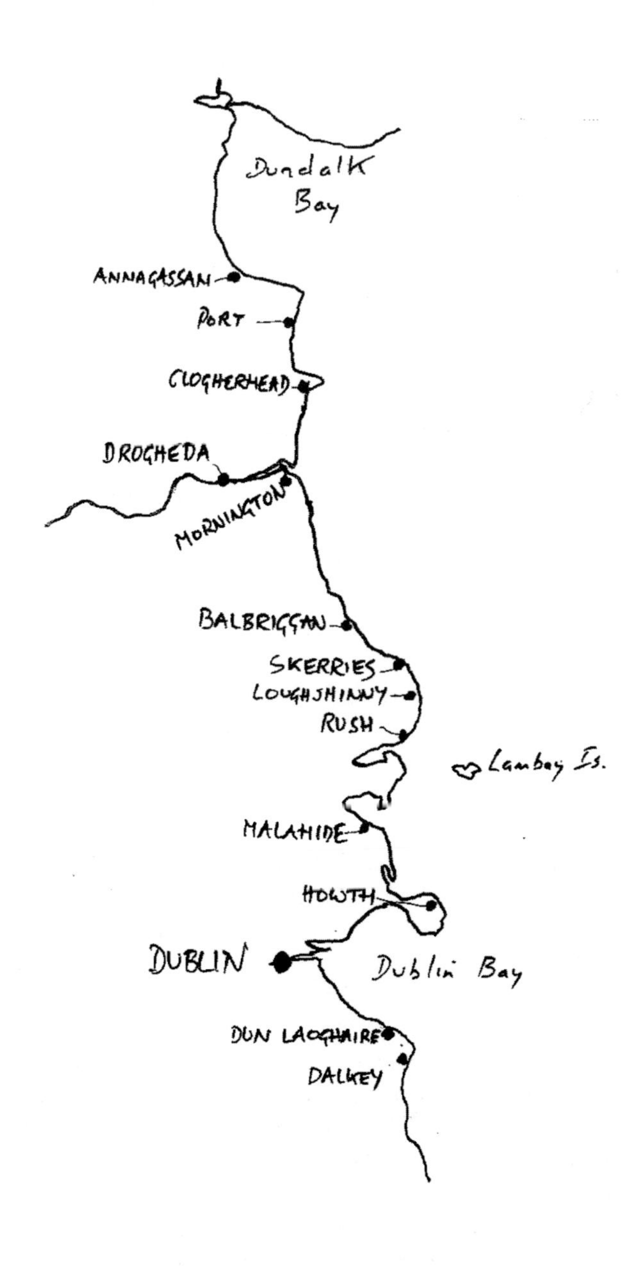

DAY TWENTY-TWO

Darina didn't get home from a visit down to Co.Wexford until pretty late in the evening, about 11.30pm I guess, and afterwards we talked well into the night so that it must have been well after 2am by the time I returned to the van to sleep. She seemed quite surprised that I'd made it around the coast so far in three weeks though I kept on explaining that I wasn't undertaking a full survey of the coast. Just enough to tease myself and, hopefully, satisfy the readers. So this morning, after breakfast and a welcome shower in her place, we walked down the road a few hundred yards to a primary and secondary school situated next door to a convent for elderly nuns. Walking around the nunnery the views were fantastic over the sea. Howth Head lay to the left and Dalkey Island was just in view to the right. Below was Coliemore harbour, built to supply the owner of the island with coal. What a view this to behold while at school. On the other hand, perhaps not, as I doubt I'd have learned so much for want of staring out of the windows.

Then we jumped into the van and drove down to Bulloch Harbour where I'd had a quick look the previous evening and admired a couple of boats. This morning the place was a hive of activity with small sailing boats preparing to sail out. The sun was out, blue skies above and a good light breeze would keep the sailors happy. Perhaps some pretence at summer was upon us. Darina sought out Monica Smyth whose family had rented out tripping boats from here for generations. Her husband and his father had fished from here. Though Darina did introduce us, she was just about to rush off in her car. But, before she did, she went back into her house and returned with a copy of her son Donal's booklet *Bulloch Harbour – Past and Present* which she kindly gave me.

Bulloch Castle towers over the harbour and dates from the twelfth century. In those days Bulloch was just a small cove where herring fishermen worked from, paying their mease of herring to the monks for the rights. It is said that the monks stored this herring in an underground system packed in ice. If so, this is the first instance I've heard of herring being stored in this was instead of being cured or smoked. Herring goes off very quickly though once frozen they can be kept for long periods. Perhaps this was the first deep freezing of herring.

The locals survived off fishing until ships started coming into Dublin port. Pilots were needed and this became one of their bases, pilot cottages being built by the Ballast Board for their exclusive use. Other boat owners worked as hobblers serving the vessels with their needs. They worked on a first come, first served basis in that the first hobbler to reach a ship and get a line aboard got the job for that vessel. Presumably some smuggled goods were brought ashore here as well as there's a tiny gully in the rock called 'Brandy Hole' nearby. At some point at Bulloch a rough quay was hewn in the rock, allowing fish to be landed more easily, and taken to Dublin market. When Captain Bligh of the Mutiny on the Bounty fame came to survey Dublin Bay in 1800, he found 'a dry harbour - it lies between Dalkey and Dunleary and has a quay on the west side where small vessels come to load with stones', though a short time afterwards the present harbour was built thus allowing the stone export business from the quarries above to expand. Coal, always a cargo brought in these small harbours along the coast, was just as vital in the nineteenth century and Downey's coal yard was for many years the central supply, with supplies brought in by sea, the yard delivering to the local houses and the surrounding area.

Bulloch had its resident boatbuilder, John Atkinson, who'd come up from the south in the 1860s, building fishing and other small boats and well as the occasional larger boat, one of the largest being *The Geraldine*, a yacht-like vessel of 60 tons. He also had the contract for servicing and repairing the lifeboats. At his death in 1922 his son Richard continued the business until about 1942.

Darina and I parted at Bulloch as she had work to do and I had to move on. I tried to drive down to Coliemore Harbour but because of road works I couldn't find the way down. Through a maze of twists and turns I eventually found myself on the south side of Dalkey overlooking Killiney Bay. In the distance I could see Bray, my next destination.

Bray was a very touristy place. At one time it had cornered the upper end of the market whilst Dalkey was very working class. These days their roles have reversed and it is Dalkey that is considered as being a bit exclusive. The Halls visited, finding it 'extensively visited by persons either in search of the sea-air or the enjoyment to be derived from the beautiful scenery, and here, in consequence, is one of the most splendid hotels in the kingdom'. That seems to confirm the earlier statement. Paradoxically, Bray had its own large number of fishermen, they reported, who lived in the neighbourhood. However the lack of any quay or harbour of any kind went against them though they suggested that something was about to be built, provided by through the generosity of Mr and Mrs Putland who had already built a school and a cluster of cottages for the fishermen and their families. The harbour was subsequently built. The turnabout in fortunes came about with the Dublin to Kingstown railway extension south, it arriving here in 1854. The day trippers and holiday-makers came in their hordes and it became the largest resort in Ireland. In the 1950s it attracted British visitors keen to get away from post-war Britain with its rationing, depression and poverty. Today, though having to compete with cheap air flight, it remains a busy place in summer though it has also become a dormitory town for Dublin commuters.

Greystones, four miles south, was a noted fishing place in 1795. The railway arrived here in 1855 and with it came visitors, though not on the same scale as at Bray. A campaign for a harbour was instigated between 1885 and 1897 to develop the fisheries and to import coal and this was eventually built in the early twentieth century. The current campaign seems to be against further development for there are plans for a marina. It seems that the community is split down the middle for those who do and do not want it. I haven't heard the outcome or even if a final decision has been made. Though presumably the outcome will be decided in the way all things are in Irish politics which, I recently read, are furtive, tribal, incestuous, tangled and thoroughly corrupted and that the largest amount of corruption is centred on one thoroughly Irish passion: land. Brown envelopes will already have been handed out as property developers and politicians survive by being in each other's pockets, so to speak. (yes, I know, I promised not to mention politics at the outset and I won't again).

As I was lounging about on the grass overlooking this harbour, wondering where the shipwrights of Greystones that I'd read about worked, I received a phone call from Darina. She had arranged an interview for me with Michael Tyrrell, the last surviving member from the famous boatbuilding company of Arklow. However Michael had to go out at 4pm and thus I had to get my skates on if I wanted this only chance of meeting him. It was now about 1.30pm and thus, from Greystones, I had to rush down the coast, briefly stopping at Wicklow which my journal described as 'hectic and industrial'. The harbour here was first built in the 1760s and added to over the next century or more at which time the pilot skiffs bringing the ships in were said to be lug-rigged craft with a jigger sail at the after end.

The beach at Greystones.

The Packet Pier dates from 1885 when a service ran over to Wales. Sixty ships worked out of here in the early twentieth century giving work to 200 dockers and today the port remains a major shipping outlet. We took the coastal road down the coast, past the three-mile expanse of Brittas Bay whose golden sands draw in plenty of tourists, before arriving at Arklow with an hour to spare.

I found Michael's house by asking some kids which one it was. At first they pointed me to the wrong house but eventually they realised who it was I was after. Michael took me into his kitchen and we sat at the table talking whilst he smoked his way through more than several cigarettes. We decided to start back at the beginning.

> I was the fourth generation Tyrrell. John Tyrrell was Arklow-born in 1836 but he went off to serve an apprenticeship in the Royal Naval Dockyard at Devonport, though he might have spent time at Chatham too. He came back here and set up his own yard on the south side of the river. That was in 1864.

Arklow is famous for its shipping and boatbuilding. How old this tradition is no one knows for sure, but Greek cartographer Ptolemy marked a place called 'Manapii' on his second-century map which historians agree is probably Arklow. A fifth-century legend refers to a healthy fishery in the area. Then came the Vikings with their seamanship skills to add to the general mix of the town and the Normans in 1169, strengthening the town and the sea continued to be treated as a place to eke a living from. When fishing bounties were introduced for herring in 1784, twenty-seven boats applied though some suggest this number might be inflated. Regardless of that, there seems to have been a thriving fishing industry with boats pulled up on the beach when not in use. There was also coastal trading with other parts of Ireland and across to Wales and the Bristol Channel. In 1791, William Chapman, when surveying the river, noted a north wall along the river and that the whole community of 1,000 people depended upon the sea. The herring season ran twice a year for six weeks, in May and November, at which time boats would come down from other parts of the coast. Larger ships came to buy fish from the small fishing boats and carry it away. Arklow was, at the time, one of the principal fishing ports in Ireland. However this seemed to be a hit and miss affair as fishing often was; still is for that matter. In 1834 it was described as one of the poorest villages imaginable and solely survived from the herring fishery and was very badly off the rest of the time. From Chapman's survey came the development and extraction of the sulphur ore from nearby mines which was shipped out through the port, a trade abruptly expanded in 1840 when the King of Naples slapped a heavy tax on exports from Sicily.

One of the first vessels known to have been built at Arklow was one of the earliest European catamarans, ordered by William Petty after he'd seen the indigenous *kattumarams* of India and Sri Lanka. This vessel consisted of two wooden cylinders supporting a wooden platform like a true raft though the cylinders were shaped at either ends. The vessel was 20 feet in length by 9 in beam with a 20-foot mast. It is said that forty men could be accommodated on board but that sounds pretty improbable on a 20-foot boat! The next boat known to have originated in Arklow was the 1788-built *Success*, a 41 ton sloop of 47 feet in length. By the early nineteenth century James Canterbury is believed to have been the principal builder. He might have built the 56-ton schooner *William*, launched in 1812 though he was renowned for his fishing smacks and small trading sloops. The port increased in trade after 1838 and a steady number of schooners were built, reaching a peak in the 1850s. However, about this time it was said there were not enough shipbuilders to keep up with the demand and it was against this background that John Tyrrell, who worked briefly in Canterbury's yard, returned after three years away. No one

The harbour at Wicklow *c.*1890.

knows for sure whether this was the reasoning behind his decision to go off to England to learn the skill, but is quite possible.

'His first boat was a fishing smack. It had a transom stern,' said Michael.

> He called it *Shipwright* and she was designed to drift-net the herring. Her mainmast was easy to lower when drifting to the nets. During the sea trials of this boat, John's father Michael was aboard. That was my great-great-grandfather and he had his own boat. Whilst they were hoisting the mast back up after hauling the nets he got knocked overboard. He couldn't swim like most of them and drowned.

Michael lit another cigarette.

When the Kinsale mackerel fishery opened up in the late 1860s it seems John Tyrrell was building typical Arklow oyster dredgers, half-decked boats working the beds offshore. Whilst building one for some local brothers, they asked John to convert her for mackerel fishing. Thus he cut her in half and added an extra 10 feet and completely decked her and she became the first of the Arklow-built mackerel boats, Dandy-rigged. They named her *Pioneer*. Many more followed. Similar vessels became known as the 'Arklow yawls'. By the early 1880s the harbour was improved after pressure from fleet owners for, though the fleet was increasing, the harbour was in a dilapidated state. At the time there were seventy-six trading vessels and 160 fishing boats belonging to Arklow and the demand was still growing. Between September 1888 and March 1889 Tyrrells built three 60-footers for the herring season, according to Michael.

John's son, also Michael, followed his father into the business and in 1904, they built their first powered boat, the 50-foot yacht *Express*.

'She had a 22 hp Gardner engine and a variable pitch propeller though they were worried that they'd put too much power into the vessel. The engine bearers were two 22ft by 12in by 2in. Massive.'

This led to one of the most important vessels to have been launched from the yard, the first purpose-built motorised fishing boat built in the British Isles. This was the *Ovoca* and she was designed by both men in 1905, plans drawn and a model made (which still exists). Plans and model were taken to the Chief Inspector of Fisheries at the Fisheries Branch of the Department of Agriculture who eventually agreed to advance the money for the building of the boat as long as they recommended fishermen to work the boat. Construction began in 1907 and the 48ft *Ovoca* was launched in the January of the following year complete with her 20 hp Dan hot bulb engine. This was innovative stuff in 1908 for the fishing fleets of Britain were just beginning to convert their old sailing boats to motorisation. To build one from scratch was almost unheard of. *Ovoca* had one other distinction - she was the first canoe-sterned fishing boat in the British Isles. She had two masts, ketch-rigged, engine room forward and cabin aft. During her first year fishing in the Irish Sea and off Donegal her gross earnings almost equalled her cost, less the fishing gear. The large sail plan was soon deemed unnecessary and shortened and bowsprit removed. During the First World War she went from Arklow to Balbriggan and worked until 1966, when her registry was closed and she became derelict which is a great shame for a boat so important in Irish maritime history. Tyrrells built variations of that boat over the next few years after her launch.

A disastrous fire swept through the yard in the first decade of the twentieth century and two boats, many half models and plans, including those of *Ovoca*, were lost. However, this didn't stop the Tyrrells from continuing.

'They just erected a new shed and carried on building,' Michael continued, fingering his packet of cigarettes. I rolled one to keep him company.

> Built a couple of steam drifters between 1910 and1915. Daniel O'Connor owned one and he went out to help when the *Lusitania* was torpedoed off Kinsale Head. They never kept all their eggs in one basket. Fishing they knew was cyclical so there were repairs going on and they were designing yachts. We did in my time too.

Two of their most well known large boats were built after the First World War. These two schooners, the *JT&S* (1919) and *Invermore* (1921) were in excess of 90 feet in length. *JT&S*, at 92 feet could carrying 220 tons of cargo whilst the slightly larger *Invermore*, at 98 feet, carried 240 tons. Timber for these came within five miles of Arklow. These two boats were again innovative for they were a stepping stone between sail and motor. Both were rigged with fore-and-aft sails but didn't carry bowsprits and had 'fishing boat' bows and canoe-sterns. They were, in fact, like nothing else. With powerful engines, they could achieve speeds of six knots fully loaded and eight under ballast. Their design was a compromise but a very successful one which persuaded many sceptics of the advantage of the internal combustion engine. We might frown upon that now with hindsight because of the environment, but in the 1920s this was ingenious stuff and it has been suggested that these boats were the only real attempt at bridging the gap between sail and steam.

Both were owned by the Tyrrell family who had always had shipping interests from well before John started his yard. They owned trading vessels and fishing boats alike. Both the *JT&S* and *Invermore* worked until they were sold off in early 1960, the former sadly catching fire in April 1960 near Start Point, just after being sold and was burnt to the waterline. The navy later bombed her as she was a danger to shipping. *Invermore* was sold to Dartmouth and the new owner invited people to contribute £200 to sail with him to Australia with a share in the boat. However, once he had received the money he disappeared with it. The boat gradually became a wreck and sank somewhere up the river there. Her remains are probably still there I reckon.

John Tyrrell died in 1932 by which time his grandson Jack was working there. He had trained as a naval architect. Times were lean in the 1930s.

'He was as good with a pencil as he was an adze. He designed hundreds of boats, took over the yard in 1948,' said Michael, obviously remembering his father with pride.

> We never wanted an engine agency. Didn't want to influence the owner with his choice of engine, didn't want him having something he didn't really want. Kelvins were good engines though, known worldwide. I remember being in Kuwait in about 1982, walking on the beach. What did I see but a K6 sitting there. Once in Dubai, down by the dhows, this fellow intimated he'd have to go and get the doctor. When he arrived he spoke English and asked whether I knew of any second-hand Kelvins or Gardners. We use to drill the injectors out by hand in Gardners.

Jack Tyrrell got the yard involved in the fishing boat building scheme partly funded by the *Comhlachas Iascaigh Mhara Na hEireann* (the Irish Sea Fisheries Association) and designed what later became the Tyrrell bow for fishing boats where the stem flares upwards from a conventional waterline, thus giving more room on deck. During the Second World War they were busy building fishing boats for Northern Ireland and the Isle of Man. These were 48-footers multi-use boats, usually with Kelvin engines fitted. Four went to the Manx Fisheries: *Manx Clover*, *Manx Lily*, *Manx Rose* and *Manx Future*.

'In the 30s they came up with two sizes of fishing boats, 32ft and 35ft, the 35-footers being the standard model.'

'What did they call the 32-footers then?' I asked

'Would you believe it: sub-standard!' He laughed for the first time before carrying on.

The Tyrrell's-built *Invermore.*

> Jack submitted a plan for a new type of lifeboat in 1964. They'd been servicing them for year. His was designed as a cruiser lifeboat, to operate where there were no harbours. Built of steel and Jack won the competition the RNLI had staged. His was built, *Grace Paterson Ritchie* she was called and went up to the Orkney Islands. Yes, he was an innovator of design. Became president of the Irish Boatbuilders Association in 1964 too, when the firm was a hundred years old. Ah, they built pilot boats for Drogheda, Wexford, Limerick, Coleraine, Waterford, Dublin, Cork.

'Was that the *Betty Brean* in Waterford?' I interrupted, having seen photos of her as a working boat and the real thing that night in Waterford.

'Yes,' he replied quickly and continued. 'Some went to Wales, Cardiff and Newport, one even to Gloucester. In Waterford the harbourmaster Capt Farrell would not let the *Betty Brean* go alongside the ships incase she bumped the rail. They had to use a punt. We wanted to send two out to Pakistan in the 1950s but the solicitors advised against it.'

In 1950 they built their first BIM 50-footer, the *James Wickham*, followed by eight more over the next four years and, of these, he knew that the *Ros Ard*, built the same year, was still fishing in County Donegal. Another was the *Vega*, owned by Captain Russell of Helvick (mentioned in chapter three) which was fished by the Kelly family of Helvick until 2000. Michael joined the company in 1953.

'I started by sweeping the floors, learnt everything by doing it. Learnt every trade.' He smiled across the table, maybe remembering those days though he didn't seem to smile too much.

'We built plenty of yachts as well as working boats, and lots of punts and pram dinghies.'

I knew all about *Gipsy Moth III* of course, launched in 1959, in which Sir Francis Chichester sailed across the Atlantic single-handedly and won the race in1960 and again in 1962. Not only that I'd seen other boats of theirs all around Ireland. Such as the Irish Lights tender *Nabro* which was in Hegarty's yard in Oldcourt.

> Jack designed and built himself a 36-foot motorsailer, *Aisling of Arklow*, in 1964 to cruise around in West Cork. Four more: *Eilis of Arklow*, *Vandara of Arklow*, *Tyrrellette* and *Serena II*. Five in total we built. One's in the river here. All during 1964 and 1965. In that time we also built the 45-foot *Shamrock* to replace an earlier ferry for Lambey Island. She's still there. Six ringers between 1958 and 1963 before that. The *Thomas MacDonagh* in 1968. She was a 65-foot fishing boat with a forward wheelhouse and transom stern. The first in Ireland and she went to Kilmore Quay. Then there were the yachts *Huff of Arklow* and *Helen of Howth*, she's now in Scotland. Both Uffa Fox designed, and *Tyaldur*. People thought we were a bit mad with *Huff*! In the 1950s I remember Laurent Giles, a lovely man. I was fortunate to have dealings with him. We'd been building *Rose of York* and then *Maid of Mourne* and he'd come over. He kept an eye on things. My mother was a nervous driver and she drove him from the airport at Dublin. The car was hiccupping along. He asked her to pull over and opened the bonnet, cleaned the plugs. Then asked if he could drive. Mother said he drove like a madman, fast. Later on, father told her that he only had one eye! But he was very quiet and unassuming. Unlike some of the designers who were tyrants.

Huff of Arklow is a revolutionary yacht regarded by many as the world's first ocean-going vessel with a 'fin and skeg' concept. Launched in 1952 for Douglas Heard, she is still considered as the grandmother of today's racing yachts. Her hull is built of two layers of mahogany, the outer running fore and aft and the inner diagonal. Today she is a recognized RYA training vessel based in Plymouth for courses from Start Yachting to Yachtmaster Offshore for adults and youngsters. Sailing on her is a unique experience; a vintage fast cruising yacht so well designed she virtually sails herself. Her cut-away after deck makes her very exhilarating on the wind and is a wonderful lounging area when sailing more upright. *Huff* belongs to Cremyll Sailing, a sail training charity dedicated to provide young people from all walks of life a sailing experience to remember; one designed to develop character, build self-esteem and promote awareness of the needs of others, through teamwork and the shared adventure. Anyone interested can see them at www.cremyll-sailing.org.uk.

He rattled the names off quicker than I could write and I'm sure I missed a few. Other than those already mentioned they built *Asgard II*, designed by Jack Tyrrell in 1974. *Asgard*, as is well known, after being sold by Erskine Childers' family in 1926, eventually came into the hands of the Irish government in 1961 because of her associations and awaits restoration. *Asgard II* is Ireland's national sail training vessel, launched by An Taoiseach Charles Haughey at the yard in March 1981 and who, as an accomplished sailor, also sailed upon her for her maiden voyage to Dun Laoghaire. (Sadly she sank in the Bay of Biscay in the period between writing and publishing this book.)

I asked about the more unconventional boats they'd built.

> In the late 60s we built a conservancy launch, the *Skomer*, for Milford Haven in 1968 and a survey vessel for Liverpool - the *Mersey Inspector* the following year. In 1991 there was a 65ft passenger boat for the lakes in Killarney, the *Pride of the Lakes*. One of the last boats we built. The last one was number 345 though that wouldn't include all the small launches and punts.

Michael had taken over running of the yard in the 1970s along with his brother James, the other brother John working for B&I Ferries. He reckons that they employed about fifty men at the time, probably the peak from that point of view. The syncro-lift system at the bottom

A model of an early Tyrrells-built motor fishing boat.

yard was installed in about 1962 which became known as John Tyrrell (slipway) Ltd. They also retained some of their shipping interests. However, with waterfront land prices booming in the 1990s, though they had work in the yard and new boats were in demand, they sold up though the syncro-lift is still in operation. Across the river another branch of the family runs a steel shipyard where, ironically, the Tyrrells-built fishing boat *Shelmalier* was scrapped in 2005 as part of the ludicrous EU policy of decommissioning fishing boats.

But Michael had to go as he'd promised his wife they'd go somewhere or other. I asked to take a photograph of him but he was the other person to decline. Now as I write this I find it hard to picture him though I have those visions of him taking another cigarette from the packet. This is so unfair because he was so gentle, a man who held the longest tradition of boat-building in Ireland between his fingers and yet was forced to stop by the market pressure of waterfront housing. And you wonder why I hate these developments so much? Yet again I was sad to leave this person, so quiet and assuming he was. We drove off but I felt as if I could cry.

After leaving Michael, I had another appointment with Eugene Wixted whom I'd first met at the London Boat Show in 2007 on the *Classic Boat* stand. I'd told him about coming to Ireland in the summer and he'd given me his phone number. It was he who actually said I should write about Tyrrells. I'd phoned him earlier and we agreed a time and a place. Meanwhile, I'd discovered that the Arklow Maritime Museum had closed down for refurbishment.

Eugene owns the yacht *Aisling of Arklow* and it was she who was afloat in the river. She was the second of the motorsailers, built in 1965 for Mr and Mrs Purvis who later lived aboard her in the Canaries. Eugene had owned her for seven years. She's iroko on oak with a teak deck, 36 foot overall, 30 foot on the waterline, 11 foot in beam and 5 foot in draught and is powered by a Ford Parsons 4-cylinder 50hp engine. He took me out to her in his new Redbay

Inside the boatbuilding shed at Tyrrell's yard.

Stormforce 8.4 metre RIB upon which he runs Arklow Sea Tours (www.arklowseatours.com; he deserves a plug for his kindness).

I looked around the boat that reminded me of a motorsailer my father had owned, the boat I've mentioned sailing in earlier. The smell was similar, and I told Eugene this, commenting on how I love it.

'The wife wouldn't agree with you,' he replied. Suddenly I remembered that first crossing of the Irish Sea in fog, me doing the navigation from Holyhead and the Kish Bank Light bang on the bow as the fog lifted near the Irish coast. Memories are often part of one's security though I didn't always feel secure whilst at sea. Those gales eh!

Eugene talked about the Tyrrell yard as he remembered it. Old style, he said, a huge shed, an equally huge workbench along one side. They were skilled workmen, everything had to be within a sixteenth of an inch. Then we toured the harbour in his RIB, him pointing out various Tyrrell-built craft including the motorsailer *Tyrrellette* standing out of the water. Of the other three motorsailers, one was in Stornoway, one in the Mediterranean and I'm not sure about the third. The lifeboat, he told me, was the first one the RNLI stationed in Ireland in 1826 though today's Trent-class boat is only ten years old. On the north side of the harbour was the old Conningbeg light vessel and jammed in the corner of the south dock, looking a bit worse for wear, one of Tyrrell's BIM 50-footers, the *Ros Bremore* lying alongside a similar 50-footer from the Killibegs yard. Before we parted he also told me about a website with photos of his boat sailing at the Glandore Festival in 2005.

'Two pictures, one with the green hulled *St Bridget*, another Tyrrell's boat built in 1938.'

That's for sure, because wherever I've been along the Irish coast, there's never a Tyrrell-built boat far away. It was time to move on once again, the sun about to dip in the west.

From Arklow I decided to find a quiet beach for what was likely to be my last night here. We headed south once again in search of the perfect beach. I found it on Kilpatrick strand. Two guys arrived in a taxi and parked alongside the van where I was overlooking the beach. Darkness fell as they gathered all their fishing gear and established a camp just below me. Dog happily danced amongst the waves as they cast out their lines. I ate well that evening, and drank too much fine wine, partly celebrating the fact that I'd almost completed my tour and partly to hide my sorrows in having done so. Offshore I could see the flashing red lights that mark either end of the seven wind turbines on Arklow Bank. Some other lights were also announcing their presence. This shoal used to be one of the greatest dangers in the Irish Sea. No longer so, though some idiots probably plough into it, fast asleep. Much later on, with the glow from their lanterns reflecting off the sand-dunes, and with the van door wide open, I fell into a deep stupor to the magical musical sounds of the waves beating themselves upon the beach.

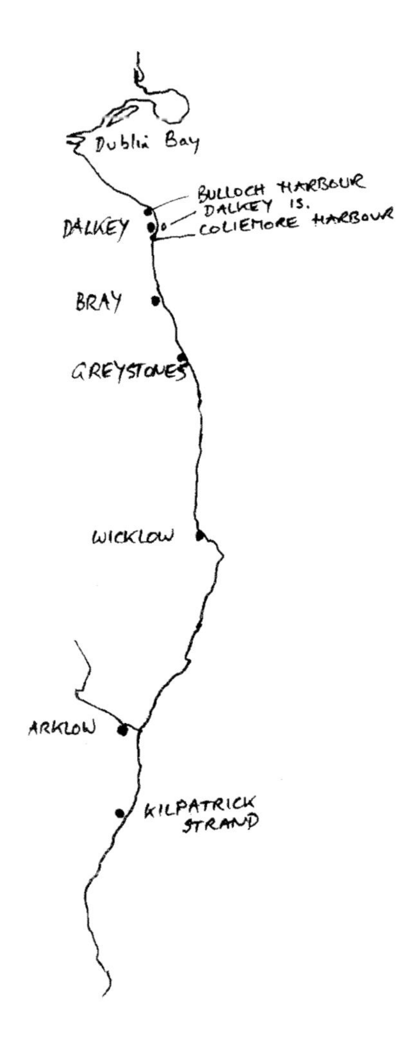

DAY TWENTY-THREE

Tis another lovely morning, blue skies and all. On waking early, I lie in the bed watching the sun effortlessly lift itself out of the horizon and gradually felt its warming rays penetrate the freshness of the morning air. Eventually I pull myself out from under the duvet and Dog and I walk along the beach. The fishermen's camp is still there and one of them was fast asleep in a chair, the other presumably snoring away inside the tent. Their rods were still propped up on tripods with the lines invisibly out into the ocean. The seated one doesn't stir as we pass and I noticed a pile of empty beer cans littered around on the sand. They'd obviously had a thicker night of it than I had with my one bottle of wine. Above their temporary camp, there's a good example of coastal erosion where the old coast road has been severed, it having collapsed into the beach and now the base lumps of gravel remain exposed, with the tarmac ending in a great big tear.

We walk to the far end of the beach and then back to my end where I swim in the wavelets, the cold water taking my breath away and the dog barking. He usually swims as soon as he sees the sea but he has this strange habit of not coming in if I swim, and stands watching and barking at the water's edge. I try to shush him as I don't want the fishermen to wake up, feeling a bit exposed in my nakedness, but he persists. The only way to silence him is to leave the water, at which time he then paddles in and stares, waiting for me to throw him sticks. There aren't any around so I chuck the odd stone for him to dunk his head into the water in his attempt to retrieve it. I then sit on my towel drying off in the warm rays and the heat increases with every minute. Why, I wondered, could we not have had endless days like this instead of the wind and rain over the past three weeks?

Over coffee I browsed through a book on County Wicklow that I'd purchased the previous day, only to realise how much I'd missed. Well, that can't be helped. That made me think about Arklow and the race to build houses. Was it unreasonable to oppose the re-development of the harbour? Is the provision of yet more blocks of waterfront apartments seven stories high a blot on the landscape or a necessary modernity? Given the multitude of housing already built here, and the perception that the economy is heading downwards (according to a phone-in radio debate programme I listened to on national radio), I'm not sure. That poses the question of 'is heritage worth saving?' Life might have been nasty, brutish and short in the past, and there's no general romance about it, but it is from where we came. Many still speak fondly of their time at the fishing eighty years on, as I'd discovered. Thus their experiences must be worth something, valid to catalogue and retain. Fifty men worked in the Tyrrell yard at any one time over the years, probably adding up to several hundred over time. So was it right simply to bulldoze the entire shed with its memories and turn it into flats? Probably, I say with sadness, for a huge wooden shed wouldn't be much use again unless someone wanted to build boats. Too big and too costly. That Tyrrell's was allowed to go to the wall, presumably forced by bankers and property developers, was an utter disgrace though. Where were the grants to help them keep a century-old firm going then? In today's world they could be benefiting from a healthy bull market in wooden craft like, for instance, Tom's Yard in Cornwall where they continue to build wooden and steel working craft, repair them and store them over winter. And Tyrrell's had that added pedigree that, not only has permeated around the Irish Sea, but makes the name known internationally. The infrastructure was still there, a big syncro-lift, shed and yard and access to the south harbour. The developers could just leave that part of the town alone, keeping also the old hardware shop that I was told was also about to be demolished even though it's a popular and thriving business. Go build your ugly housing on the north bank, alongside your shopping outlets, if you must but leave the working harbour alone. Short-sightedness in the name of greed is all it is and, come another financial boom, they'll have to knock that lot down because it's not built to last anyway.

Regretfully we left Kilpatrick. The sun was hot by then and I would have loved to have lain soaking up its rays for longer. The fishermen were still fast asleep when I left at 9.30am, maybe dreaming of the huge fish they hadn't caught, and I hoped no one was waiting for their taxi ride somewhere in rural County Wicklow. Just as I thought that, I realised we were already in County Wexford once again, three weeks and one day after leaving it. At that point I suddenly noticed the tripometer on the van had at some point zeroed itself and only read 11 miles. I knew it was reading 300 and something the previous day but wasn't sure when. It had certainly been round twice past the 1,000 mark but an accurate account of my mileage was, from then on, impossible. Probably, by the time I reached Rosslare once again, the total distance travelled, I estimated, would be 2,500 miles.

We motored down to Courtown for breakfast in a café there. Like many of these coastal communities, Courtown was a small fishing village in the early nineteenth century though, in 1820, it was said to be totally undeveloped. Fishing boats were drawn up the strand and cod was said to be the main catch which was sold around nearby Gorey. Although demands were made for the building of a harbour by the landlord the Earl of Courtown, it wasn't until 1824 that Royal Assent was given for 'the building of a harbour under Breanogue Head, in the County of Wexford, to facilitate the export of corn or other produce, import fuel and lime and to tend to the promotion of Agriculture and Fisheries as also the employment of the poor'.

Plans were prepared by Alexander Nimmo. Has there been any part of the coast where he has not been involved in harbour building? He really must have been an energetic and instrumental proponent of these harbours during the relatively short time he worked. Work began but very slowly due to site problems. By 1833 the south pier was in the process of breaking up in any storm that happens this way. When Henry Inglis arrived the following year he found the harbour under construction and that this 'when completed, will be of much use to the fishery on this coast, which has greatly suffered from the want of some refuge'. In 1837 Lewis notes some building on the quay including 'a Constabulary Police Station'. By 1846 things were almost completed and there were thirty fishing boats from 3 to 10 tons using the harbour but that there were another fifty-five vessels unable to enter. Official announcement of the harbour's completion was made the following year. Over the years the south pier continued to receive a bashing from the sea, having to be rebuilt and silting seemed an ever problem. Some say the real problem was in the original design which didn't conform to Nimmo's plan and that, if it had, it would not have continually collapsed. New sluice gates, the remains of which are still visible, were fitted in 1891 though the problem of silting up never seemed to go away. Trade diminished in the 1910s when only a couple of boats bothered to call in, mostly with coal. Fishing continued, though on a small scale and the hoped for revival of the local oyster beds never seemed to materialise. Courtown was left, after The Emergency, as many other harbours, redundant. Today, although the harbour is picturesque, it does have a handful of working boats and plenty of yachts.

Courtown got its first lifeboat in 1865 though this was withdrawn in 1925. It has had an inshore boat since 1990. Around the harbour there are today several strange and wonderful

The harbour at Courtown.

works of art such as a bronze propeller on a stand, wooden sculptures in a garden across the road, the sand bucket from the old dredger brought in to solve the silting up problem (it didn't succeed), the proverbial anchor and several Jamieson's whiskey barrels in a mock boat. There's also a lovely barometer given by the RNLI to the fishermen in 1925 in recognition of their services rendered and a memorial to those lost at sea. It's actually a very pleasant place to walk about, especially given the bright sunny day. County Wexford has the best climate in Ireland and Courtown has the doubtful honour of having the lowest rainfall. Doubtful, that is, according to the farmers! The tidal drop is only 3 or 4 feet so the surrounding beaches are renowned for their safety when it comes to the novice swimmer. And there are plenty of fine sandy expanses right along the coast. One thing I did notice about Courtown though was it had an upmarket atmosphere, and nowhere else was this highlighted so perfectly than in the public toilets. In there the toilet paper was of that embossed type, up-market and posh. None of that hard crunchy loo paper here!

From Courtown we headed down the coast to Blackwater Harbour and then cut inland to the river Slaney by Killurin where I'd arranged a morning appointment with cot builder and river fisherman Jim Devine. When I eventually found Jim I discovered that he lives in a wonderful house separated by a couple of green fields in their swoop down towards the river with an equally fantastic view up the other side, other trees with the distant Mount Leinster evident above. Looking at the map later I discovered that this 2,600-foot mountain was 20 miles away. He lives with his sister in this, his family home. He's tall and wiry with locks of ginger hair sticking out beneath his baseball cap, dressed in brown corduroy trousers looking every bit the country man. His face is earnest, his manner one of experience and hard work.

I'd come to learn about the cots, the traditional small boats of the river Slaney. Already I knew they came in various sizes for three-masted cots sailed across to Wales in earlier times but for now I was keen to hear about the small river cots.

A River Slaney cot at Killurin.

A drawing of a Wexford cot.

The word 'cot' comes from the Irish *coite* which means a log boat. Today's cots, though, are not log boats yet the suggestion is that they developed from such craft. Whether these log boats then became 'extended' by the addition of planking, craft like this are in use in many parts of the world still today, and then fully planked craft is not known, never will be I suppose, but it is improbable. More likely the term became accepted in the vernacular and continued. Cots are in fact flat-bottomed boats and display many similarities to dozens of other river and lagoon craft in use throughout Europe. What is also quite likely is that they are a combination of two influences upon boatbuilding techniques that have come about over a couple of millennia, these being a southern influence from the Roman times in Britain and a more recent influence from the northern Vikings. This is because they have a flat bottom, consisting of planks of timber butted together in a way similar to the craft of the Veneti tribe of Northern France, as described by Julius Caesar. Their upper planks are clench or clinker built, however, in the same way as the Vikings built their craft. In other words a hybrid of building techniques resulting in a strong yet easily built vessel.

Jim took me into his shed where a cot he'd recently built lay. He described the method of building in a brief and simple way. It's all white deal to the water except the garboard which is marine ply. That wouldn't have been the case before but because it tends to rot first it's easier to replace. I set up the bottom first, four planks as you can see, shaped and two inches thick. Then you have to get the rocker by weighting the middle of the bottom. I use these weighs here. Do you recognise them? he said pointing to lumps of iron. They were railway chairs that the railways used to sit in in the days of wooden sleepers. I nodded the affirmative. CIE, the national railways, they were throwing them out. I put them in the middle and jack up either ends to give a five inch rocker. That's enough on an 18-foot boat. They used to be longer: 23 1/2 feet until Pat Savage introduced the smaller boat about twenty-five years ago. Then the boards are nailed together through the floors. Elm or oak there. The stem is notched on and the sternpost just sits on the bottom with the small transom fixed. Then the planking can be added using three moulds, these planks tapering progressively more and more so that the third plank is tapered a lot more than the first. The knees are grown oak normally if I can get it, or sometimes sawn elm. The rubbing strake, two by one inches, adds an enormous amount of strength to the gunwale. As you can see the floors and the ribs are alternate. Add a few thwarts, strengthen around the rowlocks and that's it.

He made it sound all too simple though I knew it wasn't. I looked around the boat for several minutes, photographing and admiring his workmanship. Then he showed me a racing version in another shed, painted yellow, white, and black. The difference here was that the boat was pointed at both ends.

> That's how they used to be. This is a racing version, see the oars there. But when outboards came into use the fishermen wanted a small transom to fix the engine to. If you see some older craft you'll see how they've been altered at the rear end to take an outboard.

I asked about the racing.
'Ah,' he answered with a sigh.

> They used to race out on Wexford Harbour. Now it's local stuff racing, Four oars a boat and the coxswain. These are the older longer boats, 23 1/2 feet and they have more rocker on the bottom. This has nine inch. Used to be seven but nine makes them go better. No good for working the river though. There's anywhere between three and twelve racing although the river's only wide

enough here for five or six.

After chatting some more about the boat he took me down to the bottom of the field where several cots lay in the grass.

'With the salmon fishing gone some folk aren't going to the water this year. That one there is thirty-five years old.' He pointed to a grey one with a wide transom. Alongside was another green-painted one with a wooden bracket at the end to take an outboard.

'That one's longer, see, that old one.'

It certainly was and more solidly built, thicker planking but much heavier. I asked what fishing they did.

> The salmon was the best though the licence was a lot of money. €190 last year and €380 this year though we didn't have to pay with there being no fishing. There were seventy-five licences though some now handed in. Three years ago this river was one of the best salmon rivers in the country but not a lot here last year. Too much drift-netting out at sea. They're still drifting in Kerry though. There's hope it will come back here in a few years. Used to go and fish the herring in Wexford Harbour outside the bridge. Some used a ring-net. Few wildfowlers use cots still.

We walked down to the river as he explained the salmon fishing in more detail. Several cots were moored off and a couple sat on the river bank. He showed me the remains of a very old one that was almost rotted away.

'See how big she was. Look over the other side, can you see those moored there. They belong to wildfowlers.'

I looked carefully to see perhaps half a dozen right along the water's edge on the far side of the river, almost impossible to see with my poor eyesight. What else did he do to survive? Was the thatched house at the bottom of the driveway his?

'Bit of farming, cattle on the top field, work on buildings. No, the thatched house belongs to a doctor, a top eye doctor, in Dublin. He rents it out at €1,000 a week and there's a family there now.'

I asked about the bigger boats I'd heard of.

> The cots down river are bigger. You want to go and see Larry Dugan, he used to build the bigger ones. Then there's the gabbards, the trading barges of the river. They are built a bit the same way though up to 60 feet. Carried stuff all the way up the river to Enniscorthy, up to 30 tons of wet sand or whatever. Think I've found one sunk in the river, I'm waiting for Darina to come down and have a look, divers maybe. No one knows much about them. If she doesn't some soon maybe I'll have to get somebody else down to look.

It was Darina who'd given me his phone number after all so it wasn't surprising he wanted her to look. I heard a few weeks later that she had been and they were waiting for a diver. Jim described where Larry lived. Again we chatted for an half an hour or so about the river and his life living by it. It sounds all idyllic and everything, especially with the sun shining but I'm sure it's far from that when the snow's falling, it's freezing cold and he has to feed the cows. There are always two sides to everything. Probably is in the doctor's life as well for he has to put up with whining patients or whatever. No excuse for his tenant's lovely daughter to be so patronising though! It was time to go and again I had really enjoyed my time with Jim. He was so warm and open about his life, so down to earth and honest. We said our farewells before I drove on.

By the bridge across the river I found two cots on the water and three ashore above the small quay, one which looked like a racing boat and the other two working boats. One looked like it had been purposely shortened. A good example of a limestone kiln stood nearby. From there we headed towards Wexford, passing the Irish National Heritage Park where I managed to get a quick look for free under the auspices of wanting to look at their log boat which, it turned out, wasn't even there. To be honest, there wasn't any other reason to stop though there was quite a nice example of a Viking boat in an open shed.

I found Larry Dugan's house after knocking on several doors but, unfortunately, he was out. In Wexford itself I couldn't find anywhere to park it was so busy. I ended up parking in an illegal spot whilst I ran over to the 'safe harbour' to photograph a few bigger cots moored there and one turned upside down. Several mussel dredgers were moored alongside the quay that was thronged with visitors promenading up and down. Relieved at not receiving a parking ticket, we drove on to the Burrow, the strip of land on the southern side of the bay with Rosslare Point at its tip. On the inside of the spit there were several of the larger cots moored just offshore and as the tide was ebbing, two of them were soon dried out which enabled me to have a proper look. The two I measured were a little over 23 feet in length and recently built judging by their condition. A couple more lay turned over on the grassy bank. However, though these were larger than most of those at Jim's, they weren't the biggest built.

On the outside of the spit the land falls away to Rosslare and along to Rosslare Harbour. Here, bigger cots once developed in sea-going craft, being up to 40 feet in length. Holdsworth writes that these cots were used for the herring fishery and had three masts sporting three spritsails and a jib. He states their normal length was 30 feet and that there were flat-bottomed with a small bit of keel at each end and a bilge keel on either side though in his illustration these weren't very deep. A more thorough appraisal of these craft appears in *The Mariner's Mirror*, volume 75, number 1, by Owain T.P. Roberts. In this paper he discussed the influences that brought these craft into existence. He writes that forty-six of these large cots were regularly fishing in the 1920s and that they travelled a fair distance in this quest, as far as the north of the Irish Sea. As well as fishing for herring, they trawled, potted and long-lined. It is also thought they sailed over to the Welsh coast to fish. Their demise seems to have come about after the advent of motorisation when their hulls were entirely inappropriate to receive motors. The smaller cots survived purely because they could be adapted to take outboard motors, as we've seen.

In chapter one I mentioned the ancient village of Fort at the tip of this peninsula which was washed away in a storm in 1926. In those days the peninsula jutted much further out across the entrance of the river Slaney, almost shutting the bay off. Not only had the lifeboat station been here but also a high concentration of these large cots. This narrow entrance was shoal and the crews of the cots, which usually numbered four men, needed great skill to navigate in a flat-bottomed vessel. Roberts mentions Larry Dugan as being a builder in Wexford which adds to the disappointment that he was out when I called. Another builder he mentions is Patsy Brian who built the cot *Fiona* which was in Rosslare Harbour at the time. Brian learnt his trade at John Tyrrells though Roberts states this yard was on the river Slaney. I doubt there are two Tyrrells!

These early cots were double-ended with a slight rake at either end. Later boats have a transom though the bottom remains pointed at both ends. Being bigger in length, they had up to eight planks either side and five boards in the bottom and probably more in the 40-foot versions. Both the cots I studied had centreboards which they would need to be able to sail without capsizing. Although it isn't known when the first cot was fitted with a centreboard, that they existed in the nineteenth century seems pretty certain and probably a lot longer before that. Afloat a cot looks like any other boat, a point confirmed whilst watching them dry out. They appear afloat right up to the last moment so that as soon as they do dry out, only then do you notice that they are flat bottomed with the shallow rocker visible at the fore end.

I brewed a cup of tea and sat staring out over the expanse of Wexford Harbour. Mussel beds appeared the further the tide ebbed. Six mussel dredgers steamed into the harbour way over the other side though their engines echoed all around. The heat haze off the sand gave them a ghostly appearance and they seemed to be marching all in line. Three stopped short of Wexford and anchored whilst the other three continued on. Were those anchored dropping their mussel spat into the harbour to seed their grounds or simply staying put for the night? Even with the binoculars it was impossible to decide. I continued my thoughts.

With plenty of time to spare, Dog and I walked to the tip of Rosslare Point, through the golf course and amongst the sand-dunes, to a deserted beach. Dog chased sticks until I got fed up with throwing them seaward. A ferry entered Rosslare Harbour just along the coast and I presumed this would be the one to take me away. I lay on the sand with the last of the day's heat, Dog barking and I lost in reverie. I realised that this was the first time in twenty-three days that I'd not had to think about where I'd been, was going, what I was going to write. I could simply blank my mind off to the outside world if, that is, he would stop barking. This, then, was the end of the journey I thought, as Rosslare Harbour, and now my ferry home, were lurking only a few miles away.

So that's the end of my small observations on the vernacular maritime landscape of Ireland. It might be brief and certainly only touching the subject, as I've written before, but I've discovered what I think to be a good taste of what exists. The coastline stretches for some 7,500 kilometres, according to the guide book and I must have travelled almost half of that. I thought back to what I considered was my most memorable time or place. That morning, on the radio, there had been a programme about Ireland's favourite drives chosen by its listeners. 'Was it the Ring of Kerry, the Connor Pass, the coast of County Clare or the Atlantic Drive in Achill?' the presenter asked. But, I had thought, they had missed plenty of other coastal drives, not to mention those inland though I hadn't any knowledge of them. What about the road around the tip of the Beara or Dingle peninsulas? But the one that comes to mind as the most perfect was the evening drive to Keem Bay with Charlie Fadian, along the cliff top with those views and the sight of the sandy beach below, cast in shadow. The one I missed, I guess, would have been the drive up Slieve League in Donegal.

More memorable than the scenery, of course, are the people. The afternoon with Joe Teesdale and the folk he introduced me to, sailing with Nigel Towse, in the pub with Cormac Levis, the picture of Liam Hegarty next to the old bandsaw, Seamus O'Flaithearta's wobbly eye, Charlie Fadian trying to sell me his currach, chatting to Cara, Fabiene and Billy, Dave Donna's sad eyes, the sight of Jim Moore's attic or Michael Tyrrell's cigarettes. All sweet memories of people who accepted me for what I am; people who were so hospitable, so open and honest, so helpful. That's not to say that a host of other people weren't as well. They were equally so. In fact I think I can say that everyone I came across was friendly and helpful, even those I bumped into in shops or asked directions from.

As for regrets, I knew there would be plenty from the outset. To undertake such a project in such a small amount of time was asking for them. I'm sorry I didn't visit Skellig Michael and a host of other islands including Rathlin, somewhere I'd wanted to go for over twenty-five years. Bloody rain! Another major regret was not visiting the National Museum of Ireland's Folk Museum outside Castlebar and maybe meeting Séamus MacPhilib, of whom I've heard so much. I guess the biggest regret is not being able to take a more leisurely pace.

Fifty people spoken to in some detail in twenty-three days isn't a bad average though, with 100 miles to drive each day on average, it's a hard task.

And so we finally arrived at the ferry dock and were ushered aboard the same boat we'd come over on. On deck, watching the harbour slip away, I felt no sense of achievement. It felt more like an anticlimax. Although. honestly, I didn't feel much at all. Just as if I'd completed another day of interviews, photographing and learning more about this fascinating and tangible subject. Driving around Ireland in itself isn't much of an achievement in the grander way of today's world. Gaining the knowledge might be, and I'd certainly gathered plenty of that for that is the job of the ethnologist. Tomorrow I'll wake up in Fishguard and I'll probably feel a dire loss. I'm going to miss the bumpy roads, the ugly housing, the lack of public footpaths, the signposts that point in the wrong direction, the height barriers and the crazy drivers. I'll miss it all. Still, in the words of many that I met, 'Oh, by Jesus, you'll be having to come back'. I will for certain.

As an after note, I read about Arthur Young's return trip home in 1776. He had left from Waterford which normally took from twelve to fourteen hours though when the Smalls light was visible, a contrary wind blew the ship back towards Arklow. A gale arose, a violent storm even, and for thirty-six hours they sailed up and down the coast with a reefed mainsail. He was the only passenger of seven not to be sick. He had left on 19 October and arrived in Milford Haven on the 22 October. Our crossing will be much quicker, about six hours, wind or no wind!

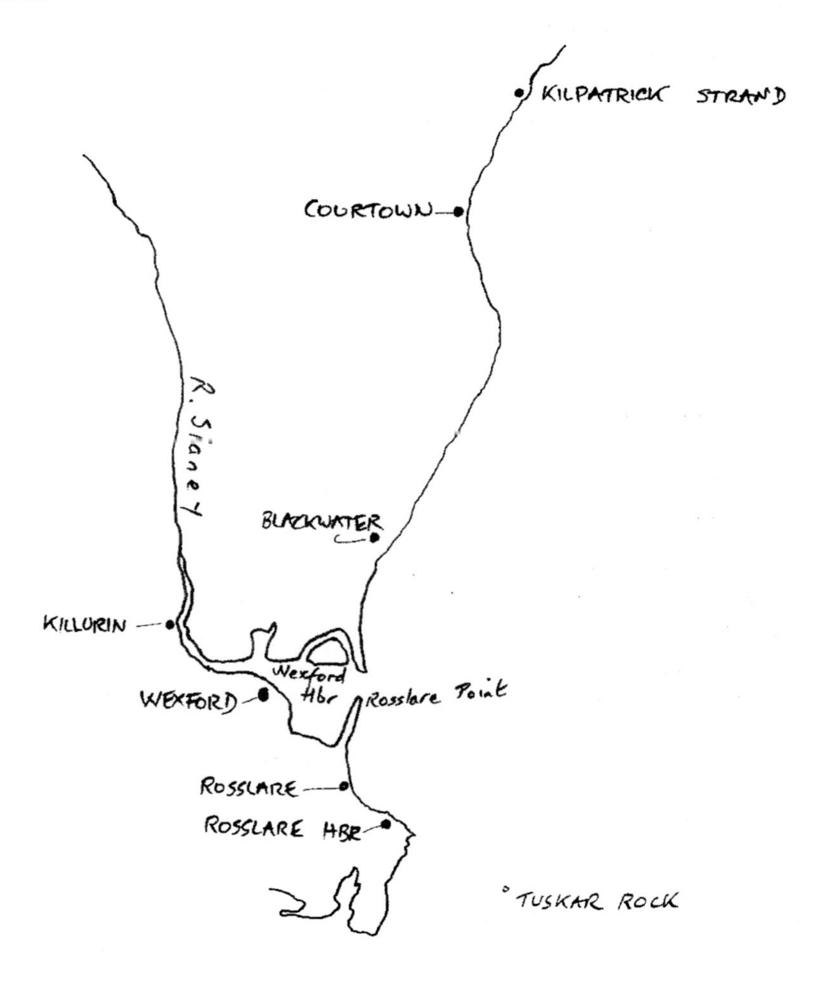

BIBLIOGRAPHY

Allen, H., *Donaghadee: an illustrated history* (White Row Press: Belfast, 2006).
Anderson, J., *An account of the present state of the Hebrides and Western Coasts of Scotland* (Edinburgh, 1785).
Beattie, S., *The Book of Inistrahull* (Lighthouse: Donegal, 1992).
Brabazon, W., *The Deep Sea & Coast Fisheries of Ireland* (James McGlashan: Dublin, 1848).
Cheekpoint F.H.G., *The Cheekpoint Prong* Cheekpoint (2005).
Conaghan, P., *The Zulu Fishermen – Forgotten Pioneers of Donegal's First Fishing Industry* (Bygone Enterprises: Killibegs, 2003).
Concannon, K. (ed), *Inishbofin Through Time and Tide* (Inishbofin Development Association: Inishbofin, 1993).
Conghail, M.M., *The Blaskets – People and Literature* (Roberts Rinehart Publishing: Dublin, 1987).
Coyne, J.S., *The Scenery and Antiquities of Ireland* (Virtue & Co.: London, 2003).
Davis, Fr C., *Deep Sea Fisheries of Ireland* (London, 1886).
De Courcy Ireland, J., *Ireland's Sea Fisheries – A History* (Glendale Press: Dublin, 1981).
Durell, P., *Discover Dursey* (Ballinacarriga Books:, Cork, 2000).
Dutton, H., *Statistical Survey of the County of Clare* (London, 1808).
Dutton, H., *Statistical Survey of the County of Galway* (London, 1824).
Estyn Evans, E., *Irish Folk Ways* (Routledge & Kegan Paul: London, 1957).
Feeney, M., *The Cleggan Bay Disaster* (Penumbra Press: Glencolmbkille, 2001).
Fitzgerald, S., *Mackerel and the making of Baltimore, Co. Cork 1879-1913* (Dublin, 1999).
Flynn, A., *A History of County Wicklow* (Gill & Macmillan: Dublin, 2003).
Fraher, W. et al, *Desperate Heaven – The poor Law, Famine & Aftermath in Dungarvan Union* (Dungarvan, undated).
Fraser, R. *Report of the County Surveys, and the best means for the Further Encouragement of the Fisheries of Ireland* (Dublin, 1818).
Hackett, M., *Brave Seamen of Youghal* (*On Stream* Publications:Blarney, 1995).
Hall, Mr & Mrs C., *Hall's Ireland – Mr & Mrs Hall's Tour of 1840* (Sphere: London, 1984).
Holdsworth, E.W.H., *Deep-Sea Fishing and Fishing Boats* (Edward Stanford: London, 1874).
Irish, B., *Shipbuilding in Waterford 1820-1882* (Wordwell: Bray, 2001).
Kinsella, A., *The Windswept Shore – A History of the Courtown District* (Courtown, 2004).
Kemp, D., *Dixon Kemp's Manual of Yacht and Boat Sailing* (Horace Cox: Southampton, 1988).
Kelly, L. et al, *Blennerville – Gateway to Tralee's Past* (Training & Employment Authority Community Response Programme:Tralee, 1989).
Lankford, É., *Cape Clear Island: Its People and Landscape* (Cape Clear Museum :Cape Clear Island, 1999).
Lankford, É., *Fastnet Rock: An Charraig Aonair* (Cape Clear Museum: Cape Clear Island, 2004).
Leach, N., *The Lifeboat Service in Ireland* (Tempus: Stroud, 2005).
Levis, C., *The Towelsail Yawls – The Lobsterboats of Heir Island and Roaringwater Bay* (Galley Head Press: Ardfield, 2002).
Lewis, S., *A Topographical Dictionary of Ireland* (S. Lewis & Co.: London, 1837).
MacCullagh, R., *The Irish Currach Folk* (Irish American Book Company: Dublin, 1992).
MacPhilib, S., *Fishing Boats of the River Boyne Estuary* (Ulster Folklife, vol 48, 2002).
MacPholín, D., *The Drontheim: Forgotten Sailing Boats of the North Irish Coast* (Playprint: Dublin, 1999).
MacPholín, D., *The Donegal Currachs* (Cottage Publications: Donaghadee, 2007).
McCaughan, M. (ed), *Sailing the Seaways* (Friar's Bush Press: Belfast, 1991).

McCaughan, M. (ed), *The Irish Sea – Aspects of Maritime History* (The Institute of Irish Studies: Belfast, 1989).

Marmion, A., *The Ancient and Modern History of the Maritime Ports of Ireland* (J.H. Banks: London, 1860).

Martin, C., *Full Fathom Five – Wrecks of the Spanish Armada* (Viking Press: London, 1975).

Martin, C., *The Spanish Armada* (Guildford, 1988).

McInerney, J., *The Gandelow – A Shannon Estuary Fishing Boat* (A. K. Ilen Company: Limerick, 2005).

McKillop, F., *Glencloy – A Local History* (Belfast, 1998).

McNally, K., *The Islands of Ireland* (London, 1978).

Molloy, J., *The Irish Mackerel Fishing and the making of an Industry* (Killibegs, 2004).

Molloy, J., *The Herring Fisheries of Ireland (1900-2005)* (Marine Institute: Oranmore, 2006).

Moore, J., *Portavogie – A History* (Portavogie, 2004).

Morris, J., *The Story of the Dunmore East Lifeboats* (Lifeboat Enthusiasts' Society: Coventry, 2003).

Nolan, P., *Sea Caress – West Cork's Fishing Industry* (Ballycastle, 2003).

O'Brien Briggs, K., *Clogherhead Port Oriel – A brief History 1886-2006* (Clogherhead, 2007).

O'Cleirigh, N., *Valentia: A Different Island* (Portobello Press: Dublin, 1992).

O'Crohan, T., *The Islandman* (Oxford University Press: Oxford, 1934).

O'Shea, T., *The Skelligs* (undated).

Power, J., *Above and Beyond the Call of Duty* (Kilmore Quay, 1992).

Quinn, T., *Turfboats* (Dublin, 2004).

Rees, J et al, *Arklow: Last Stronghold of Sail* (Arklow).

Robinson, T., *Connemara – Listening to the Wind* (Dublin, 2006).

Scott, R.J., *The Galway Hookers* (Ward Rive Press: Dublin, 1985).

Severin, T., *The Brendan Voyage* (Arrow Books: London, 1978).

Smylie, M., *Traditional Fishing Boats of Britain & Ireland* (Adlard Coles Nautical: Shrewsbury, 1999).

Smylie, M., *Herring - A History of the Silver Darlings* (Tempus:Stroud, 2004).

Smylie, M., *Working the Welsh Coast* (Tempus: Stroud, 2005).

Smyth, D., *Bulloch Harbour: Past and Present* (Dublin, 1999).

Stagles, J. & R., *The Blasket Islands: Next Parish America* (O'Brien Press: Dublin, 2006).

Symonds, T.E., *Observations on the Fisheries of the West Coast of Ireland* (London, 1855).

Synge, J., *The Aran Islands* (Penguin: London, 1906).

Taylor, R., *The Lighthouses of Ireland* (Collins Press: Cork, 2004).

Thackeray, W., *An Irish Sketch-book* (London, 1842).

Thuillier, J.R., *History of Kinsale* (Kinsale, 2006).

Villiers-Tuthill, K., *Alexander Nimmo & The Western District* (Connemara Girl Publications: Clifden, 2006).

Wilkins, N.P., *Men, Tides and Salmon: Snap-netting on the Barrow, Nore and Suir* (Southern Regional Fisheries Board: Clonmel, 1990).

Young, A., *A Tour in Ireland with general observations on the present State of the Kingdom 1776-79* (London, 1892).

Young, J., *A Maritime & General History of Dungarvan 1690-1978* (undated).